Researching Cultures of Learning

Researching Cultures of Learning

International Perspectives on Language Learning and Education

Edited by

Martin Cortazzi
University of Warwick, UK

Lixian Jin
De Montfort University, UK

First published 2013 by
PALGRAVE MACMILLAN

Palgrave Macmillan in the UK is an imprint of Macmillan Publishers Limited,
registered in England, company number 785998, of Houndmills, Basingstoke,
Hampshire RG21 6XS.

Palgrave Macmillan in the US is a division of St Martin's Press LLC,
175 Fifth Avenue, New York, NY 10010.

Palgrave Macmillan is the global academic imprint of the above companies
and has companies and representatives throughout the world.

Palgrave® and Macmillan® are registered trademarks in the United States,
the United Kingdom, Europe and other countries.

ISBN: 978–0–230–32132–8

This book is printed on paper suitable for recycling and made from fully
managed and sustained forest sources. Logging, pulping and manufacturing
processes are expected to conform to the environmental regulations of the
country of origin.

A catalogue record for this book is available from the British Library.

A catalog record for this book is available from the Library of Congress.

10 9 8 7 6 5 4 3 2 1
22 21 20 19 18 17 16 15 14 13

Printed and bound in Great Britain by
CPI Antony Rowe, Chippenham and Eastbourne

Contents

Part III   Learners' Perceptions and Expectations of Teachers

Part IV   The Dynamics of Socialization and Motivation in Cultures of Learning

List of Figures

List of Tables

List of Appendices

Acknowledgements

The editors and contributors would like to extend profound thanks to all the participants in the research projects featured here. As participants you are learning in many situations, contexts and cultures around the world with different kinds of intercultural learning, and without your help our work and our learning here would not be possible. Your needs encouraged us to research. Thus, in our many languages we give you our gratitude: Thank you.

In the same spirit, the editors would like to say how enjoyable and inspiring it has been for us to work with all the contributors from different parts of the world. We thank them all.

Finally we would like to thank the editorial team members of Palgrave Macmillan for their patience. We wish you intercultural blessings.

Notes on Contributors

Dr. Jan Abd-Kadir is Lecturer in Language Education in the Department of Education at the University of York. Her research interests include intercultural communication, classroom interaction, written discourse analysis, second-language writing and language curriculum-based research. More recently, she has been researching classroom interaction and discourse in low-income countries in Asia and Sub-Saharan Africa, focusing on the impact of the use of a first and second language on the quality of classroom talk.

Zahra Alimorad is a Ph.D. candidate of TEFL at Shiraz University, Iran, specializing in teaching English to foreign language learners. Her research interests include EFL motivation/demotivation, testing, and (critical) discourse analysis. One of her main research areas is investigation of factors contributing to Iranian EFL learners' demotivation construction. Her recent publications are 'Inflating and persuading in the discussion sections of NSs' vs. PSs' academic research articles' (2012), 'The role of grammar in L2 lexical inferencing' (2010), 'Do L2 proficiency and L1 reading strategies affect Persian EFL learners' use of English reading strategies? Threshold Hypothesis revisited' (2009), and 'A comparison of English and Persian organizational patterns in the argumentative writing of Iranian EFL students' (2009).

Prof. Nahla Nola Bacha is Professor of Applied Linguistics and Chairperson of the Department of Humanities at the Lebanese American University, Lebanon, where she has administered and taught in the academic English program for over 20 years. She has presented at regional and international conferences and published in international refereed journals. Her research interests are in English for academic and professional purposes and discourse and corpus analysis.

Dr. Rima Bahous is Associate Professor of Education and the Director of the Program and Learning Assessment at the Lebanese American University in Lebanon. She has presented at regional and international conferences and published in international refereed journals. Her main research interests are in program assessment and discourse analysis, as well as language teaching and learning.

Dr. Dat Bao is Lecturer in TESOL at Monash University, Australia, specializing in creative pedagogy, visual materials and curriculum development in second language education. He researches classroom silence, his main interests being the silent learning mode in East Asian cultures and its applications in Western educational contexts. One of his main research areas is the needs of East Asian students in Australian universities: He has gathered empirical data about what happened in the minds of Japanese, Korean, Chinese and Vietnamese learners of English, with special focus on how these groups perceive the values of silence and talk, as well as on the implications of such perceptions in classroom pedagogy in the Australian university system. He is author of *Understanding Silence and Reticence: Nonverbal Participation in Second Language Acquisition* (forthcoming), and is visual developer for *Success with English* (2003), the English textbook currently used in Guangzhou, China.

Prof. Erich Berendt was born in Canada. He obtained a B.A. (history) University of Alberta, Canada, M.A. (philosophy of religion) University of Chicago, M.S. & Ph.D. (linguistics) Illinois Institute of Technology, Chicago. He has taught in Japan at the University of Chiba (1973–93) and Seisen University (1993–2008), honoured by Seisen University as "Professor Emeritus" in 2008. He worked as a professor at the Graduate School of English, Assumption University, Bangkok (2008–2012). He has served on the editorial boards of: *Japan Assoc. of College English Teachers' Bulletin, Asian Englishes, Asia TEFL, Intercultural Communication Studies*, also as editor-in-chief of *Japan Assoc. of Applied Linguistics Bulletin* (1986–95). Research areas have focused on comparative spoken discourse (English, Spanish, Japanese, Chinese), applied speech acts in conversation, and contemporary theory of metaphor in cognitive linguistics. Recent books published in 2008 include one in *Cognitive Linguistics Metaphors for Learning: Cross-cultural Perspectives* (J. Benjamins); a book of poetry *Passageways to My Mind* (2008), and *Facing Finality: Cognitive and Cultural Studies on Death and Dying* (2011).

Prof. Martin Cortazzi is Visiting Professor at the Centre for Applied Linguistics at the University of Warwick, UK. He has taught and trained teachers in Britain, China, Lebanon, Turkey, Iran, Malaysia, Norway, Cyprus and elsewhere. He has published widely on aspects of primary education, applied linguistics, language and cultural issues, narrative and metaphor analysis. Martin Cortazzi and Lixian Jin have for many years jointly researched and published widely on a range of linguistic, cultural and educational issues related to Chinese learners. They are the writers for the teacher's books for New Standard College English series of textbooks (2009, 2010) published by the Foreign Language Teaching and Research Press/Macmillan in Beijing. They are the editors and contributors to several books: *Researching Chinese Learners: Skills, Perceptions and Intercultural Adaptations* (2011) and *Researching Cultures of Learning; International Perspectives on Language Learning and Education* (2013) *and Researching Intercultural Learning: Investigations in Language and Education* (2013).

Dr. Sami Dadi is Assistant Professor in TESOL and Applied Linguistics in the ISEAH, Kef, Tunisia. He teaches ESL/EFL, SLA, ESP, Research Methods, ELT Methodology and general English courses. His areas of research include: pidgin studies, the motivation to learn English, and the effects of social network relations on learners' attitudes. He is particularly interested in the roles of interest and self-efficacy in improving students' motivation to learn English. His research developed the Osmosis Model to explain the interaction between these factors and social interaction to determine the level of L2 learning motivation. He has published a number of articles and book chapters that include: *The Role of E-learning and Online Materials in Developing Interest in Literary Texts for Foundation Year Students* (2012) and *The Computational Metaphor Model and Interlanguage Studies* (2011).

Dr. Joseph Falout researches, publishes, and presents internationally about developmental motivational variables of language teachers and learners in English as a Foreign Language (EFL) sociocultural contexts, co-authoring 'Demotivation: Affective States and Learning Outcomes' in *System* (2009), and 'A Comparative Study of Proficiency and Learner Demotivation' in *The Language Teacher* (2004). He edits for the *OnCUE Journal*, published by the Japan Association for Language Teaching (JALT), and the *Asian EFL Journal*. His collaborations in teaching and researching include contributions to originating the theoretical and applied foundations of Critical Participatory Looping (CPL) and Present Communities of Imagining (PCOIz). He is an assistant professor at Nihon University, College of Science and Technology in Japan, where he teaches English for academic purposes and English for specific purposes to undergraduate and graduate students. Falout has also taught English composition and essay writing, public speaking, and English as a second language at colleges in the USA.

Tetsuya Fukuda is an English instructor at International Christian University, Tokyo. He has been teaching English both at the university level and at the high school level for more than 25 years, in diverse English learning settings in the Tokyo area, including Dokkyo University and Waseda University. Since receiving an MA in International Studies from Leeds University in England, he has been doing research in issues surrounding English in the context of a globalizing world. Currently, he is interested in the sociocultural and political aspects of language learning in Japan, especially factors that motivate students to learn and use English, and how students perceive varieties of English in and out of the classroom. He is enjoying making presentations and writing papers on these issues in the Japan Association for Language Teaching (JALT), Teachers of English to Speakers of Other Languages (TESOL), and the American Association of Applied Linguistics (AAAL).

Prof. Frank Hardman is Chair Professor of International Development and Education in the Institute for Effective Education at the University of York. He has published extensively in the areas of language and education, classroom learning and teacher development in high- and low-income countries and has been successful in attracting large-scale funding from research councils and government and non-government agencies in the UK and overseas.

Le Thi Thu Huyen has been a senior lecturer at Danang University in Vietnam for 15 years. Presently, she is a Ph.D. student at the Faculty of Education of Monash University doing research on TESOL discourses and methodology in EFL contexts. One of her main research interests involves English language teachers' professional identity considering transnational teaching and learning experience and English as an international language; how teachers' professional identity influences their EFL teaching practices and attitude towards their students' learning. Also, she focuses on the reconceptualization of teaching approaches with underlying concepts of 'traditional' and 'communicative' and the extent to which the conceptualization of these concepts contribute to the cultures of learning in EFL contexts.

Prof. Lixian Jin is Chair Professor of Linguistics and Intercultural Learning and the Director of the Centre for Intercultural Research in Communication and Learning (CIRCL) at De Montfort University, UK. She has taught linguistics and English in China, Britain and Turkey, and coordinated research projects in Singapore, Malaysia and China. She has led funded research projects with international teams in Malaysia, Singapore and China and with international companies. Her publications and research interests are in intercultural communication, applied linguistics, bilingual clinical assessments and narrative and metaphor analyses. She has also served as an editor or an executive editorial member on a number of international journals, including *Asian Journal of English Language Teaching, International Journal of Language Communication and Disorders* and *Intercultural Communication Studies*.

Dr. Shiva Kaivanpanah is Associate Professor of Applied Linguistics at the Faculty of Foreign Languages and Literatures, University of Tehran. Her research interests include second language learning related issues in general and L2 vocabulary learning and assessment, lexical inferencing, and teacher feedback in particular.

Dr. Jin Li is Associate Professor of Education and Human Development at Brown University, USA. Her research examines cultural learning models and how such culturally based models shape children's learning beliefs and achievement. She has studied Chinese, Taiwanese, Chinese American and European American children as well as children from other ethnicities in the United States and other countries; the age groups range from preschool age, school-aged, and adolescence, to college students. She collaborates with researchers from different countries. She has published in leading journals, such as *American Psychologist, Journal of Educational Psychology, Child Development, Developmental Psychology, Ethos,* and *Cognition and Emotion* among others. Dr. Li is author of her recent book *Cultural Foundations of Learning* (2012).

Gulnissa Makhanova is Senior Lecturer in English at Kazakh-British Technical University. Her main interests include cultural issues of learning, learning materials design, critical discourse and metaphor analysis. She also researches students' learning perceptions. She was awarded the MA (University of Warwick) with distinction. She was short listed for the British Council's ELTons award for Innovative Writing for developing students' writing skills.

Dr. Shakila Abdul Manan is Associate Professor of English Language Studies at the School of Humanities, Universiti Sains Malaysia. She researches and teaches in the areas of stylistics, critical discourse analysis, feminist and postcolonial studies. Her main research interest is in the critical study of language and the way in which it is used to constitute, maintain or challenge relationships of power. She is also interested in exploring issues of multicultural identity and their intersection with race, class and gender in Malaysian postcolonial creative writings. Her recent publications include three co-edited books: *Linguistics, Literature and Culture: Millennium Realities and Innovative Practices in Asia* (2012), *Exploring Space: Trends in Literature, Linguistics and Translation* (2008) and *Higher Education in the Asia-Pacific: Emerging Trends in Teaching and Learning* (2008).

Maaret Mattsson is a kindergarten 1 teacher and the leader of the Physical Motor Program in Australian International School of Bangkok (AISB). She is specialized in teaching swimming to young children. Her main job affiliation is to teach 3 to 4 years' old children basic English, the letters of the alphabet, the numbers and sight words. During MA-ELT studies, she wrote her Thesis about 'A Study of the Concept of a "Good Teacher" in the Learning Cultures of Finland and Thailand', in Assumption University of Thailand.

Dr. Tim Murphey, a series editor for the TESOL's Professional Development in Language Education, co-author with ZoltanDörnyei of *Group Dynamics in the Language Classroom* (2003), author of *Music and Song* (1991), *Teaching One to One* (1992), *Language Hungry!* (1998, 2006), *Teaching in Pursuit of Wow!* (2012) and a novel about Japan's entrance exam system, *The Tale That Wags* (2010, 2011 in Japanese), presently researches Vygotskian socio cultural theory (SCT) applications with particular emphasis on student voice, agency, identity and community construction at Kanda University of International Studies. He presents internationally 20 times a year, has taught graduate school courses in the US, Taiwan, and Japan; published books with a dozen publishers; and produced a dozen downloadable videos at the NFLRC, as well as 50 short YouTube teacher training Vidlets (2 to 5 minutes) University of Hawaii.

Dr. Majid Nemati received his PhD in Applied Linguistics from Leicester University (UK) in 2000. He is currently an assistant professor at the University of Tehran, Iran, where he is the Head of the English Language and Literature Department. His area of interest includes applied linguistics, writing, ESP and first language acquisition. He has published a number of articles in both national and international journals and has given lectures in a number of local and international conferences. Besides writing and translating some books, he has also supervised a large number of research projects in the department, aiming at promoting the status of applied linguistics in the country.

Dr. Phan Le Ha is Senior Lecturer in Culture and Pedagogy in the Faculty of Education Monash University, Australia. She also holds honorary positions at universities in Vietnam. She has been developing the Engaging with Vietnam Initiative over the past years. This initiative has brought together scholars, researchers, policy makers, diplomatic officials and the general public to collaboratively engage with knowledge production and scholarship building beyond the Western world. Annual scholarly conferences are a major part of the initiative. She has a range of research publications on her research themes including *Teaching English as an International Language: Identity, Resistance and Negotiation* (2008) and a co-edited special issue of *Studies in Writing* (2011, vol. 22) '*Voices, Identities, Negotiations and Conflicts: Writing Academic English across Cultures*' and gave invited presentations in countries that include Britain, the Philippines, Malaysia and Vietnam.

Dr. Hajar Abdul Rahim is Associate Professor in the English Language Studies department at the School of Humanities, Universiti Sains Malaysia. Her current research interests include L2 vocabulary and corpus-based lexis studies. She supervises postgraduate research in these areas and is particularly interested in L2/FL vocabulary learning and acquisition issues. She also researches the development of Malaysian English using corpus methods and is the principle member of the Malaysian component of the International Corpus of English project (ICE Malaysia). Her recent publications include 'Corpora in ESL/EFL Teaching', in *English in Multicultural Malaysia: Pedagogy and Applied Research* (2012), and 'The Evolution of Malaysian English: Influences from Within', in *Exploring Space: Current Trends in Linguistics, Literature and Translation* (2008). She is also the co-editor of three publications, including a recent one entitled *Linguistics, Literature and Culture: Millennium Realities and Innovative Practices in Asia* (2012).

Dr. Janette Ryan is Director of the BA in Education, University of Birmingham, Research Associate at the China Centre at the University of Oxford, and Visiting Professor at the Centre for Academic Practice and Internationalisation at Leeds Metropolitan University. Her publications include *A Guide to Teaching International Students* (2000), *Teaching International Students: Improving Learning for All* (2005), *International Education and the Chinese Learner* (with Gordon Slethaug, 2010), *China's Higher Education Reform and Internationalisation* (2011), *Education Reform in China* (2011), *Cross Cultural Teaching and Learning for Home and International Students: Internationalisation of Pedagogy and Curriculum in Higher Education* (forthcoming) and *Education in China: Historical, Philosophical, Social and Cultural perspectives* (forthcoming). Her research interests include the internationalization of curriculum and pedagogy, teaching and supporting international students, China's curriculum reform and Western and Confucian notions of scholarship and learning.

Dr. Rahman Sahragard is Associate Professor in Applied Linguistics at Shiraz University, specializing in ELT materials development, critical and mainstream discourse analysis. He studies the contribution of discourse analysis in materials development and language teaching/learning issues. He teaches graduate courses such as Discourse Analysis, Research Methods, and Materials Development. He has participated in many national and international conferences and has published 26 articles in scholarly journals and three books.

Maria Trovela works at the Center for Developing Kids, a pediatric therapy clinic, in Pasadena, California, and attends the Occupational Therapy Graduate Program at the University of Southern California in Los Angeles, California. She has authored 'Maria and the Beatles', in *Sociocultural Theory in Second Language Education: An Introduction through Narratives* (2011). She relocated to Southern California after eight valuable years of teaching English in Japanese universities. While in Japan, Maria's interests included remotivation strategies of learners and also learner autonomy. While in Japan, Maria's interests included remotivation strategies of learners and learner autonomy. She looks forward to discovering connections about remotivation in the clinical setting. She will work with people who, through disease or disability, cannot perform basic life activities.

Jing Wang is currently undertaking a PhD in the University of Hong Kong. She has a Master's degree from the University of Warwick and graduated with distinction. She has diverse learning experience in Mainland China, Finland, the UK and Hong Kong, and she also has worked in both public universities and in the private language training sector. Hence one of her research interests is on Chinese students' English language learning in the classroom from a cultural perspective. Her current research focus is on assessment and its effects on students' metacognitive development.

Prof. Junju Wang is Professor of Applied Linguistics and Dean of the School of Foreign Languages and Literature at Shandong University, China. She holds her BA in English, MA in bilingual translation and Ph.D. in applied linguistics. Her research interests include second-language acquisition, EFL teaching and learning, teacher development, and language testing and assessment. She is the author of *From Ideas to Text: A Cognitive Study of English Writing Processes*, and co-author of *Academic English Writing*. She is also the editor of several books, and her published articles appear in both domestic and international journals. She now serves as member of the National Advisory Committee on Foreign Language Teaching in Higher Education of Ministry of Education of China, councillor of the China English Education Association, vice president of the National Association of EFL Writing Teaching and Research, and President of the Shandong Association of Linguistic Studies.

Prof. Xie Qun is Professor of English and the Dean of College of Foreign Languages in Zhongnan University of Economics and Law, specializing in drama studies and English education. One of her main interests is to interpret the formation of identity in literature from different perspectives. She is also interested in cross-cultural studies in language acquisition and translation. She is the author of *Language and Divided Self – Selected Reading Eugene O'Neill's Plays* (2005), *Introduction to English Literature* (2006), and *A Cotemporary Textbook of Translation between Chinese and English* (2010).

Dr. Yuan Yuan received her PhD from the Kobe University (Japan) and is an associate professor of School of Foreign Languages, Zhongnan University of Economics and Law, China. Her doctoral dissertation has looked at the relationship between second language users and L2 user identity by employing narrative inquiry and conversation analytic approaches. She has published several papers on the discursive construction of 'L2 Learner Identity' in Study-Abroad context: 'Stereotypes and Talk-in-Interaction: The Strategies Used in Identity Negotiation' (2010); 'Identity (Re)formation in a Study-Abroad Context: The Case of a Chinese Learner of Japanese' (2011); 'Co-accomplishing an Interactional Task through Identity Ascription and Ratification' (2009). Her current research interests include identity, discourse analysis and intercultural communication.

Introduction: Researching Cultures of Learning

Martin Cortazzi and Lixian Jin

Cultures of learning, as a concept, suggests that learning is cultural: Members of different cultural communities may have different preferences, expectations, interpretations, values and beliefs about how to learn or how to teach. This idea is enormously important in international and multicultural contexts of education in which commonly students and teachers represent two or more cultures in a single classroom. Centrally, the idea of cultures of learning helps participants in education to think about learning from different angles; potentially there is new thinking about learning from the viewpoint of any culture around the globe; thus, any culture can be a resource, not only for members themselves to learn, but for any others, too, whether that culture is world-influencing or less known. In a framework of cultures of learning, teachers and researchers make an effort to ascertain perspectives in cultures of learning other than those cultures that are most familiar. This helps them to discover more, to increase their understanding of cultural commonalities and of differences in learning, and to develop ways to work positively to mediate between different cultures of learning.

Cultural ideas of learning, often subconscious and taken for granted, are absorbed in early learning in the absence of contrasting ideas and are not normally articulated; they are built up in interaction in families and through early and later schooling as cultures transmit ways of learning and children are socialized into education and then, through education, into so much else in the wider world. However, in the contemporary world members of different cultural communities interact in educational contexts; they bring with them differing cultural perceptions and values. This might be a matter of different ways of learning maths, history or science, but beyond content or syllabus differences, it includes deeper presuppositions and values – for example about the nature of maths, science or history, or about the roles of students and teachers in interaction. Learning in such interactions may go unremarked or may be simply seen as differing ways of learning; but, often, some participants experience the discernible discomfort and stress of culture gaps or clashes, misunderstandings or misinterpretations by teachers or students.

1

Developing a framework of cultures of learning means that learning is not simply seen as transmission, but is likely to be transformative and, at its best, transcendent. As open-minded travellers encountering new cultural experiences, we return home to see the familiar anew and re-engage differently. This framework of learning through alert engagement with participants of other learning cultures also leads us to reflect on our own assumptions, expectations and values for learning, in order to reassess reasons underlying actions and, at least in part, re-engage differently with others. A cultures-of-learning framework means, thus, learning about others' learning and therefore learning more about ourselves: It means learning more about ways of learning. Thus the culture of learners and teachers is not 'background'; it means sets of fore grounded and explicit cultural processes which actually have a centre-stage role, one which we can spotlight in research.

Within a framework of cultures of learning, there are advantages when teachers and learners with different cultural histories develop strategies to learn from each other about learning, in order to try to recognize, appreciate and value alternative approaches to learning. For students, this goes beyond 'learning how to learn'; in collaboration with teachers and other students they may learn from, in, with, and through different ways of learning to increase their repertoires of learning strategies. Since a range of different approaches to learning are likely to be more or less effective in any particular context, teachers – by recognizing positive features of their students' current learning cultures – can help students extend, adapt or adopt new approaches. Such recognition can be part of validating the students' individualities, social identities and cultural voices; giving a place to their culture of learning can be a positive step in helping them develop other ways of learning. With mediation, cultures of learning are, thus, potential resources for learner development. For teachers, investigating and reflecting on other cultures of learning can yield insights for professional development: Every good teacher is a learner. These advantages are more easily realized if learning cultures are discussed, so there is strong value when different voices express experiences and interpretations of learning. *Cultural synergy* is a term which captures this reciprocal learning through reflection. It suggests a holistic benefit that is larger than separated elements. It suggests the importance of peer dialogue as well as teacher–student discussion about ways of learning to develop local, contextualized ways of learning. Such synergy might be seen among small groups and, with effort, between larger communities and institutions.

The idea of cultures of learning is complex: Cultures are complex, dynamic, changing, with (obviously) shared common values but (less obviously) internal diversity of recognized differences, too, so there is no expectation that every member of a particular group thinks or must behave in identical or even similar ways, despite group trends. Thus, the notion of applying a cultures of learning framework to classroom interaction with international students, say, should not involve reducing them to an over-simplified view, or one invoking stereotypes; on the contrary, the notion of cultures of learning has been developed precisely to counter stereotypes (see Chapter 1) by focussing on specific aspects of real learning and getting those insider perspectives, preferably through research, which illumine the activities and thinking of real learners or teachers in authentic contexts through rich data.

It is important to stress this cultural side of learning, since long-standing traditions of research about learning (for example, to develop conceptions of learning in teacher education) have been based largely within psychology and, therefore, focussed predominantly on the individual or small group; only more recently has such research developed social insights and given attention to social contexts. Research broadly within frameworks of cultures of learning includes here key notions of cultural models, cultural scripts and roles of linguistic and social interaction, with motivation that is sensitive to the dynamics of social contexts and, in general, to different traditions of learning. It points up the fascinating details of how cultural groups might learn in different ways, which is vital knowledge for teachers. The orientation to cultures of learning focuses attention on shared cultural values, expectations and interpretations of behaviour in learning – while acknowledging diversity and difference within and between cultural communities.

I.1   A pedigree for cultures of learning, 1970s to 1990s

We now give the briefest sketch of an intellectual map of a pedigree for conceptions of cultures of learning with selected landmarks of classic references (1970s to 1990s), as a prelude for the chapters here, particularly Chapter 1, which focuses on the development of cultures of learning through related research. In the 1970s and 1980s, within areas of linguistics, education, anthropology, sociology and psychology, a number of streams of development of theoretical approaches rooted in studies of different cultural communities could be seen as drawing together language education, sociolinguistics, anthropological linguistics, socio-cultural approaches to development, constructivist approaches to language use in classrooms, classroom discourse studies .... We might now see these as related, having a nexus relating to the idea of *cultures of learning*: a complicated series of complementary connections between separate threads that came to be closely connected, forming an idea which now seems central to internationalization in learning and developing more equitable practices in contexts in which different cultural communities learn together.

Examples of these threads include ethnographic research about *different ways of speaking*, which shows that styles, meanings and identities connected with speech might greatly vary in different cultural communities and represent different systems of social values (Gumperz & Hymes, 1972; Bauman

& Sherzer, 1974; Hymes, 1977; Saville-Troike, 1982). This has consequences in classrooms where teachers and learners as representatives of different cultural groups use different discourse patterns and adopt *different ways of learning* and teaching, perhaps resulting in clashes (Cazden et al., 1972; Hymes, 1996). This work develops sensitivity to language and cultural communities' uses of different discourse patterns, which can also be linked to cultural literacies and contrastive rhetoric in which scholars show different cultural values in using books, reading and formulating writing texts – ways which can be evaluated quite differently by outsiders (Gumperz, 1982; Brice Heath, 1983; Street, 1984; Cook-Gumperz, 1986; Connor & Kaplan, 1987; Purves, 1988; Dubin & Kuhlman, 1992; Connor, 1996). Crucially, in such an ethnographic approach, researchers make every effort to get insider perspectives and portray participants in their own voices (words, meanings, stance, and integrity). As language use socializes across cultures in different ways (Schieffelin and Ochs, 1986) we may see language used for socializing into school cultures (not very successfully for some cultural communities) and, indeed, into wider social structures, cultural values and structures of knowledge (Bernstein, 1971; Halliday, 1978). Since education has broad functions of transmission of culture (together with functions of innovation and change), there are links we can recognize – once they are pointed out – between culture, mind, language and education, which affect individuals, groups and institutions (Bruner, 1983, 1990, 1996), but these links must vary when different cultures are considered, which leads to *different ways of learning through different cultures*. Since different uses of language in classroom interaction are seen as constructing knowledge in different ways, this has given huge importance to discussion and dialogic modes of collaboration and inquiry, which are vital when cultures differ between home and school (Edwards & Furlong, 1978; Wells, 1981, 1986; Mercer, 1995). Dialogues are considered crucial in the socio-cultural perspectives, which see outward language among peers or with advanced others as becoming internalized and social activities as mediating learning, and participation as the way towards the appropriation of concepts (Vygotsky, 1962, 1978; Wertsch, 1985, 1991; Wertsch, et al., 1995) in situated learning and communities of practice (Lave, 1988; Lave & Wenger, 1991; Wenger, 1998). This reinforces notions that representatives of diverse communities of learning in contact with each other should try to make explicit their ideas about learning and attempt to articulate the values that lie behind how they go about learning: Such dialogues create further learning and may have a goal of synergy.

By the late 1980s and early 1990s, the above streams could be expanded in *cultures of learning* in three ways that probably were not imagined by many of the foregoing scholars: First, they could be envisaged globally, with increasing significance for rapidly growing numbers of international students, exchanges, collaborations and partnerships in schools and, particularly, universities; second, with world-wide migration of families with children, they could be seen locally with multiplying recognition of diversity in multicultural communities, which was especially evident in inner city schools, later in many other schools, in receiving countries; third, there was a need for cross-cultural and intercultural research in international contexts, using a variety of research methods to establish more details. Thus, a case could be made and research carried out to explore insights into socialization and classroom expectations with international students and language learning world-wide to consider cultural expectations (Cortazzi, 1990); and to consider details of academic culture gaps with Chinese students studying in Britain in terms of cultures of learning (Jin, 1992; Jin & Cortazzi, 1993; Cortazzi & Jin, 1997) or Chinese learners in China taught by Western teachers (Cortazzi & Jin, 1996), children in multicultural primary schools (Cortazzi, 1997, 1998; Jin & Cortazzi, 1998a, 1998b), questions of equity, researcher identity, dilemmas and rights in relation to cultures of learning (Cortazzi, 2002; Cortazzi & Jin, 2002) and to consider cultural synergy in the light of academic culture gaps and English for Academic Purposes (Jin & Cortazzi, 1995, 1996, 1998a), with further research into cultural conceptions of good teachers, good students and classroom interaction (Jin & Cortazzi, 1997; Cortazzi & Jin, 2001, 2002).

In light of the above sketch, it is interesting to note that, whereas earlier books for teachers which focussed on learning said nothing about culture, by the late 1990s later books in this genre featured whole chapters on 'culture and learning', as if this is normal and natural (Jarvis et al., 1998; Biggs, 1999; Moore, 2000) – which it is. The present book of research studies takes cultures of learning in further directions.

I.2 The chapters in this book

Chapter 1 sets a general context for later chapters by providing a background which reviews over 20 years of research into cultures of learning. This work is known at least in part by all contributors to this book, though none of the writers here have felt bound to follow any particular definition or direction of thinking or method of research about cultures of learning. In this chapter, Yuan Yuan and Qun Xie, two Chinese foreign language and literature scholars, present a critical review of the developing concept of *cultures of learning* through a detailed consideration of the research of Jin and Cortazzi. These authors argue that Jin and Cortazzi's work in the early 1990s was aimed to counter stereotypes of that time, regarding Chinese learners, by raising cultural awareness and portraying learning in China through the inside voices by investigating features of classroom pedagogy. Yuan and Xie review a range of statistical and qualitative research elaborating ideas of Chinese students about good teachers, good students, the classroom interaction between them and why some students may do not ask questions in class; the results contrast with parallel investigations in other East Asian and Middle Eastern cultures. The authors show how Jin and Cortazzi have qualitatively elaborated other key elements of cultures of learning through narrative analysis and metaphor analysis, together with their explorations of Confucian heritage sources of some features of Chinese cultures of learning. Finally, Yuan and Xie give extended critical comment by consideration of whether such research superimposes characteristics on the participant groups, whether it ignores agency and overlooks diversity within a culture of learning, and how it squares with change and a dynamic view of culture.

In Chapter 2, Janette Ryan, based in the United Kingdom, builds on her research in educational reform in China to report an exploratory, rather telling, investigation of two groups of scholars regarding their views of scholarship and learning. These are Anglophone scholars and Chinese scholars, all in several countries, and all working in a range of disciplines. This is particularly interesting because most research related to cultures of learning has focussed on learners, including their perceptions of teaching. In arguing for the need to be cautious about binary lists of supposed differences between Chinese and Western students (which might reinforce myths and stereotypes, and risks treating them as homogenous groups with essentialized features), Ryan points up rapid changes in schools and universities in China which have affected some characteristics of cultures of learning there. Her research interviews confirm commonalities across the two groups' views, but also differences, including differences between individuals, within each group. This commonality may be a consequence, she thinks, of internationalization in China which has included not only global flows of students to and from China but also of academics travelling both ways. However, this is complex because there are tensions in the changing educational cultures in China between learner- and teacher-centred approaches as well as between learning for exams and teaching for broader purposes; and some scholars sense a reclaiming of features of Confucian educational ideals amid rapid modernization.

The question of the relevance of a Confucian heritage to students in contemporary China is taken further in Chapter 3. Here, Wang Junju, an applied linguistics researcher in China, reports on a large-scale investigation of Chinese students' perceptions of traditional concepts of learning which are known in the Confucian heritage. This complex heritage of several thousand years certainly held sway in examinations in China for hundreds of years and has at times been intertwined with influential Buddhist and Taoist streams of action and thought; there is a current debate about how these heritages might relate to modern education, if at all. To ascertain students' perceptions, Wang uses a substantial questionnaire survey largely based on statements about learning contained in the *Analects*, a foundational Confucian classic text which is well known in Chinese culture. The results show how the participants largely do recognize and agree with key features of this traditional educational thought. While the students seem to see such thinking as a holistic system, they put high value on traditional concepts of learning, attitudes to learning and modes of teaching; athough many have reservations about traditional learning objectives, methods of learning and student–teacher relationships, they have high expectations for traditional teachers and their practices. There are some gender differences with these perceptions and differences according to year of study. Wang implies that the Confucian heritage should not be considered an all-or-nothing package; it is a complex whole that inspires much student agreement but some disagreement with some features because educational aims and contexts have changed. She suggests that teachers of Chinese students need to take account of those features valued by the students; her research shows more precisely what are those features.

The context shifts to Kenya and Tanzania in East Africa in Chapter 4, in which Jan Abd-Kadir and Frank Hardman draw on their expertise in classroom learning and teacher development in international education to emphasize the key role of discussion and dialogue in classroom talk as being central to the quality of learners' construction of knowledge and development of different levels of thinking. This is crucial to their report of details of research into substantial teacher education and leadership programmes in Kenya and Tanzania; this research is helpful for an understanding of schooling and teachers' pre- and in-service education in these and other low income countries, especially for school-based programmes, since the quality of teaching is identified as the most important single factor in school achievement. Abd-Kadir and Hardman show how the teachers' pedagogic skills and their training in classroom exchanges (of question-and-answer sequences and elicitation from students) mediates possibilities of discussion and dialogue, which in turn are limited by the underlying beliefs, knowledge, skills and commitments of teachers and by the pedagogic practices of those who train them. Thus the socio-cultural ideas of knowledge held by many teachers leads to transmission of 'fixed' knowledge to students through rote learning; changing this in teacher education, among other characteristics, towards more dialogic practices requires, the authors argue, a holistic approach beyond training in classroom techniques. This holistic approach needs to consider factors in the socio-cultural context, such as the teachers' beliefs and what they value in education, and it includes other aspects of context, such as the end-of-primary school certificate assessments and the policies of language choice in education, where English and Kiswahili have national roles in the context of many other local languages.

The role of interaction through talk and classroom exchanges, and especially teacher feedback in the form of praise to learners, is the focus of Chapter 5, in which Jing Wang and Martin Cortazzi report on research in a university classroom in China which closely monitors how a teacher of college English attempts to change his feedback practices and how students respond to this. While this is a single large class, it represents a huge number of classes involving around nine million students in China (non-English majors) who need to take the College English Test annually for graduation and, often, to secure particular employment. In such classes, recent advances in learning materials and pedagogic practices are constrained by cultural rules of classroom talk, which tend to be teacher-centred and have cultural constraints on public praise. Wang, a Chinese teacher of English and classroom researcher, and Cortazzi, a teacher educator and applied linguistics researcher, report their intervention in the classroom with a 'distant' action research project. The project is 'distant' because data from questionnaires, interviews, learning journals and audio and video recordings were analysed, at a distance, but without directly observing the participants, all of which demands good teamwork. Wang and Cortazzi show there are differences between actual praise given and perceptions of what praise was given. Also, students perceive that they participate orally more in class when the teacher uses more praise – students believe there is a causal link. Interestingly, students show clear preferences for some types of praise rather than others. The results are discussed in the context of Chinese cultures of learning.

This question of changing aspects of cultures of learning is further explored in the context of a university in Lebanon in Chapter 6. This is a case study of multiple heritages in a cosmopolitan context: Many Lebanese have travelled or lived abroad for extended periods, and the population is multilingual, with considerable ethnic and religious diversity. For the majority, Arabic is the first language but secondary schooling is likely to be given in either an English-medium or French-medium school (with the other language as a third language), while universities are Arabic, French or English medium. In this chapter, Nahla Bacha and Rima Bahous draw on their extensive experience teaching English and on their interactions with Lebanese teachers in Lebanon. They explain the complexities of Lebanese education, with its nuanced strands of languages, cultures and identities. They use a questionnaire survey and focus group interviews to investigate students' perceptions of learning in a North American university educational environment (which encourages critical thinking and classroom interaction in a learner-centred context) compared to the Lebanese high school environment (which is widely seen to encourage memorization in a more teacher-centred lecturing approach). The first impression is that high school teachers encourage memorization and lecture in a teacher-centred approach, and that students need to make a transition to develop critical thinking and greater classroom interaction in a more student-centred approach. However, the authors present surprising results which partly counter this impression but which also overlay it with complexities of gender expectations and behaviour, features of friendship and different ideas about fairness, and a need to develop study habits and citation skills. Features of these cosmopolitan cultures of learning are thus not obvious.

In Chapter 7, Dat Bao, a Vietnamese researcher based in Australia, investigates Vietnamese students' perceptions of why many of them are reticent in the classroom. Their reluctance to speak out has been construed as 'poor speech' or a lack of motivation, but Bao develops a questionnaire and interview approach to get their inside voices and reveals how these students have a collective understanding of reticence which is surprisingly rich in detail. The student comments about causes and possible solutions to reticence, and their thoughts about active participation, are an indirect mirror which shows a great deal about their learning situation as they see it. Some comments analyse teacher–student exchanges (compare Chapters 4 and 5) and the conditions of teaching. Since Bao shows that efforts by outside teacher-training experts coming to Vietnam have been less successful than hoped in developing students' active participation, it is particularly noticeable how the students make suggestions which are, in fact, much in line with stances of contemporary Western theorists of classroom pedagogy and practice (which the students are unlikely to have heard of); however, the students' stance is balanced by a delicate attitude to maintaining respect for teachers and a regard for some traditions in their cultures of learning. Thus, these students show a reasonable attitude to remaining relatively silent under conditions which may not, in fact, encourage activity, yet most are in favour of more active pedagogies. Significantly, their conception of activity is a vibrant one of peer support which creates encouragement and depth of learning – activity, they say, that gives teachers a better opportunity to diagnose their learning.

Chapter 8 focusses on how textbooks for teaching English in Malaysia reflect features of 'glocalization'. As Hajar Abdul Rahim and Shakila Abdul Manan explain and elaborate, this term blends global and local processes to recognize the globalization of the local which may be expected to be seen as a transformative potential in education or, here, in the content of secondary school textbooks. Since these sample books are officially approved and very widely used, a culturally based analysis would show features of an endorsed culture of learning, although in actual practice this might be mediated by both teachers and learners. Rahim and Manan give a detailed portrayal of the evolving context of English teaching and the changing nature of syllabuses in Malaysia which inform the design of the textbooks. Using their respective expertise in linguistics and local usage and practices of English in Malaysia, and in English studies, culture and literature, the authors use the framework of Intercultural Communication Competence (intercultural attitudes, knowledge, skills and critical cultural awareness) to analyse the books as crucially influential pedagogic documents. Their analysis reveals some predominance of the local in the area of the major category of cultural knowledge, which develops multicultural competence within the nation, but with strong representation of the global in some content themes and personalities and places featured. An interesting aspect of the textbooks is how the literature embodied in them is both Eastern and Western and reflects universal values and cultural diversity, and through this content skills of discovery are developed. To further realize the transformative potential of glocalization as it is evolving, they suggest the books (or, we may say, teachers using the books) would need to develop the framework features of critical cultural awareness and a more intercultural learning environment, which could be achieved, they comment, through the inclusion of more non-literary text elements and through the use of associated technology and social media.

The potentially globalizing role of English in a local context of different cultural heritages is a feature of Chapter 9, in which the focus is on the students' perceptions and expectations of English teachers in the Central Asian country of Kazakhstan. Gulnissa Makhanova, a Kazakh- and Russian-speaking university teacher of English, and Martin Cortazzi, first review the country's heritages: an ex-Soviet educational tradition with Russian as a lingua franca and people of Russian heritage; Kazakh people as the major ethnic group of the population plus other indigenous minorities (each with their own language and traditions) and residents from outside; an Islamic heritage; and several choices of language for the medium of schooling but with English (post-1990) as the major foreign language with potentially, an internationally mediating prestigious influence on cultural perceptions of teachers through its associated pedagogies. Additionally, students' ideas about teachers may derive from notions of teacher professionalism and from students' socialization in childhood and earlier schooling. The data for this study are elicited through students' essays about their expectations of 'good' English teachers and follow-up interviews; the major responses are succinctly reported (compare Chapters 10 and 11) as high expectations for teacher knowledge; their learning; qualities of dedication, caring and being fair; their teaching of the cultures of English-speaking peoples; and their guidance for students to be better people. However, the value of this study is in the extended illustrated discussion which elaborates and comments on the features expected of teachers as overlays of different traditions within a culture of learning with multiple heritages such that some features are under tension and others cannot, so far, be traced to a single source.

The theme of perceptions of 'good' English teachers continues in Chapter 10, in terms of teacher efficacy, not only through the views of students but of teachers, too, with some focus on gender, so teacher participants in the study reported here are in part asked to evaluate co-professionals of the same or opposite gender – an innovative research step in this context. Majid Nemati and Shiva Kaivanpanah report on their research in Iran, where learning English as a foreign language has a strong role in schools and is crucial for university entrance exams. Importantly, teachers here are the chief source of language input. The researchers, as English specialists in a university in Iran, are insiders, and they seek insider perspectives about good English teachers through questionnaires filled out by students and English teachers at university; they also interview male and female teachers regarding gender aspects (no easy task in this context). While female teachers tend to teach in girls' schools and male teachers in those for boys, at university level teachers of both genders teach male and female students together and, notably, female students outnumber males at university. While there are no statistically significant gender differences (a lack of bias and absence of stereotyping), students of both gender seem to value male teachers as more effective; a follow-up investigation shows that many students do not consider gender to be relevant in judging efficacy (factors like teacher knowledge and the quality of their teaching are much more important), while other students are split in preferring male or female teachers (giving different sets of reasons, with intriguing comments), with some preference for male teachers. Similar splits among the teachers themselves are discussed. As in other studies in this book, the details of the results and discussion points are worth particular attention.

Chapter 11 also looks at expectations of teachers with a cross-cultural comparison of students' perceptions in Finland and Thailand, using a very different research approach to explore both cultural contexts which seem dramatically different. Here, Erich Berendt, a Canadian cognitive applied linguist, known for long-standing work in Japan but here researching in Thailand, and Maaret Mattson, a Finnish teacher with professional experience in Thailand, first collected proverbs about teaching and student teachers' essays in the two countries. These were analysed to make a questionnaire with balanced numbers of Finnish- and Thai-origin statements for other students in both places to rate. The statements can be seen as conceptual metaphors about teachers (they underlie different actual sayings and metaphoric statements about teachers in language use), which later can be grouped in conceptual patterns of cultural use and related to protocols of classroom expectations, roles, ideas about knowledge and learning which underlie behaviour. While details of the rationale and procedures in this kind of research are technical, Berendt and Mattson present and discuss their results in relation to the cultures, in an unfolding picture of some ideas common to both cultures, some overlapping ones and some which are dramatically different. Common concepts show a teacher as a key to knowledge, sharing and learning; learning is hard, but should be a joy, an endless journey. For the Finnish students, a teacher is a professional, a guide, an ordinary person who is strict; for Thai students a teacher is superior, a master, leader, friend or parent, who has heart and is compassionate and caring for students. This study implies many comparisons with other cultures of learning.

Chapter 12 has a focus on the identity of English teachers in Vietnam. This chapter (complementing Chapter 7) takes as a starting point the common labelling of Vietnamese learners as passive, reluctant and reticent in the English as a Foreign Language (EFL) context, but argues that English as an International Language (EIL) frames both learners and teachers differently, not only pedagogically but with reference to their identities since EIL is far more flexible about including local self-positioning regarding language learning rather than simply making comparisons with native speakers (as EFL often does). A stance of critical pedagogies reinforces notions that teaching EIL should employ culturally situated pedagogies in which teacher agency and identity have a significant role in relation to local perspectives. To explore these issues, Le Thi Thu Huyen and Phan Le Ha, Vietnamese scholars and education specialists in Australia, study ethnically Vietnamese, Australian-trained teachers of English who have returned to teach in Vietnam. Le and Phan investigate how the enhanced professional training of completing specialist ELT postgraduate degrees might have changed the teachers' sense of identity and how this impacts the nurturing of a more locally appropriate culture of learning for their students. Analysing interviews, classroom observation and teachers' reflective journals, the authors give details of how these teachers have grown professionally, although their identity is not simply as a Western-trained teacher; while their overall pedagogic approaches have shifted away from a traditional Vietnamese approach, their views of learners remain somewhat entrenched within stereotypes. Their teacher identities are partly constructed in comparison with of those of other local teachers and local ideas about status, power and respect. These fluidities and continuities of identity might be further developed through the space developed in this study, which gives further consideration to EIL and concepts of cultural synergy of these teachers with their Vietnamese students.

In Chapter 13, attention moves to children's learning beliefs and their socialization regarding cultural models of learning acquired from their parents. Here Jin Li, a Chinese researcher in education and human development in the United States, uses her previous research analysing elicited associations with 'learning' to contrast the cultural models of learning held by Euro-Americans with those held by Chinese in order to show how the former is more mind-oriented while the latter is more virtue-oriented. To explore how young children might acquire such models, she first investigates children's learning beliefs through story completion activities to find a similar basic contrast and then moves, through research with parents in the United States and Taiwan, to explore the children's socialization into the cultural models. Using prompts, the parents talk with their young children about positive and more negative learning situations; these conversations are analysed in a topic analysis over sequences of mother–child turns in an innovative research study. Amid interesting details, overall the Euro-American parents emphasize positive affect and a mental orientation, while the Chinese parents emphasize virtue, but not positive affect (see Chapter 5 on praise in a Chinese classroom). Li concludes thought-provokingly by raising doubts about Westernization and traditions in Chinese contexts, and she wonders what a successful mixture of cultures would look like (compare Chapter 1 and others on cultural synergy), especially in light of the ways in which second- or third-generation descendants of migrants in the United States may not maintain features of the non-American cultural models of the previous generations.

Parents of students also feature in Chapter 14, but as part of a social network along with relatives, friends and teachers, in an investigation of how the enacted attitudes within such social networks have an effect on secondary school students' motivation to learn English in Oman. Sami Dadi, a Tunisian teacher of English working in Oman, with Lixian Jin, an applied linguistics researcher from China working in Britain, investigate these social networks locally. These networks are recognized as strongly reflective of Omani values of social relations, social support and integrity, and they are enacted within occasions of social interaction – largely out-of-class and out-of-school interactions that are thus informal features of a culture of learning. Using questionnaire and interview data, the authors show statistically how the networks affect students' motivation mainly through two aspects which depend on the influence of others: interest and self-efficacy (evaluations of the capability of performing a task). Analysis of interview data shows how teachers, parents, close friends and family members other than parents are, in that order, the main influences within the networks. The study shows how network members meet a student's need for help, support and advice by urging them on and giving encouragement and reassurance, but this is mediated by trust and may be reciprocal when one student encourages another. An 'osmosis model' brings together motivational factors related to social networks in Oman.

Chapter 15 takes the issue of motivation further by examining what demotivates high school students in Iran from learning English (see Chapter 10 on perceptions of teachers in Iran). Demotivating factors include external influences that reduce learners' motivation and internal factors that affect learners' confidence and lead to negative attitudes; this has been much researched in Japan (see Chapter 16). Here, Rahman Sahragard and Zahra Alimorad, Iranian university teachers of English who are also applied linguistics researchers, review the culture of learning English in Iranian schools to show the need for this study: English is given strong attention as a compulsory course, but teaching is largely 'traditional' and 'teacher-centred', and students have relatively little opportunity to engage in active use of the language in class and even less opportunity outside school. The authors statistically analyse questionnaire data with a factor analysis to identify seven demotivating factors. Lack of self-confidence was one main factor demotivating many students, especially for those who were less motivated in the first place. In contrast to other research, the perceived competence of teachers and teaching styles were not strong causes of demotivation in comparison to the following: the learning contents and contexts, students' lack of interest in English, the focus on usage rather than on real uses of English, and teachers' methods of teaching. These were major factors, both for those groups initially more motivated and groups less motivated: notably these are both external and internal causes. The lack of facilities in schools, the perceived inappropriateness of books and teaching materials also lead to demotivation. When teachers overlook affective factors this leads to the students' lack of self-confidence and lack of interest in English. The authors argue that the conjunction of these demotivating factors points to a systemic need to make changes in English teaching in schools in order to minimize the effects of these factors.

A further stage of complementary studies in motivation, sensitive to social interaction and with dynamic conceptualizations of motivation which can see changes over time (see Chapters 14 and 15), is reported in Chapter 16. Here, the focus is on remotivation in Japan: students in a demotivating situation who take up strategies for coping, finding meaning in this context and in their actions, revive their motivation for learning English. In Japan, widespread initial enthusiasm for learning English in primary schools declines dramatically during the 6–8 years learning period as students face exams in English (particularly for university entrance), meet ambiguous or indifferent attitudes among parents or in society and unhelpful teaching methods in large classes, and who do not engage in contexts of real use for the language. Extensive motivation studies in Japan are reported here, crucially through the work of a team of creative scholars – North American long-term resident teachers with Japanese co-researchers, and experts in the field of the (de/re)motivation of students of English: Joseph Falout, Tim Murphey, Tetsuya Fukada and Maria Trovela. They employ the key idea of 'antecedent conditions of the learner' and examine whether these are internal or external to the learners, positive or negative, stable or changing. Using questionnaires and motivation timelines and grids with university students, they investigate in some detail how various antecedent conditions develop over time, with unintentional or intentional short- or long-term coping strategies. Among their conclusions: Students need a longer-term social vision of learning, with more incremental ways of learning and teaching, so that learners can cope better with the inevitable ups and downs of study. Teachers can offer strategies to recognize demotivation and help students do something positive, and peers can be supportive.

The present book can usefully be seen in conjunction with:

Jin, L. & Cortazzi, M. (Eds) (2011) *Researching Chinese Learners: Skills, perceptions and intercultural adaptations.* Houndmills: Palgrave Macmillan.

Jin, L. & Cortazzi, M. (Eds) (2013) *Researching Intercultural Learning: Investigations in language and education.* Houndmills: Palgrave Macmillan.

References

Bauman, R. & Sherzer, J. (Eds) (1974) *Explorations in the ethnography of speaking.* Cambridge: Cambridge University Press.

Bernstein, B. (1971) *Class, codes and control; vol. 1, Theoretical studies towards a sociology of language.* London: Routledge & Kegan Paul.

Biggs, J. (1999) *Teaching for quality learning at University, what the student does.* Milton Keynes: SRHE/Open University Press.

Bruner, J. (1983) *Child's talk, learning to use language.* Oxford: Oxford University Press.

Bruner, J. (1990) *Acts of Meaning.* Cambridge, MA: Harvard University Press.

Bruner, J. (1996) *The culture of education.* Cambridge, MA: Harvard University Press.

Cazden, C. B.; John, V. P. & Hymes, D. (Eds) (1972) *Functions of language in the classroom.* New York: Teachers College Press.

Connor, U. (1996) *Contrastive Rhetoric, cross-cultural aspects of second-language writing.* Cambridge: Cambridge University Press.

Connor, U. & Kaplan, R. B. (Eds) (1987) *Writing across Language: Analysis of L2 text.* Reading, MA: Addison-Wesley.

Cook-Gumperz, J. (Ed.) (1986) *The social construction of literacy.* Cambridge: Cambridge University Press.

Cortazzi, M. (1990) Cultural and educational expectations in the language classroom. In B. Harrison (Ed.), *Culture and the language classroom.* London: Modern English Publications/The British Council, pp. 54–65.

Cortazzi, M. (1997) Classroom Talk: communicating within the learning relationship. In N. Kitson and R. Merry (Eds), *Teaching in the Primary School, a learning relationship.* London: Routledge, pp. 139–56.

Cortazzi, M. (2002) Cultures of Learning and Equitable Education, challenges from China. In K. J. Solstad (Ed.), *Equitable education – Utopia or realism?* Bodo: Nordlands Forskning, pp. 93–108.

Cortazzi, M. & Jin, L. (1996) Cultures of learning: Language classrooms in China. In H. Coleman (Ed.), *Society and the language classroom.* Cambridge: Cambridge University Press, pp. 169–206.

Cortazzi, M. & Jin, L. (1997) Communication for learning across cultures. In D. McNamara and R. Harris (Eds), *Overseas students in Higher education, issues in teaching and learning.* London: Routledge, pp. 76–90.

Cortazzi, M. (1998) Curricula across cultures: Contexts and connections. In J. Moyles and L. Hargreaves (Eds), *The Primary Curriculum, learning from international perspectives.* London: Routledge, pp. 205–16.

Cortazzi, M. & Jin, L. (2001) Large Classes in China: 'good' teachers and interaction. In D. A. Watkins and J. B. Biggs (Eds), *Teaching the Chinese Learner: psychological and pedagogical perspectives.* Hong Kong: CERC, The University of Hong Kong, pp. 115–34.

Cortazzi, M. & Jin, L. (2002) Cultures of Learning: The social construction of educational identities. In D. C. S. Li (Ed.), *Discourses in search of members, in honor of Ron Scollon.* Lanham: University Press of America, pp. 49–78.

Dubin, F. & Kuhlman, N. (Eds) (1992) *Cross-cultural Literacy, global perspectives on reading and writing.* Englewood Cliffs, NJ: Regents/Prentice Hall.

Edwards, A. D. & Furlong, V. J. (1978) *The Language of Teaching, meaning in classroom interaction.* London: Heinemann.

Gumperz, J. J. (1982) *Discourse strategies.* Cambridge: Cambridge University Press.

Gumperz, J. J. & Hymes, D. (Eds) (1972) *Directions in sociolinguistics, the ethnography of communication.* New York: Holt, Rinehart and Winston.

Halliday, M. A. K. (1978) *Language as social semiotic, the social interpretation of language and meaning.* London: Edward Arnold.

Heath, S. B. (1983) *Ways with words*. Cambridge: Cambridge University Press.

Hymes, D. (1977) *Foundations in sociolinguistics, an ethnographic approach*. London: Tavistock Publications.

Hymes, D. (1996) *Ethnography, linguistics, narrative inequality, towards an understanding of voice*. London: Taylor & Francis.

Jarvis, P., Holford, J. & Griffin, C. (1998) *The theory and practice of learning*. London: Kogan Page.

Jin, L. (1992) *Academic cultural expectations and second language use: Chinese postgraduate students in the UK, a cultural synergy model'*, unpublished PhD thesis, University of Leicester, U.K.

Jin, L. & Cortazzi, M. (1993) Cultural orientation and academic language Use. In D. Graddol, L. Thompson and M. Byram (Eds) *Language and culture*. Clevedon: Multilingual Matters, pp. 84–97.

Jin, L. & Cortazzi, M. (1995) A cultural synergy model for academic language use. In P. Bruthiaux, T. Boswood and B. Du Babcock (Eds), *Explorations in English for professional communication*. Hong Kong: City University, pp. 41–56.

Jin, L. & Cortazzi, M. (1996) 'This way is very different from Chinese ways' EAP needs and academic culture. In M. Hewings & T. Dudley-Evans (Eds), *Evaluation and course design in EAP*. Hemel Hempstead: Prentice Hall Macmillan/The British Council, pp. 205–18.

Jin, L. & Cortazzi, M. (1997) Expectations and questions in the intercultural classroom. *Intercultural Communication Studies, 7* (2) 37–62.

Jin, L. & Cortazzi, M. (1998a) The culture the learner brings: A bridge or a barrier? In M. Byram and M. Fleming (Eds), *Language learning in intercultural perspective, approaches through drama and ethnography*. Cambridge: Cambridge University Press, pp. 98–118.

Jin, L. & Cortazzi, M. (1998b) Dimensions of dialogue: Large classes in China. *International Journal of Educational Research, 29*, 739–62.

Lave, J. (1988) *Cognition in practice: Mind, mathematics and culture in everyday life*. Cambridge: Cambridge University Press.

Lave, J. & Wenger, E. (1991) *Situated learning: Legitimate peripheral participation*. Cambridge: Cambridge University Press.

Mercer, N. (1995) *The guided construction of knowledge, talk amongst teachers and learners*. Clevedon: Multilingual Matters.

Moore, A. (2000) *Learning and teaching, pedagogy, curriculum and culture*. London: Routledge/Falmer.

Purves, A. (Ed.) (1988) *Writing across languages and cultures, issues in contrastive rhetoric*. Newbury Park: Sage.

Saville-Troike, M. (1982) *The ethnography of communication, an introduction*. Oxford: Blackwell.

Schieffelin, B. S. & Ochs, E. (1986) *Language socialization across cultures*. Cambridge: Cambridge University Press.

Street, B. (1984) *Literacy in theory and practice*. Cambridge: Cambridge University Press.

Vygotsky, L. S. (1962) *Thought and language*. Cambridge, MA: The MIT Press.

Vygotsky, L. S., Cole M., John-Steiner V., Scribner S. & Souberman E. (Eds) (1978) *Mind in Society, the development of higher psychological processes*. Cambridge, MA: Harvard University Press.

Wells, G. (1981) *Learning through interaction, the study of language development*. Cambridge: Cambridge University Press.

Wells, G. (1986) *The meaning makers, children learning language and using language to learn.* London: Hodder & Stoughton.

Wenger, E. (1998) *Communities of practice: Learning, meaning and identity.* Cambridge, MA: Harvard University Press.

Wertsch, J. (Ed.) (1985) *Culture, communication & cognition.* Cambridge: Cambridge University Press.

Wertsch, J. V. (1991) *Voices of the mind, a socio-cultural approach to mediated action.* London: Harvester Wheatsheaf.

Wertsch, J. V., del Rio, P. & Alvarez, A. (Eds) (1995) *Sociocultural studies of mind.* Cambridge: Cambridge University Press.

Part 1

Some Issues of Research and Its Application

Part 1

Some Issues of Research and Its Application

1
Cultures of Learning: An Evolving Concept and an Expanding Field

Yuan Yuan and Qun Xie

Cultures of learning, as a concept, suggests that learning is cultural (as well as psychological) and that people from different cultural groups might therefore learn in different ways. The concept focuses on the cultural values, expectations and interpretations relating to learning which are shared within a cultural community. Further, it proposes positive strategies for teachers and students to learn from each other about learning, and to recognize, appreciate and value different approaches, especially in intercultural contexts in which participants who use different cultural ways of learning engage with each other. This goes beyond 'learning how to learn'; it asserts a need for both teachers and students to learn from different ways of learning and thus implies the value of different voices. Cultures of learning is a positive concept for both learner development of their individuality, social identity and awareness of others, and for teacher development of professional insights into alternative ways of learning.

The related concept for *cultural synergy* stresses reciprocal learning between and among different students and teachers through raising awareness and engaging in reflection. It suggests the importance of a dialogue about ways of learning: such a dialogue becomes more than the sum of the differences and will develop local, contextualized ways of learning. In contexts of the globalization of learning, this allows a strong role for local voices and values.

In this chapter we trace the research related to cultures of learning carried out by Lixian Jin, Martin Cortazzi and others between 1990 and 2012.

1.1 The context: Stereotyped Chinese learners

Briefly, the context of the proposal for the concepts of cultures of learning and cultural synergy stems from an encounter with a predominant misunderstanding of Chinese learners in the literature about international students. The central purpose of the concept of cultures of learning is to counter the stereotypes about Chinese learners in the TESOL (Teaching

English to Speakers of Other Languages) profession by portraying their ways of learning using insider voices. Since the 1980s, the developments within the global economy, with greatly increased migration patterns and international movements of students and teachers, has resulted in an increasing interest in understanding ESL learners (using English as a Second Language) in Western classrooms. The large number of Chinese students studying in Western classrooms provokes a research interest in Chinese learners; in applied linguistics there has been an emerging discourse on 'Chinese learners', 'Asian learners', or sometimes 'East Asians'. These discourses have constructed Chinese learners as a stereotyped group who are obedient to teachers' authority, passive in class, lacking in critical thinking and adopt inadequate learning strategies (Atkinson, 1997; Ballard & Clanchy, 1991; Carson, 1992; Flowerdew, 1998; Fox, 1994). Meanwhile, some scholars have observed that stereotyping Chinese or other Asian learners can have a disastrous effect on pedagogy. Alast Pennycook (1998), in a critique that includes data from mainland China and Hong Kong, argues that colonial stereotypes of the 'Other' continue to resurface in public discourse such as travel writing and the media, thus influencing the ways in which Western educators form opinion about, position and 'fix' their students. Likewise, 'Some unreflected response might take all these testimonies from the Chinese learners as an easy ideological proof that they are more immature, passive, illiterate and less sophisticated than [W]estern learners' (Klitgard, 2011: p. 177). The overwhelming conclusion sets the relationship between educators and students as one of power status, which in fact results in anxiety among students in the classroom (Tsui, 1996). Such a misunderstanding of Chinese learners could result in an impasse of teaching and learning in international contexts. A two-fold solution is to examine insider perspectives on learners from China and take the diversity of Chinese learners into consideration.

1.2   Phases in investigating culture of learning

Based on a series of empirical studies on Chinese learners, Jin and Cortazzi point out how the traditional perspective of the isolated and distinct Chinese learner is a fallacy. The negative attitudes towards Chinese learners, as apparently held by some Western educators, should not be attributed to the students' or educators' personalities; instead, educators should recognize the cultural orientations to learning in language and in other subject classrooms. Jin and Cortazzi argue that a different cultural orientation, whether a particular Western or a Chinese one, should not imply in itself either inferiority or superiority, but needs to be understood empathetically as something from which educators can learn. If, when and how Chinese students may adapt, modify or transform this orientation (say in Western educational institutions) is a separate question which can best be examined when we have a research-based understanding of the two (or more) cultural orientations. In order to argue for this perspective more convincingly, Jin and Cortazzi explore three phases: first, awakening cultural awareness by providing snapshots of the cultural gap between Chinese learners and British academic staff; second, proposing solutions after critically examining the relative models of learning; and, in the third phase, developing possible solutions by scrutinizing the key elements of cultures of learning from various angles, using several research methods. Based on findings from a series of studies, they criticize the stereotyping of Chinese learners and argue for respect and greater equality in multicultural and international contexts (by definition, TESOL is inevitably situated in such multiple contexts).

The underlying questions, as exemplified in relation to Chinese learners, that Jin and Cortazzi have asked are:

(1) Chinese learners of English are constantly measured against native speakers, for example as passive versus active learners. What are the appropriate cultural standards for investigations in applied linguistics and education research?
(2) What kinds of features in classroom interaction are crucial in understanding Chinese learners' behaviour in language learning and language use?
(3) What kinds of stance or attitudes should educators take in encountering the diversity of Chinese learners internationally?

1.3   Awakening cultural awareness

To awaken cultural awareness, Jin and Cortazzi first explored cultural differences in attitudes and behaviour between Chinese postgraduate learners in the United Kingdom and their British academic tutors and supervisors (teachers). Drawing on data gathered through questionnaires and interviews with a sample of 101 students, Jin and Cortazzi (1993, 1996) outline some major features of the cultural orientation of Chinese postgraduate students and visiting scholars studying at six British universities and one polytechnic (which later became a university). They focus on the students' experiences and beliefs about academic culture, their expectations of learning and teaching, their academic language use (ALU) and their orientation to teacher–student relationships. This is contrasted with the cultural orientation of 37 British academic staff, who taught the students and also completed questionnaires and were interviewed.

The results of these studies demonstrated that there was an academic cultural gap between Chinese students and their British teachers. Such a cultural gap is exemplified in the two parties' perceptions of the tutor–student relationships; in asking for help or expecting an offer of help; in being independent or dependent; and in discourse patterns in writing.

For example, Chinese students show great respect towards supervisors, who are expected to be moral and social leaders and, therefore, their relationship is considered similar to parent-and-child relationships; students expected to be offered help and to receive care in the community whereas, for the British teachers, offering help unasked was considered intrusive: students should show independence rather than rely on a kind of parental guidance; academic leadership is separated professionally from social and moral leadership (which is more likely a personal matter). This relationship can explain some reasons why Chinese students seldom report their difficulties to teachers and why British teachers rarely ask in detail about the students' difficulties in learning and living. Meanwhile, Chinese discourse patterns in writing were often different from the ones expected in English. These findings interpret difficulties and problems that Chinese learners have in English academic writing and in studying in Britain in terms of academic–culture gaps, which participants on either side often felt but were unable to make explicit easily because they were not fully aware of the differing perspectives and cultural orientations.

This work on culture awareness created the groundwork to develop the concept of cultures of learning.

1.4   Cultures of learning

A series of papers published in the 1990s by Jin and Cortazzi provided the needed theoretical support for differing conceptions of cultures of learning. In the concept of cultures of learning, the word *culture* is central. In the TESOL and applied linguistics literature, *culture* is a term that often has been overlooked or taken for granted. Jin and Cortazzi defined a culture of learning through combinations of a wide range of features:

> A 'culture of learning' might be defined as socially transmitted expectations, beliefs and values about what good learning is, what constitutes a good teacher and a good student and what their roles and relationships should be; about learning and teaching styles, approaches and methods; about classroom interaction and activities; about the use of textbooks; about what constitutes good work. (Cortazzi & Jin, 1996a, 1996b; Jin & Cortazzi, 1993, 1995)

Thus, the concept of cultures of learning includes a cluster of values, expectations, attitudes of both learners and teachers within the teaching context. To achieve a more comprehensive understanding of what the concept of cultures of learning means in practice, Jin and Cortazzi, in different contexts, adopted various research methodologies and approached the key elements in terms of expectations: of learning; of good teachers; of good students; of asking questions in classrooms.

Jin's and Cortazzi's survey-based study (1998c) indicates significant statistical differences in the perceptions of Chinese, British and Japanese students concerning the expectations of a good teacher, a good student and students' explanations of why students do not ask questions in class. This survey shows that for the Chinese and Japanese students, a deep knowledge, warm heartedness and understanding are considered as dominant expectations of a good teacher; these contrasted with a British emphasis on various personal qualities and professional skills with which teachers relate to learners. Based on such results, Jin and Cortazzi infer a teacher knowledge-pedagogy contrast in which 'the Chinese and Japanese students' cultures of learning seem more knowledge-centred, while the British culture of learning centres more on skills, methods and organization' (p. 46). The implication is reinforced by the differing perceptions of a good student. The survey results about student perceptions of good students reveals that being hard working and showing respect to the teacher are highly valued by the Chinese students, while the British students emphasize paying attention to the teacher, and Japanese students value the development of good character and asking questions in class. The results are intriguing: both the Chinese and Japanese students place significantly more emphasis than the British do on answering teachers' questions, on asking questions after class (rather than in class), and place significantly more emphasis on asking questions in class and volunteering comments in class. These results are in contrast to the comments often heard from Western teachers that East Asian students are 'passive' and that it is difficult to stimulate them to engage in 'active participation'. For the Chinese students, however, 'being active' includes paying close attention, listening well, and thinking about what the teacher is saying. Jin and Cortazzi (1998c) conclude that expectations of teachers and students clearly affect learning in intercultural classrooms. 'Cultures of learning define the ways in which learning takes place, they define how teachers and students deal with the curriculum and with each other, they define how classroom participants learn intercultural communication' (p. 57).

The evidence was extended in studies comparing Chinese, Malaysian, Japanese, Turkish and British students (Cortazzi, 1998, 2000; Cortazzi & Jin, 2001, 2002; Jin & Cortazzi, 2002); these studies show there can be some dissonances and tensions between cultures of learning, while (importantly) there are also shared common elements. The researchers also considered practical ways in which awareness of cultures of learning and communication can be raised (Cortazzi, 1990, 1993; Cortazzi & Jin, 1996c), ways which were developed for student workshops and teacher development programmes they conducted in China, the United Kingdom, Malaysia, Turkey and Lebanon.

In order to achieve a more comprehensive picture, they developed the use of various innovative methodologies, including narrative analysis and metaphor analysis. In narrative analysis, Cortazzi and Jin (1992) apply William Labov's model of narrative to analysing cultural perception. According to

Labov (e.g., Labov, 1972; Labov & Waletsky, 1967), there are two main functions of an oral narrative of personal experience: a referential function and an evaluation function. The evaluation function is the key in applying this model to culture studies. In this function, 'the teller communicates the meaning of the narrative by establishing some point of personal involvement. This is the evaluation: the speaker's perspective on what it all means. Within most personal stories, one part, at least, can usually be clearly identified as having and evaluative function' (Cortazzi & Jin, 1994, p. 77). Based on this consideration, Cortazzi and Jin believe that if we analyse large numbers of stories, we can extract the story tellers' observation and understanding of culture by analysing evaluations *in, of* and through *narrative* (Cortazzi & Jin, 2000). For example, Cortazzi (1991) analysed around 1,000 classroom stories from 123 primary school teachers in order to reveal the teachers' cultural perceptions about their work. Adopting a similar narrative approach, Jin (1992) analysed the British supervisors' and Chinese students' cultural orientations with regard to each other, and also their perceptions of British and Chinese academic cultures. Her study illustrates how personal autonomy is highly valued in British academic culture but not necessarily emphasized in other cultures of learning. A further paper by Cortazzi and Jin (1994) aims at introducing narrative analysis in culture studies: they focus on the procedures of applying narrative analysis to cultural observation and understanding, especially how to extract a culture of learning model from the stories. Later, their framework was elaborated within ethnography, comparative education and qualitative research in education (Cortazzi, 2001; Cortazzi & Jin, 2006, 2012) to develop a framework of 19 questions which researchers can ask about narratives.

In more recent work, Cortazzi and Jin adapted the George Lakoff approach to conceptual metaphors (e.g., Lakoff, 1993; Lakoff & Johnson, 1980) for analysis in education and applied linguistics (Cortazzi & Jin, 1999b) to examine concepts of learning and teaching in different cultures. Against their analysis of educational metaphors in Confucian traditions of education and in modern China, they investigated Chinese learners' ideal expectations of teachers through a detailed study of the metaphors the students used to describe the characteristic of teachers (Cortazzi et al., 2009; Jin & Cortazzi, 2008). The researchers proposed a cultural model of core characteristics of teachers found in Chinese metaphors which centres on underlying values of knowledge, cultivation and morality, each of which is realized in clusters of metaphors, such as those relating to light, water, nutrition or tools. The analysis shows some surprising results; for example, different metaphors of a teacher as a 'bee', a 'silkworm', 'a ladder' or 'ice' seem to be unrelated; however, analysis of them shows that throughout these metaphors are underlying conceptions which show deep appreciation of the teachers' devotion and sacrifice. In viewing the role of the teacher, such a cultural model bridges the students' perceptions (revealed in previous studies) and the influences of heritage. In continuing work on Chinese students' and teachers' metaphors for learning (Jin & Cortazzi, 2011a, 2011b), they pick out the metaphor of *learning as a journey* for a rich analysis to derive an elaborate model of student 'learning as a journey from hell to heaven' in which teachers not only guide and direct their studies, but also show students 'the way in life' and 'give light and hope' (2011b: p. 86). This model is potentially helpful in international contexts and has been used to support Chinese students studying in the United Kingdom (ibid.: p. 89).

Jin and Cortazzi (1998a, 1988b, 1988c) probe the implications of the culture the learner brings to a language classroom. After a detailed description of the possible difficulties with teaching and learning in an intercultural classroom, they compare the difference between Western cultures and Chinese cultures of learning, as illustrated by a detailed analyses of classroom transcriptions and comments from Chinese teachers (Cortazzi & Jin, 2001; Jin & Cortazzi, 1998b). Although there are enormous differences within the 'Western' and 'Chinese' cultures, Jin and Cortazzi focus on the common ground these two groups of cultures share.

Taking issue with the notion of Chinese students as 'passive recipients', Jin and Cortazzi (1995) point out that the term of 'passive' and 'active' is a relative one which should be interpreted according to the expectation of the 'culture of learning' into which one has been socialized.

In the Anglophone West, 'learner-centred' pedagogies encourage students to 'learn by participating, through talking and active involvement' (Jin & Cortazzi, 1995: p. 6). By extension, students who are not verbally participatory tend to be considered problematic. This contrasts with the 'more cognitive-centred, learning–listening approach' favoured by Chinese educators (Jin & Cortazzi, 1998: p. 744). Within this tradition, being 'active' suggests 'cognitive involvement, lesson preparation, reflection and review, thinking, memorization and self-study' (Cortazzi & Jin, 1996a: p. 71). (Grimshaw, 2007: p. 302)

Another implication of *cultures of learning* concerns the ways teachers use English textbooks. According to Cortazzi and Jin (1999a), a given culture of learning is not only reflected in the expectations concerning ideal teachers or good students, but also in the expectations of what kinds of texts are chosen and how they are used. The researchers employ photographic and observational evidence to comment on contrasts in the physical stances to learning in China and Lebanon, as shown in the uses of texts in class by the teachers and students, and also by students out of the classroom for spare reading (Jin & Cortazzi, 1998a, 2006). They conclude that, 'Cultural mismatches can occur, but knowledge and awareness of cultural approaches may alleviate problems. Ethnographic stances [towards practices] and explicit teaching may develop both students' and teachers' cultural knowledge' (Cortazzi & Jin, 1999a: p. 219).

1.5   The roots of a Chinese culture of learning

Jin and Cortazzi go deeper to consider the roots of a Chinese culture of learning. They suggest that traditional culture can be used as an effective resource in understanding, at a deeper level, the Chinese students' behaviour in the language classroom. They ponder the relationship between culture in general, academic culture and second language use in English for Academic Purposes (EAP) setting, and especially focus on the influence of the culture background of Chinese students on their use of English in British universities (Jin & Cortazzi, 1996). Drawing on questionnaire and interview data, they suggest that the academic cultural background of Chinese learners from mainland China studying in the United Kingdom derives from three major roots: Confucianism, Taoism and modern Chinese intellectual development. Later Jin and Cortazzi (1998a) elaborate a model of how the traditional cultures related to Confucianism and Taoism contribute to the Chinese learners' cultures of learning and how the implications are manifested in the Chinese learners' academic performance. After constructing a further model of student learning activity in Confucian heritages (Jin & Cortazzi, 2006), they argue that this is 'significant' for modern attitudes in China towards learning, as 'one part' of changing practices (p. 14).

A central argument of Confucianism is the collectivism in contrast to individualism in Western culture. For example, Chinese students' expecting offers of help or offering help can be tracked from the collectivist perspective they have.

> In individualist cultures people focus on 'I' for their identity, while in collectivist cultures they focus much more on 'we'. In individualist cultures people look after themselves and their immediate family only, whereas in collectivist cultures, people belong to in-groups or collectives which look after them in exchange for loyalty (Hofstede & Bond, 1984: p. 419).

Cultures emphasizing the collective orientation focus more on 'in-groups'. Individualist cultures have many specific in-groups but these exert less influence on individuals than the wider in-groups of collectivist cultures. Members of collectivist cultures tend to draw sharper distinctions between in-groups and out-groups relationship: in-group relationships are seen as being more intimate and more important (Jin & Cortazzi, 1993: p. 85).

The emphasis of Taoism on paradox and ambiguity could be well reified in written discourse patterns. Chinese students believe that the background part should indicate the direction of present and future work, so they tend to write a lengthy background at the beginning of a paper. However, this pattern of writing in an article could be viewed as irrelevant and be the cause of ambiguity and confusion (Jin & Cortazzi, 1998a: p. 112).

1.6 From one-way to two-way acculturation

It has been long observed that there is a particularly wide variation among language learners in terms of their background cultures, especially that of language learning motivation and learners' identity. An example of a rival explanation proposed by researchers sharing the same overall theoretical allegiances concerns John Schumann's (1978, 1986) Acculturation Model which 'invokes a combination of social, psychological and social-psychological variables to explain success and failure in SLA [Second Language Acquisition] at the level of the group, mostly as a function of group membership and intra- and intergroup relations. Each attributes greater importance to affective and situational factors than to linguistic or cognitive variables' (Long, 2007: p. 24).

Jin and Cortazzi (1995, 1998a) critically reviewed Schumann's Acculturation Model, suggesting that two major developments are needed. First, except the two kinds of distance Schumann has observed (social distance and psychological distance), a new direction should be considered for both academic language use and English for professional communication contexts – academic distance. Second, which locates the new direction centrally in the cultural synergy model, is that the movement envisaged by Schumann is one-way, by the learner towards the target culture. Jin and Cortazzi point out that using Schuman's Acculturation Model of SLA to examine the Chinese learners does not account for the advanced Chinese learners they have investigated, as explained:

> The Acculturation Model was put forward to account for the SLA of subjects with lower or intermediate language levels acquiring language in non-instructional setting, i.e., their language levels and cultural level, in terms of TL [Target Language] culture, were low. However, the Chinese subjects in this research have high levels of competence in English (a minimum of 550 on TOEFL and 6.5 on IELTs [International English Language Testing System] tests) to start their study here. They are all successful academics or professionals who have strong motivation and clear aims for studying – in China they would be considered the cream of the intellectual elite. Learning strategies which they developed in China helped them to high academic success there. However, the same strategies used in the U.K. will not reveal their academic strengths in the context of British academic culture. (Jin & Cortazzi, 1993: p. 94)

Instead, Jin and Cortazzi suggest we should abandon the one-way concept, 'the acculturation is only considered from the SLL's [Second Language Learner] point of view'; and try to take a *two-way* approach, 'to consider the tutor's lack of culture knowledge of the students' background and how this leads to a measure of misunderstanding which affects ALU [Academic Language Use]' (Jin & Cortazzi, 1993: p. 94).

In the classroom research literature, there are voices which advocate learning from Asian classrooms, since they represent a good example for whole-class interactive teaching (Biggs, 1996, Gardener, 1989; Reynolds & Farrell, 1996; Stevenson & Stigler, 1992). While a large number of Western educators consider what can be transferred from the success of East Asian classrooms, they take a critical perspective on this movement. Jin and Cortazzi (1998b) first investigate the reasons for success with large classes in China, with special focus on ways in which talk (such as in-class discussions) and culture mediate learning in large classes averaging between 40 and 70 students in primary and middle schools. They point out that the cornerstone of the success of large classes is the underlying Chinese culture of learning – specifically, the collectivism of Confucian values. As they conclude, 'Part of the foundation of a Chinese culture of learning is a range of Confucian values…. Much of the successful Chinese management of large classes can be understood as applying collective principles' (p. 757).

Likewise, Cortazzi (1998) explicitly appeals for a critical attitude towards learning from Asian lessons. Drawing on data collected from the Asian kindergarten and primary schools, he argues that we might better learn from Asian classrooms by studying learners' behaviour within their own multicultural setting. The 'whole-class interactive teaching model' in the East Asian countries results in significant achievements in both math and science, while in Britain the individualism contributes to the creativity and critical thinking. He finally concludes that 'we cannot simply uproot some apparently successful classroom approaches from elsewhere in the world without considering the interactional and cultural contexts in which they are found. This context may be crucial to the success of the practices we wish to emulate' (Cortazzi, 1998: p. 48).

Cortazzi concluded by referring to how Asian students in Britain learn: 'A final paradox, then, is that some successful Asian lessons may already be right here in Britain for the learning, but most of us have failed to see them. To see them might be the first step towards a cultural synergy' (Cortazzi, 1998: p. 49). If we wish to learn from other cultural lessons, the first thing we need to do is to observe and analyse the major factors for success, especially attending to the cultures of learning.

The evidence and concepts outlined above are then used as a rationale for an advocacy of a cultural synergy model which we will discuss in the next section.

1.7   Cultural Synergy

As an alternative solution Jin and Cortazzi suggest, from a multiculturalist stance, applying a concept of cultural synergy from business (Moran & Harris, 1991: pp. 91–92) into language teaching.

The *cultural synergy model* was initially built from the study of Chinese students studying in British universities and working with British supervisors

(Jin, 1992), and then was inductively developed through a series of studies relating to Chinese students in China and other students in other countries. The model arises from Jin's and Cortazzi's understanding of various cultures of learning, and the recognition that one useful method or approach to teaching may not work effectively in another educational and text. In order to bridge the different perceptions and attitudes, ciate the cultures of learning, this model suggests the need for erstanding of participants who have been enculturated into dif-res, communication styles and academic cultures.

el's emphasis is on *synergy*, a term originating from Greek, which ork together. The implications of the model include: *culture is viewed e*, which indicates the need to recognize and make positive use of ultures of learning; *mutual understanding* refers to the need to avoid of imperialism, of imposing the values of native-speakers on non–aking learners; *two-way acculturation*, which means that participants mutual awareness and understanding of each other's culture and, ly, of two or more cultures of learning. The model is defined:

> ral synergy means that people from two or more cultures inter-stematically, cooperating for a common purpose with an attitude ing willing to learn, understand and appreciate the other's culture out loss of their own status, role or cultural identity. In this concept, adaptation, rather than assimilation, is emphasized, otherwise it is likely that learners will fear that their original culture will be downgraded, which may create a psychological barrier to learning the target culture and language'. (Jin & Cortazzi, 1993: p. 95)

This contribution from Jin and Cortazzi features their attitude toward others' cultures of learning. The fundamental attitude is one of curiosity to learn about different cultures of learning without presuming superiority on any side, or that students studying internationally would necessarily have to adopt a different way of learning (though they may choose to do so). Rather, they ask whether, because cultures of learning are deeply embedded in identity and emotion, students 'should have the right to learn according to their own culture of learning' (Cortazzi & Jin, 2002: p. 72).

The cultural synergy model can be applied to academic language use, inter-cultural communication, language teaching and learning, and other fields. For academic language use, this model is helpful. The aspect of two-way adaptation rather than assimilation means diversity and variety should not be merged into one, but that natural diversity exists and academic cultural practitioners should have an open mind to be aware of the operation of other styles and appreciate their emphasis and strengths. This aspect is important as it helps the second language users such as Chinese postgraduate students or Chinese professionals to avoid the anxiety evoked by the cultural gap in the language classroom. Only by believing that all cultures in the classroom have something of value to contribute, can the participants engage in mutual learning without anyone being frustrated or feeling inferior to others.

For intercultural communication, this model is crucial. In globalizing education, for both international students and academic staff, developing inter-cultural communication skills is crucial. The cultural synergy model can be applied to the skills development, as it aims at fostering intercultural competence in the sense that participants will be socially and educationally effective across cultures, not only communicating appropriately in inter-cultural contexts, but further understanding the communication patterns, expectations and interpretations of others as 'cultures of communication' (Jin and Cortazzi, 1998a). The situation of communicating for learning across cultures thus invites *cultural synergy* (Jin, 1992; Jin & Cortazzi, 1995). This could be defined as the mutual effort of both teachers and students to understand one another's academic cultures, cultures of communication and cultures of learning. This would include the effort to understand others' principles of interpretation (Cortazzi & Jin, 1997: p. 88). Not surprisingly, they extend the model to researchers in intercultural research teams (Cortazzi & Jin, 2002) and comment on the reciprocal learning among researchers in collaborative partnerships.

For language teaching, the cultural synergy model can equip teachers to meet the needs of learners' diversity and to appreciate their differences in the global classroom context. A cultural synergy model encourages conscious awareness of differences in learning and teaching through explicit discussion so that all participants are clear about their expectations of one another. Then, inside the classroom, teachers could make use of their own and others' culture-of-learning resources to create a context-based pedagogy or teaching method. Cultural synergy in this context stresses the need for teachers and students to learn more about each other's cultural expectations, values and beliefs regarding learning, but not necessarily with the need to surrender their own (Jin & Cortazzi, 1995).

1.8   Evaluation

A systematic and critical reading of their academic publications shows that Jin and Cortazzi have not only contributed to the concept of culture of learning, but also have cultivated several related academic areas that demonstrate promising potential for further exploration. The areas they probe include cultures of learning and their relation to learners' national or community cultures and classroom interaction; cultures of pedagogy around the world and their foregrounding in international or multicultural classrooms; the cultural implications of content and design in textbooks; learners' and teachers' identity construction; diverse quantitative and qualitative research methods with learners in different cultural contexts; cultural adaptation and the creative application of cultural synergy; intercultural learner studies; and cultural studies in L2 and L3 teaching. This chapter now examines some arguments and counter-arguments to assist future global classroom researchers to develop other investigations. The conceptual underpinnings of culture of learning and culture synergy models are multidisciplinary in the sense that the interweaving threads of language, culture and learning come not only from the feeder disciplines of sociology, education and linguistics, but also from psychology and cultural studies, as well as ethnography and pragmatics.

However, the world is changing rapidly, and in many ways is growing ever more transcultural. Despite our admiration for Jin and Cortazzi's effort, and given the complexity of the changing contexts in which many practitioners are engaged, we want to reflect on the limits of the large-culture perspective, even though Jin and Cortazzi have explored 'Chinese learners' so much more empathetically and imaginatively than most previous researchers.

From a methodological point of view, much of their research is based on interviews and questionnaires; in future work, if they or others can include more video-taped classroom interaction (beyond Cortazzi & Jin, 2001; Jin & Cortazzi, 1998b, 2008), it would enrich the data and also the understanding of classroom activity. Take the students' silence in the classroom as an example: this might have nothing to do with the cultures of learning but simply be the result of the teacher not providing the students with a chance to ask a question in class.

Major points of a possible critique include the following. First, by attributing the Chinese students' behaviours in the classroom in part to the Confucian heritage, Jin and Cortazzi risk presuming a deterministic relationship between the superposed characteristics of Chinese national or ethnic culture and the attitudes and practices of individual Chinese students and educators. Their argument relies crucially on the 'large-culture' (Holliday, 1999) assumption which ignores individual agency. The large culture 'entails a sense of cultural fixity and a notion of historicisation only in the sense that cultures are determined by a historical heritage rather than emerging through history and thus dynamically evolving' (Clark & Gieve, 2006: p. 55). A possible consequence of the research done from the large-culture perspective will be that teachers attribute all the students' behaviours in the class to their background culture, which would minimize any efforts to improve class teaching because there is nothing teachers can do to change cultural heritage. As Dwight Atkinson (1999) has argued, '[S]uch research must always be balanced with, and ideally incorporated into, perspectives that reveal the individuality and agency of those who have already been deeply socialized and enculturated' (p. 646).

A counter-argument is that Jin and Cortazzi (1998) have not made deterministic claims: they fully recognize diversity and modernity within a culture of learning and have only argued for 'broad trends' and acknowledge that 'not every learner will follow them and many depend on contexts and circumstances' (p. 113). Much of their work is rooted in observations of classrooms from which, in a bottom-up approach, a model of 'influential features' is developed (Cortazzi & Jin, 2001: p. 123) that makes extensive use of interview quotations and classroom transcripts (Jin & Cortazzi, 1998b) in which 'the local' should be evident.

Second, applying a framework of the dichotomy of individualism versus collectivism tends to essentialize and polarize the 'Western' culture and 'oriental' culture. This dichotomy 'tends to exclude the possibility that self-expression associated with individualism exists in cultures that are often viewed as collectivist. Further, these constructed dichotomies manifest certain power relations' (Kuboda, 1999: p.750).

A counter-argument is that Jin and Cortazzi recognize the dangers of drawing up lists of characteristics which might be construed as dichotomies, although their lists are labeled cautiously as 'contrasting interpretations' (Cortazzi & Jin, 1996b: p. 200), 'Chinese students' views' (Jin & Cortazzi, 1998a: p. 105) or as 'different emphases' which 'illustrate trends' (Jin & Cortazzi, 1998b: p. 747). Their analysis of individual collective perspectives was not imposed, but was derived from student interview data and thus reflected participants' perspectives at the time (Jin & Cortazzi, 1993); they have not used the concept as an analytic construct since then. Further, their research has featured many cultures in China, the United Kingdom, Malaysia, Japan, Turkey and Lebanon and so should be interpreted as multiple, not binary (Cortazzi & Jin, 2001, 2002; Jin & Cortazzi, 1998a, 2008).

Third, using a label of 'Chinese learners' runs a risk of reinforcing the stereotype of students from China, as Ruth Spack (1997) points out:

> Students are remarkably diverse, and thus no one label can accurately capture their heterogeneity. Yet that does not stop teachers and researchers from labeling. It may be that we use labels such as ESL – even if they do not match students' profiles – to provide us with a shared shorthand by which we can talk about learners. But even if our reasons are well intentioned, we need to consider that, in the process of labeling students, we put ourselves in the powerful position of rhetorically constructing their identities, a potentially hazardous enterprise. At worst, a label may imply that we sanction an ethnocentric stance. At the very least, it can lead us to stigmatize, to generalize and to make inaccurate predictions about what students are likely to do as a result of their language or cultural background. (p. 765)

A counter-argument here is that, in an extended discussion of the term 'Chinese learners', Jin and Cortazzi (2011c: pp. 4–7) argue strongly that this is a plural term which includes much diversity, including a diversity of cultures (plural) within China, and that it should not be interpreted in reductionist, essentialist or simplistic terms. Notably, their concept of 'cultural model' is distinct from personal models of individual experience, and cultural models 'represent socially distributed knowledge widely shared and transmitted within a community'; they are 'complex and cannot be easily reduced to simple labels' and 'we do not imagine a one-to-one correspondence between a cultural model and particular individuals; that is, the models allow for some diversity within a cultural community for which the model is proposed' (Cortazzi et al., 2009: p. 111). The diversity and individuality among the participating students from China are highly evident in their research on metaphors in cultures of learning (Cortazzi et al., 2009; Jin & Cortazzi, 2008, 2011a, b).

A more recent paper titled 'Different waves crashing into different coastlines? Mainland Chinese learners doing postgraduate dissertations in UK' (Pilcher et al., 2011), seems to represent a conceptual change. This is not surprising, since some papers specifically focus on changes in cultures of learning (Cortazzi & Jin, 1996d; Jin & Cortazzi, 2006). First, they adopt the term of 'learners from China' instead of 'Chinese learners' with the consideration of reinforcing the notion of diversity. As Cortazzi and Jin (2011) conclude:

> The term 'Chinese learners' is a trade-off between generalization and diversity. There is always a need for some level of generalization in research, and related to Chinese learners there is a need to take account of Chinese perceptions and self-identification with linguistic, ethnic and cultural aspects of being recognized as 'Chinese'. However, there is another need to recognize the clear diversity and differences between individuals, groups, local communities and geographic, economic, social and cultural diversity that must characterize Chinese learners. Those who make generalizations need to avoid reduction and over-simplification through labelling as 'Chinese' or a false sense of sameness and homogeneity. (p. 314)

Second, in viewing the cultures of learning, they move from a co-existing perspective to a co-shaping dynamic perspective. This movement and change is manifested in their elaboration of waves and coastlines as a metaphor to indicate the reciprocal relationship between supervisors (coastlines) and students (waves). These two changes arguably indicate a conceptual moving from the previous large-culture perspective to a middle ground between large-culture and small-culture approaches. Drawing on research with 45 learners from China and their supervisors' experiences and perceptions' of completing MSc dissertations, they show much variation in learners from China, and in how they are perceived and supervised in the United Kingdom. As Nick Pilcher et al. (2011) conclude:

The learners were described as being different 'waves' as their previous educational experiences varied greatly, and they had differing views and experience of the dissertation. Their supervisors were described as different 'coastlines' to represent the different experiences of the learners, as 'waves', when they met them. Nevertheless, there were a number of core ideas and experiences, and learner did indeed adapt to their department over the course of the dissertation. Many supervisors also changed through encountering these different 'waves' of learners; their views and perceptions varied, and changed over time, although not as greatly as those of the students. (pp. 310–11)

On the surface, these changes seem to be contradictory to cultural synergy: 'This does not mean that diversity and variety will be merged into one' (Jin & Cortazzi, 1998a: p. 114); however, if we expand the notion of culture to include small cultures which individuals in small groups create, it follows the initial purpose of their study which is to 'bridge the different perceptions and attitudes [toward classroom events and interaction]', therefore they suggest that there is a 'need for mutual understanding of different cultures, communication styles and academic cultures' (Jin & Cortazzi, 1998a: p. 114).

In asking about the intercultural adaptation and cultures of learning, they note: 'The question of learners' *agency* is crucial' (Cortazzi & Jin, 2011: p. 316). We can expect that focusing on a balance between agency and large culture will be a potential direction of Jin and Cortazzi, and we feel strongly that their advocacy for a cultural synergy model will result in what they have expected: that 'both or many sides gain'.

1.9 Conclusions

In this chapter, we traced the research related to cultures of learning carried out by Lixian Jin and Martin Cortazzi, giving attention to how the definition of cultures of learning has been elaborated and redefined, and how its content is enriched by the joint efforts of these two scholars and others to develop research on themes of intercultural issues in global classrooms. We discussed the contributions the concept brings to TESOL and some potential criticisms. We pondered the notion of 'culture' and considered what it might contribute to conceptualizing the characteristics of international students in the global classroom. Finally, we presented a possible future direction which we consider is worth addressing.

In our understanding, the cultures of learning and the cultural synergy models proposed are not just a specific theory or a certain model; rather they present a way of looking at the vexing notion of culture, of taking into account a wide range of cultural understandings and critiques, trying to show that differences in cultural practices and beliefs do not necessarily need to be viewed as oppositional or mutually exclusive; instead, they can be dynamically inclusive while respecting individual and group identities.

References

Atkinson, D. (1997) A critical approach to critical thinking in TESOL. *TESOL Quarterly,* 31 (1), 71–94.

Atkinson, D. (1999) TESOL and culture. *TESOL Quarterly,* 33 (4), 625–54.

Ballard, B. & Clanchy, J. (1991) *Teaching students from overseas: A brief guide for lectures and supervisors.* Melbourne: Longman Cheshire.

Biggs, J. B. (1996) Learning, schooling, and socialization: A Chinese solution to a western problem. In S. Law (Ed), *Growing up the Chinese way.* Hong Kong: The Chinese University Press, pp. 147–67.

Carson, J. (1992) Becoming biliterate: First language influences. *Journal of Second Language Writing,* 1, 37–60.

Cortazzi, M. (1990) Cultural and educational expectations in the language classroom. In B. Harrison (Ed.), *Culture and the language classroom.* London: Modern English Publications and The British Council, pp. 54–65.

Cortazzi, M. (1991) *Primary teaching: How it is, a narrative account.* London: David Fulton.

Cortazzi, M. (1993) Using activity cards on training courses for language teachers. *The Teacher Trainer,* 7 (1), 15–19.

Cortazzi, M. (1998) Learning from Asian Lessons: Cultural expectations and classroom talk. *Education,* 3–13, 24 (2), 42–49.

Cortazzi, M. (2000) Languages, cultures, and cultures of learning in the global classroom. In H. W. Kam and C. Ward (Eds), *Language in the global context: Implications for the language classroom.* Singapore: DEAMEO Regional Language Centre, pp. 75–103.

Cortazzi, M. (2001) Narrative analysis in ethnography. In P. Atkinson, A. Coffey, S. Delamont, J. Lofland and L. Lofland (Eds), *Handbook of ethnography.* London: Sage publications, pp. 384–94.

Cortazzi, M. & Jin, L. (1994) Narrative analysis: Applying linguistics to cultural models of learning. In D. Graddol and J. Swann (Eds), *Evaluating language.* Clevedon: The British Association for Applied Linguistics and Multilingual Matters, pp. 75–90.

Cortazzi, M. & Jin, L. (1996a) State of the art article: English teaching and learning in China. *Language Teaching,* 29 (2), 61–80.

Cortazzi, M. & Jin, L. (1996b) Cultures of learning: Language classrooms in China. In H. Coleman (Ed.), *Society and the language classroom.* Cambridge: Cambridge University Press, pp. 169–206.

Cortazzi, M. & Jin. L. (1996c) Cross-cultural communication, a foreign language perspective. *The Fountain,* 15, 26–31.

Cortazzi, M. & Jin, L. (1996d) Changes in learning English vocabulary in China. In H. Coleman and L. Camerin (Eds), *Change and language.* Clevedon: Multilingual Matters, pp. 153–65.

Cortazzi, M. & Jin, L. (1997) Communication for learning across cultures. In D. McNamara and R. Harris (Eds), *Overseas students in higher education.* London: Routledge, pp. 76–90.

Cortazzi, M. & Jin, L. (1999a) Cultural mirrors: Materials and methods in the EFL classroom. In E. Hinkel (Ed.), *Culture in second language teaching and learning.* New York: Cambridge University Press, pp. 196–219.

Cortazzi, M. & Jin, L. (1999b) Bridges to learning: Metaphors of teaching, learning and language. In L. Cameron and G. Low (Eds), *Researching and applying metaphor.* Cambridge: Cambridge University Press, pp. 149–76.

Cortazzi, M. & Jin, L. (2000) Evaluating evaluation in narrative. In S. Hunston and G. Thompson (Eds), *Evaluation in text: Authorial stance and the construction of discourse.* Oxford: Oxford University Press, pp. 102–20.

Cortazzi, M. & Jin, L. (2001) Large classes in China: 'Good teachers' and interaction. In D. A. Watkins and J. B. Biggs (Eds), *Teaching the Chinese learner: psychological and pedagogical perspectives.* Hong Kong: Comparative Education Research Centre, University of Hong Kong, pp. 115–34.

Cortazzi, M. & Jin, L. (2002) Cultures of learning: The social construction of educational identities. In David. C. S. Li (Ed.), *Discourses in search of members: In honor of Ron Scollon.* New York: University Press of America, pp. 49–78.

Cortazzi, M. & Jin, L. (2006) Asking questions, sharing stories and identity construction: Sociocultural issues in narrative research. In S. Trahar (Ed.), *Narrative research on learning: Comparative and international perspective.* Oxford: L Symposium Books, pp. 27–36.

Cortazzi, M., Jin, L. & Wang, Z. (2009) Cultivators, cows and computers: Chinese learners' metaphors of teachers. In T. Coverdale-Jones and R. Rastall (Eds), *Internationalising the university: The Chinese context.* London: Palgrave Macmillan, pp. 107–29.

Cortazzi, M. & Jin, L. (2011) Conclusions: What are we learning from research about Chinese learners? In L. Jin and M. Cortazzi (Eds), *Researching Chinese learners: Skills, perceptions and intercultural adaptations.* London: Palgrave Macmillan, pp. 304–18.

Cortazzi, M. & Jin, L. (2012) Approaching narrative analysis with 19 questions. In S. Delamont (Ed.), *Handbook of qualitative research in education.* Cheltenham: Edward Elgar, pp. 474–88.

Clark, R. & Gieve, S. N. (2006) On the discursive construction of the Chinese learner. *Language, culture and curriculum,* 19 (1), 54–73.

Flowerdew, L. (1998). A cultural perspective on group work. *ELT Journal,* 52 (4), 323–28.

Fox, X. (1994) *Listening to the world.* Urbana, IL: National Council of Teachers of English.

Gardener, H. (1989) *To open minds: Chinese clues to the dilemma of American education.* New York: Basic Books.

Grimshaw, T. (2007) Problematizing the construct of 'the Chinese learner': Insights from ethnographic research. *Educational Studies,* 33 (3), 299–311.

Hofstede, G. & Bond, A. M. (1984) An independent validation of Hofstede's culture dimensions using Rokeach's value survey. *Journal of Cross-cultural Psychology,* 15, 417–33.

Holliday, A. (1999) Small cultures. *Applied Linguistics,* 20 (2), 237–64.

Labov, W. (1972) *Language in the inner city: Studies in the Black English vernacular.* Philadephia: University of Pennsylvania Press.

Jin, L. (1992) *Academic cultural expectations and second language use: Chinese postgraduate students in the UK – A cultural synergy model.* Unpublished doctoral dissertation, University of Leicester.

Jin, L. and Cortazzi, M. (1993) Cultural orientation and academic language use. In D. Graddol, L. Thompson and M. Byram (Eds), *Language and culture.* Clevedon: Multilingual Matters, pp. 84–97.

Jin, L. & Cortazzi, M. (1995) A cultural synergy model for academic language use. In P. Bruthiaux., T. Boswood and B. Du-Babcock (Eds), *Explorations in English for professional communication*. Hong Kong: City University of Hong Kong, pp. 41–56.

Jin, L. & Cortazzi, M. (1996) This way is very different from Chinese ways. In M. Hewings and T. Dudley-Evans (Eds), *Evaluation and course design in EAP*. Hemel Hempstead: Prentice Hall Macmillan in association with The British Council, pp. 205–16.

Jin, L. & Cortazzi, M. (1998a) The culture the learner brings: a bridge or a barrier? In M. Byram and M. Fleming (Eds), *Language learning in intercultural perspective: Approaches through drama and ethnography*. Cambridge: Cambridge University Press, pp. 98–118.

Jin, L. & Cortazzi, M. (1998b) Dimensions of dialogue: Large classes in China. *International Journal of Education Research*, 29, 739–61.

Jin, L. & Cortazzi, M. (1998c) Expectations and questions in intercultural classrooms. *Intercultural Communications Studies*, 7 (2), 37–62.

Jin, L. & Cortazzi, M. (2001) Cultural Synergy: a model for dilemmas in cultures of learning. In D. Killick, M. Parry and A. Phipps (Eds), *Poetics and Praxis of Language and intercultural communication*. Glasgow: University of Glasgow; Leeds: Leeds Metropolitan University, pp. 39–47.

Jin, L. & Cortazzi, M. (2006) Changing practices in Chinese cultures of learning. *Language, Culture and Curriculum*, 19 (1), 5–20.

Jin, L. & Cortazzi, M. (2008) Images of teachers, learning and questioning in Chinese cultures of learning. In E. Behrendt (Ed.), *Metaphors for learning: Cross-cultural perspective*. Amsterdam: John Benjamins, pp. 177–202.

Jin, L. & Cortazzi, M. (2011a) The changing landscapes of a journey: Educational metaphors in China. In J. Ryan (Ed.), *Education reform in China: Changing concepts, contexts and practices*. London: Routledge, pp. 113–31.

Jin, L. & Cortazzi, M. (2011b) More than a Journey: 'Learning' in the metaphors of Chinese students and teachers. In L. Jin and M. Cortazzi (Eds), *Researching Chinese learners: Skills, perceptions and intercultural adaptation*. Houndmills: Palgrave Macmillan, pp. 67–92.

Jin, L. & Cortazzi, M. (2011c) Introduction: Contexts for researching Chinese learners. In L. Jin and M. Cortazzi (Eds), *Researching Chinese learners: Skills, perceptions and intercultural adaptations*. Houndmills: Palgrave Macmillan, pp. 1–18.

Klitgard, I. (2011) Plagiarism in the international university: From kidnapping and theft to translation and hybridity. In B. Preisler, I. Klitgard and A. Fabricius (Eds), *Language and learning in the international university: From English uniformity to diversity and hybridity*. Bristol: Multilingual Matters, pp. 169–92.

Kubota, R. (1999) The author responds… . *TESOL Quarterly*, 33 (4), 749–57.

Labov, W. & Waletsky, J. (1967) Narrative analysis: Oral versions of personal experience. In J. Helm (Ed.), *Essays on the verbal and visual arts*. Proceedings of the 1966 Annual Spring Meeting of the American Ethnological Society. Seattle: University of Washington Press, pp. 12–44.

Lakoff, G. (1993) The contemporary theory of metaphor. In A. Ortony (Ed.), *Metaphor and thought*, (2nd edn). Cambridge: Cambridge University Press, pp. 205–51.

Lakoff, G. & Johnson, M. (1980) *Metaphors we live by*. Chicago: The University of Chicago Press.

Long, M. H. (2007) *Problems in SLA*. Mahwah, NJ: Lawrence Erlbaum.

Pennycook, A. (1998) *English and the discourses of colonialism*. Routledge: London.

Pilcher, N., Cortazzi, M. & Jin, L. (2011) Different waves crashing into different coast-lines? Mainland Chinese learners doing postgraduate dissertations in the UK. In L. Jin and M. Cortazzi (Eds), *Researching Chinese learners: Skills, perceptions and intercultural adaptations*. London: Palgrave Macmillan, pp. 292–313.

Reynolds, D. & Farrell, S. (1996) *Worlds apart? A review of international surveys of educational achievement involving England*. London: Office for Standards in Education.

Schumann, J. H. (1978) The acculturation model for second language acquisitic R. Gingras (Ed.), *Second language acquisition and foreign language teaching*. Arlin Centre for Applied Linguistics, pp. 27–50.

Schumann, J. H. (1986) Research on the acculturation model for second lar acquisition. *Journal of Multilingual Development*, 7, 379–92.

Spack, R. (1997) The rhetorical construction of multilingual students. *Quarterly*, 31 (4), 765–74.

Stevenson, H. W. & Stigler, J. W. (1992) *The learning gap: Why our schools are fa what we can learn from Japanese and Chinese education*. New York: Summit I

Tsui, A. (1996) Reticence and Anxiety in second language learning. In K. Bail Nunan (Eds), *Voices from the language classroom*. Cambridge: Cambridge I Press, pp. 145–67.

2

Comparing Learning Characteristics in Chinese and Anglophone Cultures: Pitfalls and Insights

Janette Ryan

Much of the literature on cultures of learning takes a binary view of the attributes of learning in different cultures, emphasizing differences between these cultures. A close examination of notions of scholarship and learning in Anglophone and Chinese education contexts shows that there are often more differences to be found within cultures than between them. Binary descriptions of learning characteristics can stereotype learners within what can be very large, complex and dynamic systems of cultural practice and risk homogenizing and essentializing individuals within them. Cultures of learning in contexts such as China are undergoing rapid and radical change, and contemporary external views of the cultures of learning within such contexts can be outmoded or unhelpful for those teaching and learning across these systems.

Rather than taking the conventional research approach of identifying the learning characteristics and learning experiences of international students from countries such as China entering Anglophone learning environments, this chapter looks at both the possible differences as well as the commonalities of these systems of educational practice by identifying the views and practices of expert scholars working within these systems. It reports on a qualitative research study of the views of expert scholars in a range of Anglophone and Chinese universities on their definitions of scholarship and learning, their ideas about the differences and commonalities between these systems and their views on changes occurring within their own systems. The study was conducted in universities across China and in a range of Anglophone universities in the United Kingdom, the United States and Australia, and it includes interviews in English and Chinese with senior scholars in a range of disciplines.

This chapter also reports on recent developments in the reform of curriculum and pedagogy in China at the higher education and school education levels to demonstrate the rapid changes occurring in the contexts within which the scholars from China are working. It outlines the changing nature of learning contexts in China and the changing characteristics of learners within areas of China and points to the implications of these changes for those working with international students from China in more intercultural and transcultural learning environments.

2.1   Introduction

Educational cultures derive from the wider historical, social, cultural and political contexts within which they are situated. No culture is static and, hence, educational systems – their structures, systems, organization, management, and teaching and learning practices – undergo constant change. These changes sometimes occur in rapid bursts, such as in periods of major curriculum change, and sometimes more slowly and less perceptibly, but the systems experience considerable shifts all the same.

This chapter examines some of these shifts in relation to China and the Anglophone countries with which it is most actively engaged through academic mobility of students and scholars, with a focus on the United Kingdom, the United States and Australia as case studies. Large numbers of internationally mobile academics and students from China are engaging with these educational systems and take home what they have learnt. These travelling scholars carry knowledge and learning around the world, like their predecessors of a thousand years ago when knowledge was carried mainly from East to West (Gordon, 2008). This phenomenon is often referred to as 'brain circulation' (Johnson & Regets, 1998), and the scholars change both the systems that they come from (on their return) and those that they visit. Yet, to date, this movement of ideas and people has been mostly one-way, and Anglophone systems, such as those in the United Kingdom, the United States and Australia, often fail to take advantage of these new epistemologies and practices that newcomers are bringing to their teaching and learning contexts. Often these newcomers are seen as 'empty vessels' in need of filling up with Western knowledge and skills to bring them up to particular academic standards. Too often, their knowledge and skills on arrival are ignored, assumed to be non-existent, or of a lesser standard. Assumptions about Chinese learners in Anglophone countries are generally made on the basis of judgments about newly arrived Chinese international students who are struggling to adapt to the requirements of their new teaching and learning environments. Their lecturers generally have little understanding of their previous educational experiences and expectations (Jin & Cortazzi, 2006: p. 6) and often have little interest in finding out (Ryan, 2002).

Western views on Chinese *cultures of learning*, defined by Lixian Jin & Martin Cortazzi (2011) as 'the often implicit values, expectations and inter- pretations of learning and teaching which frame ideas and pedagogic prac- tices' (p. 114), are often based on outmoded, inaccurate or stereotyped views of the 'Chinese' or 'Confucian-heritage culture' (CHC) learner. Western lec- turers' views of Chinese international students in countries like the United Kingdom, United States and Australia are often based on observations of students trying to 'decode' and adjust to new and unfamiliar requirements and whose behaviours may thus be misinterpreted by lecturers. Although views of Chinese learners as passive, rote learners have been effectively debunked by a large body of research (see Li & Cutting, 2011), such negative views prevail (Edwards, 2007; Rizvi, 2010; Singh, 2009) and, according to Edwards (2007), we are 'still having the same conversation we were all hav- ing in the 1970s' (p. 373).

The lack of interest shown by lecturers in Anglophone universities in exploring their students' previous cultures of learning may in part be due to their belief in the superiority of their own academic traditions and cultures of learning and to complacency about the continued flow of international students. Yet, no education system can afford to remain static, particularly in the face of rapidly changing student cohorts in those countries receiv- ing large numbers of international students; the increasing competition for internationally mobile students and academic staff; and changing world economic and political relations of power. Those countries that actively seek to respond to contemporary realities and take a positive stance towards the re-examination and rejuvenation of their education systems can take advantage of these shifts in the global financial and knowledge economies.

As I have shown elsewhere (Ryan & Louie, 2007), lecturers need to be cau- tious about focusing on supposed 'differences' in academic cultures since, for several reasons, these often arise from inaccurate assumptions about Chinese or CHC learners. These reasons include a lack of understanding of the vast diversity to be found in educational settings in China; contempo- rary views of Chinese learners in the West, which are increasingly outdated because culture is dynamic; and because China is undergoing such deep and rapid educational and social reform.

Prevailing stereotypes of Chinese learners are generally based on Western teachers' interpretations of specific behaviours of international students from China when they are still learning to cope with their new learning contexts and its expectations. Lecturers might misinterpret students' lack of English language proficiency as lack of ability, and their initial lack of sophisticated language use as lack of criticality. They may misunderstand their questions about assignments and the 'correct' answer as a tendency towards 'rote' or dependent learning rather than an active process of find- ing out expectations. Finally, they may misinterpret their students' rela- tive silence in the classroom as lack of connection with ideas rather than a deeper, internal engagement with ideas or a reluctance to display their as yet underdeveloped language skills. Apparent plagiarism by students may arise from as yet underdeveloped skills at paraphrasing in another language rather than as deliberate cheating, or even as a result of desperation stemming from the overwhelming stress involved in experiencing such steep learning curves early in their study. As these lecturers generally have no direct experience of learning in authentic Chinese contexts, they may instead base their assumptions about Chinese learners and Chinese cultures of learning on these partial and early observations.

This chapter explores some of these issues and draws on research into contemporary cultures of learning in both Western and Chinese cultures to demonstrate that neither Chinese nor Anglophone cultures are static, and that cultures of learning in both systems are undergoing massive change. Current binary views of scholarship and learning in all of these cultures are increasingly out of date and unhelpful for those working with Chinese students, now and into the future. This chapter focuses on the *changes* in cultures of learning stemming from broader social and cultural change in China and in the Anglophone countries that are receiving the largest numbers of Chinese international students. It provides evidence of, and an in-depth discussion about, the radical changes occurring in China's education system and, as a result, in Chinese cultures of learning.

2.2 Changing cultures of learning

Cultures of learning are undergoing significant change both in China (Guan & Meng, 2007; Jin & Cortazzi, 2006, 2011; Ryan et al., 2009; Zhong, 2006) and in the Anglophone countries that accept large numbers of international students from China. This is occurring through major curriculum reform in the case of China and through transformation of the student population, especially at university level in countries such as the United Kingdom, United States and Australia, as well as through the internationalization agendas of all of those education systems. However, both continuity and change coexist within all of these systems and, as systems struggle to define what to retain and what to transform in the face of major challenges from globalization and internationalization, apparently contradictory values and aspirations can be found amongst those working within these systems.

Too often, however, engagement between Chinese people and Westerners is inhibited by out of date stereotypes of China and the 'Chinese', or 'CHC', learner that bear little resemblance to the contemporary realities of China and the pace of change that it is experiencing. As I have argued (Ryan & Louie, 2007; Ryan, 2011a, 2011b), a more nuanced examination of cultural differences and commonalities shows that not only are Chinese cultures of learning rapidly changing, but that these cultures of learning are diverse and complex and vast differences exist between different parts of China. This chapter rejects the 'binary divide' view of culture and instead examines the ways that cultures and those participating within them have common goals and aspirations.

Curriculum and broader educational reforms in China stem from changing social and economic conditions and aspirations. Over the past decade, China has been undertaking major 'root and branch' reform of all levels of its education system. This is aimed at bringing about substantial and enduring changes to Chinese educational philosophies and classroom practices. The reform programme is radical and ambitious and encompasses systematic transformation of educational curricula, teaching and learning approaches, and assessment and administrative structures. This has led to far-reaching changes in the operation of schools and universities (Hannum & Park, 2007; Morgan & Bin, 2011; Ryan, 2011a, 2011b) and adult and vocational education and distance learning (Jin & Cortazzi, 2006).

The areas covered by the reform encompass all areas of education, including curriculum aims, design, content, structure assessment and administration (Ryan, 2011a, 2011b; Ryan et al., 2009). The overall intention of the reform programme is to encourage and enable a move away from a transmission approach in teaching and learning and towards developing a 'new kind of learner' (Paine & Fang, 2007: p. 282) and the encouragement of students' independence, creativity, problem solving skills and collaborative learning. This is designed to be better aligned with students' real-life experiences and interests and to the needs of the nation for skills relevant to a more globalized world. Universities in China have responded to the need identified by the Chinese government for its future workforce to develop learners who are more globally aware (Morgan & Bin, 2011), and China's young people are now often more 'internationalized' than their Western counterparts (Ryan, 2011a).

China has thus drawn upon Western (and other) models of education in the internal reform of its institutions as well as through external means by sending university faculty and students abroad to research and study. These intellectual 'flows' between Chinese and overseas universities, especially in Anglophone countries, have grown rapidly. The outward movement of Chinese students and scholars has provided unprecedented opportunities for intercultural contact and reciprocal learning and understanding.

These reforms in China – though so far unevenly enacted and unfinished – are having considerable impact on cultures of learning there and, in turn, on its academics and students. As Keqin Liu & Changyun Kang (2011), key players in the school level reform programme in China, argue relationships between teachers and students are now more equal; the classroom atmosphere is more democratic; students are treated with more respect; curriculum content has moved closer to students' own experiences; and knowledge acquizition is no longer the only goal of learning. Liu and Kang acknowledge that reform has been uneven in different areas and that there is still much to do before the aims of the reform are fully achieved.

As these changes continue to have an impact, Chinese international students are likely to display very different learning and teaching expectations and behaviours, and there is already evidence of this occurring. In their study of Chinese international students at the University of Northumbria, Junxia Hou et al., (2011) found that the 'gap' in students' expectations and experiences was narrowing; the differences between social and cultural conditions and academic norms in China and the U.K. were becoming less pronounced and were less than what both the students and their lecturers had expected. There are now many examples of innovative curriculum and pedagogy being introduced in universities across China, including service learning, experiential learning and liberal arts programmes (Slethaug, 2011; Stone, 2011); universities across China are undertaking sweeping reforms of their models of teaching, learning and assessment, as well as management and organization (Fang, 2011; Ryan, 2011a).

Yet, in the midst of these radical changes, there is a desire among both staff and students to retain Chinese intellectual traditions and the continuity of Chinese cultural and educational ideas and values. Change programmes have led to major challenges 'on the ground' in terms of how to introduce reform into the educational system in ways that respect and retain the best aspects of traditional teaching and learning values and practices while simultaneously learning from educational practices and curriculum reform in other countries. There is renewed pride in China's history of scholarly excellence, high student achievement and economic strength. Moreover, the reforms are overlaid on conventional teaching and learning practices in ways that sometimes make for 'hybrid' models that draw from Western or other models but have 'Chinese characteristics'. Sometimes they have been introduced in ways that have caused tensions and challenges (Kang et al., 2011; Liu & Kang, 2011; Ryan, 2011b), especially in relation to 'student-centred' versus 'teacher-centred' classrooms and the roles and relationships between teachers and students. Many of the reforms involve seemingly intractable problems, such as how to align the new curriculum programme with a system of evaluation in the context of high-stakes assessment and fierce competition for school and university places via the national entrance examinations (Liu & Kang, 2011).

Even in educational systems that are undergoing major changes there is continuity as well as change. Jin and Cortazzi (2011) argue that although the 'external landscape' of education in China appears to have changed during the reform programme, the enduring nature of Chinese 'cultures of learning' means that the 'internal landscape' (held in the 'heads' and 'hearts' of students and teachers in China) of individuals' expectations, values and beliefs about teaching and learning continue to have significant impact. They conclude that there is much continuity of the ways that students in China talk about and conceptualize teaching and learning, and that traditional values and conventional practices continue to have an influence. An interesting feature of contemporary Chinese education is an attempt to reclaim China's intellectual heritage through the rejuvenation of Confucian educational ideals and a 're-traditionalizing' of education through the re-introduction and renewed emphasis on 'moral education' (Phan et al., 2011; Ryan, 2011b). Nevertheless, it is clear that deep and sustained change is also occurring within universities in China at not only the structural and systemic levels but also at the level of individual university programmes and teaching and learning pedagogies.

Although Jin and Cortazzi (2011) draw attention to both continuity and change in students' views, they also point to the fact that there is much diversity and difference within cultures, hence their term *cultures of learning*. As I have argued previously, vast differences can be found amongst learners and teachers and educational contexts within China, and respondents from the one country can give significantly differing and even contradictory accounts of their experiences in those contexts as well as differing accounts of their educational values and practices.

2.3   Mutual learning or one-way traffic between 'East' and 'West'?

To date, the movement between Western and Chinese knowledge systems has been mostly unidirectional, from the West to China, with large numbers of Chinese students and scholars travelling abroad to learn in Anglophone countries. The United Kingdom, United States and Australia account for nearly 45 per cent of the destinations of all international students worldwide (U.K. International Unit, 2011) but this trend is changing. In a major study of current and future trends in international student mobility, the Institute of International Education (2011) predicts that as international students now have a greater choice of countries offering English language courses, and as students are increasingly likely to choose destinations within their own regions, 'we may begin to see less of an "East to West" movement' (U.K. International Unit, 2011). China is also investing heavily in its higher education system (U.K. International Unit, 2011; Ryan 2011a, 2011b), and the number of international students *going to* China to study has overtaken the number of Chinese students *going abroad* to study. Young people from South Korea, the U.S. and Japan (the three top source countries of international students in China) are seeking to learn about China and take advantage of opportunities there as the country becomes more powerful economically and politically.

Given the rise of China and increasing recognition of its importance to the future of the rest of the world, there is an urgent need to also learn from China. The terms 'East' and 'West' themselves are of limited value in a world of increasing interconnections, and their simplistic use runs the risk of essentializing and stereotyping individuals within these large civilizations and systems of cultural practice. The boundaries between 'East' and 'West' are becoming increasingly fuzzy and less useful as analytical frameworks, as have the labels 'international' and 'local' or 'home' student, because many 'local' students may have come as international students during high school, and different modes of teaching, such as mixed mode and transnational education, make 'home' a less clear-cut category. Arjun Appadurai (1996, 2001) argues that as national and cultural boundaries become less permeable, the notion of nation states is being replaced by international or transnational flows of people, ideas, languages and media.

2.4   Change and continuity

Educational systems are becoming less static, and the accelerating interconnections between systems – such as through academic and student mobility, joint ventures and international collaborative research – means that educational cultural boundaries are becoming less permeable and previous 'labels' less useful. There are now more learners of English in China than there are native speakers of English worldwide, and more speakers of English as a second language (or third or fourth language) in the world than speakers of English as a first language: this gives rise to questions about the nature of the English language itself and definitions of 'native speakerdom' (Ryan & Viete, 2009).

There have also been calls by several theorists such as Raewyn Connell (2007), Michael Singh (2009), Jeroen Huisman (2010) and Fazal Rizvi (2010) for Western cultures of learning to become less ethnocentric and to take more account of other academic values. Theorists such as these are critical of current Western notions of 'internationalization' with Simon Marginson (2010) arguing that 'equal cultural respect is hard to secure in Anglo-American countries in which systems are monocultural; there is usually an innate belief in Western superiority'. Jeroen Huisman (2010) goes further, arguing that internationalization has become a 'synonym' for the 'export of the Anglo/American model'. An alternative view is that internationalization needs to become an endeavour of mutual enterprise between educational cultures and civilizations, as argued by Gu Mingyuan, a leading educationalist in China:

> The internationalization of education can be expressed in the exchange of culture and values, mutual understanding and a respect for difference…. The internationalization of education does not simply mean the integration of different national cultures or the suppression of one national culture by another culture. (Gu, 2001: p. 105)

This macro-level conception fits the smaller scale notion that Jin and Cortazzi (1993: p. 96) developed about *cultures of learning*: they called for teachers and learners (especially in international contexts) to learn reciprocally about each other's cultures and cultures of learning, arguing that this is mutually beneficial and a *cultural synergy* in learning (for more details, see Cortazzi & Jin, 1996: pp. 201–02).

International education that is genuinely reciprocal provides universities and individuals with opportunities for respectful dialogue and can act as a springboard for the generation of new ways of working and new ways of thinking. Teachers within these systems also need to become aware of and mindful of their own cultures of learning and whether they need to change or broaden these to better suit the future needs of (all) of their students in the context of the rapid changes in education systems worldwide and the likely future acceleration of these changes. This dialogue needs to be informed by knowledge of contemporary realities within those systems. This means understanding how core academic concepts and values, such as the nature of scholarship and learning and how teaching and learning are conceptualized, are articulated and practised by scholars within those academic traditions. Rather than the usual approach of investigating supposed differences between Chinese and Western cultures of learning through a focus on the behaviours of Chinese students in Western classrooms, the study reported here seeks to investigate the views of expert scholars in a range of authentic and diverse settings within each system.

2.5 Methodology

The study reported here is a work in progress, and preliminary results are described in part below. The study investigates the differences and similarities between (and within) Western and Chinese (or Confucian-heritage) academic cultures, and how notions of scholarship and learning are understood and practised in these systems. It uses qualitative methodology and involves semi-structured interviews with senior academics in the United Kingdom, United States and Australia, and across China. Twenty-six interviews have been conducted to date.

Experienced academics (at associate professor equivalent level or above) with at least 10 years' teaching experience are asked their views about:

- How they define 'good' scholarship and 'effective' learning
- What differences and commonalities they believe exist in paradigms of scholarship and learning between Western and Confucian-heritage cultures (CHC) such as China
- Whether they believe that these paradigms are changing or should change

The study seeks to identify what precisely are these views and definitions, how common or different they are within and between these systems, and what contemporary changes and complexities are found in these views. It aims to provide an empirical basis for judgments about these traditions and a basis for potential cross-fertilization across these systems through the identification of common aspirations. The study examines whether Chinese 'cultures of learning' or the 'internal landscape' (as described by Jin and Cortazzi, 2011) are changing in the 'heads' and 'hearts' of experienced academics working in universities across China and in Anglophone contexts. Experienced academics were chosen for study because it was anticipated that their views and practices would be more representative of authentic practices in their academic cultures than would those of newly arrived students, in unfamiliar settings, entering the Western academy and, therefore, more likely to represent their previous school level attributes and behaviours.

Respondents come from diverse discipline areas, including education, humanities, law, health and medical sciences and fine arts. The sample includes large and smaller universities and those with long academic traditions as well as newer ones. Interviews have been conducted in English or Chinese. Chinese participants have been offered the choice of being interviewed in either Chinese or English (if they speak both) so that: they are able to more freely and accurately express their views; to ensure quality and fidelity; and to identify the precise language and terms used (see Cortazzi et al., 2011 for a discussion of how this can make a difference). Most of the Chinese participants have chosen to be interviewed in Chinese.

Nine universities have been chosen in each system:

- Chinese universities include Tsinghua, East China Normal, Nanjing, Harbin Normal, Zhejiang, Sun Yat-sen and Beijing Language and Culture Universities, Shijiazhuang Vocational Technology Institute in Hebei and the University of Hong Kong.
- Anglophone universities include Oxford, Oxford Brookes, Bristol and Cardiff in the United Kingdom, Columbia, New York and Indiana in the United States, and Monash and Charles Sturt in Australia.

2.6   Study findings

The views expressed by respondents in the interviews conducted to date show that, despite prevalent beliefs to the contrary amongst Western academics, there are many commonalities between these systems of academic practice, although there are also differences amongst individuals within these systems. There is much overlap in the actual terms and words that Western and Chinese academics use to describe good scholarship and effective learning, as can be seen in Table 2.1. Almost all respondents report that it is difficult to precisely define the terms 'scholarship' and 'learning' but, as can be seen below, even though the language differs slightly there are clear

Table 2.1 Definitions of 'good scholarship' and 'effective learning'

	Western	Chinese
Definitions of 'good' scholarship ('好的' 学术)	Original, original ideas Creative	Original, innovative (创新) Creative, passion for pursuing knowledge
	Adds value, makes a difference	Has some value(价值), beneficial (有意义)
	Advances knowledge or thinking, application to existing knowledge	Contribution to knowledge, application (运用) of knowledge
	Sound theories and methods, innovative methodologies	Includes theory, methodology and subject knowledge, innovative methodologies (研究方法上的创新)
Definitions of 'effective learning' ('有效' 学习)	Understanding and applying knowledge	Deep and broad knowledge framework (既有深入,又有广泛 ... 知识), applying knowledge (知识应用),
	Think for yourself Work independently	Critical thinking (思考) Independent learner (有独立学习能力)
	Challenge and interrogate authorities	Challenge authorities' views (不能 迷信权威)
	Build on what's known, develop new schema	[Combines] old and new academic knowledge

parallels in the terms and concepts that respondents use, even amongst respondents who have had no contact with the other system.

When asked about differences and similarities between Western and Chinese systems, most of the Chinese respondents were able to comment on this, even including those who had not worked outside China. Almost all of the Chinese respondents expressed a desire to learn more about Western paradigms of scholarship and learning. Only a small number of the Western respondents were able to answer this question, usually as a result of some kind of direct experience in China or through contact with Chinese colleagues. Chinese respondents tend to report that there were more commonalities than differences between the systems:

> I don't think there are fundamental differences. I mean, both of them [the Confucian and Aristotelian traditions] emphasize combining theory and practice and collaborating in learning and being a good person. (History professor, Nanjing University)
> I think there are more commonalities between Western and CHC paradigms of scholarship and learning. In other words, there are commonalities that good scholarship and effective learning share in both paradigms.

An oft-cited belief in China is that the Western paradigm emphasizes critical thinking whereas the CHC paradigm emphasizes rote learning, memorization and breadth of knowledge. I believe that differences exist only amongst individual scholars whether Eastern or Western. They should not be taken as differences between the paradigms. (Professor of foreign languages, Sun Yat-sen University)

Several respondents commented on what they see as differences between the systems, sometimes involving a different focus or method while pursuing similar goals overall. Two respondents felt that although there were many similarities between the systems, there was different emphasis placed on mastery of academic skills:

Both Western and CHC paradigms of scholarship and learning emphasize critical thinking during the learning process. Both emphasize applying what you learnt into practice and learning methods, like to learn and practise good learning methods. The differences are that in CHC ideology, the practice of skills is fundamental, even a priority. Learning is a process which requires considerable hardship. However, it seems to me that Western paradigms put creativity as a priority. (Professor of education, East China Normal University)

The best Chinese students are experts at knowing things; for example, in a research context, they know how to do specific statistical techniques. But they have trouble knowing when they should use that knowledge. (Senior lecturer, medical education, Cardiff University)

The fact that respondents report more commonalities than differences is due largely to the rate and trajectory of change in Chinese cultures of learning, a phenomenon often referred to by the Chinese respondents. Western respondents with more experience of China also often comment on the radical changes occurring within China and, therefore, on the increasing similarities between the two systems, although some believe that this is happening at slower pace than they would like:

[Chinese cultures of learning] are changing, but very slowly. The Chinese move to project-based instruction, although just starting to take hold, is a move in a positive direction. But it will take a long time for those changes to take place. And, again, the move seems motivated by a desire to be more Western in thought and approach to learning and research, which strikes me as a mistake. My hope is that globalization will create new forms of scholarship and learning that emerge from our combined approaches across cultures – but I worry that it is currently more about copying other cultural approaches. Perhaps that's just a necessary first stage ... but it does concern me. (Professor in education, Indiana University)

[T]here are similarities and differences in the two systems[;] ... there is a paradigm shift with the CHC paradigm adopting much more Western characteristics. I would like to see this as a two-way street with the Western paradigms acknowledging the merits of CHC and learning from them. (Senior lecturer in medical education, Bristol University)

Several other respondents have similarly commented that they are concerned that China does not just slavishly copy Western cultures of learning and, instead, nurtures and develops its own strengths in the hope that greater globalization and increasing collaboration between the different cultural systems will produce new forms of scholarship and learning. Other respondents criticize the current binary characterizations of Western and Chinese, or Confucian-heritage, paradigms:

[T]hey are both often based on stereotypes and are de-contextualized, homogenized and essentialized constructs; as discursive constructs they are themselves constitutive of individual and group identities and of versions of social reality; they need to be understood as having fluid, overlapping boundaries rather than being hermetically sealed off from each other or from the multiple contexts in which they are embedded; they need to be understood as having developed historically and in relation to the wider social, political, institutional and economic contexts including globalization. (Education professor, Bristol University)

Responses to the third question about changes within academic cultures provided the most illuminating responses. Without exception, academics on both sides say that the paradigms are changing (this has also frequently been mentioned in responses to the second question, see above). Western academics with direct experience in China describe the pace of change as *breathtaking*. Chinese academics express positive opinions about the direction of change in China but almost universally express a desire for this to be accelerated, acknowledging that there is still much to be done.

Although the changes are not obvious, teachers do emphasis these ideas and the changes do exist, however, the changes are slow[;] ... change is necessary but the current speed is too slow (知识目前的变化太慢) (History professor, Nanjing University)

Western academics also almost unanimously believe that Western paradigms are changing but by contrast were generally pessimistic about the nature of these changes, describing the move towards more managerialist, *market-driven* approaches driven by a *consumerist agenda*.

It is also apparent that within one system there are often differences amongst individuals, and they sometimes express very different definitions of scholarship and views on teaching and learning approaches. Respondents from the same culture interpret academic values differently when referring to the same principle, showing that these values can be understood and enacted upon differently by individuals within the same culture:

> Confucius placed emphasis on teaching students according to their individual characteristics. He adopted different teaching methods according to students' characteristics and personalities. Western education emphasizes the students' characteristics and developing their own interests.... Therefore, in this aspect, Confucius' thought is the same as Western education thought, which also advocates adopting different methods and strategies according to students' different learning interests and backgrounds. The difference between these two ideas is that Confucius focused on 'teaching' while Western countries emphasize 'learning' according to students' own interests. (Law professor, Tsinghua University)
>
> The key point of Confucian education philosophy is that differential teaching methods [should be used for] different students. What [Confucius] means is that if there are fifty students, you need to teach them by fifty different methods to accommodate them. You should not use one method to teach all fifty students. The metaphor is clear. This is Confucius's point. I think his view is very insightful[, however,] Chinese teachers have already forgotten Confucius's words. What our teachers are doing is one method for fifty students, even for one hundred students. (Lecturer in languages, Beijing Language and Culture University)

The first respondent used a reference to Confucian educational values and practices to illustrate his view that Chinese teachers, while recognizing the need for different teaching methods for individuals, focus on teaching rather than learning, whereas the second respondent criticizes Chinese teachers' lack of focus on teaching students as individuals. The first respondent used this reference to provide evidence of differences in approaches between the two systems, while the second respondent claimed that this Confucian educational principle was *not* being practised in China.

The evidence presented above shows, therefore, that it is difficult to provide simple, binary descriptions of Western, or even Anglophone, and Chinese cultures of learning, and that such descriptions are becoming less useful, especially in view of the strong evidence of change reported by the respondents within both Western and Chinese systems.

Although differences between systems do exist, they may not be as great as is often believed. As can be seen from the evidence presented above, there can be an overemphasis on perceived 'differences' between educational cultures of learning rather than recognition of shared values and aspirations. Although it is clear that these systems are moving in directions in which they have much more in common than before, it must be acknowledged

that there are, nevertheless, perceptible differences between , ﹍﹍, ﹍﹍
even within national systems sharing a common language such as in the
United Kingdom, United States and Australia.

There are significant differences as well as similarities even amongst
Anglophone countries (Ryan and Louie, 2007). Students from the U.S. and
Australia studying in the U.K., for example, often report differences, such as
less formative and less continuous assessment and feedback, a much more
conservative marking scheme, and different attitudes to mastery of the
'canon' versus the encouragement of creative writing and the expression of
original ideas. Many British lecturers are critical of cultures of learning that
focus on the acquisition of a canon of facts, yet Australian and American students in the U.K. are often surprised to find that they are expected to master
the canon through knowledge of foundational and definitive works before
writing about their own ideas and arguments and are expected to write in less
personally expressive ways (a sentiment sometimes shared by international
students from other countries studying in the United Kingdom). Aspects of
needing to learn the canon appear at differing levels in all educational systems and across difference discipline areas within systems. According to Jin
and Cortazzi (2006), the Confucian tradition combines the practice of moral
'self-cultivation' with careful study of a canon of texts. In the U.K. in subjects
such as English literature and philosophy, especially at the upper secondary
school level, students are also expected to master the canon before they are
allowed to write creatively or express their own opinions.

2.7   Discussion: Possibilities for the future

In a period of unprecedented change and growing academic mobility worldwide, it is incumbent on all educators and education systems to learn about
what happens elsewhere in the world. China is sending its intellectuals
aboard on this quest. Although British universities recognize the need for
U.K. students to become more global learners, this recognition has yet to
be translated into larger numbers of British students travelling abroad for
study. Also, British universities are not taking advantage of the opportunities
afforded by the large numbers of international students on U.K. campuses
for internationalized learning experiences or 'internationalization at home'
for all students and for mutual learning and understanding. Learning is still
often regarded by many as one-way, from teachers to learners and from the
West to the East.

China is seeking to maintain its own indigenous intellectual traditions
and wisdom while adopting and adapting international models. This
has occurred while there has been unparalleled interest in, and engagement with, China from the outside world as its economy and consequent
influence in the world grows. However, as Dolly MacKinnon & Catherine
Manathunga (2003) argue, Western universities value 'Western ways of

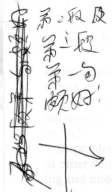

l learning' and ignore diverse cultural values and literacies. stern academic ethnocentrism, such as Michael Singh (2009) vi (2010), have called for two-way learning and for an 'examina's diverse heritage of intellectual disputation' and traditions

ts in the study reported above who have the most experience ures of learning are aware of the possibilities for mutual learning and understanding. Shijing Xu (2011) points to the possibilities for new theories and ways of being and knowing by drawing parallels between Eastern and Western education systems and between Confucian concepts of 'being' and Deweyian concepts of 'knowing', through the increased transnational flows of not just capital and goods but also of people and ideas. She calls for a move away from simply one-way learning and adaptation from West to East and a dichotomized 'East/West' view of the world and, instead, towards a focus on mutual understanding and adaptation and two-way flows of knowledge and interactions.

As cultures of learning change, intermingle and are regenerated across and within education systems, Western educators need to explore new approaches to curriculum and pedagogy to take advantage of the opportunities offered by increased academic mobility in multiple directions. International education 'flows' between China and Western universities provide opportunities for the generation of new knowledge and of ways of working between and among systems. 'Two-way' flows of knowledge rather than unidirectional learning can mean that Western academics and students can learn from the wealth of experience and knowledge that Chinese students and academics bring to the Western academy. As a precursor to this new stance, however, there needs to be a re-examination of the myths and stereotypes about Chinese cultures of learning and a re-examination of how academic values are defined and practised. This can give rise to broader and more diverse academic practices, such as styles of expression and forms of knowledge. Rather than putting Chinese students and Chinese cultures of learning 'under the microscope', as occurs in much of the literature on international students and the 'Chinese learner', the Western academy instead needs to examine Western academic traditions and practices to uncover whether current and future opportunities for the generation of new knowledge and expression are being grasped.

References

Appadurai, A. (Ed.) (2001) *Globalization*. Durham, NC: Duke University Press.
Appadurai, A. (1996) *Modernity at large: Cultural dimensions of globalization*. Minneapolis: University of Minnesota Press.
Connell, R. (2007) *Southern theory: The global dynamics of knowledge in social science*. Crow's Nest: Allen & Unwin.

Cortazzi, M., Pilcher, N. & Jin, L. (2011) Language choices and 'blind shadows': Investigating interviewing with Chinese participants. *Qualitative Research*, 11, 505–35.

Cortazzi, M. & Jin, L. (1996) Cultures of learning: Language classrooms in China. In H. Coleman (Ed.), *Society and the language classroom*. Cambridge: Cambridge University Press, pp. 169–206.

Edwards, J. (2007) Challenges and opportunities for the internationalisation of higher education in the coming decade: Planned and opportunistic initiatives in American institutions. *Journal of Studies in International Education*, 11, 373–81.

Fang, H. Q. (2011) Reform and development of teaching assessment in China's higher education institutions. In J. Ryan (Ed.), *China's higher education reform and internationalisation*. London: Routledge, pp. 48–63.

Gordon, S. (2008) *When Asia was the world*. New Haven and London: Yale University Press.

Gu, M. Y. (2001) *Education in China and abroad: Perspectives from a lifetime in comparative education*. Hong Kong: Comparative Research Education Centre, University of Hong Kong.

Guan, Q. & Meng, W. J. (2007) China's new national curriculum: Innovation, challenges and strategies. *Frontiers in Education in China*, 2 (4), 579–603.

Hannum, E. & Park, A. (2007) *Education and reform in China*. London: Routledge.

Hou, J. X., Montgomery, C. & McDowell, L. (2011) Transition in Chinese–British Higher Education articulation programmes: Closing the gap between East and West? In J. Ryan (Ed.), *China's higher education reform and internationalisation*. London: Routledge, pp. 104–19.

Huisman, J. (2010) *Internationalisation in higher education: Local responses to global challenges*. Keynote address at the Inaugural Seminar Internationalisation and globalisation in higher education, Society for Research in Higher Education International Research and Researchers Network, London, 30 March 2010.

Institute of International Education (2011) *Who goes where and why? An overview of global educational mobility*. New York: Institute of International Education.

Jin, L. & Cortazzi, M. (2006) Changing practices in Chinese cultures of learning. *Language, Culture and Curriculum*, 19 (1), 5–20.

Jin, L. & Cortazzi, M. (2011) The changing landscapes of a journey: Educational metaphors in China. In J. Ryan (Ed.), *Education reform in China: Changing concepts, contexts and practices*. London: Routledge, pp. 113–31.

Jin, L. & Cortazzi, M. (1993) Cultural orientation and academic language use. In D. Graddol, L. Thompson and M. Byram (Eds), *Language and culture*. Clevedon: Multilingual Matters, pp. 84–97.

Johnson, J. & Regets, M. (1998) International mobility of scientists and engineers to the United States: Brain drain or brain circulation? *SRS Issue Brief*, 22 June 1998, U.S. National Science Foundation.

Kang, C. Y., Erickson, G., Ryan, J. & Mitchell, I. (2011) Constructing a cross-cultural teacher professional learning community in the context of China's basic education curriculum. In J. Ryan (Ed.), *Education reform in China: Changing concepts, contexts and practices*. London: Routledge, pp. 41–60.

Li, X. & Cutting, J. (2011) Rote learning in Chinese culture: Reflecting active Confucian-based memory strategies. In L. Jin and M. Cortazzi (Eds), *Researching Chinese Learners: skills, perceptions and intercultural adaptations*. Houndmills: Palgrave Macmillan, pp. 21–42.

Liu, J. & Kang, C.Y. (2011) Reflection in action: Ongoing K–12 curriculum reform in China. In J. Ryan (Ed.), *Education reform in China: Changing concepts, contexts and practices*. London: Routledge, pp. 21–40.

MacKinnon, D. & Manathunga, C. (2003) Going global with assessment: What to do when the dominant culture's literacy drives assessment. *Higher Education Research and Development*, 22 (2), 131–44.

Marginson, S. (2010) *International student security: Globalization, state, university.* Keynote address to the World Universities Forum, Davos, 9–11 January 2010.

Morgan, J. & Bin, W. (Eds) (2011) *Higher education reform in China: Beyond the expansion.* London: Routledge.

Paine, L. & Fang, Y. P. (2007) Challenges in reforming professional development. In E. Hannum and A. Park (Eds), *Education and Reform in China*. Oxford: Routledge.

Phan Le Ha, McPherron, P. & Phan Van Que (2011) English language teachers as moral guides in Vietnam and China: Maintaining and re-traditionalising morality. In J. Ryan (Ed.), *Education reform in China: Changing concepts, contexts and practices.* London: Routledge, pp. 132–57.

Rizvi, F. (2010) International students and doctoral studies in transnational spaces. In M. Walker and P. Thomson (Eds), *The Routledge doctoral supervisor's companion: Supporting effective research in education and the social sciences.* London: Routledge, pp. 158–70.

Ryan, J. (2002) *University education for all: Teaching and learning practices for diverse groups of students.* Unpublished doctoral thesis. Ballarat: University of Ballarat.

Ryan, J. (Ed.) (2011a) *China's higher education reform and internationalisation.* London: Routledge.

Ryan, J. (Ed.) (2011b) *Education reform in China: Changing concepts, contexts and practices.* London: Routledge.

Ryan, J., Kang, C. Y., Mitchell, I. & Erickson, G. (2009) China's basic education reform: An account of an international collaborative research and development project. *Asia Pacific Journal of Education*, 29 (4), 427–41.

Ryan, J. & Louie, K. (2007) False dichotomy? 'Western' and 'Eastern' concepts of scholarship and learning. *Educational Philosophy and Theory*, 39 (4), 404–17.

Ryan, J. & Viete, R. (2009) Respectful interactions: Learning with international students in the English-speaking academy. *Teaching in Higher Education*, 14 (3), 303–14.

Singh, M. (2009) Using Chinese knowledge in internationalising research education: Jacques Rancière, an ignorant supervisor and doctoral students from China. *Globalisation, Societies and Education*, 7 (2), 185–201.

Slethaug, G. (2011) Cross cultural team teaching in China: A retrospective view. In J. Ryan (Ed.), *China's higher education reform and internationalisation.* London: Routledge, pp. 87–103.

Stone, L. (2011) Preparing for the 21st Century: Liberal education and undergraduate educational reform at Sun Yat-sen University. In J. Ryan (Ed.), *China's higher education reform and internationalisation.* London: Routledge, pp. 69–86.

U.K. International Unit (2011) Who goes where and why? *International Focus*. Issue 26 May 2011.

Xu, S. J. (2011) Bridging the East and West dichotomy: Harmonising Eastern learning with Western knowledge. In J Ryan (Ed.), *Education reform in China: Changing concepts, contexts and practices.* London: Routledge, pp. 224–42.

Zhong, Q. Q. (2006) Curriculum reform in China: Challenges and reflections, *Frontiers in Education in China*, 1 (3), 370–82.

Part II

Exploring Changes in Cultural Heritages and Learning

3
Understanding the Chinese Learners from a Perspective of Confucianism

Junju Wang

The learner phenomenon of students with a Confucian heritage culture has attracted many studies in recent years. To understand this group of learners better, this chapter explores how well Chinese students receive traditional educational thought, which is mostly embedded in Confucianism.

3.1 Introduction

For decades, the Confucian Heritage Culture (CHC) learner phenomenon has aroused the interest of sociologists, educators and psychologists (e.g., Bond, 1996; Cortazzi & Jin, 1996; Watkins & Biggs, 2001; Wong & Wong, 2002; Xu, 2004). A considerable body of research has explored CHC learners' orientation to examinations, achievement motivation, use of repetitive learning and recitation, and synthesis of memorization and understanding (e.g., Morris, 1988; Stevenson & Stigler, 1992; Stigler & Hiebert, 1999). It has been found that memorization is considered a significant part of learning in the Confucian tradition and that CHC learners approach academic study in a qualitatively different way that is somewhat inadequate in the academic context of Western universities.

To a large extent, learning and teaching traditions in CHC contexts are negatively stereotyped as authoritarian teaching, bird-cage teaching, and an examination culture. Students are perceived as passive in learning and heavily reliant on memorization and recitation (Yang, 2004). They are portrayed as being weak in skills of analysis and reflection, unable to think independently, and unable to organize ideas in a logical and linear manner (Bradley & Bradley, 1984; Ballard & Clanchy, 1991; Carson & Nelson, 1996).

However, recent years have seen re-interpretations and new understandings of CHC learning and teaching (Wan, 2001). The focuses of these studies are primarily on 'Confucian confusions' (e.g., Cheng, 2000; Biggs, 1991; Kennedy, 2002), a family relationship between student and teacher (e.g., Cortazzi & Jin, 1997; Pratt et al., 1999), a mixture of authoritarianism and student-centredness (e.g., Gao & Watkins, 2002; Kember et al., 2001), and the 'Chinese learner paradox' (e.g., Dahlin &Watkins, 2000; Zheng, 2001). It has been noted that although the 'Confucian values' of collectivism and conformity are often stressed, individualized learning strategies are favoured by many Chinese students. More contradictorily, Chinese students show high levels of understanding, even though they are perceived as passive rote learners (Watkins & Biggs, 2001).

It is the case, however, that many previous studies on Chinese learners were conducted in second language (ESL) contexts and mostly from cross-cultural perspectives. Primarily focused on observable phenomena, most of the studies resorted to qualitative methods, such as open-ended questions, interviews, and classroom observations. As a consequence of these method-ologies, conclusions drawn are often limited by the small size of the sample, and the quantitative features of Chinese students remain largely unknown in the absence of larger scale studies.

In response to such restrictions, this present study included a large number of participants to investigate a range of learner characteristics of Chinese students and explore possible sources from the perspective of Confucianism. By combining quantitative and qualitative methods, it is aimed at answer-ing the following questions:

(1) How well do Chinese students receive traditional educational thought?
(2) How do they perceive traditional concepts of learning, attitudes towards learning, methods of learning, aims of learning, modes of teaching, and roles of the teacher?
(3) What could be the factors which influence their perceptions of tradi-tional educational philosophy?

It is recognized that the Confucian traditions of learning are complex and dynamic: Over the centuries they include diversity of philosophical approach and practice and, not surprisingly, they have changed over time. The present study does not investigate such features but aims to gain con-temporary students' perspectives – that is, their received knowledge and attitudes, whether or not they are historically contextualized or accurate. It is this received knowledge which is likely to be influential (if there is an influence) on their orientations and practices regarding learning.

3.2   Method

3.2.1   Participants
The participants in the study were from the school of foreign languages and literature at a comprehensive and national key university in Shandong Province, China. Taking students from all over the country, the school

offers BA programs in English, Russian, Japanese, Korean, French, German, Spanish and translation studies. At the postgraduate level, it offers MA and PhD programs in English language and literature, with streams in literary studies, linguistics, applied linguistics and translation studies. In this sense, students from this school are representative of their peers in terms of age and educational backgrounds.

A total of 691 students from 26 provinces participated in a questionnaire survey. The sample was composed of 175 graduate students and 516 undergraduates; 150 were male and 541 were female. Table 3.1 provides more details about these students.

Ten students joined in interviews conducted after questionnaire administration. One student from each major was selected for the interviews. Four were graduate students and six were undergraduates (referred to by their initials).

3.2.2 Sources of data

The sources of data for the study were a questionnaire survey and semi-structured interviews. The questionnaire, in Chinese, (see Appendix 3.1 for a translation) consisted of two sections. The first section elicited students' personal information, such as gender, grade, major, and hometown. The second section included 40 structured items with five-point Likert scales ranging from a scale point of 1 for 'strongly disagree' to 5 for 'strongly agree'. Classified into six categories (A to F), it entailed items about traditional Chinese educational thought concerning *concepts of learning* (A), *attitudes towards learning* (B), *aims of learning* (C), *methods of learning* (D), *roles for the teacher* (E) and *modes of teaching* (F).

The questionnaire was validated three times before it was finalized. The initial version consisted of 35 items, all directly quoted from the *Analects*,

Table 3.1 Profiles of the participants in the study

Postgraduates				Undergraduates			
Grade	No. of Students	Major	No. of Students	Grade	No. of Students	Major	No. of Students
Year-1	81	Linguistics	48	Year-1	154	English	156
		Applied linguistics	64	Year-2	150	Korean	70
						Japanese	107
Year-2	94	Literature	35	Year-3	132	Russian	58
		Translation studies	28	Year-4	80	French	65
						German	60
Subtotal	175			Subtotal	516		

the seminal work of Confucianism. Written during the Spring and Autumn Period through the Warring States Period (475–221 BC), this well-known classic consists of a record of the words and acts of Confucius and his disciples. However, a pilot study with ten students found that some ancient Chinese expressions were difficult to understand. Adjustments were then made by putting these difficult items in more accessible language. Ten more items were added to strengthen the reliability of the questionnaire, since these items are commonly accepted as traditional educational thought derived from Confucianism. Experts in Confucian studies were consulted about the inclusiveness and categorization of the questionnaire. Finally, a 45-item questionnaire was piloted again, this time with 50 students. Five items were deleted due to their low inter-item reliability.

Semi-structured interviews in Chinese, guided by some questions (see Appendix 3.2 for a translation) prepared beforehand, were used to elicit information for the sources of students' conceptualization and the possible reasons for their perceptions.

3.3   Data collection and analysis

The questionnaire was administrated in 2008. With the help of the student monitors of different classes, the questionnaires were distributed to 750 students. After assurances about the confidentiality of their responses, the students were informed of the purpose of the study and were asked to provide honest answers applicable to their own situations. The avoid hasty responses possibly affecting the validity of the study, the questionnaires were collected two days later so that students could have sufficient time to respond. In all, 691 of them were found valid and 59 were found either incomplete or invalidly ticked with the same scale point throughout.

Then the data were analysed using the Statistical Package for the Social Sciences (SPSS 13.0) to obtain the tendencies of students' responses in general and by category, as well as to ascertain the most and least received educational thought. Correlation analysis was used to investigate the relationship between different categories of educational thought and to explore possible contributory factors to students' judgment, such as age, gender, major, and hometown. A T-test was conducted to explore if there were any gender differences in students' perceptions. Reliability analysis indicated that the questionnaire is highly reliable, with alpha = 0.8648 and standardized item alpha = 0.9288.

The interviews were conducted in Chinese after the administration of the questionnaire. The interviews were digitally recorded and checked twice for useful information. All relevant interview comments were selectively transcribed and analysed in accordance with the research questions. The excerpts quoted here are translated into English.

3.4   Results and findings

3.4.1   Tendency of students' responses in general

Results of the descriptive analysis indicate that the educational philosophy embedded in Confucianism was broadly well received by the students in this study. Table 3.2 shows that the grand mean of questionnaire items was 4.3495 with range of means extending from 4.8249 to 3.5171. Of the 40 items, 34 (85 per cent) had mean values larger than 4.000. This suggests strongly that students in this study acknowledged the value of most educational thought expressed in Confucianism, as represented by the questionnaire items, and in general they had positive attitudes towards this traditional Chinese educational philosophy.

[A = *concepts of learning*, B = *attitudes towards learning*, C = *aims of learning*, D = *methods of learning*, E = *roles for the teacher* and F = *modes of teaching*; see Appendix 3.1 for numbered items]

3.4.2   Patterns in students' perceptions by category

By category, students' perceptions of traditional Chinese educational thought were ranked in order of most positive responses: F>B>A>D>E>C

Table 3.2   Descriptive results of students' responses

Category	Item	Mean	Std Dev.	Category	Item	Mean	Std Dev.
F	4	4.8249	2.3520	E	8	4.4165	0.8289
D	5	4.7445	0.6198	F	28	4.4024	0.7874
A	1	4.7404	0.6920	F	21	4.3803	2.4226
D	7	4.7223	2.3699	B	24	4.3501	0.8389
F	9	4.6901	2.3854	B	17	4.3400	0.9064
C	20	4.6787	0.6503	D	22	4.3400	0.8419
B	19	4.6660	0.6758	A	6	4.3300	1.5657
F	11	4.6459	2.3834	A	34	4.3159	2.0178
D	10	4.6076	0.7302	F	35	4.3139	0.8742
F	3	4.5755	0.7586	E	31	4.1414	0.8727
C	27	4.5755	0.6860	E	2	4.1348	0.9796
B	33	4.5634	2.4047	A	16	4.1046	2.4710
D	32	4.5252	0.7377	E	23	4.0865	0.8768
B	26	4.5010	0.7702	E	29	4.0161	0.9979
D	12	4.4970	0.8258	D	37	3.9678	1.0544
C	25	4.4728	0.7592	D	40	3.9256	1.0103
B	14	4.4628	0.7875	E	39	3.8209	1.1457
A	18	4.4588	0.8025	C	30	3.6640	1.1152
A	38	4.4286	0.8563	C	15	3.6143	1.1861
D	36	4.4185	0.7841	C	13	3.5171	1.1658
Grand Mean						4.3495	

(see Table 3.3). Such a sequence means that the traditional modes of teaching (F) are best received by Chinese students, whereas the traditional aims of learning (C) were, they thought, the least applicable. This may suggest, as might be expected, that Chinese students are studying for life goals that are different from their ancestors, although they still prefer more or less the same teaching methods, and that some traditional learning attitudes and concepts of learning are applicable nowadays, whereas learning methods and social roles for teachers are expected to change.

Results of the correlation analysis in Table 3.4 show that the six categories were all positively correlated with one another at a very significant level. This indicates that students' perceptions of all the categories are mutually interactive within a system, so that any change in perceptions of one category will lead to perceptional changes of the other five. This confirms how the integrity of the traditional Chinese educational philosophy is strengthened by interwoven ideas of different kinds and confirms how these current students perceive this philosophy as a holistic system.

Table 3.3 Results of students' perceptions by category

Category	Mean	Rank
Modes of teaching (F)	4.5476	1
Attitudes towards learning (B)	4.4806	2
Concepts of learning (A)	4.4165	3
Methods of learning (D)	4.3964	4
Roles for the teacher (E)	4.1027	5
Aims of learning (C)	4.0876	6

Table 3.4 Results of correlation analysis by category

		A	B	C	D	E	F
A	Pearson Correlation	1.000	0.518	0.514	0.623	0.583	0.592
	Sig. (2-tailed)	.	0.000	0.000	0.000	0.000	0.000
B	Pearson Correlation	0.518	1.000	0.573	0.707	0.572	0.603
	Sig. (2-tailed)	0.000	.	0.000	0.000	0.000	0.000
C	Pearson Correlation	0.514	0.573	1.000	0.680	0.681	0.571
	Sig. (2-tailed)	0.000	0.000	.	0.000	0.000	0.000
D	Pearson Correlation	0.623	0.707	0.680	1.000	0.708	0.735
	Sig. (2-tailed)	0.000	0.000	0.000	.	0.000	0.000
E	Pearson Correlation	0.583	0.572	0.681	0.708	1.000	0.629
	Sig. (2-tailed)	0.000	0.000	0.000	0.000	.	0.000
F	Pearson Correlation	0.592	0.603	0.571	0.735	0.629	1.000
	Sig. (2-tailed)	0.000	0.000	0.000	0.000	0.000	.

3.4.3   The most recognized educational thought

As illustrated in Table 3.5, 14 of the 40 items have mean values larger than 4.500, covering five of the six categories classified in the questionnaire. In the list of the highest received items, one involves *conception of learning*; three are about *attitudes towards learning*; two are concerned with *aims of learning*; three are options for *methods of learning*; five are in line with *modes of teaching*; and none are about *roles for the teacher*.

Such results mean that these Chinese students are broadly in strong agreement with traditional concepts of learning and highly value the traditional teacher roles and modes of teaching. They expect teachers to take students' individual abilities into consideration and in the meantime teach with devotion, entertainment, enlightenment and guidance. To them, learning should be life-long, strongly motivated, and achieved with reflection, by analogy, and in a step-by-step way. In the process of learning, students should work hard together with modest and earnest attitudes towards what is known and what is unknown.

Table 3.5   List of the best received educational thought

Category	Item	Content	Mean	Std Dev.
F	4	To suit the teaching to the ability of the students	4.8249	2.3520
F	5	Learning and reflection should be integrated	4.7445	0.6198
A	1	There is no end to learning	4.7404	0.6920
D	7	Learning by analogy and infer other things from one fact	4.7223	2.3699
F	9	To teach without reservation	4.6901	2.3854
C	20	Learning is aimed at broad knowledge, deep questioning, careful thinking, clear clarification and faithful action	4.6787	0.6503
B	19	It's wise to pursue life-long learning	4.6660	0.6758
F	11	To provide enlightenment and guidance in teaching	4.6459	2.3834
D	10	To learn step by step	4.6076	0.7302
F	3	To make entertainment a medium of education	4.5755	0.7586
C	27	Learning without thinking leads to confusion; thinking without learning ends in danger	4.5755	0.6860
B	33	The true knowing is to acknowledge what is known as known and what is not known as not-known	4.5634	2.4047
D	32	Achievements are reached by hard work rather than recklessness	4.5252	0.7377
B	26	Among any three people walking, one will find something to learn for sure	4.5010	0.7702

Table 3.6   List of the least acknowledged educational thought

Category	Item	Content	Mean	Std Dev.
D	37	The deeper-meaning will become evident once you read the book a hundred times over	3.9678	1.0544
D	40	To learn by rote	3.9256	1.0103
E	39	He who teaches me for one day should be treated as my father for life	3.8209	1.1457
C	30	With learning, one can make high pay	3.6640	1.1152
C	15	Within books, one can find houses of gold; within books, one can find ladies as fair as jade	3.6143	1.1861
C	13	Officialdom is the natural outlet for good scholars	3.5171	1.1658

3.4.4   The least acknowledged educational thought

Students had relatively less-positive opinions on some features of traditional educational thought. Table 3.6 shows that six items of the questionnaire had mean values smaller than 4.000, involving *aims of learning* (C), *methods of learning* (D) and *roles for the teacher* (E).

Interestingly, the three items (13, 15 and 30) with the smallest mean values were all about what learning could bring about in the end, implying that high pay, officialdom and happy family life are no longer what some students truly expect from learning. The low ranking of items 37, 39 and 40 suggest that some Chinese students are not in favour of having an intimate, yet hierarchical, relationships with teachers, and that for some rote learning and repetitive learning are no longer so applicable to present situations. Notably, while these items receive fewer acknowledgements from students, they nevertheless receive some agreement by many students, since the means are over 3.5.

3.4.5   Contributing factors to students' perceptions

As to what may influence students' perceptions, results of the correlation analysis (see Table 3.7) show that students' perceptions of traditional Chinese educational thought are in negative correlation with grade (year of study) at a significant level ($r = -0.098$, $p = 0.01 < 0.05$) but not significantly correlated with their major ($r = 0.018$, $p = 0.63$) and hometown location ($r = -0.01$, $p = 0.79$). This may suggest a move away from the unswerving appreciation of the traditional Chinese educational philosophy. It is possible that the more the students are exposed to a foreign language, the more they identify with the value of target cultures.

As to the role of gender, results of the T-tests indicate that significant differences exist between male and female students. For all six categories, as Table 3.8 shows, the mean values of male students' perceptions are

Table 3.7　Results of correlation analysis for contributing factors

Category		Major	Grade	Hometown location
A	Pearson Correlation	−0.020	−0.071	0.014
	Sig. (2-tailed)	0.605	0.066	0.723
B	Pearson Correlation	0.042	−0.062	−0.034
	Sig. (2-tailed)	0.269	0.103	0.396
C	Pearson Correlation	0.040	−0.107	0.021
	Sig. (2-tailed)	0.296	0.005*	0.590
D	Pearson Correlation	0.016	−0.102	−0.026
	Sig. (2-tailed)	0.674	0.008	0.508
E	Pearson Correlation	0.034	−0.083	−0.019
	Sig. (2-tailed)	0.372	0.030*	0.638
F	Pearson Correlation	−0.027	−0.060	−0.008*
	Sig. (2-tailed)	0.488	0.119	0.842
Perceptions	Pearson Correlation	0.018	−0.098	−0.010
in General	Sig. (2-tailed)	0.630	0.011*	0.796

Note: * Denotes level of significance $p < 0.05$.

Table 3.8　Effects of gender on students' perceptions

	Mean		Std. Deviation					
Category	Male	Female	Male	Female	F	Sig.	t	Sig.
A	4.1870	4.4143	0.8290	0.5828	24.731	0.000	−3.724	0.000**
B	4.2722	4.5010	0.7743	0.6190	15.821	0.000	−3.672	0.000**
C	3.9930	4.1161	0.7902	0.5303	33.524	0.000	−2.179	0.030*
D	4.1586	4.3841	0.7495	0.4572	43.215	0.000	−4.466	0.000**
E	4.0072	4.1125	0.8082	0.5555	29.096	0.000	−1.840	0.066
F	4.2950	4.5704	0.7383	0.4470	37.224	0.000	−5.562	0.000**

Note: * $p < 0.05$; ** $p < 0.001$.

consistently smaller, suggesting that gender plays a role in students' perceptions, both in general and by category. It seems that female students are more ready to accept the traditional educational philosophy embedded in Confucianism.

3.5　Discussion

3.5.1　Well-received traditional educational thought

This study has found that these Chinese students hold positive attitudes towards the value of traditional educational thought, particularly those of teacher responsibilities, teaching modes and learning methods. This confirms that Confucianism (as represented in a carefully constructed questionnaire) has had a lasting and pervasive influence on the development and characteristics of the system of student attitudes within Chinese education (Bush & Qiang, 2000; Wong, 2004). Even though the teachers and students are often unaware of the sources, these aspects of education in China are still primarily based on, or at least fully consonant with, Confucian principles that continue to have currency for contemporary explanations of the learning culture in the Chinese context (Cortazzi & Jin, 1997; Jin & Cortazzi, 1998).

For centuries, the Confucian tradition prioritized education as important both for personal improvement and societal development. It is often stated that the salient characteristics of learning in the CHC include social-achievement orientation, maintaining diligence, attributing success to effort, learning in a competitive spirit, and holding a strong belief in the maxim, 'practice makes perfect' (Wong, 2004). Understandably, students in such a cultural context have high expectations of education. Compared with their Western counterparts, they are likely to have stronger achievement motivation and to demonstrate greater levels of diligence in studies (Goyette & Xie, 1999). For many Chinese students, learning is a painstaking process of gaining knowledge (Cortazzi & Jin, 2007; Jin & Cortazzi, 2011), but making an effort in learning is the essential preparatory step to achieving future success.

3.5.2 High expectations from teachers and teaching

Students in this study were found to expect teachers to teach without reservation, to suit teaching to students' abilities, to make entertainment a dimension of teaching, and never to be weary of teaching. This is in agreement with the Chinese tradition that teachers should take responsibility for cultivating talent for the benefit of society. Typically, Chinese teachers are expected to have a broad scope of knowledge (Nield, 2004), convey knowledge in a disinterested fashion, express ideas elegantly and in lively fashion, cultivate their own personal morality, and match deeds with words (Xu, 2004; Yang, 1993). As teachers, they should be passionately and conscientiously committed to their work in the way that candles light up others while burning out themselves (Jin & Cortazzi, 2011: p. 124).

One student interviewee commented on this:

> School education is so important that teachers play crucial roles for one's development and cultivation. We often say students are the subjects of education and teachers are the leading force. Universities in China are investing so much money to send teachers overseas for professional development and to attract talents from abroad. All this indicates the important roles of teachers for education and the society. Isn't it often for us to say, 'A teacher passes on knowledge, educates on various subjects, and solve problems?' This is an ancient maxim as old as a thousand years! But still it has realistic significance today. (LM)

However, too much reliance on teachers and teaching may prevent students from participating fully or responsibly in the learning process (Bradley & Bradley, 1984; Zhao & McDougall, 2008). This might explain why students within a Confucian cultural heritage are often associated with lacking independent thinking and deep understanding. More often than not, they are observed to be passive, compliant learners. They do not actively participate in classroom discussion, and prefer non-critical reception of information (Peng, 2007). This lack of willingness to communicate does not necessarily mean, of course, that students lack understanding or independent thinking, although these are apparently not demonstrated.

3.5.3 Changed attitudes towards methods of learning

Rote memorization has been seen as a salient characteristic of Chinese students (e.g., Gu & Johnson, 1996; Martinsons & Martinsons, 1996), but this image is made shaky by the relatively low ranking of rote learning and repetitive learning in this study. In other words, some students have changed their attitudes towards some traditional learning methods. Memorization and rote learning for education are no longer universally regarded as important as in the past.

One student shared a negative story of rote memorization:

> I have a relative who is now studying at this university as an engineering student. He told me he was a victim of rote learning. For the first year, he tried hard to memorize everything he took down from teachers' lectures, but got three courses failed for the year. He just couldn't infer other things from one fact…. This is an era of 'knowledge explosion', so we have to give up some inefficient ways of learning and build up our ability to selectively gain knowledge in a quicker way. (ZL)

Another student, while acknowledging the significance of education, explained why rote learning has lost its realistic value. The student begins with acknowledgement of the value of learning:

> Important? Of course. The whole society is emphasizing learning, not only in China but also in the Western world. If you don't study, how can you make progress?…However, I don't think memorization works well now. Because it is an information era. There is so much to learn, how can we recite everything? We just can't do that even if we wanted to. Also, if you are the person who wants to memorize everything, others would think you are crazy, rigid, old-fashioned and lagged behind…(WJ)

Such comments suggest a need to update the stereotyped picture of Chinese students as surface learners (Zheng, 2001). As a matter of fact, Confucian traditions of education stress the significance of reflective thinking in the process of learning and take deep knowledge as the goal of learning (Jin & Cortazzi, 2006: pp. 12–14). Instead of acquiring knowledge superficially, Chinese students often adopt the deep approach to learning by promoting reflection and enquiry (On, 1996) and by synthesizing memorization and active understanding (Li & Cutting, 2011; Stevenson & Stigler, 1992). More often than not, they are mentally active. although they are observed to be physically passive (Jin & Cortazzi, 2006).

In addition, it is worth mentioning that repetition or memorization practice by Chinese students might not be the same as previously perceived (Watkins & Biggs, 2001). Even though memorization is seen as a significant part of learning, it should by no means be equated with rote learning. Whereas rote learning is not intended for understanding and deep thinking, memorization is supposed to precede understanding and lead to deeper understanding (Biggs, 1996; Lee, 1996; Li & Cutting, 2011). To better understand the Chinese cultures of learning, it is advisable to regard memorization, understanding, reflection, and questioning as the basic components of interactive learning.

3.5.4   Downgraded roles for the teacher

Traditionally, the attitude of Chinese students towards their teachers is one of respect, obedience and reliance. Teachers are supposed to be superior in class, but after class they are encouraged to have personal relationships with students. So teachers and students typically have a family-like relationship, though in a dominance–obedience hierarchy. Responsibility, authority, and morality are all part of the relationship (Jin & Cortazzi, 2009; Pratt, 1992).

However, this study found that of the six items in the questionnaire for teacher roles, five of them had mean values smaller than the grand average, indicating that some students in contemporary Chinese society are less in favour of having the traditional parent–child relationships with their teachers.

Two students explained why:

> We are encouraged to have our own personalized characteristics. We can't extensively listen to other people, including our parents and teachers. Definitely, we should have respect for them, but it doesn't mean that we should listen to them for everything. It's just not wise to do that! (SF)
>
> The relationship between teacher and student is becoming somewhat functional... Of course, teachers are still caring about us, and we still pay due respect to our teachers. But we're not like family members as you just said. We are teacher and students. They don't behave in a fatherly way, and students then do not treat him as a father. (LQ)

It can be noted that students' expectations of teaching approaches and of teacher roles are somewhat inconsistent. Whereas they value highly the

Interviews with a larger number of students could make the findings more valid and generalizable.

Acknowledgements

This study was supported by Shandong Provincial Planning Project of Education Science (2010GZ079) and The Innovation Fund for Young Scholars of Shandong University. The author would like to specially thank Professor Tony Silva for his insightful comments and suggestions for the earlier drafts, and for his careful proofreading of the final draft. Thanks also go to the participants for their cooperation and contribution.

Appendix 3.1: Questionnaire items

A   Concepts of learning

(1) There is no end to learning.
(2) Men are born about the same, but learning makes them different.
(3) Learning is like rowing upstream: not to advance is to drop back.
(4) There are no fixed teachers in learning.
(5) There is no royal road to learning.
(6) Learning makes wisdom obtainable.

B   Attitudes towards learning

(7) In learning, be modest enough to consult one's inferiors.
(8) It's necessary to realize that diligence is the path through the mountains of books and hard work is the ship for sailing through the endless ocean of learning.
(9) It's wise to pursue life-long learning.
(10) Isn't it a pleasure to learn and review from time to time?
(11) Among any three people walking, one will find something to learn, for sure.
(12) The true knowing is to acknowledge what is known as known and what is not known as not known.

C   Aims of learning

(13) Officialdom is the natural outlet for good scholars.
(14) Within books, one can find houses of gold. Within books, one can find ladies as fair as jade.
(15) Learning is aimed at broad knowledge, deep questioning, careful thinking, clarification, and faithful action.
(16) The gentleman keeps learning, to the betterment of his future endeavors.
(17) Learning without thinking leads to confusion; thinking without learning ends in danger.
(18) With learning, one can earn high pay.

D   Methods of learning

(19) To learn step by step.
(20) Skilfulness comes from practice.
(21) To gain knowledge of the new by reviewing the old.
(22) Achievements are reached by hard work rather than recklessness.
(23) To inquire for knowledge with earnestness and reflect on it with self-practice.
(24) The deeper meaning will become evident once you read the book a hundred times over.
(25) To learn by rote.
(26) Learning and reflection should be integrated.
(27) To learn by analogy and infer other things from one fact.

E   Roles for the teacher

(28) Teachers are the superiors, whereas students are the inferiors.
(29) Teachers should set good examples for students.
(30) Teachers and elders are those who deserve due respect.
(31) In the pursuit of virtue, do not be afraid to overtake your teacher.
(32) He who teaches me for one day should be treated as my father for life.
(33) Teacher should never be weary of teaching.

F   Modes of teaching

(34) To provide enlightenment and guidance in teaching.
(35) To instruct only when someone bursts with eagerness for learning; enlighten only when someone bubbles to speak but fails to express himself.
(36) To learn things by heart in silence, to retain curiosity despite much study.
(37) To make entertainment a medium of education.
(38) To enrich teaching with literature, conduct, loyalty, and trustworthiness.
(39) To suit the teaching to the ability of the students.
(40) To teach without reservation.

Note: Items were randomized without headings before the questionnaire was administered to students.

Appendix 3.2:   Guiding questions for interviews

(1) What do you think of traditional Chinese educational thought in general?
(2) What aspect of educational thought is best applicable to your situation? Why?
(3) What educational thought does not appeal to you?

(4) What factors may influence your opinions on educational thought?
(5) What are the most effective ways of learning in your situation?
(6) What do you think about the influence of Confucianism on Chinese education?
(7) How do you find the teacher–student relationships nowadays? For example?
(8) What do you expect from teacher and teaching?
(9) What is your life goal? What do you expect from learning/education?
(10) What kind of teachers are ideal teachers in your opinion?

References

Ballard, B. & Clanchy, J. (1991) *Teaching students from overseas: A brief guide for lecturers and supervisors.* Melbourne: Longman Cheshire.

Biggs, J. B. (1991) Approaches to learning in secondary and tertiary students in Hong Kong: Some comparative studies. *Education Research Journal*, 6, 27–39.

Biggs, J. B. (1996) Western misperceptions of the Confucian-heritage learning culture. In D. A. Watkins and J. B. Biggs (Eds), *The Chinese learner: Cultural, psychological and contextual influences.* Hong Kong: CERC and ACER, pp. 45–67.

Bond, M. H. (1996) Chinese values. In M. H. Bond (Ed.), *The handbook of Chinese psychology.* Hong Kong: Oxford University Press, pp. 208–26.

Bradley, D. & Bradley, M. (1984) *Problems of Asian students in Australia: Language, culture and education.* Canberra: Australian Government Publishing Service.

Bush, T. & Qiang, H. (2000) Leadership and culture in Chinese education. *Asia Pacific Journal of Education*, 20 (2), 58–67.

Carson, J. & Nelson, G. (1996) Chinese students' perceptions of ESL peer response group interaction. *Journal of Second Language Writing*, 5, 1–19.

Chen, C. S., Lee, S. Y. & Stevenson, H. W. (1996) Academic achievement and motivation of Chinese students: A cross-national perspective. In S. Lau (Ed.), *Growing up the Chinese way: Chinese child and adolescent development.* Hong Kong: The Chinese University Press.

Cheng, X. (2000) Asian students' reticence revisited. *System*, 28, 435–46.

Cortazzi, M. & Jin, L. (1996) Cultures of learning: Language classrooms in China. In H. Coleman (Ed.), *Society and the language classroom.* Cambridge: Cambridge University Press, pp. 169–206.

Cortazzi, M. & Jin, L. (1997) Communication for learning across cultures. In D. MacNamara and R. Harris (Eds), *Overseas students in higher education.* London: Routledge, pp. 79–90.

Cortazzi, M. & Jin, L. (2007) *A journey from hell to heaven? Continuity and change in Chinese students' metaphors for learning.* Keynote speech at The Third International Conference on Chinese and East-Asian Learners, Jinan: 16–19 November 2007.

Dahlin, B. & Watkins, D. (2000) The role of repetition in the processes of memorising and understanding: A comparison of the views of German and Chinese secondary school students in Hong Kong. *British Journal of Educational Psychology*, 70, 65–84.

Gao, L. & Watkins, D. A. (2002) Conceptions of teaching held by school science teachers in P. R. China: Identification and cross-cultural comparisons. *International Journal of Science Education*, 24 (1), 61–79.

Goyette, K. & Xie, Y. (1999). Educational expectations of Asian-American youth: Determinants and ethnic differences. *Sociology of Education*, 72, 22–36.

Gu, Y. & Johnson, R. (1996) Vocabulary learning strategies and language learning outcomes. *Language Learning*, 46 (4), 643–79.

Ho, I. T. (2001) Are Chinese teachers authoritarian? In D. A. Watkins and J. B. Biggs (Eds), *Teaching the Chinese learner: Psychological and pedagogical perspectives*. Melbourne: Australian Council for Educational Research, pp. 99–114.

Jin, L. & Cortazzi, M. (1998) The culture the learner brings: A bridge or a barrier? In M. Byram and M. Fleming (Eds), *Language learning in intercultural perspective, approaches through drama and ethnography*. Cambridge: Cambridge University Press, pp. 98–118.

Jin, L. & Cortazzi, M. (2006) Changing practices in Chinese cultures of learning. *Language, Culture and Curriculum*, 19 (1), 5–20.

Jin, L. & Cortazzi, M. (2009) Cultivators, cows and computers: Chinese learners' metaphors of teachers. In T. Coverdale-Jones and P. Rastall (Eds), *Internationalizing the University, the Chinese context*. Houndmills: Palgrave Macmillan, pp. 107–29.

Jin, L. & Cortazzi, M. (2011) The changing landscapes of a journey: Educational metaphors in China. In J. Ryan (Ed.), *Education reform in China: Changing concepts, contexts and practices*. London: Routledge, pp. 113–31.

Kember, D., Kwan, K.-P. & Ledesma, J. (2001) Conceptions of good teaching and how they influence the way adults and school leavers are taught. *International Journal of Lifelong Education*, 20 (5), 393–404.

Kennedy, P. (2002) Learning cultures and learning styles: Myth-understandings about adult (Hong Kong) Chinese learners. *International Journal of Lifelong Education*, 21 (5), 430–45.

Lee, W. O. (1996) The cultural context for Chinese learners: Conceptions of learning in the Confucian tradition. In D. A. Watkins and J. B. Biggs (Eds), *The Chinese learner: Cultural, psychological and contextual influences*. Hong Kong: CERC and ACER, pp. 25–41.

Li, X. & Cutting, J. (2011) Rote Learning in Chinese culture: reflecting active Confucian-based memory strategies. In L. Jin and M. Cortazzi (Eds), *Researching Chinese learners: Skills, perceptions and intercultural adaptations*. Houndmills: Palgrave Macmillan, pp. 21–42.

Martinsons, M. G. & Martinsons, A. B. (1996) Conquering cultural constraints to cultivate Chinese management creativity and innovation. *Journal of Management Development*, 15 (9), 28–35.

Morris, P. (1988). Teachers' attitudes towards a curriculum innovation: An East Asian study. *Research in Education*, 40, 75–87.

Nield, K. (2004) Questioning the myth of the Chinese learner. *International Journal of Contemporary Hospitality Management*, 16 (3), 189–96.

On, L. W. (1996) The Cultural context for Chinese learners: Conceptions of learning in the Confucian tradition. In D. A. Watkins and J.B. Biggs, (Eds), *Chinese learner: Cultural, contextual and psychological influences*. Hong Kong: CERC and ACER.

Peng, J. E. (2007) Willingness to communicate in the Chinese EFL classroom: A cultural perspective. In J. Liu (Ed.), *English language teaching in China; new approaches, perspectives and standards*. London: Continuum, pp. 250–69.

Pratt, D. D. (1992) Chinese conceptions of learning and teaching: A Westerner's attempt at understanding. *International Journal of Lifelong Education*, 11 (4), 301–19.

Pratt, D. D., Kelly, M. & Wong, W. S. S. (1999) Chinese conceptions of 'effective teaching' in Hong Kong: Towards culturally sensitive evaluation of teaching. *International Journal of Lifelong Education*, 18 (4), 241–58.

Salili, F. (1996) Accepting personal responsibility for learning. In D. A. Watkins and J. B. Biggs (Eds), *The Chinese learner: Cultural, psychological and contextual influences*. Hong Kong: CERC and ACER, pp. 85–105.

Smith, P. J. & Smith, S. N. (1999) Differences between Chinese and Australian students: Some implications for distance educators. *Distance Education*, 20 (1), 64–80.

Stevenson, H. W. & Stigler, J. W. (1992) *The Learning gap: Why our schools are failing and what we can learn from Japanese and Chinese education*. New York: Simon & Schuster.

Stigler, J. W. & Hiebert, J. (1999) *The Teaching gap: Best ideas from the world's teachers for improving education in the classroom*. New York: The Free Press.

Tang, C. (1996) Collaborative learning: the latent dimension in Chinese students' learning. In D. A. Watkins and J. B. Biggs (Eds), *The Chinese learner: Cultural, psychological, and contextual influences*. Hong Kong: CERC and ACER, pp. 183–204.

Wan, G. (2001) The learning experience of Chinese students in American universities: A cross-cultural perspective. *College Student Journal*, 35 (1), 28–44.

Watkins, D. A.. & Biggs, J. B. (2001) The paradox of the Chinese learner and beyond. In D. A. Watkins and J. B. Biggs (Eds), *Teaching the Chinese learner: Psychological and pedagogical perspectives*. Hong Kong: CERC and ACER, pp. 3–23.

Wong, N. Y. (2004) The CHC learner's phenomenon: Its implications on mathematics education. In L. Fan, N. Y. Wong, J. Cai and S. Li (Eds), *How Chinese learn mathematics: Perspectives from insiders*. Singapore: World Scientific, pp. 503–34.

Wong, N. Y. & Wong, W. Y. (2002) The 'Confucian Heritage Culture' learner's phenomenon. *Asian Psychologist*, 3 (1), 78–82.

Woodrow, D. & Sham, S. (2001) Chinese pupils and their learning preferences. *Race Ethnicity and Education*, 4 (4), 377–94.

Xu, R. (2004) *Chinese mainland students' experiences of teaching and learning at a Chinese university: Some emerging findings*. Paper presented at the BERA 2004 Conference, UMIST, Manchester, 15–18 September 2004.

Yang, H. (1993) Confucius Prospects: the quarterly review of comparative education. *UNESCO: International Bureau of Education*, 23 (1/2), 211–19.

Yang, Y. B. (2004) *Characteristics of good English learners – urban key senior secondary school students learning English in Yunnan – China*. Unpublished M.A thesis. Melbourne: La Trobe University.

Zhao, N. & McDougall, D. (2008) Cultural Influences on Chinese Students' Asynchronous Online Learning in a Canadian University. *Journal of Distance Education*, 22 (2), 59–79.

Zheng, Y. (2001) Paradox of Chinese learners. *Journal of Mathematics Education*, 22 (1), 6–10.

4

Reforming Teacher Education in East Africa: The Importance of Socio-cultural Context

Jan Abd-Kadir and Frank Hardman

4.1 Introduction

Enabling pupils to become proficient at using spoken language is seen as one of the major goals of education. Pupils are expected to express their thoughts and engage with others in joint intellectual activity so as to advance their individual capacity for productive, rational and reflective thinking. The guided co-construction of knowledge, in which a teacher talks with pupils in whole class, group and individual situations to guide their thinking, together with opportunities for collaborative learning to promote critical thinking and problem solving, is, therefore, seen as being central to the educational process (Hardman, 2008a).

The role that classroom talk can play in learning is reflected in the distinctions that Alexander (2008, pp. 33–34) makes in the repertoire of teacher–pupil interaction, moving from talk that promotes lower to higher levels of cognition:

- *rote*, or the drilling of facts, ideas and routines through constant repetition;
- *recitation*, or the accumulation of knowledge and understanding through questions designed to test or stimulate recall of what has previously been encountered, or to cue pupils to work out answers from clues provided in the question;
- *expository instruction*, or imparting information and/or explaining facts, principles or procedures;
- *discussion*, or open exchanges between teacher and pupil, or pupil and pupil, with a view to sharing information, exploring ideas or solving problems;
- *dialogue*, or using authentic questioning, discussion and exposition to guide and prompt, minimize risk and error, and expedite the 'uptake' or 'handover' of concepts and principles.

However, while international research suggests the last two forms of peda-gogical interaction provoke the most cognitive engagement and under-standing, research from sub-Saharan Africa suggests that the underlying pedagogy of primary school teachers is largely made up of teacher explana-tion and questions, and brief answers often chorused by the whole class or by individual pupils, a process which promotes the transmission of knowl-edge and rote learning (Arthur, 2001; O-saki & Agu, 2002; Abd-Kadir & Hardman, 2007; Barrett, 2007; Wedin, 2010). Research also suggests such instructional practices are often perpetuated in teacher colleges where the training is largely lecture-based (usually from trainers who lack experience and expertise in primary education) with little in the way of modelling practical application of learning theory in the classroom (Lewin & Stuart, 2003; O'Sullivan, 2010, Hardman et al., 2012).

The stakes for improving the quality of pedagogical interaction through teacher development are particularly high in low income countries as research suggests that teaching is the most important factor in pupil achieve-ment (Dembele & Lefoka, 2007). In sub-Saharan Africa the teacher is said to account for 27 per cent of pupil achievement, which is much higher than in high income countries. It also reflects the fact that, in the absence of textbooks and other learning resources, the teacher is the primary source for learning academic content and, therefore, key to improving the quality of education in resource-poor environments.

In light of these research findings, the promotion of a more 'child-centred' form of pedagogy has been high on the agenda of primary teacher educa-tion reform in many countries in Eastern and Southern Africa. However, a major issue facing those charged with reforming teacher education in low income countries like Kenya and Tanzania has been how to implement such an approach to learning in classrooms where learning resources are limited, classes are large and teachers inadequately trained. There are also recognized dangers if the adoption of such 'best practices', often driven by the agendas of international donors and adapted from high income coun-tries, ignores the everyday realities of the classroom and the motivations, capacity and cultural beliefs of the teachers charged with delivering such reforms. Comparative research shows that teacher reform needs to combine that which is culturally or nationally unique with what is universal in class-room pedagogy if internationally driven reforms to teacher education are to be embedded in the classroom reforms (Avalos, 2011).

Drawing on baseline studies of classroom interaction and discourse prac-tices in Kenya and Tanzania, this chapter explores how reforms to pre- and in-service education need to combine the culturally or nationally unique with what is universal in classroom pedagogy if educational innovations are to be embedded in the classroom; the chapter explores the way in which contextual factors interact with pedagogical practices, depending on the traditions, culture mores, policy environments and school conditions of the respective countries. It concludes that acknowledging the importance of local cultural and educational circumstances is necessary if we are to avoid the simplistic polarization of pedagogy into 'teacher-centred' versus 'child-centred' that has characterized much of the educational discourse in the international donor community which provides aid to less developed countries.

4.2   Background

The difficulties teachers and pupils face in Kenyan and Tanzanian primary schools are due to the lack of resources and to the socially and economically deprived environment in which most children live, but these difficulties are compounded by the policy of teaching through the medium of an international or national language following the first three years of primary education (Arthur, 2001). In Kenya more than 40 different languages are spoken in addition to English, the official language, and Kiswahili, the national language used by speakers of different languages outside the home and in the larger community. English and Kiswahili predominate in urban areas, and this is reflected in most urban schools where English or Kiswahili may be used as an initial medium of instruction, although most use English from the beginning. In rural areas vernacular languages are widely used, and this is reflected in the fact that for the first three years instruction in primary schools is normally in one of these vernaculars. While the importance of English is apparent in urban areas, for those who remain in rural areas to live and work, it is not as apparent. A similar situation prevails in Tanzania where over 110 native languages are spoken, and although Kiswahili is the national language other mother tongues are used on a regular basis.

The poor quality of teaching and learning in many Eastern and Southern Africa countries is very apparent. An estimated 8.8 million children remain out of school, and around 50 per cent of children are failing to complete primary education. For those who do complete five or six years of basic education, the quality and relevance of the provision appears to be low, since many leave without having achieved a functional level of literacy and numeracy. A regional assessment of 15 countries conducted by the Southern African Consortium for Measuring Educational Quality (SACMEQ) found that a significant percentage of pupils in the region are being taught by teachers who are themselves not qualified beyond a junior secondary school level, and that only 57 per cent of pupils are attaining basic levels in reading and 25 per cent of expected levels for mathematics (SACMEQ, 2010).

In discussing the quality of education in Eastern and Southern Africa, it also has to be acknowledged that by international standards average teacher academic qualifications and levels of training are low: Many teachers are unqualified or underqualified. Not only is it the case that a significant percentage of pupils in the region are being taught by teachers with a junior secondary school qualification or lower (SACMEQ), but where teachers have received pre-service education and training it is judged to be of poor quality. It is found to be largely lecture-based (usually from trainers who themselves lack experience and expertise in primary education), with little supervised practical teaching for the trainees: This creates a large gap between theory and actual classroom practice, and a repetition of secondary education at several times the cost (Lewin & Stuart, 2003; Mattson, 2006; O'Sullivan, 2010). Similarly, the provision of in-service education and training is also judged to be of poor quality, with little transferability to the classroom, and where such provision does exist, it is often found to be ad hoc and mainly concentrated in urban areas (Penny et al., 2008; Mulkeen, 2010).

Such identified weaknesses at the pre-service (PRESET) and in-service (INSET) stages have led to calls for a radical overhaul of teacher education, an overhaul that moves away from a largely college-based pre-service to a more long-term sustainable vision of continuous professional development that would systemically update the key competences that teachers require in the classroom (Timperley, 2008; Mulkeen, 2010). In response to this need, development partners in Kenya and Tanzania have been assisting the governments to develop national in-service strategies and continuing professional systems for teachers.

4.3   Reforming teacher education in Kenya and Tanzania

In line with other countries in Eastern and Southern Africa, Kenya and Tanzania have expanded their primary education provision in order to achieve universal primary education by 2015. In Kenya Universal Free Primary Education was announced in 2003 by the National Rainbow Coalition. Efforts to cope with the subsequent surge in enrolment focussed attention on the scaling up of a countrywide in-service training and the provision of free textbooks to primary schools. The Ministry of Education set up a national, distance-led teacher education scheme for classroom teachers, called the School-based Teacher Development (SbTD) programme.

The aims of the programme, which ran from 2001–05, were primarily to improve the quality and cost-effectiveness of teaching and learning in primary schools through the acquisition by teachers of new skills that promote active learning and training in the use of new textbooks (Hardman et al., 2009). It was developed as a programme of self-study, using distance-learning modules combined with regular face-to-face cluster meetings. It successfully graduated over 47,000 primary school teachers throughout Kenya in the three core subjects of English, mathematics and science. Also, 18,000 primary head teachers were given training in curriculum leadership and whole school development in an initiative entitled School Empowerment Programme, which built on the earlier primary school management programme (Crossley et al., 2005). The programme was supported by a zonal-based teacher advisory system of over a thousand tutors in teacher advisory centres, who were trained to provide cluster and school-based support to the teachers participating in the in-service training. Building on the success of this initiative, the five-year Kenyan Education Sector Support Programme was launched in 2005 and included the teaching of Kiswahili, training in guidance and counselling and the launching of a national textbook programme called the Instructional Materials Programme.

Similarly, in Tanzania, given the need to address the quality of a rapidly expanding teaching force following the launch of the donor-supported Primary Education Development Programme in 2002 – a programme designed to expand access to primary education by up to 50 per cent by 2010 – the Tanzania Ministry of Education and Vocational Training set about developing its national in-service and teacher education provision as part of the Teacher Development and Management Strategy (MoEVT, 2009). The Continuing Professional Development programme was officially launched in February 2011.

4.4 Baseline studies

In order to inform the design of teacher education programmes in Kenya and Tanzania, baseline studies of the underlying pedagogical practices of primary school teachers and teacher educators were commissioned. The baseline studies used systematic observation and discourse analysis of digitally recorded lessons to study classroom interaction and discourse practices in both countries. The coding systems primarily focused on the three-part teaching exchange first revealed by Sinclair and Coulthard (1992). In its prototypical form, a teaching exchange consists of three moves: an *initiation*, usually in the form of a teacher question; a *response*, in which a pupil attempts to answer the question; and a *follow-up* move, in which the teacher provides some form of feedback (very often in the form of an evaluation) to the pupil's response. The interaction and discourse analysis, therefore, investigated the types of teacher questions (i.e., open or closed), whether questions were answered (and by whom), and the types of follow-up given in response to answers. The analysis also recorded the number of pupil initiations in the form of questions. Responses were coded according to whether a boy or girl answered, or whether there was a choral reply. Teacher follow-up to a pupil response was coded according to whether it was affirmed, praised or elaborated upon.

In addition to teacher questions designed to elicit an answer from the pupils, one prominent 'questioning' move found in both baselines was the use of a mid-sentence rise in voice intonation that acted as a teacher elicitation, designed to get a response from the pupils during, or at the end of, an explanation or following a pupil response (Pontefract & Hardman, 2005; Wedin, 2010). Usually, the elicitation was in the form of a repetition or completion of a phrase or word. It was often direct, and pupils often knew from the intonation whether it required an individual answer or a choral response. This was categorized as a *cued elicitation*. Teachers would also use a tag question categorized as a *teacher check*, but rather than being a genuine check, often the only possible response was an affirmative answer from the pupils.

Cued elicitations and teacher checks, therefore, largely functioned as ritualized participation strategies designed to keep the pupils involved rather than to require an answer to a question. Only teacher elicitations that went beyond a strategy to get the pupils to participate were classified as *teacher questions*. The interaction analysis system also recorded whether teacher questions were *open* (i.e., defined in terms of the teacher's reaction to the pupil's answer: Only if the teacher accepted more than one answer would it be judged as open) or *closed* (i.e., calling for a single response or offering facts). The system also recorded *teacher directs*, in which the teacher directed the class to do something that did not require a verbal response. Pupil questions, and teacher responses to such questions were also recorded.

The first Kenyan baseline study of classroom interaction and discourse practices was commissioned in 1999 and subsequently, in 2005 and 2006, used to evaluate the SbTD in-service and instructional material programmes (Ackers & Hardman, 2001; Hardman et al., 2009). While the 1999 national primary baseline made up of an analysis of 102 lessons covering the teaching of English, mathematics and science found an overwhelming level of directive teaching and rote learning, the 2005 baseline analysis of 144 lessons suggested that there had been major changes in pedagogic practices in Kenyan primary schools. For example, 34 per cent of teachers in the 2005 sample used paired/group work in their lessons compared to only 3 per cent in 1999. The findings also showed that a greater range of organizational arrangements were being deployed by teachers to meet different educational goals: In the 1999 national primary baseline most classrooms (97 per cent) were organized using a traditional classroom layout (i.e., desks organized in rows), compared to 42 per cent of classrooms in the 2005 evaluation using an alternative classroom layout. Textbooks were also far more in evidence compared to the national primary baseline, with an average pupil–textbook ratio of 2:1 at grade 6 and 3:1 at grade 3.

However, findings from the 2005 baseline suggested that the 'cascade' model of school-based training, whereby trained teachers worked with other colleagues in the school to pass on their training, was having less impact than had been anticipated by the programme's designers. It was found that 62 per cent of those who had undertaken in-service training used some form of peer interaction in their lessons, compared to 17 per cent of the non-trained teachers. A similar picture emerged with the use of open-ended questions (i.e., questions eliciting a range of responses): Trained teachers were twice as likely to ask an open question: 11 per cent compared to 5 per cent asked by non-trained teachers. This suggested the need for all teachers to undergo in-service training with official time being set aside for school-based training, and for teachers to be observed, coached and given feedback on their classroom practices.

Similarly, the 2009 Tanzanian baseline study of interactional and discourse practices in 276 lessons covering the teaching of Kiswahili, English, science and mathematics showed that teacher directed activities (explaining, question and answer, writing on the chalkboard, reading to the class, asking pupils to read, giving a lesson summary) took up over half (55 per cent) of the lesson time (Hardman et al., 2011; Hardman et al., in press). Individual seat work, whereby pupils worked on exercises from the chalkboard or textbooks and teachers marked the exercises, accounted for 25 per cent of the lesson time. More 'pupil-centred' forms of learning (i.e., pair or group work, pupil demonstration) accounted for just 14 per cent of the lesson time. Non-curricular activities (i.e., administration, interruptions) took up a further 6 per cent of the time. There also appeared to be little variation in teaching approaches across all four subjects at both stages of the primary curriculum.

Closer analysis of the classroom discourse revealed that teacher questions made up 38 per cent of teacher initiations and 97 per cent of these questions were closed, followed by cued elicitations (25 per cent) and teacher explanations (23 per cent). Pupil questions were extremely rare: in all 40 lessons, only nine pupils asked questions, making up less than 1 per cent of the total initiation moves. Choral responses were the dominant method of responding to a teacher initiation, making up 62 per cent of the response moves, compared to 35 per cent individual responses. It was also found that boys were twice as likely as girls to be asked to answer a question. Follow-up moves were coded to analyse the teacher's follow-up to a pupil response: whether there was a response; whether it was affirmed (i.e., acknowledging that the teacher accepts or rejects the answer); whether it was praised; whether it was probed; whether the answer was commented upon; whether the teacher asked another pupil to answer. The analysis found that it was common for an answer to receive no follow-up in 60 per cent of the questioning exchanges, particularly when a teacher elicitation called for a choral response. When follow-up did occur, teachers usually affirmed an answer (19 per cent of the time) or praised it (in 11 per cent of follow-ups, often by asking the class to clap). Teacher comments on pupil answers, whereby they would rephrase, build or elaborate upon an answer, were rare, as were teacher probes (i.e., when the teacher continues to focus on a pupil who has answered and asks for further elaboration upon the answer).

Given the central role that college tutors were being expected to play in the Tanzanian in-service strategy, a review of pedagogical practices in three colleges of education was also conducted. Twelve college sessions were observed and the lessons transcribed for analysis: that is, four each of English, mathematics and science lessons (Hardman et al., in press). As in the primary school baseline, this analysis revealed that tutor-fronted interaction made up of explanation, question and answer, and use of the chalkboard, took up nearly 80 per cent of the time; the rest was made up of individualized work, group work, administration and interruptions. The absence of teaching and learning resources in the form of textbooks, charts and practical equipment also meant that the students had to copy notes from the chalkboard. Nine of the classes observed were focused on the development of student subject knowledge, with only three covering teaching methodology which would address the knowledge, skills and attitudes needed to teach the subject matter. Even here, a transmission model dominated, resulting in little blending of theory with practice. For example, in two science lessons, students were lectured about the use of practical work and, in an English lesson, they were lectured about the use of group work (rather than using practical work and group work as ways of teaching these student teachers about how to manage a class and teach content through these methods). In these sessions, college tutors appeared to be offering idealized images of schools rather than the reality of the Tanzanian primary classroom.

Overall, the analysis of the twelve college sessions suggested that the pedagogical knowledge, skills and attitudes that are needed to teach primary subjects effectively through a mixture of theory and practice were rarely being practiced. The model of teaching with which the students were presented was essentially transmission-based, stressing a hierarchical learning of knowledge and conventional teacher-fronted classroom organization (O'Sullivan, 2010). Since teachers (at least initially) tend to teach in the way in which they have been taught, it is not surprising that – as the baseline study of interactional and discourse practices in Tanzanian primary schools showed – such transmission-based practices are perpetuated in schools from which the students emerge and into which they will return as teachers, thereby maintaining the status quo.

4.5   Changing pedagogical practices

Overall, the Kenyan and Tanzanian baseline studies suggest that improving the quality of primary education in such poorly resourced contexts presents a considerable challenge. Many of the teachers observed were working in an environment of genuine constraints caused by inadequate funding: Schools lacked electricity, learning resources and other facilities. Where material conditions are poor in terms of the availability of teaching and learning resources and classrooms are often overcrowded, there are clearly limits on what teachers can do to change their teaching practice. However, findings from the 2005 Kenya baseline support the view that bringing about changes in teachers' beliefs, knowledge, understandings, skills and commitments is possible through a well designed and supported school-based INSET system and programme that takes into consideration the contextual reality in which teachers work.

Helping teacher educators and teachers transform classroom talk from the familiar rote, recitation and exposition to include a wider repertoire of dialogue and discussion in whole class, group-based and one-to-one interactions to improve the quality of instruction will require training in alternative classroom interaction and discourse strategies (Hardman & Abd-Kadir, 2010). Research into teacher development suggests improvements in pedagogical practices requires professional development programmes that upgrade pedagogic knowledge and skills over a sustained period of time rather than through disjointed one-off courses; such programmes bring together initial teacher education, induction and continuing professional development so as to create a lifelong framework for teachers. Teachers also need opportunities to work together at the school level so as to learn from one another through mentoring or peer coaching, and by conducting whole school training to collectively guide curriculum, assessment and professional learning decisions.

Research into classroom talk raises the possibility that pedagogic change can be achieved within the cultural context in which teachers operate by developing the classroom talk repertoire through more effective teacher training programmes. Transforming teachers' beliefs, knowledge, understanding, skills and commitments – in what they know and are able to do in their individual practice as well as in their shared responsibility – is, therefore, viewed as being central to teacher professional development (Moon, 2007; Schwille et al., 2007). As discussed above, research suggests it is best to focus on the school as the most effective level of intervention to improve the quality of teaching and learning by involving the school head teacher and all the teachers in creating a genuine learning community through ownership of the process.

4.6   Emerging lessons

Overall, the findings from the baseline studies support the view that enhancing the capacity of the teaching profession is crucial if the quality of teaching and learning in primary schools in the region is to improve. By focusing on the classroom, school-based training can help teachers develop more of a dialogic pedagogy to broaden the repertoire of whole class teaching currently found in many sub-Saharan African classrooms. In this way dialogue and discussion can be included alongside the more traditional drilling, closed questioning and telling, thereby raising cognitive engagement and understanding. Such an approach builds on the traditional model of whole class teaching found in many African primary classrooms, but it avoids the simplistic polarization of pedagogy into 'teacher-centred' versus 'child-centred' that has characterized much of the educational discourse in the international donor community (O'Sullivan, 2006; Barrett, 2007; Alexander, 2008; Hardman et al., 2009). It will also help to ensure there is a better balance and blending of local cultural practices with internationally informed teacher education reforms.

However, it is apparent from the baseline studies that there is no quick fix to the reforming of teacher education in Kenya and Tanzania. New ideas for methods and structures have to recognize the realities of differing needs, circumstances, resources and cultural beliefs in the two countries and must be formulated within the assumptions, processes and expectations of the wider national education systems. Teacher education will have only limited success if there is a disjuncture between the training teachers receive and the particular cultural mores, policy environments and school conditions of the country (Avalos, 2011).

Research into teacher development in East Africa suggests that changing pedagogic practices is difficult because of the strong cultural and social influences that shape teachers' assumptions about the purpose of schooling, the nature of the teaching and learning process and adult–child relationships (O-saki & Agu, 2002; Tabulawa, 2003; Abd-Kadir & Hardman, 2007). It has been found that teachers often view knowledge as fixed, objective and detached from the learner, so that they see it as their role to transmit this knowledge to pupils through rote-learning techniques. The notion that pupils might question teachers is also difficult in a culture in which teachers are perceived as figures of authority and respect. However, while recognizing that teaching is a cultural activity, and acknowledging the influence of contextual factors on the teaching and learning process, international studies of classroom interaction and discourse show that teachers can be helped to broaden their repertoires of classroom talk beyond just explanation, rote and recitation (Alexander, 2008).

In terms of changing interactional and discourse practices as revealed in the current study, research into classroom talk suggests teachers can make a difference by, for example, using both open and closed questions, sharing questions at the start of a lesson, encouraging pupils to ask questions, asking pupils in pairs to discuss a question for a minute before they answer, getting a pair or group of pupils to set questions for another pair, or beginning a lesson by giving pairs or groups a question to answer from the last lesson. In following up a pupil answer, teachers can use effective alternatives to simply giving direct feedback; these include probing, commenting on a response to exemplify, expand, justify or add additional information, and building a pupil response into a subsequent question, thereby acknowledging its importance to the classroom discussion (Hardman, 2008b).

In order to bring about such changes, school-based teacher development programmes need to start by helping teachers to explore their own beliefs and by getting them to reflect on their classroom discourse practices as a way of enhancing expert thinking and problem solving so as to bridge the gap between theories and actual classroom practice. Therefore, in the context of Kenya and Tanzania, a model of in-service training which builds on existing systems and structures at school and school cluster level has been adopted as the most effective way of providing support and development to teachers. Working at the school and cluster level will also help to ensure that teacher education is part of a broader capacity development strategy that supports all actors in the education system, including, for example, head teachers, district education officers and teacher trainers, and that it is cost-effective against all the other competing demands in a resource-poor environment.

While there are many good pedagogic and professional development reasons why teacher education and professional learning should be largely located in the school environment, it should also be recognized that such provision requires a significant investment of time and money in building partnerships, collaboration and delegation. The capacity and training needs of those charged with organizing and providing the training, mentoring and coaching, such as district officers and college tutors, is key to the success of school-based training, as is the creation of incentives and accreditation for those college tutors and teacher mentors who will be working with teachers in school. It also requires a clear division of roles and responsibilities amongst national, regional and district offices, and amongst head teachers, schools, tutors and local colleges. Mattson (2006) therefore questions the common assumption amongst governments in the region that school-based training is a cheaper alternative to traditional college-based courses because of the need to provide in-class support from trained supervisors and mentors. As the baseline studies suggest, most schools are not appropriately resourced as training sites, as they lack textbooks and expertise in observation, coaching and mentoring as tools of professional development. The Kenyan baseline suggests, however, that with enough support, some elements of school-based training are possible even in very resource-poor circumstances, so that primary teachers are better prepared to bring about effective learning in the classroom (Hardman et al., 2009).

The baseline studies also revealed that the policy of teaching through the medium of English in Kenya and Kiswahili in Tanzania appears to be having a major impact on the discursive patterns found in many of the Kenyan and Tanzanian classrooms. In the case of Tanzania, Wedin (2010) argues that Kiswahili, like English, is a second language for the majority of primary pupils, and which few have mastered when they start school, which leads to similar communication difficulties. Because of the disparity that often exists between the teacher and pupils in terms of proficiency in the use of English or Swahili, code switching to other languages known to teacher and pupils is common (Arthur 2001). Such difficulties have led to what Hornberger and Chick (2001) call 'safe talk', in which the chorusing of answers is used as a 'participation' strategy in response to a cued elicitation by the teacher, often with little understanding on the part of the pupils. Weaknesses in teachers' use of English or Kiswahili also appeared to encourage teachers to see whole class teaching as a safer option because of the control it affords over their own language choice and that of the pupils. It is therefore used to save face on the part of teachers and pupils and mask the language difficulties and conceal the fact that little academic learning is taking place (Pontefract & Hardman, 2005; Abd-Kadir & Hardman, 2007).

The policy of teaching the primary curriculum through a national or international language in many low income countries is, therefore, exerting a powerful influence on the quality of teaching and learning by presenting communication difficulties for both teachers and pupils. Recent studies point to the advantages of using the mother tongue as the medium of teaching and learning in the early stages of education (Pinnock, 2009). For the preschool and primary years in particular, teaching in a language which is not familiar to a child is often too demanding for them to cope with – particularly when they face other barriers to education, such as poverty, hunger and poor learning conditions. Not having access to primary schooling in a familiar language is leading to the exclusion of large numbers of children from education.

These problems can be addressed successfully by providing at least six years of mother tongue education, with gradual introduction of other languages from an early stage. It also requires the appropriate training of teachers in the use of both the mother tongue and second language teaching to make the curriculum more relevant by connecting the learning to the pupil's experience, environment and culture. However, the linguistic complexity and financial implications of providing for mother tongue teaching in contexts in which there are many local languages has to be recognized (Penny et al., 2008). Such an approach, therefore, requires an analysis of how a country's language policy is affecting children's participation and success in education so as to determine which language(s) would be most likely to increase enrolment, retention and pupil learning, and the findings need to be shared and discussed with stakeholders, followed by information programmes to explain the policy.

In addition to the effects that a monolingual policy has on classroom interaction and discourse in Kenyan and Tanzanian primary classrooms, the end-of-primary certificates continue to exert a powerful influence on instruction and on the patterning of classroom interaction because they focus on memorization and factual recall, leading to transmission forms of teaching (Somerset, 2011). It is important that other approaches (such as those suggested above) supplement the current normative evaluation, and that teachers have a thorough understanding of formative and competency-based assessment (Wiliam, 2010).

4.7   Concluding remarks

This chapter does not conclude that school-based pre- and in-service training alone can address the problems faced by teachers and learners in Eastern and Southern Africa classrooms where resources are scarce and the education systems are likely to continue to face many constraints. Rather, it has been argued that a holistic approach to building an education system is required, an approach which recognizes the socio-cultural context in which teachers work and emphasizes capacity building and the equitable distribution of resources at national, regional, district and school levels. However, the quality of the teachers' expertise is essential to raising standards in the region's primary schools, and systematic school-based training, together with management and career structures that result in consistent and high quality performance by teachers, could contribute to teachers' sense of professionalism and classroom practice and raise educational achievement.

References

Abd-Kadir, J. & Hardman, F. (2007) The discourse of whole class teaching: a comparative study of Kenyan and Nigerian primary English lessons. *Language and Education,* 2 (1), 1–15.

Ackers, J. & Hardman, F. (2001) Classroom Interaction in Kenyan Primary Schools. *Compare: A Journal of Comparative and International Education,* 31 (2), 245–61.

Alexander, R. (2008) *Education for all, the quality imperative and the problem of pedagogy.* London: DFID.

Arthur, J. (2001) Perspectives on educational language policy and its implementation in African classrooms: A comparative study of Botswana and Tanzania. *Compare: A Journal of Comparative and International Education,* 31 (3), 347–62.

Avalos, B. (2011) Teacher professional development in Teaching and Teacher Education over ten years. *Teaching and Teacher Education,* 27, 10–20.

Barrett, A. M. (2007) Beyond the polarization of pedagogy: models of classroom practice in Tanzanian primary schools. *Comparative Education,* 43 (2), 273–94.

Crossley, M., Herriot, A., Waudo, J., Mwirotsi, M., Holmes, K. & Juma, M. (2005) *Research and evaluation for educational development: Learning from the PRISM experience in Kenya.* Oxford: Symposium Books.

Dembele, M. & Lefoka, P. (2007) Pedagogical renewal for quality universal primary education: Overview of trends in Sub-Saharan Africa. *International Review of Education,* 53, 531–53.

Hardman, F. (2008a) The guided co-construction of knowledge. In M. Martin-Jones, A. de Mejia and N. Hornberger (Eds), *Encyclopaedia of language and education.* New York: Springer Publishing, pp. 253–64.

Hardman, F. (2008b) Opening-up classroom discourse: The importance of teacher feedback. In N. Mercer and S. Hodgkinson (Eds), *Exploring talk in school.* London: Sage, pp. 131–50.

Hardman, F. & Abd-Kadir, J. (2010) Classroom discourse: towards a dialogic pedagogy. In D. Wyse, R. Andrews and J. Hoffman (Eds), *The international handbook of english, language and literacy.* London: Routledge and Taylor and Francis, pp. 254–64.

Hardman, F., Abd-Kadir, J., Agg, C. Migwi, J., Ndambuku, J. & Smith, F. (2009) Changing pedagogical practice in Kenyan primary schools: The impact of school-based training. *Comparative Education*, 45 (1), 65–86.

Hardman, F., Ackers, J., O'Sullivan, M. & Abrishamian, N. (2011) Developing a systematic approach to teacher education in sub-Saharan Africa: Emerging lessons from Kenya, Tanzania and Uganda. *Compare: A Journal of Comparative and International Education*, 41 (4), 1–17.

Hardman, F., Abd-Kadir, J. & Tibuhinda, A. (2012) Reforming teacher education in Tanzania. *International Journal of Educational Development*, 32 (6), 826–834.

Hornberger, N. & Chick., K., (2001) Co-constructing school safetime: Safetalk practices in Peruvian and South African classrooms. In M. Heller and M. Martin-Jones, M. (Eds), *Voices of authority, education and linguistic difference*. USE: Ablex Publishing, pp. 31–55.

Lewin, K. M. & Stuart, J. S. (2003) *Researching teacher education: New perspectives on practice, performance and policy*. Multi-Site Teacher Education Research Project (MUSTER) Synthesis Report. London: DFID.

Mattson, E. (2006) *Field-based models of primary teacher training: Case studies of student support systems from Sub-Saharan Africa*. London: DFID.

MoEVT (2009) *In-service education and training strategy for primary school teachers 2009–13*. Dar Es Salaam: Ministry of Education and Vocational Training.

Moon, B. (2007) *Research analysis: Attracting, developing and retaining effective teachers: A global overview of current policies and practices*. Paris: UNESCO.

Mulkeen, A. (2010) *Teachers in Anglophone Africa: issues in teacher supply, training and management*. Washington, D.C.: The World Bank.

O-saki, K. M. & Agu, A. O. (2002) A study of classroom interaction in primary schools in the United Republic of Tanzania. *Prospects*, 32 (1), 103–16.

O'Sullivan, M. C. (2006) Lesson observation and quality in primary education as contextual teaching and learning processes. *International Journal of Educational Development*, 26 (3), 246–60.

O'Sullivan, M. C. (2010) Educating the teacher educator – A Ugandan case study. *International Journal of Educational Development*, 30 (5), 377–87.

Penny, A., Ward, M., Read, T. & Bines, H. (2008) Education sector reform: The Ugandan experience. *International Journal of Educational Development*, 28 (3), 268–85.

Pinnock, H. (2009) *Language and education: The missing link – How the language used in schools threatens the achievement of education for all*. London: CfBT and Save the Children.

Pontefract, C. & Hardman, F. (2005) Classroom discourse in Kenyan primary schools. *Comparative Education*, 41 (2), 87–106.

SACMEQ (2010) *Southern African Consortium for Measuring Educational Quality III Project Results: Pupil achievement levels in reading and mathematics*. Available at: www.sacmeq.org

Schwille, J., Dembele, M. & Schubert, J. (2007) *Global perspectives on teacher learning: Improving policy and practice*. UNESCO – International Institute for Education Planning, Paris.

Sinclair, J. & Coulthard, M. (1992) Towards an analysis of discourse. In M. Coulthard, M. (Ed.), *Advances in spoken discourse analysis*. London: Routledge, pp. 1–34.

Somerset, A. (2011) Strengthening educational quality in developing countries: The role of national examinations and international assessment systems. *Compare: A Journal of Comparative and International Education*, 41 (1), 141–44.

Tabulawa, R. (2003) International aid agencies, learner-centred pedagogy and political democratisation: A critique. *Comparative Education,* 39 (1), 7–26.

Timperley, H. (2008) *Teacher professional learning and development.* Brussels: The International Academy of Education.

Wedin, A. (2010) Classroom interaction: Potential or problem? The case of Karagwe. *International Journal of Educational Development,* 30 (3), 145–50.

Wiliam, D. (2010) The role of formative assessment in effective learning environments. In H. Dumont, D. Istance and F. Benavides (Eds), *The nature of learning: Using research to inspire practice.* Paris: OECD, pp. 135–55.

5

Changing Cultural Ways with Praise: A Distant Action Research Project in China

Jing Wang and Martin Cortazzi

5.1 Introduction

Praise is like penicillin: It is beneficial when administered with 'rules about timing and dosage' and with care regarding 'possible allergic reactions'; teacher praise, as a significant 'antibiotic' in classrooms, can benefit the process of learning (Ginott, 1965: p. 39; Thompson, 1997). Unlike antibiotics, however, there are different views among educational researchers and teachers about the functions of verbal praise. Since the 1980s, corrective feedback and learner uptake of correct language items has been well investigated by researchers working in classroom second language acquisition, yet the effects of positive verbal feedback are comparatively under-researched internationally. The majority of extant studies regarding verbal praise have been conducted on school-age populations; there is a relative gap regarding research related to adults, and an even larger gap concerning English language teaching (ELT) in Chinese universities. Crucially, in China the teacher generally acts as 'an authority, a knowledge-giver and moral example' (Cortazzi & Jin, 1996a) and the 'relationship hierarchy' (Chang & Holt, 1994: p. 105) is firmly maintained, so the praise given in Chinese practice may yield a picture different to that of North American or European contexts, where most previous research has been conducted. Thus, this study is positioned to investigate links between teacher praise and university students' participation within Chinese cultures of learning.

5.2 Context

Unlike some periods in the past when English was not at all favoured (e.g., much of 1950s–1980s), ELT in Chinese society currently enjoys a boom: Learning English has practically become a national obsession. In the forefront of this urge to learn is tertiary level ELT which, however, retains Chinese-specific characteristics. University English – the learning of English by non-English majors in universities – is centrally planned but locally flexible in organizing teaching and assessment, yet nationally assessed through the College English Test (CET). University English students are expected to pass the CET band 4 after a compulsory two-year English language course as a requirement to graduate. Yet, increasingly, students see passing the higher-level CET 6 as a necessity, since employers are known to prefer job applicants with this certificate. CET is one of the world's largest examinations (in 2009 it involved about 9 million participants); however, this enterprise has brought few changes to ELT practices in tertiary classrooms. Apart from the obvious exam pressure, participants are implicitly constrained by the cultural rules and sanctions within their educational traditions which, as the Chinese proverb says, discourage the 'nail that sticks up' since to stand out in this way is 'to be beaten with a hammer' (Anderson, 1993). Thus, despite considerable innovations in the most recent generation of University English teaching materials, classroom practices remain largely teacher-centered, test-oriented, linguistic-based, with much focus on detailed grammar, some translation, and extensive memorizing of vocabulary (Cortazzi & Jin, 1996a). Institutional emphasis on the CET passing rates tends to distort the value of ELT and constrains classroom practices: For many students the CET is their main motivation for learning English.

There are real issues in teaching University English courses: Two problems frequently mentioned are the limited class hours and large class sizes. In most universities, two 45-minute English classes are given weekly on each of two separate days, over two 20-week semesters for two years – only three classroom hours per week for teacher–student interaction. Students can rarely access their English teacher after class, for busy teachers can hardly chat outside the classroom. With limited opportunity, the intensity and quality of interaction is what matters for student learning. Time constraints are exacerbated by the widely recognized factor of large class size. Normal numbers of students per class can be anywhere between 50 and 70, and sometimes much greater. This teaching situation highlights the importance of interaction for language learning within careful use of time to involve participants.

In this ELT context, building teachers' capacities to interact with – and motivate – students has become increasingly important. Some Chinese teachers of English have indeed developed activities, such as daily reports, presentations and classroom discussions, as a means to activate students to share the teaching and learning responsibility; and thus they develop a more learner-centred, activity-oriented pedagogy. However, those teachers find it hard to step out of the influential circle of the teacher-centred stereotype; it is challenging to play down the traditional emphasis on the relationship hierarchy in which teachers have authoritative status; they still metaphorically (and often quite literally) stand centre-stage on a classroom platform to teach. Even when teachers employ motivation, many students seem to follow such activities passively rather than actively engaging in them; many lack confidence to participate verbally and are reluctant to take greater responsibility for their own learning. Most Chinese teachers find it hard to deal with these situations; many just let things be. If there is no effective stimulant for practice, teachers with no consistent interactive response from students may gradually lose heart and, perhaps, just go through the motions. Thus, there is a need for effective and sustained professional development to modify student–teacher interaction – the teacher's praise is one aspect of achieving this interaction.

Perhaps surprisingly, there are long-standing Chinese traditions involving teachers' self-examination, reflection, cultivation and learning (Cortazzi & Jin, 1996a, 1996b, 2001; Ivanhoe, 2002; Hayhoe, 2006) which might support efforts to modify teaching practices through teacher development. This counteracts the views of some researchers who characterize Chinese teachers and learners in supposedly typical Confucian-heritage terms, in which there is a teacher–student relationship hierarchy and the teacher is the authority (see Chang & Holt, 1994; Ryan, 2010). Crucially, though, the various Confucian traditions do not attempt to develop arbitrary authoritarianism; rather, they promote the central idea that teaching and learning are for mutual growth and improvement, that is: 'Teaching is a way of learning and self-cultivation' (Cortazzi et al., 2009: p. 115), and it follows that learning is a way of self-cultivation (Li, 2003). Thus, where teachers are willing to take action to modify their feedback and practices of giving praise to enhance interaction, they engage in developing their own and their students' self-cultivation and show the humane Confucian quality of care regarding student progress and success. Self-cultivation echoes strengths of Chinese education in moral and human terms which have been emphasized for centuries (Yao, 2000) but may still endure despite recent changes (Jin & Cortazzi, 2006). This tradition links closely to self-motivated learning, but self-cultivation can be nurtured by a teacher's actions, including the act of praise; this is clearly shown in the *Analects*, one of the central ancient Chinese classics in which, in a number of teaching interactions, Confucius praises his students (Huang, 1997).

5.3 Praise

The term 'praise' derives from the Latin verbs *pretiare*, which means to value highly (Shepell, 2000) it involves 'commending the worth of' something or 'expressing admiration or approval' (Brophy, 1981a: p. 5). Here, praise refers to an positively evaluative teacher response to students' degree of success by a simple praise statement (like 'okay', 'good' or 'correct') or similar notions conveyed by body language (e.g., nodding, smiling, using positive eye contact) or repeating the correct answer. Praise expresses positive affect (surprise, delight, excitement) or information about the value of a student's behaviour in context with implications about the student's status (Brophy,

1981b). As praise is a branch of feedback, a brief review of feedback studies paves the way for research on praise.

5.3.1   Feedback within IRF patterns

Feedback here refers to oral comments to students through which the teacher directly or indirectly reflects on the adequacy, appropriateness or correctness of students' solicited or self-initiated statements in relation to subject content (Zahorik, 1970). Two broad pedagogical roles of feedback emerge: an evaluative and a discoursal role (Cullen, 2002). Evaluatively, the teacher provides information to students about their performance; in language classrooms, teacher feedback allows learners 'to confirm, disconfirm and modify their inter-language rules' (Chaudron, 1988: p. 133). Discursively, feedback picks up students' contributions and incorporates them into the flow of classroom discourse to develop teacher–student interaction (Mercer, 1995: p. 26).

The role of feedback can be exemplified in the IRF exchange: a three-part prototypical sequence of I as teacher *initiation*, R as student *response*, F as teacher *feedback*, which typifies much classroom communication (Edwards & Westgate, 1994). This somewhat ritualized framework of classroom interaction is not as prevalent today in Western classrooms as it was, say, 40 years ago (Griffin & Mehan, 1981; Mayher, 1990), yet these structured classroom exchanges survive in communicative ELT. Still, the use of the IRF exchange might be promoted as a way in which teachers can guide a large number of students towards the common goal of dialogic learning (Nassaji & Wells, 2000; Hellermann, 2003; Seedhouse, 2004). In a Chinese context of large class sizes, the use of IRF patterns emphasizes the teacher's role and fits some teachers' notions of 'performance' through demonstrating, explaining and questioning (Paine, 1990) but this can be positive in a listener-oriented culture since these exchanges can effectively help teachers to scaffold learning and engage large numbers of students in interaction, provided learners engage mentally and pay attention to the IRF patterns involving others (Cortazzi & Jin, 1998).

In an attempt to better understand the 'timing', 'dosage', 'allergic reactions' and 'rules' of providing praise (following the penicillin analogy), three aspects of teacher praise are addressed: the functions, the frequency and attributing factors.

5.4   Functions of praise

Many studies show how praise can function as a reinforcer when made contingent upon behaviour performance (Lipe & Jung, 1971; O'Leary & O'Leary, 1977). While the behaviourist overtones of this view are outdated, there remains a strong view of praise as positive reinforcement which encourages desirable behaviour if praise is consistent, descriptive, appropriate and precise (Thomas, 1991). A teacher's praise can routinely enhance learners' intrinsic motivation (O'Leary & O'Leary, 1977; Cameron & Pierce, 1994).

Besides many studies with children, research with adults also supports this view of motivational praise (Catano, 1975, 1976; Deci, 1975). A contrasting view is that praise is unnecessary or might actually harm intrinsic motivation, presumably because others' praise is an external factor (Gordon, 1989; Kohn, 1993). Praise as a complex construct may have a negative impact if it focuses attention on the self rather than on the task itself (Black & William, 1998). This is supported by claims that the function of feedback on learning achievement is low when feedback focuses on praise (Hattie & Timperley, 2007; Chaudron, 1988: p. 152), unconvinced by studies on positive feedback, comments on the ambiguity of the effects of praise on language learning and calls for longitudinal research to determine the extent of learning possible from feedback. Thus, an exploratory investigation into the relationship between the use of verbal praise, motivation and learning gains is needed, especially in Chinese contexts.

5.4.1 Frequency

Many classroom studies of praise indicate that it occurs infrequently (Thomas et al., 1978). Dunkin and Biddle, (1974) analysed 10 studies including the rate of praise to claim that praise comprised on average only 6 per cent of total class time. However, different investigators use different coding definitions of praise and analytic procedures. Additionally, Brophy (1981a) argued that there are cultural differences in the positive effects of praise; the effectiveness of praise depends much on context: on teaching styles, personality and teacher perceptions of students' need for praise. The critical point is that the context of most of these studies is North American, and it is reasonable to presume that praise in a Chinese context may present a different picture.

5.4.2 Attributing factors

Arguably, there is a need for the teacher to praise well, rather than praise often, since the meaning of evaluative feedback can be influenced by attributing factors: whether the praise is directed towards students' ability factor or effort (Brophy, 1981 a and b). In attributional theory, ability and effort are often perceived as compensatory causes of achievement among adults (Kun & Weiner, 1973; Nicholls, 1978): that is, the greater one's effort, the lower one's perceived ability and vice versa. Nevertheless, praise is complex interactive communication across cultures, and the effectiveness of praise depends on the type of students and the context (Henderlong & Lepper, 2002). Since the 1990s, researchers have argued that American students perceive progress in terms of talent and ability rather than effort, while Chinese students regard effort as more important than ability (Stevenson & Stigler, 1992). This claimed difference in attribution reinforces the interest of the present study, whether effective teacher praise is directed towards student ability or effort (or both).

5.5   Praise in Chinese cultures of learning

In Chinese education, there are some culturally rooted assumptions and expectations of educational practice (Cortazzi & Jin, 1996a), so it seems plausible that classroom practices of praising students may, in part, be culturally located. Chinese conceptions of education are widely held to have been much influenced by Confucian thinking (Biggs, 1996; Lee, 1996; Scollon, 1999), including a traditional emphasis on maintaining a hierarchical relationship between teacher and students, characterized by Chang and Holt, (1994: p. 105) as a *relationship hierarchy*. A number of scholars have observed strong social relations and hierarchy in Chinese culture (Hsu, 1985; Chu, 1985), and this helps us to understand Chinese students' respect for the teacher as an authority figure and, generally, their apparent reluctance to function in roles of classroom negotiators or discoverers. Meanwhile, those Chinese teachers of English who may be more communicatively inclined towards more classroom interaction find it hard to step out of the circle of influence of this stereotype and play down the relationship hierarchy (Hu, 2001, 2002); they still need to act as a monitor, dominator, instructor and knowledgeable authority. Thus, we might presume that praise from a Chinese teacher to students is rarely given in public.

However, closely related to respect for authority is the much-observed Chinese pre-occupation with *face*. The multiple meanings and importance of face have been much discussed cross-culturally (e.g., Ho, 1976; Hwang, 1987; Scollon & Scollon, 1994). In particular, in Chinese communication one must 'protect the other's self-image and feelings' (Chang & Holt, 1994: p. 115). This helps to explain why many Chinese students, respectful of their teachers and wishing to maintain their teachers' face, will not challenge the teacher in the classroom – or they lose face themselves by doing so. With similar concern for self-image, the teacher is reluctant to admit publicly any mistakes, inadequacies relating to knowledge, or poor pedagogic skills. However, face is not just a negative loss but can be positively given to others, and is thus necessary for their self-worth. In a traditional saying, 'Every person needs face as every tree needs bark' (*ren yao lian, shu yao pi*). One might, therefore, expect praise to be given by Chinese teachers in order to give face to worthy students. Many researchers (Bond & Lee, 1981; Redding & Ng, 1982; Harrington, 1992) indicate that Chinese values of face do have an impact on feedback-seeking behaviours in learning. Some Western experience with Chinese students explicitly reveals students' sensitivity to feedback from teachers (Dougherty & Wall, 1991). Students express the desire to gain honour and prestige and stress the need to manage their impressions and self-image in front of peers so that their peers respect them (Hwang et al., 2002). Correspondingly, students may make strong verbal efforts in classroom interaction in order to elicit teacher praise and gain face publicly. Thus, raising teachers' awareness of providing praise to students is potentially to give face to students, which is one way to motivate students in Chinese contexts.

5.6   The present study: distant action research

This project was conducted in Hunan University of Science and Engineering (HUSE), a full-time comprehensive public university in central south China. A cooperating teacher and his entire class of College English students (50 students) were involved in a three-week teaching period with three stages: pre-observation, observation and post-observation. Various data were collected via three research tools: classroom observation, interviewing and questionnaires administered not only to the focal class but also to 30 English teachers and to 129 students in other classes.

Whereas in conventional action research teacher-researchers (individually or collaboratively) typically attempt to improve educational practice on site in their own classrooms through cycles of planning a change or solution to a problem, teaching and observing, analysing relevant gathered evidence and reflecting (Nunan, 1990; Holly, 1991; McNiff, 1995; Thorne & Wang, 1996; Koshy, 2010), in this project the researchers were not actually present; they were off-site, distant. The first author – the main researcher – remained in Britain, while the focus teacher, whose class was researched, remained in China. With close collaboration and communication, however, other characteristics of action research applied, hence our term *distant action research*.

First, the focal teacher sent an initial video recording of a normal English class; we studied the teacher's classroom talk and identified the problem of praise with the focal teacher in terms of his own practice. He reconsidered his practice by adopting the researchers' suggestions, and they framed a joint action plan of change that was informed by his reading of teacher development materials, which we sent. Enacting the plan over a three-week observation period, data to monitor teaching were gathered through video and audio recordings, interviews and student questionnaires. Three classes (six hours) were video recorded ('Class As') and three classes (six hours) were audio recorded ('Class Bs'). The focal teacher was interviewed for a stimulated recall after watching recordings of each previous class, and six audio-recordings of these interviews constituted further data. The focal teacher reflected on each class, prompted by questions in a 'teaching journal', and the 50 students were each asked to record perceptions of their participation in a 'learning diary'. Students gave suggestions for the teacher in anonymous questionnaires collected after each class and shown to the teacher for his further improvement (thus giving feedback to the teacher). For further assistance, a collection of expressions of verbal praise (Thomas, 1991; Spratt, 1994) was provided at the focal teacher's request: These gave English language examples of typical classroom expressions of praise. Importantly, this breaks a vicious circle: Chinese teachers do not use much praise, so they encounter few examples in their observation, training and experience, which means that they may lack model examples and practice and, hence, are likely to be less confident using praise in English, even when they want to increase the amount of praise. Thus, six action research cycles of *plan-act-collect-reflect* emerge at this stage (see Figure 5.1).

Overall, distant action research involved a process of designing, modifying, carrying out and reconstructing a series of systematic, problem-solving activities in which the researchers were not physically present. Though far from the research site, the researchers cooperated closely with the focal teacher in planning, designing, directing and data gathering. The first author was responsible for the overall research, data analysis and reporting, and communication, while the second author advised on design, research strategies, student engagement, teacher development and cultural issues. Specifically, as 'outsiders', we investigated the teaching process by collecting, analysing and presenting data from/to/for the teacher via audio/video recording; We were vicariously immersed in the context as 'learners'; whereas the focal teacher, as an 'insider' engaged in the action process of change, became a 'co-investigator' and 'learner' or self-cultivator through the interpretation and guidance from the researchers to reflect on and modify his practice. Thus, researchers and the teacher complemented each other's efforts to make reflective practitioners. The relations within this distant action research are illustrated in Figure 5.2.

Accomplishing distant action research requires solid cooperation between researchers and participants; this underlines the importance of choice of research tools and timing communication to overcome the geographical

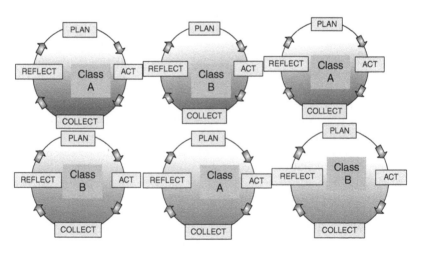

Figure 5.1   Cycles of the distant action research

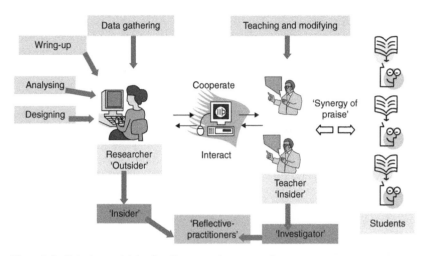

Figure 5.2 Relations within the distant action research

distance. Collaboration raises ethical issues about potentially interfering in students' learning (e.g., making video recordings); cooperation implies not intervening in the teaching beyond the scope of the research design. It involves a dilemma of *subjectivity* (researchers are immersed in the context as vicarious participants and committed to change) versus *objectivity* (researchers are independent and trying to be impartial). In this project, the researchers were far off-site, but remained in daily contact with participants via electronic communication, through the transcribing of video and audio recordings of classes and analysing collected questionnaires. A technical assistant helped with the recording process.

5.7 Results of the study

Results along with qualitative comments gathered from the research process will be categorized into four areas: (a) the changes of the focal teacher's verbal praise; (b) the changes of students' participation; (c) statistical correlation;(d) the contributing factors.

5.7.1 The changes of the focal teacher's verbal praise

Data include one 40-minute video recording of the initial 'normal' class before any changes and six video recordings (90 minutes each) of the focal teacher's classes when he was trying to implement more praise. All the teacher-fronted activities in these classes were transcribed; examples of praise were coded following Brophy's categorization (1981). Two aspects of classroom talk were specifically analysed: *actually given praise* (AP) and *praise-potential points* (PPP). The PPPs are the recognized transition points where the teacher might – potentially – be expected to give praise, if warranted. The obvious place for this is the third part (F) of an I–R–F exchange. The number of APs and PPPs were counted, calculated and tabulated in order to see the interrelation between the two as percentages.

Figure 5.3 shows the fluctuation of the amount of verbal praise used by the focal teacher in seven transcriptions. Surprisingly, there was no verbal praise (AP) in the initial video recording, despite the teacher's perception that he did use praise at this stage. Suddenly, there was a dramatic increase in the occurrence of the praise in the first two observed sessions – a jump from zero to 32 per cent. Although this falls to 7 per cent in the first observed session of the second week, the use of praise swiftly reaches a maximum in the very next class (May 26), accounting for 42 per cent. However, in the last two observed sessions there was a continuing decrease, and the teacher's use of praise almost returns to the starting point. The increased amount of praise during the initial phase of the distant action research was not sustained.

Interestingly, despite the focal teacher's claim that he often used verbal praise, the actual occurrence of praise, as Figure 5.4 shows, took only a relatively small proportion of the praise in the IRFs which only account for an average of 20 minutes of the total class duration (90 minutes). Specifically, on May 26, when most of the praise occurred, the students can hear praise from the teacher on average only once every 11 minutes; on June 2, when the least praise was used, the students can receive praise on average only once every 100 minutes: They probably hear no praise at all in a 90-minute class. However, there is a discrepancy between the amount of praise observed by the researchers from the actual class and what the teacher perceived in

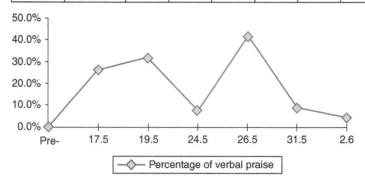

The dates	Pre-observation	17 May	19 May	24 May	26 May	31 May	2 June
APs	0	10	15	2	15	5	1
PPPs	44	38	47	26	36	59	24
Percentage	0%	26.3%	31.9%	7.7%	41.7%	8.5%	4.2%

Figure 5.3　The changes of the focal teacher's verbal praise

Dates	17 May	19 May	24 May	26 May	31 May	2 June
Scale	2	4	4	5	4	4

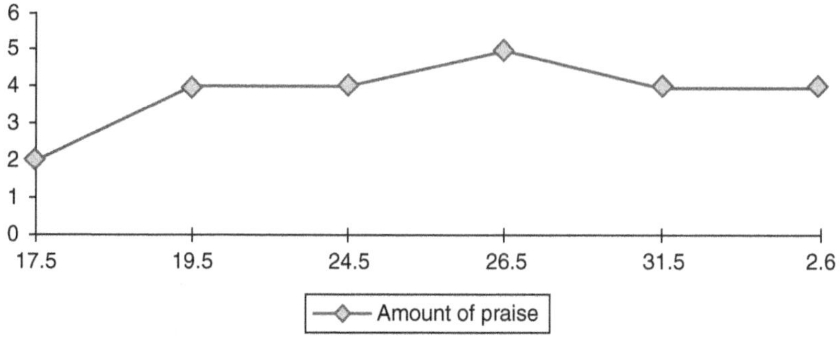

Figure 5.4 The teacher's perception of the amount of verbal praise used

recall after class. He gave a self-perception of the degree of change in the use of verbal praise in the observed class in a 'teaching journal' using a Likert scale (5–much more; 4–more; 3–no change; 2–less; 1–much less). Figure 5.4 shows that the teacher indicated a more positive opinion about the amount of verbal praise than there actually was. It is likely that his perception was affected by his growing awareness, through the project, of the value of praise.

5.7.2 The changes of students' participation

The tabulated data in Figure 5.5 show the changes in the students' perception of their participation over the six sessions. In the 'learning diary', every student was asked to give a self-perception of his/her participation, using a Likert scale.

The red line in Figure 5.5 shows a tendency of average rate of the total self-perception over the six sessions. As the graph shows, there is a surprisingly high level of participation, and it is relatively stable in the average rate perceived by the total students.

5.7.3 The correlation

Figure 5.6 depicts the correlation between the change in the focal teacher's use of praise (the lower line) and of the students' participation (the upper line). In the second week (24 May and 26 May) both curves drop down, first on 24 May, and then rise up to the peak on 26 May. A correlation coefficient (R) of 0.23 suggests statistically that the correlation between the two variables is indicative but not significant ($p = 0.07$). On this evidence we cannot definitely conclude that the students' participation changed alongside the change in the teacher's use of praise, but there is other evidence.

Dates		17 May	19 May	24 May	26 May	31 May	2 June
Points	Students'	3.71	4.07	3.98	4.07	4.07	4.02

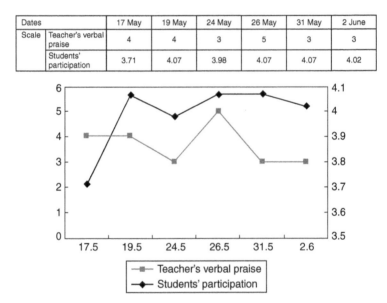

Figure 5.5 The change of the students' perception of their participation

Dates		17 May	19 May	24 May	26 May	31 May	2 June
Scale	Teacher's verbal praise	4	4	3	5	3	3
	Students' participation	3.71	4.07	3.98	4.07	4.07	4.02

Figure 5.6 Comparison between the teacher's changing praise and student participation

5.7.4 Ways of praise which affect learners' participation

As a supplement to observation, a questionnaire asked the 129 students from different classes to choose the most important ways of praise that would have a positive effect on their classroom participation. Students could choose several ways from an extensive list. From the results here, it

Rank	No. of mentions	Student preferred ways to receive praise for positive participation
1	104	Giving me eye contact and smiling when praising me
2	86	Providing praise first even when I accidentally give a wrong answer
=3	81	Attributing success to my ability
=3	81	Highlighting my progress
4	79	The praise should be specific, simply 'good' or 'well done' is not enough
5	77	Using English for simple praise and Chinese to extend the content of the praise
6	69	Saying my name when praising me
7	63	Using a variety of vocabulary for praising me
7	63	Implying that similar successes can be expected of me in the future
8	56	Attributing success to my internal interest, rather than to an external reason
8	56	Showing me spontaneity and other signs of credibility
9	48	Indicating that I have answered a very difficult question
10	41	Attributing success to my efforts
11	27	Using my past accomplishments as the context for describing my present accomplishments
12	23	Only using English to praise me
12	23	Making me as an example for other students
13	8	Only using Chinese to praise me

Figure 5.7 Rank order of students' preferred ways to receive praise

is clear that students think there *is* a causal relationship between teacher praise and student participation. In the resulting rank order of preferred ways (Figure 5.7), the highest ranked is to receive non-verbal signals from the teacher while praising, for example showing a smiling face and using eye contact. Other highly ranked ways show a preference for the teacher to attribute success to ability rather than to effort (perhaps effort is taken for granted), to highlight progress, to be specific, to use English if the praise is simple but Chinese if it is extended and to use students' names.

When the same students were asked how their English teacher could improve the use of praise, the highest ranked items were remarkably similar: the use of non-verbal signals, providing praise first, even when the student is wrong, attributing success to ability, being specific and highlighting progress. When the 50 focus class members were asked these questions, the highest ranked items were again similar, except that a higher proportion of students wanted a variety of vocabulary in praise and wanted praise in Chinese. Since many also wanted praise in English or in both languages, the language choice for praise remains unclear: English is preferred as the target language; receiving praise in Chinese has social-affective aspects.

5.8   Discussion and implications

The results of this study show that the use of Chinese teachers' praise presents a picture different to Western classrooms, as characterized in the literature. Three major themes derived from the findings will be discussed from a cultural perspective.

5.8.1   'Very good' is very good

The results here revealed that the teachers and most of the students recognized the positive functions of teacher's verbal praise. They wanted more praise. Importantly, they consider that praise promotes better teaching and learning, and that it is a factor in developing participation in interaction. Students showed clear preferences about particular ways that praise might be used to do this. Praise is valued, notwithstanding a traditional respect for the teacher as an authority figure: Most students here expressed a wish to receive teacher praise in the classroom as a way to *stand out*, to be *activated* and *encouraged*. This seems to support the 'face-gaining' phenomenon in which students desire to gain honour and prestige and need to manage their self-image in front of peers so that their peers respect them. This can be enacted publicly through the receipt of teacher praise as long as the praise is warranted. These findings imply that teachers in China should raise their awareness of providing verbal praise: If students do or say something that is very good, the teacher should find interesting ways to say so. Praise can build students' confidence, stimulate the classroom atmosphere, build closer teacher–student relationships, spark greater learning motivation and promote participation.

5.8.2   'A little' seems like 'a lot'

Based on our extensive previous experience of observing Chinese classrooms, we had expected relatively less praise from English teachers. Paradoxically, participants perceive there is quite a lot of praise – most teachers (N = 30), including the focal teacher, claimed that they often use verbal classroom praise, and most students agreed with this statement – whereas analysis of video and audio recordings reveals relatively little praise. There was a relatively small proportion of APs (actual praise) in the PPPs (praise-potential points) observed, and only moderate changes in the actual classes, yet the focal teacher continually indicated a much higher estimation of the number of APs he used (Figures 5.3 and 5.4). Moreover, the stable and high level of the average perception rate of students' participation (in their learning diaries) supports the teacher's estimation; most students demonstrated positive attitudes toward the teacher's use of praise in the questionnaire and finally showed they wanted even more praise.

Firstly, these results may reflect participants' subjectivity and a difficulty to judge their own language performance accurately: Standard sociolinguistic findings show skewed self-perceptions of participants' own speech behaviour (Labov, 1972; Trudgill, 1978; Romaine, 1982). Secondly, we may need to re-interpret the cultural norm of what is *a little* and *a lot*. Studies of Western classrooms state that praise occurs infrequently – *a little* (Luce & Hoge, 1978). However, this low norm may not be recognized by Chinese teachers and students; perhaps their concept of *a lot* of praise is *a little* in Western terms. Feedback in the large classes in China is not the same as that in Western classrooms (it is much *less*) due to the large class size and the underlying Chinese teaching values (Cortazzi & Jin, 1996b, 1999, 2001; Hu, 2002). However, whereas Western researchers in China generally have a comparative yardstick of broad international experience in classroom observation, Chinese students and most Chinese teachers without this breadth of experience inevitably make restricted and local comparisons. Third, there is the aspect of praise impact. Many Chinese language teachers have become more aware of the importance of verbal praise and wish to adopt more communicative oriented approaches since they seem to lead to improved performance in language skills (Cortazzi & Jin, 1996b; Jin & Cortazzi, 2006). Thus, there is a slight shift of actual teaching practice from *rather little praise* to *a little*, which may make a difference to students and may be perceived as *a lot* by teachers. For Chinese students, the praise from teachers is a relatively rare treasure: Chinese teachers use praise very sparingly, and only when something is exceptional (Cortazzi & Jin, 1998). On being praised, even if it is *a little*, the students feel a great honour, a sense of truly being recognized and standing out. Thus, even if the praise rate is not as frequent as western practitioners promote, the addressees will still feel enough impact to label it *a lot*, since through a little praise they can gain a lot of face. The salience and impact of praise (rare examples of praise are significant and memorable) may be more impressive to students than its frequency. The scale of praise in China may be short – from *none* to *rather little* to *a little bit more*; while in the West it may be extended – from *none* to *a little* to *a lot* to *a great deal*. This may help to explain the unexpected findings mentioned above, while the speculative question of salience remains to be researched.

This finding can encourage teachers in China to take steps to change their use of verbal praise with the confidence that students will welcome the change: a little more verbal praise would mean a lot to the students.

5.8.3 'Praise well'

Three most important contributing factors in relation to effective verbal praise given to Chinese university students emerged from the data analysis: The students' most favoured way of being praised is to receive non-verbal signals from the teacher while praising; their second preferred choice is that teachers give praise before correcting students; and, third, Chinese students like teachers to attribute the success to their ability (rather than to effort). The reasons for these preferences seem culturally embedded, which can have implications for the Chinese teachers as well as for foreign teachers in China.

5.8.4 'Non-verbal' sounds aloud

China is generally recognized as a typical high-context culture (Gao & Ting-Toomey, 1998), which means that 'most of the information is either in the physical context or initialized in the person, while very little is in the coded, explicit, transmitted part of the message' (Hall, 1976: p. 79). Accordingly, much information is unsaid, and interpretation depends on the relationship between the speakers, who are able to read between the lines. In China, most people believe that non-verbal behaviour represents more genuine characteristics, attitudes and feelings about people than does verbal behaviour, and that one can determine 'others' feelings' from their actions. When seeing a teacher smiling, nodding or just looking at them while being praised, Chinese students receive a sincerity signal and it adds credibility to the teacher's praise. We can note how sincerity and credibility are included in criteria of effective verbal praise (O'Leary & O'Leary, 1977).

5.8.5 Saying 'good' before saying 'no'

Given the value of *face* in Chinese culture, corrective feedback might be a possible face-threatening act, since it can include negative evaluation of a student's contribution to interaction. However, in a situation in which a negative evaluation is about to be given by a teacher, if the teacher gives praise by acknowledging the student's participation and contribution before pointing out the mistake, this is likely to be a good strategy to avoid violating the student's face. The finding here that most students wish to be praised before receiving corrective feedback echoes Dougherty and Wall's finding (1991) revealing that students in China show great sensitivity to feedback. Thus, teachers need a second thought before directly correcting Chinese students. Maintaining a student's face via teacher praise is not just an end in itself; it is a means through which teachers' recognition, support and encouragement can be provided to meet students' needs, and thus to promote positive learning outcomes.

5.8.6 'You're smart'

Chinese students are well-known internationally for their diligence, which is highly valued in Chinese culture. A poem by Han Yu (768–824) says 'diligence is the path to the book mountain, and pain is the boat for the knowledge ocean' (*shu shan you lu qin wei jing, xue hai wu ya ku zuo zhou*). Evidence shows hard-working diligence is the principal feature of a good learner in Chinese students' perceptions of 'good' students (Cortazzi & Jin, 1996b; Jin & Cortazzi, 2011). However, results here show that most university students prefer that the teacher attributes success to their ability rather than to their effort. This appears to echo attributve principles that ability and effort are compensatory causes of achievement among learners: The greater one's effort, the lower one's perceived ability, and vice versa (Weiner & Kukla, 1970). In this case, providing ability feedback to Chinese students can impact on the development of their self-concept (Craven et al., 1991), generate higher expectations for future performance, greater skill acquisition, a higher self-concept, enhanced satisfaction with their own performance and a further striving for achievement (Weiner, 1986). It is thus arguably more effective for teachers to tell students, 'you are smart', than to say, 'you are hard-working'. Possibly, being praised for ability seems more long-lasting: One can make greater or lesser efforts, so effort is changeable, but ability seems relatively constant; hence, perhaps praise for ability is more lasting in effect. Nevertheless, according to the attributional principle, teachers are advised to give more effort-attributed positive feedback to Chinese university students.

5.9   Conclusion

This study used distance action research to investigate the attitudes of participants in a Chinese university English class toward the value of verbal praise; it explored their perceptions of the amount and frequency of praise used, and the factors that might contribute to effective praise. Findings indicate that teachers and students are positive toward the amount of verbal praise used by most teachers in China; yet, there is a discrepancy on the amount of praise between what the focal teacher perceived he gave and what he actually did give; the focal class indicated a stable and high level of participation in their 'learning journal', no matter whether the focal teacher had changed his use of praise or whether he felt upset about the class's lack of participation. Several contributing factors associated with effective verbal praise were found which may help Chinese and foreign teachers in China to use verbal praise for students more effectively.

Two clear limitations of this study are that the focus is mainly on one teacher in one class (though this is commonplace in action research, and questionnaires with further participants extended the data), and the short time of three weeks for monitoring the enactment of praise and perceptions of change (this was a serious constraint, since such educational change in general may be expected to take months rather than weeks). Teachers will need time to establish a kind of stable pattern in the use of verbal praise to make consistent impact on learners.

The main implication for Chinese teachers of English is to consider using more praise, where warranted, to give students confidence and face, and to develop this with a focus on enhancing feedback in teacher development programmes. For those teaching Chinese students internationally, however, some caution may be needed if our speculations about differential cultural scales of praising prove valid; we have noticed how some Chinese learners in Western contexts feel that Western teachers over-praise students, which – they conclude – devalues praise so that it means little and just seems part of a routine formula. As we have mentioned, praise is needed but must be seen to be merited or it will be seen as unwarranted: To return to the analogy, no one wants to receive penicillin unnecessarily. Clearly, there is open space in these aspects for more intercultural research.

References

Anderson, F. E. (1993) 'The enigma of the college classroom: nails that don't stick up'. In P. Wadden (Ed.), *A handbook for teaching English at Japanese colleges and universities*. New York: Oxford University Press, pp. 101–10.

Biggs, J. B. (1996) 'Western misperceptions of the Confucian-heritage learning culture'. In D. A. Watkins and J. B. Biggs (Eds), *The Chinese learner: Cultural, psychological and contextual influences*. Hong Kong: CERC and ACER, pp. 45–67.

Black, P. & William, D. (1998) Assessment and classroom learning. *Assessment in Education*, 5 (1), 7–75.

Bond, M. H. & Lee, P. W. H. (1981) 'Face-saving in Chinese culture: A discussion and experimental study of Hong Kong students'. In A. Y. C. King and R. P. L. Lee (Eds), *Social life and development in Hong Kong*. Hong Kong: Chinese University Press, pp. 288–305.

Brophy, J. (1981a) 'Teacher praise: A functional analysis'. *Review of Educational Research*, 51, 5–32.

Brophy, J. (1981b.) 'On praising effectively'. *Elementary School Journal*, 81, 269–27.

Cameron, J. & W. D. Pierce (1994) Reinforcement, reward, and intrinsic motivation: A meta-analysis. *Review of Educational Research*, 64, 363–423.

Catano, V. M. (1975) 'Relation of improved performance through verbal praise to source of praise'. *Perceptual and Motor Skills*, 41, 71–74.

Catano, V. M. (1976) 'Effectiveness of verbal praise as a function of expertise of source'. *Perceptual and Motor Skills*, 42, 1283–86.

Chang, H. & R. Holt (1994) A Chinese perspective on face as inter-relational concern. In Ting-Toomey, S. (Ed.), *The challenge of facework*. Albany: State University, pp. 95–132.

Chaudron, C. (1988) *Second language classrooms: research on teaching and learning*. Cambridge: Cambridge University Press.

Chu, G. (1985) 'The changing concept of self in contemporary China'. In A. Marsell, G. De Vos and F. Hsu (Eds), *'Culture and self': Asian and western perspectives*. London: Tavistock Publications. University of New York Press, pp. 252–77.

Cortazzi, M. and Jin, L. (1996a) English teaching and learning in China. *Language Teaching*, 29, 61–80.

Cortazzi, M. and Jin, L. (1996b) 'Cultures of learning: Language classrooms in China'. In H. Coleman (Ed.), *Society and the language classroom*. Cambridge: Cambridge University Press, pp. 169–206.

Cortazzi, M. and Jin, L. (1998) Dimensions of dialogue: large classes in China. *International Journal of Educational Research*, 29, 739–61.

Cortazzi, M. and Jin, L. (2001) 'Large classes in China: "good" teachers and interaction'. In D. Watkins and J. Biggs (Eds), *Teaching the Chinese learner: Psychological and pedagogical perspectives*. Hong Kong: CERC and ACER, University of Hong Kong.

Cortazzi, M., Jin, L. & Wang, Z. (2009) Cultivators, cows and computers: Chinese learners' metaphors of teachers. In T. Coverdale-Jones and P. Rastall (Eds), *Internationalizing the University: The Chinese context*. London: Palgrave Macmillan, pp. 107–29.

Craven, R. G., Marsh, H. W. & Debus, R. L. (1991) Effects of internally focussed feedback and attributional feedback on enhancement of academic self-concept. *Journal of Educational Psychology*, 83, 17–27.

Cullen, R. (2002) Supportive teacher talk: the importance of the F-move. *English Language Teaching Journal*, 56 (2), 117–27.

Deci, E. L. (1975) *Intrinsic motivation*. New York: Plenum.

Dougherty, T. W. & Wall, J. A. (1991) Teaching in China during the age of reform. *Journal of Management Education*, 15 (2), 232–43.

Dunkin, M. & Biddle, B. (1974) *The study of teaching*. New York: Holt, Rinehart & Winston.

Edwards, A. & Westgate, D. (1994) *Investigating classroom talk*. London: Falmer.

Gao, G. & Ting-Toomey, S. (1998) *Communicating effectively with the Chinese*. Thousand Oaks: Sage Publications.

Ginott, H. G. (1965) *Between parent and child*. New York: Macmillan.

Gordon, T. (1989) *Teaching children self-discipline*. New York: Times Books.

Griffin, P. & Mehan, H. (1981) Sense and ritual in classroom discourse. In F. Coulmas (Ed.), *Conversational routine*. The Hague: Mouton, pp. 189–213.

Hall, E. T. (1976) *Beyond culture*. New York: Doubleday.

Harrington, C. L. (1992) Talk of embarrassment, exploring the taboo – repression – denial hypothesis. *Symbolic Interaction*, 15 (2), 203–25.

Hattie, J. & Timperley, H. (2007) The power of feedback. *Review of Educational Research*, 77 (1), 81–112.

Hayhoe, R. (2006) *Portraits of influential Chinese educators*. Hong Kong: CERC/The University of Hong Kong.

Hellermann, J. (2003) The interactive work of prosody in the IRF exchange: Teacher repetition in feedback moves. *Language in Society*, 32, 79–104.

Henderlong, J. & Lepper, M. R. (2002) The effects of praise on children's intrinsic motivation: A review and synthesis. *Psychological Bulletin*, 128, 774–95.

Ho, D. (1976) On the concept of face. *American Journal of Sociology*, 81, 867–84.

Holly, P. (1991) Action research: The missing link in the creation of schools as centers of inquiry. In A. Lieberman and L. Miller (Eds), *Staff development for education in the '90s; new demands, new realities, new perspectives*. New York: Teachers College Press, pp. 133–57.

Hsu, F. (1985) The self in cross-cultural perspectives. In A. Marsella, G. De Vos and F. Hsu (Eds), *'Culture and self': Asian and western perspectives*. London: Tavistock Publications, pp. 24–55.

Hu, G. (2002) Potential cultural resistance to pedagogical imports: The case of communicative language teaching in China. *Language, Culture and Curriculum*, 15 (2), 93–105.

Hu, G. W. (2001) *English language teaching in the people's Republic of China*. Country report for the Six-Nation Education Research Project on Pedagogical Practices in English Language Education. National Institute of Education, Nanyang Technological University.

Huang, C. (1997) *The analects of confucius*. Oxford: Oxford University Press.

Hwang, A., Ang, S. & Francesco, A. M. (2002) 'The silent Chinese: The influence of face and kiasuism on student feedback-seeking behaviors'. *Journal of Management Education*, 26 (1), 70–98.

Hwang, K. (1987) 'Face and favour: The Chinese power game'. *American Journal of Sociology,* 92 (4), 944–74.

Ivanhoe, P. J. (2002) *Confucian moral self cultivation.* Indianapolis: Hackett Publishing Company.

Jin, L., & Cortazzi, M. (2006) 'Changing practices in Chinese cultures of learning'. *Language, Culture and Curriculum,* 19(1), 5–20.

Jin, L. & Cortazzi, M. (2011) More than a journey: 'learning' in the metaphors of Chinese students and teachers. In L. Jin and M. Cortazzi (Eds), *Researching Chinese learners: Skills, perceptions and intercultural adaptations.* Houndmills: Palgrave Macmillan, pp. 67–92.

Kohn, A. (1993) *Punished by rewards: The trouble with gold stars, incentive plans, A's, praise, and other bribes.* New York: Houghton Mifflin.

Koshy, V. (2010) *Action research for improving educational practice.* London: Sage Publications.

Kun, A. & Weiner, B. (1973) Necessary versus sufficient causal schemata for success and failure. *Journal of Research in Personality,* 7, 197–207.

Labov, W. (1972) *Sociolinguistic patterns.* Oxford: Blackwell.

Lee, W. O. (1996) The cultural context for Chinese learners: Conceptions of learning in the Confucian tradition. In D. A. Watkins and J. B. Biggs (Eds), *The Chinese Learner: Cultural, psychological and contextual influences.* Hong Kong: CERC and ACER, pp. 25–41.

Li, J. (2003) 'The core of Confucian learning'. *American Psychologist,* 58, 146–47.

Lipe, D. & Jung, S. (1971) Manipulating incentives to enhance school learning. *Review of Educational Research,* 41, 249–80.

Luce, S. & Hoge, R. (1978) Relations among teacher rankings, pupil-teacher interactions, and academic achievement: A test of the teacher expectancy hypothesis. *American Educational Research Journal,* 15, 489–500.

Mayher, J. (1990) *Uncommon sense.* Portsmouth: Boynton Cook.

McNiff, J. (1995) *Action research: Principles and practice.* London: Routledge.

Mercer, N. (1995) *The guided construction of knowledge: Talk among teachers and learners.* Clevedon: Multilingual Matters.

Nassaji, H. & Wells, G. (2000) What's the use of 'triadic dialogue'?: An investigation of teacher–student interaction. *Applied Linguistics,* 21 (3), 376–406.

Nicholls, J. (1978) The development of the concepts of effort and ability, perception of own attainment, and the understanding that difficult tasks demand more ability. *Child Development,* 49, 800–14.

Nunan, D. (1990) Action research in the language classroom. In J. C. Richards and D. Nunan (Eds), *Second language teacher education.* New York: Cambridge University Press, pp. 62–81.

O'Leary, K. D. & O'Leary, S. G. (1977) *Classroom management: The successful use of behavior modification* (2nd edn). New York: Pergamon Press.

Paine, L. W. (1990) The teacher as virtuoso: A Chinese model for teaching. *Teachers College Record,* 92 (1), 49–81.

Redding, S. G. & Ng, M. (1982) The role of face in the organizational perceptions of Chinese managers. *Organization Studies,* 3 (3), 210–19.

Romaine, S. (Ed.) (1982) *Sociolinguistic variation in speech communities.* London: Edward Arnold.

Ryan, J. (2010) Chinese Learners: misconceptions and realities. In J. Ryan and G. Slethaug (Eds), *International education and the Chinese learner.* Hong Kong: Hong Kong University Press, pp. 37–56.

Scollon, R. & Scollon, S. (1994) *The post confucian confusion*. Research Report No. 37. Department of English, City Polytechnic of Hong Kong.

Scollon, S. (1999) Not to waste words or students: Confucian and Socratic discourse in the tertiary classroom. In E. Hinkel (Ed.), *Culture in second language teaching and learning*. Cambridge: Cambridge University Press, pp. 13–27.

Seedhouse, P. (1994) *The interactional architecture of the language classroom: A conversation analysis perspective*. Oxford: Blackwell Publishing.

Shepell, W. (2000) Health Quest: A quarterly newsletter focusing on mental health issues and concerns. Http://www.warrenshepell.com/articles/praise.html [retrieved on 20/07/10].

Spratt, M. (1994) *English for the Teacher: A language development course*. Cambridge: Cambridge University Press.

Stevenson, H. W. & Stigler, J. (1992) *The Learning Gap: Why our schools are failing and what we can learn from Japanese and Chinese education*. New York: Summit Books.

Thomas, J. (1991) You're the greatest! A few well-chosen words can work wonders in positive behavior reinforcement. *Principal*, 71, 32–33.

Thomas, J., Presland, I., Grant, M. & Glynn, T. (1978) Natural rates of teacher approval and disapproval in grade-7 classrooms. *Journal of Applied Behavior Analysis*, 11, 91–94.

Thorne, C. & Wang, Q. (1996) Action research in language teacher education. *ELT Journal*, 50 (3), 254–62.

Thompson, T. (1997) Do we need to train teachers how to administer praise? Self-worth theory says we do. *Learning and Instruction*, 7 (1), 49–63.

Trudgill, P. (Ed.) (1978) *Sociolinguistic patterns in British English*. London: Edward Arnold.

Weiner, B. & Kukla, A. (1970) An attributional analysis of achievement motivation. *Journal of Personality and Social Psychology*, 15, 1–20.

Weiner, B. (1986) *An attributional theory of motivation and emotion*. New York: Springer-Verlag.

Yao, X. (2000) *An introduction to confucianism*. Cambridge: Cambridge University Press.

Zahorik, J. A. (1970) Pupils' perceptions of teachers' verbal feedback. *Elementary School Journal*, 71, 105–114.

6

Cultures of Learning in Academia: A Lebanese Case Study

Nahla N. Bacha and Rima Bahous

6.1 Introduction

Lebanon is a mosaic of cultures and thus a mosaic of different ways of living intertwined with political, ethnic, religious diversity and social subcultures which affect the learning and teaching situation. Most Lebanese students are first language (L1) speakers of Arabic, but a large proportion have been educated in the country's French-medium or English-medium secondary schools and thus have considerable bilingual or multilingual experience. Additionally, many students are from Lebanese families which have lived abroad for extended periods, giving them wider knowledge of other languages and cultures. Arguably, Lebanon is thus distinctive in the region for its multicultural, or internationalized, population. An additional subculture of vital importance, recently studied in many parts of the world, is the academic culture of learning in higher education, which has been found to influence students' learning and subsequent achievement levels. As English increasingly becomes the language of choice for students as a medium in which to pursue higher education, many learners from different cultures of learning find it difficult to adapt to institutions that follow the North American model. This study concerns students in an American university in Lebanon. It analyses data from over 150 university students plus comments given by 20 students in focus groups. The research surveys L1 Arabic university students' cultures of learning, specifically regarding their learning of writing conventions for academic purposes, of test-taking behaviour, and interpersonal relationships. It investigates to what extent the students are adapting to the 'new' culture of learning in this private English-medium university in Lebanon, which is based on the American model and yet sees itself as having an increasing international role in the region. The chapter further discusses the extent to which learners who come from different and diverse cultural educational backgrounds adapt to the academic-learning culture of the North American model, and it draws implications for the teaching/learning situation in light of this multifaceted language and cultural milieu.

6.2   Classroom culture

In our globalized world, it is not surprising to find a multilingual/multicultural group of students in one classroom. Such is the case in many higher education institutions in Lebanon. Badgera and MacDonald (2007) mention that many writers have claimed that nations are not the only entities that relate to cultures and these writers report that academic classrooms are also linked to cultures in their different approaches and methods. Given this, it is not surprising to find some teaching methodologies are not compatible with some educational cultures (Jin & Cortazzi, 1998). In Lebanon, the culture of learning which dominates in the high schools contrasts with that of 'Western' educational cultures which – not surprisingly – dominate the American universities in Lebanon and stress critical thinking, classroom interaction, and student centeredness. The Lebanese educational culture in schools, on the other hand, tends to emphasize memorization, teacher centeredness, and lecture methods. Thus, it is to be expected that students entering a Western type of higher education institution would find difficulties and challenges even within the same country. A further factor which might hinder many of these students in adapting to the educational culture in which they find themselves could be the social identity associated with their first language (L1), Arabic, which is different from the academic identity the students are expected to adopt when they learn through the medium of another language (L2), which in the American universities is English (Chami-Sather & Kretschmer, 2005). There have been many studies that investigate L1–L2 differences and how students can best adapt linguistically (e.g., Odlin, 1989; Connor, 1996), but so far, none have to the authors' knowledge been conducted in the L1 Arabic context with a focus on cultures of learning. This chapter explores this area in order to better understand the problems of students in higher education who are expected to become acculturated into an institution with a culture of learning different to the one they have been socialized into in their L1 and which defines much of their L1 identity.

6.3   Cultures of learning

Thus, for these students another type of culture they encounter in higher education is that of learning. Cortazzi and Jin (1996) have defined *culture of learning* as what teachers and students expect to happen in classrooms and how participants interpret the format of classroom instruction, the language of teaching and learning, and how interaction should be accomplished as part of the social construction of an educational discourse system.

Hofstede (2001) presents evidence of studies that have investigated what is involved in adapting to a different culture of learning, and argues that cultures can be distinguished along five dimensions: power distance, uncertainty avoidance, masculinity versus femininity, long term versus short term, and individualistic versus collectivist. In these terms, Lebanon is considered a collectivist society (see Ayyash-Abdo, 2001) and, thus, students from Lebanese schools entering an American university in Lebanon must face the challenge of entering a university, which is mainly oriented to a more individualistic culture of learning.

6.4   Languages and education in Lebanon

The formal school system in Lebanon is from kindergarten (K) to Grade 12 (G12). The Lebanese education system (since 1994) is divided into five different cycles. Each cycle encompasses three levels: the preschool (nursery, K1–K2); Cycle 1, lower elementary (grades 1–3); Cycle 2, upper elementary (G4–6); Cycle 3, Intermediate/ Middle (G7–9); Cycle 4, secondary (G10–12). All students have to sit for the official 'brevet' exam in grade 9 and the Lebanese Baccalaureate in grade 12. Students, however, may choose different strands: humanities and philosophy; sociology and economics; general sciences or life sciences. The baccalaureate class is considered equivalent to the freshman year of college. Thus, students entering universities start as sophomores (second year) if they have the Lebanese Baccalaureate, the French Baccalaureate, or an equivalent to the International Baccalaureate. At the tertiary level, most universities in Lebanon use English or French as a medium of instruction. However, some universities, such as Beirut Arab University, use Arabic. Most Lebanese students are first-language speakers (L1) of Arabic but a large proportion have been educated in French-medium or English-medium secondary schools and thus have considerable bilingual or multilingual experience. Others are from Lebanese families who have lived abroad for extended periods and these students have learned other languages. In secondary schools, a third language (L3) is taught: In English-medium schools this is French and in French-medium schools this is English. If the second language is used as a medium of instruction, then it is used for all subjects during the school year except in Arabic courses. The third language is taught between three to five hours per week over the course of the year.

Education in Lebanon is perceived regionally as being very high quality, especially because so many students speak three languages, which is a mandate from the Ministry of Education. Many students continue their studies in Europe, Canada or the United States. In many French-medium schools, students study two programs (Lebanese and French), and they sit for two official exams, the Lebanese and the French baccalaureates. Schools in general put more emphasis on the second language and less on the first. Teacher-training programs help to ensure that high levels of second-language proficiency are maintained in schools by employing native speakers of French and English and having most activities in the second languages.

Bacha's (1997, 2000) composition studies of L1 Arabic students studying in either the medium of French or English indicated that the French-educated students at the high proficiency level do as well as the English-educated students, and that the French-educated students have a wider lexical repertoire than the English-educated at the lower proficiency levels. This could be attributed to positive transfer of lexical items from French to the learning of English (see Odlin, 1989). All Lebanese schools (public and private) are implementing content-based cooperative learning in language study and learner-centred communicative approaches in subject study. However, it is often difficult for some teachers to change from their 'traditional' ways, which emphasize lecturing and rote memorization of material. Thus, while English proficiency levels can be expected to be high in Lebanese universities, it is nearly always an L2 or L3 for students; however, study in an American university, even for those from English-medium schools, means encountering a different culture of learning, since the disciplines are taught according to American requirements and pedagogic approaches. However, this situation is still more complex, due to other variables which are introduced below.

6.5   Culture shock and learning in a different educational culture

International students in American universities, because of their limited English language proficiency, struggle academically in essay tests and in taking notes (Deressa & Beavers, 1988; Parr et al., 1992). They may experience a social struggle involving social isolation, loneliness, homesickness, irritability and fatigue (Das et al., 1986; Wehrly, 1986) and possibly psychological stress, including sense of loss, inferiority, uncertainty, communication problems and culture shock (Bennet 1993; Sandhu, 1995). These counselling studies recommend that students should engage in informal and formal English whenever possible (language shock is similar to culture shock), form international groups and seek comfort from culture and society.

6.5.1   Teachers' influence on students' learning styles

Teachers may exert a positive influence under such circumstances. EFL (English as a Foreign Language) teacher characteristics are predictors of students' academic achievement, and their teaching styles, say in Iranian junior and senior schools, can help the learners (Akbari & Allvar, 2010). Findings from a few studies (Pennington, 1995; Miglietti & Strange, 1998; Good & Brophy, 2003) show a high correlation between teacher reflectivity and student outcomes as well as a positive relationship between the teachers' sense of efficacy and student achievement. Furthermore, Hofstede (1986, 2001) points out that a high-power distant society expresses certain social hierarchies acceptable to the society; thus, a teacher would be ranked higher than students in terms of knowledge and authority, and teachers' wisdom and teaching are not questioned; they are taken as highly authentic. This is the case in Lebanon, where the teacher is widely considered the sole authority.

6.5.2   Differences in speaking behaviour

Different cultural groups have different expectations concerning verbal interaction. Chami-Sather and Kretschmer (2005) explored the discourse moves made by young children from Lebanese and American cultural backgrounds: The Lebanese repeated the same word; the Americans created an adjacent utterance. Children seemed to help each other to find solutions. Lebanese verbal communications reflected strong counter evidence of possible alternatives and confirmation of their responses.

6.5.3   Gender differences in adapting to a culture of learning

Not surprisingly, students benefit socially and academically if supported by a caring classroom and school environment; however, in a new culture of learning there may be gender differences in the intercultural awareness between girls and boys. In one study, girls reported higher intercultural sensitivity than boys, and students who were academically above average estimated their own intercultural sensitivity to be higher than did students of average ability (Tirri & Husu, 2006).

6.5.4   Language use and language attitudes among learners

Many researchers focus on approaches to learning in order to explore the relationship between dominant approaches to learning in different cultures and the generic attributes of the cultures. Approaches to learning depend on the learning context, incentives to learn and experimentation, such as the consequences of failing (see Entwistle, 1992). Many students pursue university studies in countries different from their own (Manikutty et al., 2007), and teachers may use this context to gain a better understanding of the complexity of differences in learning behaviour that they experienced in their classrooms even within one country (Hofstede, 2001; Coffield et al., 2004). This is similar to the case in Lebanon, where students are coming from a culture of learning in the high schools different to the university, which is based on a Western type education and is considered different to the culture of learning to which they have been exposed.

Thonhauser (2000) shows the complexity of the multilingual context in Lebanon and notes that the situation of *diglossia* adds to it. He reports that many students prefer to follow a career in English-medium universities, as it gives them more career opportunities; they prefer to write in English and/or French rather than in Arabic, as the latter usually requires the literary form which they do not like. He quotes Ghaith and Shaaban (1996), who point out that according to a Lebanese government decree of 1994, schools may choose to use any foreign language as the language of instruction.

The Lebanese have a bilingual, trilingual and multilingual profile, and code-switching is highly predominant in both private and public sectors – a natural characteristic of Lebanese daily social interaction (Shaaban & Ghaith, 1999; Jebejian, 2003). However, this multilingual situation may be negative if it leads to a circumstance in which some students may not have real proficiency in any of the languages. An added concern is the possibility that Arabic (L1 for most) might lose popularity compared to the foreign languages; the use of foreign languages is said to be limited to educational contexts and is not widely used in societal and daily communicative functions (Ghaith & Shaaban, 1996). This, however, is debatable. Exploration attitudes of university students in Lebanon towards the multilingualism in Arabic, French and English showed that students perceived the two main foreign languages, English and French, as more useful than Arabic, especially in the fields of business, science and technology (Shaaban & Ghaith, 2003). Further, students' linguistic attitudes were influenced by their religion and by the first foreign language they studied at school. Lebanese learners are very much part of a multilingual milieu which greatly impacts their lives.

6.5.5 Methods for teaching languages in Lebanon

It is common knowledge in Lebanon that government and private schools have diverse policies concerning language teaching methods. Some stipulate the sole use of the foreign language (L2) in class and activities; others introduce Arabic and the L2 concurrently, while still others reinforce Arabic during early years and introduce the L2 gradually, allowing teachers to communicate with students in both. Cummins (2008: p. 65), in an overview of language teaching methods, argues for using bilingual instruction and encourages 'cross-language transfer' in teaching bilingual learners, rather than the exclusive use of the target language and discarding the native language. For example, translation and bilingual and monolingual dictionaries could be used for 'two way transfer across languages' within the framework of a communicative approach whereby students use multimedia texts in authentic ways in both L1 and L2. He cites the 'two solitudes assumption', which was popular a century ago and rooted in the 'direct method' of teaching languages. This copies the 'way children learn their first language, emphasizing the avoidance of translation and the direct use of the foreign language as the medium of instruction in all situations' (Yu, 2000: p. 176) and focuses on understanding and speaking the target language with correct pronunciation and grammar and with less attention to reading and writing skills. This method was reflected in the communicative approach and task-based methods in language teaching with minimal use of L1 in teaching the L2. This decreases teachers' use of L1 in the L2 class; however, L1 use may be positive when teachers are not fluent enough in the

L2. Cummins (2008) notes that neither the direct method nor the translation method is supported by a language teaching research base. In practice, using students' L1 background knowledge can be a powerful tool in addition to using bilingual instructional strategies which complement monolingual strategies: it can engage learners in L2 learning.

6.6　Societal factors, identity and language

The various religious and political groups in Lebanon have frequently disagreed on which language to use in education because choices of Arabic, French or English are seen to be associated with particular ideologies and religious communities. Thus with the post-war education reforms of the 1990s, the Lebanese government exerted a conscious effort to create new policies in language education to which all parties agree, such as teaching the language that best suits Lebanese 'students in their learning contexts' (Shaaban & Ghaith, 1999: p. 1).

The three major languages in Lebanon have seen fluctuations in their use, depending on changing political, social, and economic situations (Shaaban & Ghaith, 2002). Before the arrival of the Christian missionaries in the second half of the nineteenth century, Arabic was used for social and education purposes; however, under the French mandate (1925–43), French replaced Arabic in government and education spheres, but after independence in 1943 and with recent globalization, English became more popular in social, economic and education fields. Many Lebanese groups currently debate the impact on local cultures of the widespread use of foreign languages, the status of national and international languages, and national identity. Thus, in results from a questionnaire survey of students, Arabic is viewed as main language for daily communication, French is associated with Christians and English with Moslems, but English has become more widespread in Christian communities than French in Moslem communities (Shaaban & Ghaith, 2002). This is attributed to the impact of Catholic missionaries on Lebanese Catholic and Maronite communities, followed by Protestant missionaries who introduced education in English at school and university levels. An educated Christian elite was created that dominated political and economic domains and supported the authority of the French in Lebanon. Arabic is perceived as a symbol of identity and a tool in religious activity. French predominates in cultural activities and self-expression. Due to its status as a global language, English was viewed as the most vital in education, especially at university level, in business, science and technology, and in mass communication. Students also believed that proficiency in English makes them marketable in the job markets of Lebanon and the Arabian Gulf. However, French was seen as more vital than Arabic as a language medium at the elementary level, which was attributed to the involvement of French educators in developing the new Lebanese curriculum and training teachers, and to the recognition of Lebanon as a Francophone country. English and French are considered more vital than Arabic as symbols of status abroad, but English remains as an international language; higher socioeconomic groups perceived French and English as more vital than Arabic, compared to perceptions of lower socioeconomic groups.

An important issue often discussed by researchers is how the language and the culture of a people are inextricable and how this might affect the teaching situation (see Diab, 2000, 2009a, 2009b). As shown above, cultural, religious and political factors have combined variously to influence the educational system in Lebanon, and this has made educational research a complex task, with overlays of the difficulties, disruptions and dislocations, which were experienced during the period of the Lebanese civil war (1975–91) and its aftermath (Serriyeh, 1989; Yazigi, 1994). Notably, young people in Lebanon have a lot to tell from their perspectives and experiences after the war, stories which have been collected in narratives of their culture and education (Saad Khalaf, 2009).

6.6.1 The school's role in maintaining the culture of learning

A study undertaken by Holm et al. (2009) on gender, academic achievement and Finnish high school students' intercultural sensitivity showed how schools are responsible for establishing and maintaining school cultures; this empowers both teachers and students to negotiate the diverse values and social norms of the communities.

Aware of the foregoing research and of the difficulties students face in adapting to the university culture of learning, this chapter's authors carried out the present study to elicit students' views on aspects of the culture of learning in two levels of education: high school and university; the transition from one to the other is often talked about as challenging by the students themselves, their parents and teachers.

6.7   Aim and research question

The purpose of the present study is to find out how students view their learning in the context of high school and university in order to see whether the likely differences between the cultures of learning at these two educational levels might pose an issue for students in adapting to higher education. Specifically, we want to find out the students' viewpoints about differences in pedagogies regarding:

- Language conventions (writing, reading, speaking)
- Testing conventions
- Conventions of teacher–student interaction in classrooms
- Adaptation strategies

6.8   Method

6.8.1   Context and participants

The study was carried out in one English-medium university situated in Lebanon in which courses are organized and taught according to the American model. The participants were 188 students, ages 17–22, following various disciplines in the university and in different years: the first, freshman (N = 59); second, sophomore (N = 50); third, junior (N = 40) and fourth, senior (N = 39). Arabic is their first language, English their second, and French their third. Males made up N = 104 (55.3 per cent) of the sample and females N = 84 (4.7 per cent).

6.8.2   Instruments and data analysis

In order to obtain students' views on learning behaviour in the classroom, a questionnaire was designed with 20 questions (see Appendix A) adapted from relevant literature and the cultural issues that we see in classrooms. Each question was answered on a Likert scale from 1 to 4 (from none to a lot) for parallel items focusing on the students' viewpoint about frequency of behaviour in high school (retrospectively recalled) and, currently, in university. Questions 1–3 focused on language conventions, 4–6 on testing, 7–15 on classroom relationships, and 16–20 on adaptation. Two hundred and fifty questionnaires were distributed in class through teachers across disciplines; this yielded 188 completed questionnaires (a response rate of 75.2 per cent). Ethical considerations of anonymity, confidentiality and informed consent were accounted for.

The data were analysed using the Statistical Package for Social Sciences 6 (SPSS v.19). Descriptive information, including means and standard deviation, was obtained. A parametric paired sample T test was applied to ascertain significant differences between the students' views of high school and university behaviour (at a two-tailed level of p = less than 0.05).

Focus group interviews were carried out with 20 randomly selected students from the sample. They were asked to respond freely to three questions on their views about similarities, differences and difficulties in learning between high school and university (see appendix B). Discourse analysis was done on the comments by categorizing them by theme.

6.9   Results and discussion

The results are given and discussed according to the four themes of the research questions by considering paired numbered questions (P) about learning methods in high school (H) and those in university (U) from the learners' perspectives regarding:

- Language conventions (writing, reading, speaking) (P1–3)
- Testing conventions (P4–6)

- Classroom teacher/student interaction conventions (P7–15)
- Adaptation strategies (P16–20)

6.9.1   Student questionnaire

6.9.1.1   *Language conventions*

The results in Table 6.1 indicate students' perceptions that they write research papers (P1), without plagiarizing, significantly more often at university than they did in high school (p = 0.010). Students' mean scores indicated significantly more plagiarism in high school. The reason for students admitting to more plagiarism in high school could be that at university they are taught the conventions of writing a research paper. With this raised awareness, the university students realize that just mentioning references at the end of a paper, but copying pasted chunks of material from references without documentation, is not appropriate scholarship. The latter practice by high school students has been mentioned by many a university student when challenged with plagiarism: They do not find it wrong to cut and paste without acknowledging sources, which is part of the learning culture in pre-university institutions (personal communication with many teachers). Evidently, conventions of citing sources should be taught in schools in Lebanon.

Students perceive that they engaged in written projects in groups (P2) more often at high school than at university, but the difference was not significant. Only the freshman students significantly indicated (p = 0.01) more of such projects done in high school (M = 2.82) than at university (M = 2.06). This result is not surprising as in high schools it is part of the culture to work together and help friends. Given this result, it is expected that the freshman students would have a similar view. However, in general, high schools emphasize traditional lecture methods, and students have little or no space for working in teams although they like to do so. Some private schools (American and British), however, are implementing communicative approaches, and teamwork is becoming more popular.

Students perceive that they give more oral presentations (P3) in high schools than in university, but statistically this is not significant. Oral reports are not an integral part of the high school curriculum and, in university (perhaps surprisingly), they are not stressed as much as one might expect. Lecture methods are still predominant as part of the culture of learning; the teacher still remains a centre of authority and instruction, and students are not really given much time to speak. Language conventions in research are not emphasized sufficiently in schools and still need to be focused on in university as there were not high incidences of research papers without plagiarism mentioned at both educational levels. Writing in groups and giving oral reports, an integral part of the New National Curriculum in Lebanon and effective according to recent recognized pedagogy, are not done a lot it seems.

Table 6.1 Mean student views on language conventions in High School and University

Pairs of questions and topics	H/U	Mean	Standard Deviation	Two tailed sig.
Pair 1	H1	2.5988	1.00676	0.010*
Plagiarism	U1	3.2326	3.30045	
Pair 2	H2	3.0380	2.38934	0.132
Group writing projects	U2	2.7174	1.70711	
Pair 3	H3	2.9297	3.57230	0.191
Giving oral presentations	U3	2.5730	0.97597	

* denotes level of significance $p < 0.05$.

6.9.1.2   Testing conventions

Table 6.2 indicates that students viewed memorizing for tests (P4) at a higher frequency in high school than that in university, but not significantly. There were similar results by year, except in the senior year, where memorizing for tests in high school was viewed as a lot (M = 3.6) in comparison with university, but not significantly. Males indicated significantly higher test memorization in high school than in university. However, females indicated doing more memorization than males in both high school and university. Memorizing material for tests is a traditional way of preparing for tests in the high schools. Although an emphasis on critical thinking skills began in the schools along with the new National Language Curriculum, teachers find it difficult to change, and most students still resort to old habits; the results here confirm these observations of this cultural learning practice. Students who enter university might find it difficult to adapt to the different style of learning for tests based on application and critical thinking. In fact, our experience suggests that many students in university try to memorize the material and regurgitate it in exams without critically answering the questions. It is also common knowledge that females are higher achievers in high school than males, and females resort to memorization more in an effort to remain high achievers (according to personal communications from teachers). Teaching critical thinking to help students adapt to the university learning culture is thus a challenge for teachers in both contexts.

Students confirm that there is no or very little punishment (P5) in both high school and university if they do not well on tests, although they indicated more punishment in high school, if any. Punishing students is not part of the culture in Lebanon. This is consistent with our observation that young people seem pampered by their parents, who exert pressure on the schools to look after their children and help them as much as possible. It seems the culture of 'pay for the degree' and 'it is important who you know' affects the way students are treated.

Table 6.2 Mean student views on testing practices in High School and University

Pairs of questions and topics	H/U	Mean	Standard Deviation	Two tailed sig.
Pair 4	H4	2.9071	3.20321	0.168
Memorizing for tests	U4	2.5792	0.96249	
Pair 5	H5	1.5989	1.10178	0.465
Punished for poor test results	U5	1.5385	0.90190	
Pair 6	H6	2.1676	1.78125	0.072
Helping friends with tests	U6	1.9189	1.02624	

Also regarding tests, some students perceived that they were 'allowed to help their friends on tests' (P6) more in high school than in university (although the frequency of both is low) with no significant differences. Although the culture of solidarity supports friends helping friends, the learning culture in university (and school) does not condone this for tests, where students must of course work individually. This makes it hard for students to separate friendship and formal educational assessment, where sometimes a student who does not help his friend on an exam would be thought of by his friends as a 'traitor' and become an outcast from the group. At both school and university, students need to become aware of the academic culture, in which social friendship does not overlap with academic fairness and individual assessment in tests.

6.9.1.3 Classroom teacher/student interaction conventions

Table 6.3 shows that students were punished (P7) significantly more often in high school than in university; males and sophomore students also significantly indicated this. It is not surprising that students, especially the males, would indicate such views. Some high school students, notably males, have been known not to do their homework (according to personal communications with teachers). At the university in this study, teachers warn students that homework assignments are important for success, but university students are left to develop their own study habits and practices, supposedly being mature. This freedom at university is a challenge for many students who find themselves with a lot of time and independence; often they do not know how to manage things. Awareness of study skills and time management are important in the transition from high school to university.

There is a high frequency, in both high school and university, of being able to ask questions in class (P8), with seniors showing the highest mean frequency (3.8). Males, though, showed higher mean frequencies in high school than did the females, though not significantly. This result is not similar to some contexts like China where students often feel their questions are not encouraged (Cortazzi & Jin, 1996). In Lebanon, the fact that males are favoured over females in society, in many areas of daily life, spills over to the schools where boys are encouraged to speak as a sign of 'manhood'. Girls are usually encouraged to be passive listeners, which may be a challenge to overcome once they begin university life where interaction and speaking is part of the culture of learning.

Although there are very high frequencies, students viewed being allowed to give their opinions in class (P9) significantly more often in high school than in university. There were similar differences by gender and year, but with no significant differences. Surprisingly, the females, however, showed the highest mean frequency (3.9) on their views between high school and university compared with males: Giving opinions in high school has not been the traditional practice but in the past 10 years schools have been subject to the new National Curriculum which encourages class discussion. The highest frequency for females could be due to their wanting to prove to teachers that are just as good as males and should be equally accepted.

Regarding teachers who treat students of different nationalities equally (P10), students confirmed that they had had such teachers at a higher frequency in university than in high school, but not significantly. This is probably due to the fact that in high school there is not such a wide mix of nationalities as in the university. Since these students are in an American-affiliated university, there are many students who come from the Middle East, United States, Australia and Europe.

Students showed a higher perceived frequency of teachers who treated girls and boys equally (P11) in high school than in university, but the difference was not significant. This was the same by gender and year, although all means were high. These results are probably due to teachers' attempts in high school to go along with the new culture that boys and girls are equal and to counteract the traditional conception of families favouring boys.

A common perception by teachers is that both high school and university teachers favour the higher achievers and focus on their learning more than on others; these results (P12) show a more equitable treatment of all in university. Students considered that fewer teachers in high school (than in university) favour both high and low achievers equally. Any differences were not significant.

It may be supposed that university teachers would tend to lecture more rather than give group work; this is confirmed by the results (P13). Students perceive significantly many more teachers in university than in high school lecture in class. This result may reflect a traditional culture of learning in university, although efforts are being made to have alternative classroom practices to lecturing so that students participate more interactively in the learning process.

Although not very high, results indicate that students view more group work (P14) in high school than in university, but not significantly. This result confirms previous findings (P1 and P13) and indicates that slightly more group work and interaction are happening in the schools. If so, students will

Table 6.3 Mean student views on classroom interaction in High School and University

Pairs of questions and topics	H/U	Mean	Standard Deviation	Two tailed sig.
Pair 7	H7	2.2989	3.30140	0.010*
Being punished	U7	1.6413	0.91235	
Pair 8	H8	3.4595	0.77300	0.974
Students able to ask questions	U8	3.4541	2.32175	
Pair 9	H9	3.8043	3.14578	0.029*
Students give opinions in class	U9	3.2989	0.78427	
Pair 10	H10	3.3736	0.85590	0.306
Teachers treat nationalities equally	U10	3.6099	3.11945	
Pair 11	H11	3.6066	3.09526	0.198
Teachers treat genders equally	U11	3.3115	0.82291	
Pair 12	H12	2.8424	0.88221	0.183
Teachers treat different achievers equally	U12	3.1576	3.16438	
Pair 13	H13	2.8579	2.81314	0.023*
Teachers lecture in class	U13	3.5628	3.23360	
Pair 14	H14	2.8967	2.75308	0.609
Students do group work in class	U14	2.7609	2.40841	
Pair 15	H15	2.9779	2.38736	0.521
Teachers enforce discipline	U15	2.8177	2.39790	

find a difference when they enter university. In any case, the dominating lecture style at the university presumes proper note taking and independent study skills, into which students should be initiated.

Students perceive that teachers often enforced strict discipline (P15) in both the high school and the university, without a significant difference. Discipline is a complex topic, but it is known (from teachers' communications and our personal observations) that teachers in both high school and university attempt to keep order in the classroom, and that this is difficult.

6.9.1.4 *Adaptation strategies*

Table 6.4 shows how students understand the rules and regulations (P16) a little more in high school than in university, but not significantly. Although results showed similar mean frequencies by gender and year, males significantly understand the rules and regulations more in university than they do in high school; juniors showed similar results.

Although this indicates that many students understand the rules and regulations, it is common experience among university teachers (from personal communications and our observations) that many petitions are regularly submitted to teachers to request special consideration on certain issues such as grade review or extension of deadlines for work. This may show an element of the local culture of learning in which students believe they can adapt the system in favour of individual exceptions for themselves, rather

Table 6.4 Mean student views on adaptation strategies in High School and University

Pairs of questions and topics	H/U	Mean	Standard Deviation	Two tailed sig.
Pair 16	H16	3.2291	0.71740	0.050
Students understand rules and regs.	U16	3.3464	0.78799	
Pair 17	H17	3.6033	0.70918	0.602
Students accept varied nationalities	U17	3.5761	0.77154	
Pair 18	H18	3.7880	3.07354	0.435
Students accept varied societies	U18	3.6141	0.73031	
Pair 19	H19	3.1902	0.83745	0.102
Students accept varied teaching styles	U19	3.2935	0.81029	
Pair 20	H20	2.9727	0.95751	0.000*
Students accept scheduling class time	U20	3.3825	0.83608	

than American concepts of fair grading and fair treatment for all according to agreed institutional procedures.

Students accept other students from different nationalities (P17) and societies (P18) in high school more readily than in university. Any statistical differences were not significant. Students in high school usually establish friendships rapidly; most students are of Lebanese nationality and usually go to schools of the same socio-economic background as that of their families, whereas the social spectrum at university is more diverse.

Students accept teachers' varied teaching styles (P19) in high school slightly more than in university: Any differences were not significant. This result is expected because we observe how students at university find it difficult to adapt to many teaching styles after being exposed to fewer teachers in high school. The challenge is for university teachers to try to find out how their students learn best.

Students accept more significantly how class time is scheduled (P20) in university compared to high school. This is surprising, since there are more demands and requirements for independent study at university, but perhaps students value the relative freedom to pick and choose courses and to manage to some extent their own timetable at university.

6.4.2 Focus interviews

There were three interview questions with 20 randomly selected students from the sample. Here we give representative answers and comments on these questions:

1. What are two differences between teaching and learning in high schools and universities?

2. What are two similarities between teaching and learning in high schools and universities?
3. What are two difficulties you have in studying at university that you did not have in high school?

6.9.2.1 Question 1

On the first question, 90 per cent of the students agreed on the three main differences between high school and university. First, the type of work was different, studying was harder in university and students had to take notes and write research papers; in school they had to memorize. Teachers did not follow up on their work in university as closely as in high school.

> In universities most of the classes are lectures. They give lectures and leave (in university).... The ability to have each his own responsibility (in university).... Write research proposal....
>
> Schools: easier; universities harder.... I think that teaching and learning in all our Arab countries is the same and go down! We memorize and study things we will never use in real life, against [contrasted with] the [W]estern system of education.

Second, these comments showed that students were more independent in choosing their own courses, managing their own time and being responsible for following up on their education. The students sounded happy that, now in university, they feel they have 'the upper hand'. However, the representative comments below are of concern and imply that students entering university should be oriented towards the new culture of learning to understand that with independence comes more responsibility: Although there might not be direct punishment, failing a course is punishment enough.

> You're independent on the teacher at the University vice versa for Schools.... Learning in school is a must; learning in university is optional.... No punishment if the homework isn't done.

Third, comments indicated a closer relationship with the teachers in high school than in university.

> The types of people in university are different than in high school.... Classmates in schools are much good.... It is more personal in high school, teachers know their students.... The relationship between the teacher and student is more close in school that in university.
> We know better the teacher, in high schools.

6.9.2.2   Question 2

On the second question, there were surprisingly few similarities among the answers; however, this confirms many of the complaints from students and teachers about the difficulties that students are facing in university (from personal communications with teachers and students).

6.9.2.3   Question 3

On the third question, 75 per cent of the students mentioned the difficulty of writing: writing research papers, note taking, and covering much material. They had to write well in order to succeed. This they found hard to do: The research writing was different; answering on tests required thinking, rather than rote memorization of the material. Getting passing grades seemed to be a concern and a difficulty. This confirms previous research in the field (Bacha, 1997, 2000) and the survey results above.

> Research papers…. Larger material must be covered in a short period of time…. Lecturing…. Strict in grades.

Figure 6.1 summarizes the students' views on the main differences between high school and university in work and languages required. As can be seen, students in high school form a complex multilingual and thus multicultural

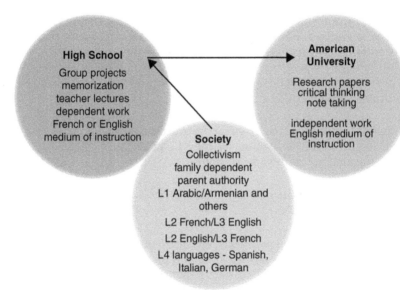

Figure 6.1   Three cultures of learning in Lebanon

mix. The difficulty of initiation into university is self-evident. Arguably, two further circles would need to be added for the French-medium and Arabic-medium universities in Lebanon: These would probably overlap but not be congruent with the American circle.

6.10 Implications and conclusions

This study investigated differences between students' perceptions of learning behaviours in high school and university. There are major implications from the results for teaching/learning. First, according to language conventions, students need to become aware of documentation skills and practice them consistently, something which seems lacking in their pre university schooling. Although the culture of learning in schools has some collectivist characteristics whereby students help their friends in group efforts, this is less evident at the university level, where it may be difficult for some to work individually, a feature of the American universities. Giving oral reports is also perceived as not done often at the university; taking into account that L1 Arabic students traditionally come from a 'speaking culture' which has adapted to the written form poses a challenge for some university students. Second, concerning testing, students need to develop critical thinking and problem-solving skills rather than undertake the heavy memorization that they were used to in high school. Furthermore, in academia students need to work independently and form a modified concept of friendship. Third, classroom teaching in university requires note-taking skills from lectures, interacting with more students from different cultural backgrounds, and adapting to an environment in which there is relatively more 'freedom' in time and choice. Finally, although students mentioned that they understood the rules and regulations more often in university than in high school and they accept students from different societal and national backgrounds, the mean frequencies were not high. There is room for more adaptability to the foregoing and to the scheduling of their classes which implies time management.

Although these results cannot necessarily be generalized to the French-medium or Arabic-medium universities in Lebanon, it is clear that students entering other universities would need to adapt to a different culture of learning. This research confirms that there are different cultures of learning within a single education system where there are international elements and awareness of these cultures might affect the students' achievement and success. Future research could focus on comparing students' socio-economic levels and investigating gender differences in relation to students' adaptation strategies and achievement levels. Teachers need to investigate the factors that affect student learning and, themselves, adapt to different cultures of learning in a cultural synergy (Jin & Cortazzi, 1993) rather than simply judge or label differences negatively. We all agree that our students deserve that much.

References

Akbari, R. & Allvar, N. K. (2010) L2 teacher characteristics as predictors of students' academic achievement. *TESL EJ*, 13 (4), 1–22.

Ayyash-Abdo, H. (2001) Individualism and collectivism: The case of Lebanon. *Social Behavior and Personality*, 29, 503–51.

Bacha, N. N. (1997) *Patterns of lexical cohesion in EFL texts: A study of the compositions of students at the Lebanese American University.* Unpublished PhD thesis, University of Leicester, U.K.

Bacha, N. N. (2000) Academic writing in a multilingual context: A study of learner difficulties. *International Journal of Arabic–English Studies*, 2 (2), 239–68.

Badgera, R. & MacDonald, M. (2007) Culture, language, pedagogy: The place of culture in language teacher education. *Pedagogy, Culture & Society*, 15 (2), 215–27.

Bennett, M. J. (1993) Towards ethnorelativism: A developmental model of intercultural sensitivity. In M. R. Paige (Ed.), *Education for the intercultural experience.* Yarmouth, ME: Intercultural Press, pp. 21–71.

Chami-Sather, G. & Kretschmer, R. (2005) Lebanese/Arabic and American children's discourse in group-solving situations. *Language and Education*, 19 (1), 10–31.

Coffield, M., Moseley, D., Hall, E. & Ecclestone, K. (2004) *Should we be using learning styles? What research has to say to practice.* London: The Learning and Skills Research Center (Monograph).

Connor, U. (1996) *Contrastive rhetoric, cross-cultural aspects of second-language writing.* Cambridge: Cambridge University Press.

Cortazzi, M. & Jin, L. (1996) Cultures of learning: Language classrooms in China. In H. Coleman (Ed.), *Society and the language classroom.* Cambridge: Cambridge University Press, pp. 169–206.

Cummins, J. (2008) Teaching for transfer: Challenging the two solitudes assumption in bilingual education. In J. Cummins and N. H. Hornberger (Eds), *Encyclopedia of Language and Education* (2nd edn), vol. 5. *Bilingual education.* London: Springer, pp. 65–75.

Das, A. K., Chow, S. Y. & Rutherford, B. (1986) The counseling needs of international students. *International Journal for the Advancement of Counseling*, 9, 167–74.

Deressa, B. & Beavers, I. (1988) Needs assessment of international students in college of home economics. *Educational Research Quarterly*, 12, 51–56.

Diab, R. (2000) Political and socio-cultural factors in foreign language education: The case of Lebanon. *Texas Papers in Foreign Language Education*, 5 (1), 177–87.

Diab, R. (2009a) Lebanese university student's perceptions of ethnic, national, and linguistic identity and their preferences for foreign language learning in Lebanon. *Linguistics Journal*, 4, 101–20.

Diab, R. (2009b) Lebanese EFL teachers' beliefs about language learning. *TESL Reporter*, 42 (2), 13–34.

Entwistle, N. J. (1992) *The impact of teaching on learning outcomes in higher education.* Sheffield: Universities and Colleges Staff Development Unit.

Ghaith, G. & K. Shabaan (1996) Language-in-education policy and planning: The case of Lebanon. *Mediterranean Journal of Educational Studies*, 1 (2), 95–105.

Good, T. L. & Brophy, J. (2003) *Looking in the classroom.* Boston: Allyn & Bacon.

Hofstede, G. (1986) Cultural differences in teaching and learning. *International Journal of Intercultural Relations*, 10 (3), 301–20.

Hofstede, G. (2001) *Culture's consequences: International differences in work related values.* Thousand Oaks, CA: Sage Publications.

Holm, K., Nokelainen, P. & Tirri, K. (2009) Relationship of gender and academic achievement for Finnish students' intercultural sensitivity. *High Ability Studies,* 20 (2), 187–200.

Jebejian, A. (2003) Attitudes towards code-switching among Armenians in Lebanon. In R. Bahous and N. N. Bacha (Eds), *Proceedings of second regional conference on language and change.* Beirut: Librairie du Liban Publishers, pp. 94–100.

Jin. L. & Cortazzi, M. (1993) Cultural orientation and academic language use. In D. Graddol, M. Byram and L. Thompson (Eds), *Language and Culture.* Clevedon: Multilingual Matters, pp. 84–97.

Jin, L. & Cortazzi, M. (1998) Dimensions of dialogue: Large classes in China. *International Journal of Educational Research,* 29, 739–61.

Manikutty, S., Anuradha, N. S. & Hansen, K. (2007) Does culture influence learning styles in higher education. *International Journal of Learning and Change,* 2 (1), 70–87.

Miglietti, C. & Strange, C. (1998) Learning styles, classroom environment preferences teaching styles, and remedial course outcomes for underprepared adults at a two-year college. *Community College Review,* 26 (1), 1–19.

Odlin, T. (1989) *Language transfer: Cross-linguistic influence in language learning.* Cambridge: Cambridge University Press.

Parr, G., Bradley, L. & Bingi, R. (1992) Concerns and feelings of international students. *Journal of College Student Development,* 33, 20–25.

Pennington, M. (1995) The teacher change cycle. *TESOL Quarterly,* 29 (3), 705–31.

Saad Khalaf, R. (2009) Youthful voices in post-war Lebanon. *Middle East Journal,* 63 (1), 49–68.

Sandhu, D. (1995) An examination of the psychological needs of the international students: Implications for counseling and psychotherapy. *International Journal for the Advancement of Counseling,* 17, 229–39.

Serriyeh, H. (1989) *Lebanon: Dimensions of conflict, Adelphi papers 243.* Oxford: Nuffield Press Ltd.

Shaaban, K. & Ghaith, G. (1999) Lebanon's language-in-education policies: From bilingualism to trilingualism. *Language Problems and Language Planning,* 3, 1–16

Shaaban, K. & Ghaith, G. (2002) University students' perceptions of the ethnolinguistic vitality of Arabic, French and English in Lebanon. *Journal of Sociolinguistics,* 6 (4), 557–74

Shaaban, K. & Ghaith, G. (2003) Effect of religion, first language, and gender on the perception of the utility of language. *Journal of Language, Identity and Education,* 5 (1), 53–78

Thonhauser, I. (2000) Multilingual education in Lebanon: 'Arabinglizi' and other challenges of multilingualism. *Mediterranean Journal of Educational Studies,* 6 (1), 31–47.

Tirri, K. & Husu, J. (2006) Pedagogical values behind teachers' reflection of school ethos. In M. Klein (Ed.), *New teaching and teacher issues.* New York: Nova Science Publishers, pp. 163–82.

Wehrly, B. (1986) Counseling international students: Issues, concerns and programs. *International Journal for the Advancement of Counseling,* 19, 11–22.

Yazigi, R. (1994) Perception of Arabic as a native language and the learning of English. *Language Learning Journal,* 9, 68–74.

Yu, W. (2000) Direct method. In M. Byram (Ed.), *Routledge Encyclopedia of language teaching and learning.* New York: Routledge, pp. 176–78.

7
Voices of the Reticent? Getting Inside Views of Vietnamese Secondary Students on Learning

Dat Bao

This chapter presents the outcome of an empirical investigation in Vietnam into the phenomenon of student reticence in six classrooms at two secondary schools, namely Bui Thi Xuan and Le Hong Phong schools. It seeks for a solution to the lack of effectiveness of education, in order to gear it towards a more successful pedagogy. Many Vietnamese students, after over ten years of schooling toward intellectual maturity, have not demonstrated their basic communicative skills; rather, there is an identifiable reticence, a reluctance to speak out in class and an apparent unwillingness of students to express themselves which, to outsiders, may be construed as a lack of motivation or shyness. While some educators point to the speech output of students and wonder why it remains so poor, this study attempts to look ethnographically into the process of what students actually do when they are learning in the classroom, a process which seems to lead to such poor results. The research responds to the current context of Vietnam, where recent academic publications and government policies express increased dissatisfaction with students' lack of interaction in many Vietnamese schools and universities. Although educational experts from outside the country have been invited to provide teacher training, such training has been much less successful than intended: Since it is externally generated, it is largely detached from the country's socio-cultural and institutional context. With this likely reason for teacher training failure in mind, this project engages in the classroom learning process from the perspective of an educational and cultural insider. The Vietnamese researcher interacts with the voices of Vietnamese students to develop insights into the phenomenon of reticence. On the basis of taking many Vietnamese socio-cultural values into consideration, the study then recommends ways to develop students' learning styles while respecting their cultural identity. Finally, the study raises the important question of whether Vietnamese teachers have the right and responsibility to bring about internally generated change within their own educational context rather than waiting for decontextualized counsels from external experts.

7.1 Context and background

Ever since Vietnam's economic reform in 1986, which opened the door to a wider range of foreign-invested businesses, the country has hoped for a gradual shift to parallel new dimensions in educational reform. Having made significant economic progress (with a remarkable growth rate of 8.4 per cent per annum) to accelerate its integration into the global economy, the previously war-torn nation achieved its new economic position when it joined the World Trade Organization (WTO) and gained Permanent Normal Trade Relations (PNTR) status. Such development increases demands on the Vietnamese education system for enhanced brainpower to serve as a major factor for the nation's further development. Although economic achievements are evident, they cannot be sustained unless the country develops a more dynamic, creative and skilled workforce. Arguably, such changes have to begin in the educational system and need to start from the foundation of everyday learning conditions.

In the classroom, Vietnamese students' culture of learning can be described as one in which students depend heavily on the pedagogical tendency of many teachers to transmit knowledge about the subject content. According to Bui Ngoc Anh (2004: p. 242), the interactive pattern often found in Vietnamese classrooms is: 'Teacher initiates – learner responds – teacher comments'. This model restricts learning because it is the teacher who has the final say or who makes the concluding evaluation. If the learner takes the initiative to complete the interaction, so that the pattern becomes, 'teacher initiates – learner responds – teacher comments – learner responds again', the nature of the discussion will change fundamentally. The last step 'learner responds again' rarely takes place in the Vietnamese classroom because it is likely to be perceived by some teachers as an act of challenging authority, which seems to undermine many values in the traditional teacher–student relationship.

7.2 IRF exchanges in Vietnam

This pattern of interaction is familiar in Western studies of classroom language as an Initiation–Response–Follow-up (IRF) exchange, frequently seen in teachers' questions and student answers. The pattern seems remarkably well-established and has long been researched as a basic discourse structure (Sinclair & Coulthard, 1975; Coulthard & Brazil, 1981; Hoey, 1993); it has been criticized as a teacher control mechanism which gives learners insufficient opportunities for expression (Edwards & Furlong, 1978; Walsh, 2006), but it can be productively extended and re-evaluated for more active and dialogic learning for different learners, including second language learners (Willis, 1992; Wells, 1993, 1999; Hall, 1998). It cannot be presumed, however, that this apparently similar pattern in Vietnamese classrooms functions in the same way as in Western classrooms, or that it has similar social and cultural inner workings. In some East Asian contexts, such as in China, the pattern has been positively evaluated for effective teaching with large classes, although it needs to be complemented with more interactive and learner-centred patterns (Jin & Cortazzi, 1998).

In the Vietnamese context, this mode of learning fails to respond to the need for complex discourse required by the increasing demands of business negotiation, educational exchange and international communication in Vietnamese daily life. Many students remain deeply reticent during classroom discussion and conduct themselves according to models long acquired from their experience of lecturing modes. Although it is appropriate in many socio-cultural situations, their reticent behaviour often collides with the need for a classroom environment which may require more verbal interaction, sharing of problem-solving skills and self-motivated debates. Actions that meet these needs are called for by Vietnamese scholars such as Hoang Co Chinh (2000) and Bui Ngoc Anh (2004) as ways to expand the Vietnamese learning repertoire in response to the country's changing economic and educational contexts.

According to Tran Vui (2009), Vietnamese teachers' response to students' contribution in many classrooms is often evaluative, and the content of such feedback is heavily driven by textbooks coupled with considerable concern for following the pre-determined syllabus. Teacher-training workshops conducted by international experts have not led to any fundamental change in the interaction in Vietnamese classrooms: Although they argued skilfully about learner-centeredness, the experts failed to position learners' participation within the country's educational and cultural context or the physical constraints, limited resources, large classes, teacher's traditional beliefs and hierarchical values, among other multifarious forces that local teachers need to work with. As a result, local teachers returned from these training workshops to their schools to implement a detached, unmodified method borrowed from a different Western context only to realize that it did not work in their classrooms, and so they reverted to their traditional teaching mode (insights into the difficulties of transferring pedagogic practices from one context to another internationally are discussed in Wagner, 1991; Holliday, 1994; Clamb, 1996; Sullivan, 2000; Maley, 2000; Lantolf, 2000). After all, it is unrealistic to try to repair a didactic approach without linking it to a wider cultural context (Holliday, 1994). As Clamb (1996: p. 221) emphasizes, 'classrooms are not isolated islands from the mainland of the educational institute to which they belong'. Maley (2000: p. 1), speaking as an outsider in an Asian context, also warns: 'We know very little about many of the contexts in which English is taught, and certainly less than those who face the day-to-day problems of teaching in them'. Any form of innovation can only match reality if researchers and practitioners take the institutional context into consideration (Wagner, 1991).

7.3 The need for student voices

Research in speech communication in Vietnam began embarrassingly late. This is because in Vietnam many French scholars dominated the publications in the field up to 1945, mostly in such activities within linguistics such as compiling dictionaries and writing grammars. In 1946, after the country gained its independence from France, Vietnamese replaced French as the official language of instruction in the education system (Hoang Tue, 2002). Despite this, it was not until the 1960s that Vietnamese scholars from the National Linguistics Institute began to pay attention to teaching and learning methodology (Huu Dat, 2002). Such a relatively short period of development in the educational research field somehow has contributed to the lack of well-established methods of teaching languages and communication skills. In the traditional Vietnamese classroom, it is the teacher who decides who talks, when to talk, what to say, how to say it and when to stop talking. This model implicitly leads students to believe that the teacher is the centre of knowledge, ideas and information. This situation prompts a demand for more systematic, empirical study into the real, everyday classroom where an aim is to investigate the voices of students and teachers to ascertain their thoughts about how they cope with the phenomenon of teacher-centred classroom interaction. Academic discussions among Vietnamese educators as well as appeals from policy makers at ministerial and metropolitan levels in the 2000s show that this area is becoming a strong research interest for educational development in the country.

Many Vietnamese teachers' favorite technique of helping students to speak is by directing questions. In such an environment, dominated by teachers' questions, getting learners to voluntarily voice their own thoughts or raise their own questions proves to be a real challenge. Some local linguists believe that focusing on different questioning methods to increase verbal responses is helpful but not sufficient. Educational scholars, such as Le Phuong Nga (2002) and Le Xuan Thai (1995), highlight the need to increase learners' emotional involvement as well as the need to link the content of classroom discussion to students' everyday concerns. Arguably, to involve students emotionally takes a high degree of cultural sensitivity, and linking discussion content to students' concerns calls for a deep level of tacit knowledge about everyday life in the country.

In a recent report from Hue University, Tran Vui (2009) highlighted the need to move Vietnamese classroom interaction to two teaching modes: interpretive and generative. In this view, interpretive teaching values the social aspect of learning by asking fewer testing questions and more genuine and thought-provoking questions in order to increase opportunities for classroom participation and discussion. The generative teaching mode emphasizes the need for students to participate, interpret and negotiate meanings in an inquiry-driven mode of instruction. Through this process teachers respond to students by stimulating further discussion as they probe, give feedback, comment and redirect questions. Generative teaching also means that key beliefs are not presumed or anticipated in advance, but teachers question their own practices and beliefs and revise their own knowledge while exploring and constructing ideas together with their students. By and large, how to create more profound conditions for students to develop more vigorous involvement in the learning process is the burning question in Vietnamese education today (Bui Ngoc Anh, 2004). The concept of active involvement is understood by Vietnamese scholars as the act of sharing curiosity and the ability to raise new questions. Such dispositions and skills should be demonstrated through some degree of talk: Being reticent arguably restricts these skills.

7.4   Research focus

To explore what Vietnamese students really want and need in relation to the need to re-evaluate the existing culture of learning, this study was conducted in six classrooms at two major high schools in urban Ho Chi Minh City, namely Bui Thi Xuan and Le Hong Phong, which are among the most prestigious schools in the city and, thus, teachers and students are more inclined to welcome opportunities for innovation. The project does not focus on any particular course but encompasses student participants with experiences in classroom learning across a variety of school subjects, including languages, social studies and sciences. Data collection tools include an open questionnaire for students and also focus-group interviews. The study invites detailed reflection from 65 secondary students. The project focuses on the following issues:

- Students' perception of their own learning behaviour and factors influencing such behaviour
- Potential obstacles to verbal participation in the classroom
- The teacher factor that governs the level and nature of verbal participation by students
- Students' perspectives on whether, and how, to move the classroom to a more interactive mode
- The relationship between students' verbal participation and traditional roles, beliefs and values regarding teachers

The project attempts to construct a picture of classroom interaction at the time of the research and investigate invisible factors that discourage students from verbal participation in the learning process. The student participants were encouraged to be as reflective and detailed as possible in their responses to the questionnaires. Interesting issues arising in their responses would then be further pursued in face-to-face, in in-depth focus group interviews. A selected group of 15 students, whose questionnaire responses gave interesting views that caught special attention, were invited to the interviews, conducted in two sessions. These sessions yielded further explanation and in-depth information as well as attitudes and feelings of the students. There was also scope for the students to raise other issues that seemed to concern them the most and to add their own further suggestions. Basic statistical means are employed to determine the significance of data information (for example, the weighting of an opinion from informants can be gauged by the number of people who shared it), and to help compare the frequency of certain behaviour that occurred as well as the relationship between different variables.

By elucidating what happens in procedural classroom interaction, the study hopes to make a contribution to the understanding of how pedagogy can better support students' learning within accepted socio-cultural behaviour in Vietnam. It also hopes to advance the overall knowledge of the relationship between the traditional values of Vietnamese teachers and students, and their performance is modified towards educational reform, which has not previously been studied in detail. Sullivan (2000), in her observation of English classrooms in Vietnam, points out that many Vietnamese socio-historical values, which in Western views are often dismissed as classroom distractions, should in fact be respected (not undermined) and should be organized to operate as mediators of the learning process. It has been reported that over recent decades a large number of TESOL innovation projects have suffered failure simply because they attempt to 'introduce practices within school cultures that promote a different type of social order in the classroom' (Karavas-Doukas, 1998: p. 49). Findings from this research when they are made accessible to local teachers and learners could serve as a way of contributing to educational reform in the country.

7.5 Outcomes and results

7.5.1 Students' perspectives on their participation

These research data reveal that the nature and level of students' participation are influenced by five key factors: their needs and interests, individual learning agendas, external forces, the classroom atmosphere and individual moods. Although Vietnamese teachers are notorious for their heavy reliance on the lecturing mode in classrooms, not all the students under study view themselves as verbally passive. In particular, 12.31 per cent of the respondents consider themselves to various degrees active communicators during the lesson, while 7.70 per cent – though admitting they tend to stay silent – claim that they can participate if they choose to, rather than seeing themselves as passive learners. One student even remarked that the level of learner participation alone is not a sufficient signal to detect whether someone should be considered an active or passive learner. In contrast, 58.46 per cent see themselves as reticent learners most of the time; they contribute to the lesson only when forced to do so. In between these two groups, 6.15 per cent feel that they are neither verbal nor silent students but vary their behaviour flexibly as a result of their individual interest levels or based on the interactive or non-interactive nature of particular subjects. A number of influential factors are identified below to explain when and how students decide to participate in classroom discussion. The figures in brackets indicate the percentage of students who share the ideas considered.

Student need and interest are the first factors that govern participation (10.79 per cent). Discussion topics which reflect the student's interest often lead to participation, as they are found to be significant and enjoyable enough to deserve the extra effort put into the lesson. Lesson content which requires intensive memorization and subsequent regurgitation offers no motivation for spontaneous contribution from anybody in the class. It seems clear that the students are acutely aware of the interactive or non-interactive nature of learning content in which interpretation of new knowledge is welcomed by everyone.

The individual learning agenda is the second influential factor (3.08 per cent). Different students may contribute differently as a result of their learning styles and diverse preferences for various issues. Some students come to class prepared to generally listen rather than to talk. Others are more willing to voice their opinions but do so only with inspiring discussion themes which allow for more divergent thinking rather than convergent solutions. The third factor is external forces (7.70 per cent). It is a policy among a number of teachers that students' contributions in class can be rewarded with marks. Once this decision has been made a rule, many students would feel motivated to volunteer their contribution in the lesson. Students' mood and energy constitute a small factor (3.08 per cent). Students' contribution in class may reflect their changeable frames of mind at the time of the lesson, which means that if some are not in the mood to speak they continue to remain quiet despite the teacher's effort to interact with them. In many cases, students tend to lose energy toward the end of the day and classes scheduled for the later hours may suffer from a greater lack of student cooperation.

7.5.2   Potential obstacles to verbal participation

In the students' views, the obstacles to classroom participation fall into three main categories: the learner factor, the teacher factor, as well as the syllabus and classroom factor.

- The learner factor includes students' concern about accuracy in their contribution (55.38 per cent), their inability to cope with lesson challenges (10.77 per cent) and their pre-established quiet nature (9.24 per cent).

- The teacher factor includes a lack of a rewarding system, such as teachers' marks, compliments and recognition (1.54 per cent); teachers' undesirable personality and behaviour (4.62 per cent); teachers' lecturing mode which does not create conditions for students to express individual concern (7.70 per cent); and teachers' inability to raise effective questions (10.77 per cent) since questions do not vary in type (information questions, referential questions, convergent question, divergent questions and so on) to tap into students' different reasoning skills as well as to meet their various preferences and thinking styles.
- The syllabus and climate factor includes limited class time (1.54 per cent) in many high school classrooms where the pressure of covering the syllabus leaves little time for spontaneous interaction, as well as the stressful or boring nature of the lesson (10.77 per cent) which takes away students' curiosity and contributes to the inertia in their learning behaviour.

7.5.3 Measures to enhance the level and quality of verbal participation

This section presents the respondents' proposal, in which the students suggest the kinds of conditions they think should be provided so as to help them become verbally active to communicate better in the classroom. The proposal requests adjustment in curriculum, management, pedagogy and sociability.

Curriculum innovation would help improve classroom communication (32.31 per cent); 3.8 per cent of the students voice concerns toward adjusting the curriculum to consider more room for teachers and learners' interaction and exchange of knowledge. The syllabus needs to be adapted to allocate more time for students' talk, and there should be a balance between learning a pre-determined body of knowledge and generating knowledge in a teacher–student exchange of ideas. In addition, the curriculum should include clear-cut policies regarding continuous assessment that takes into account individual students' class participation; 29.23 per cent of the students feel more motivated if they are aware that their contribution is not only recognized but also earns them points toward getting a positive result at the end of the course. However, it is suggested (7.69 per cent) that the awarding of marks for classroom participation should not be overdone because if a large amount of points go to verbal contribution students would be too score-conscious and thus would suffer from pressure rather than enjoying the interaction.

Management of classroom interaction can be improved (12.31 per cent). Methods of contribution should vary depending on the complexity of the contribution. For instance, questions that are easy and require short responses can be answered in chorus by the whole class because such a contribution would be too simple to discuss and would delay class time. Questions that are easy but which require longer responses can be answered by individuals without the need to raise their hands to ask for permission because long answers would be hard to hear from the whole class. For questions that are challenging and require elaborate responses, students may raise their hands to signal their contribution because such thoughtful answers may deserve more classroom time and attention. It is particularly interesting to hear such analytical recommendations from high school students who are often not expected to be so overtly judicious about the complexities of the classroom management process.

Elicitation techniques should be improved (32.32 per cent). Teachers' questions should be both intelligent and inspiring to stimulate imagination, interest and creativity. If questions are too demanding they need to come with prompts or can be broken down into small, manageable questions which lead into the main focus. Such sequences of mini-questions would have the potential to invite students at different levels to participate and thus support one another's contributions (4.62 per cent). Besides, there should be more open questions which allow for flexible answers and invite multiple solutions rather than closed questions which ask for one correct fact or a single option: all students should be kept informed of this expectation. Students' contributions need to be warmly received and nothing should be imposed without a reasonable explanation (3.08 per cent). Teaching methods should be inspiring with the aid of examples, illustrations, stories and visuals as well as with technology such as PowerPoint slides (21.54 per cent). It was also suggested by 4.62 per cent of the students that, after they finish lecturing on each section of the lesson, the teachers should pause, ask consolidation questions and leave time for students to reflect on their understanding before the class moves on to the next stage of the lesson.

There is the need for students to connect well with the teacher and with real-world communication (41.00 per cent); 26.15 per cent of students feel that teachers should be more approachable than they are at present. The majority of this group feels that classroom discussion once in a while needs to stretch beyond the classroom and connect with down-to-earth application in the real world; 20 per cent of the respondents suggest that when a classroom discussion implies some degree of controversy about values and contains issues that touch on life experience, students would become more attentive and would debate the concerns.

To ensure that the above behaviour happens more frequently, the schools need to loosen up the existing curriculum and leave room for more spontaneous discourse that will train students to become more mature thinkers and effective communicators; 4.62 per cent of the students suggest organizing games, competitions and collaborative activities that would require them to make team contributions. To push this process further, depending on the nature of the subject matter, students can be organized to shift the classroom setting to an outdoor surrounding such as in the school grounds or to go on an excursion outside school. Such a change of learning environment, as stated by 1.54 per cent of the respondents, could generate novelty that would inspire further changes in students' routine behaviour.

The results show that 4.62 per cent of the students need support to feel more confident, accepted and welcome through receiving interactional support, such as when they receive compliments and rewards from teachers. In their view, all of this should be realized in a friendly, conducive classroom climate to provide the most positive experience possible in connection with moments of participation. This scenario would create an enormous improvement from the status quo of many existing classrooms in which, according to 3.8 per cent of the respondents, some teachers instead of encouraging students often give warnings and threaten to downgrade students with poor marks or to provide negative comments in school reports.

7.5.4 Students' attitudes toward the silent learning mode

Two distinctive trends co-exist regarding whether students should be more verbally involved in the learning process. While the majority of students (87.69 per cent) enthusiastically support a belief in the value of active participation, a minority of students (12.31 per cent) feel that they have the right to remain either quiet or speak only when they feel truly interested in making a contribution. The majority group that advocates more learner-centred behaviour suggests four main justifications for this ideology. They suggest that increased verbal participation would activate their multiple senses during the learning process (75.39 per cent); it would inform the teacher's pedagogical decisions (6.16 per cent), enhance both student–student and teacher–learner communication (4.62 per cent), as well as promote a positive classroom relationship (9.23 per cent). Meanwhile those who prefer to stay quiet are acutely aware of what performance works best for them (7.69 per cent); they believe in the teacher's respect for students' maturity in decision making (1.54 per cent) and in the students' right to make their own judgments rather than be told what to do (3.08 per cent).

Most interestingly, a large number of students feel that those who talk and those who keep silent are in a position to support each other's learning, whether they are conscious of this mutual agreement or not (87.69 per cent). Some feel that a classroom characterized by students' verbal participation represents a vibrant learning environment which can stimulate the brains of others, including the silent members (75.39 per cent).

According to these students, peer interaction creates depth of learning (76.93 per cent); 3.08 per cent of the students believe that learning does not happen via the teacher alone, but peers can initiate and teach one another through thoughtful interaction to stimulate one another's thinking. In addition, participation is viewed by the majority as a way to inform the teacher's pedagogical decisions. Not only does verbal participation allow knowledge to be acquired interactively but it also supports instructional performance by allowing the teacher to gain information about how well students understand, interpret, apply and make connections between themselves and the lesson content. These types of feedback from students have a moment-by-moment influence over the teacher's decision to adapt the lesson content and pedagogy in directions that are desirable and suited to the learning preferences of the class.

Participation promotes teachers' professional development (4.62 per cent). Learner participation exerts positive pressure which has a corresponding influence over how much effort teachers would put in during their lesson preparation on a regular basis. Being conscious of how deeply students want to gain knowledge about every topic has the potential to keep teachers on the alert and makes them read, research and plan the lesson well ahead of time. Besides, the enthusiasm from the students also has a motivational effect on the teacher, which creates a virtuous circle to make every lesson more interesting and inspiring for all.

Participation cultivates students' self-esteem and confidence (13.85 per cent); 4.62 per cent of the students yearn for a positive environment which promotes confident communication so that nobody is afraid of speaking out the truth or expressing their own views. Students further commented that such interaction also plays a role in promoting positive teacher–student rapport and active peer collaboration (9.23 per cent). Many highlight their awareness that, as Vietnam is increasingly integrating into the global community in every way, there is the need to project the image of the young generation as being sociable, confident, convincing and verbally eloquent people who not only incubate good ideas but are also capable of speaking up and raising their concerns.

To trained and experienced teachers, especially many in Western contexts, the above may be familiar ideas about classroom interaction and pedagogy, since there is a widespread understanding (strongly promoted in much teacher training) that knowledge in school settings is constructed and mediated through active participation in focused classroom discussions in which students are encouraged to express their developing thinking (e.g., Tharp & Gallimore, 1988; Newman et al., 1989; Wertsch, 1991; Mercer, 1995). What is interesting and insightful about this study is that these ideas are from school learners in a context in which they (and many of their teachers) have not been exposed to pedagogies informed by such theories and student reticence holds a large and significant role in the dominant culture of learning.

7.5.5   Beliefs in the right to decide on one's own learning behaviour

Students should not be judged simply by their physical behaviour (12.31 per cent). Many feel that there is no right or wrong per se in being verbally active or passive, but what seems to them to be more important is their right to make choices about how to behave during the lesson. Some emphasize that what should be nurtured and encouraged in school culture is a sense of self-discipline in which individuals are trained to choose maturely to learn in ways that work best for them. In other words, both verbal and non-verbal modes may work equally well in the minds of many learners, and they think these modes should not be subject to value judgments about which is better. As discussed above, such choices would, in practice, be informed by their interest, motivation and perceptions of the interactive demands of the classroom context and of particular school subjects.

7.5.6 How student participation influences teachers' traditional role

Regarding the view of these students on how their active participation may exert influence over the teacher's traditional roles, beliefs and values there are three distinctive attitudes toward the relationship between learner performance and teacher role. The first view states that participation can only develop in line with teacher–learner collaboration which allows for the most fruitful effect on learning. The second view supports a classroom hierarchy and holds that teachers' traditional role is important and should be maintained through learners' humble, respectful participating behaviour. The third view indicates a revolutionizing attitude which puts students' freedom of self-expression before the traditional teacher authority and hopes that teachers open-mindedly modify their role to make discussion as stress-free as possible.

Of the participants, 24.62 per cent feel that there is no real relationship between increasing the learners' participation and teachers' values, which means that learner participation would do no harm to teacher's traditional roles, beliefs and values. Many yearn for autonomy in gaining and applying knowledge in self-regulating ways; 3.08 per cent of the students feel that they should be allowed the freedom and the confidence to share their own knowledge related to the lesson content. Although the teacher's role is to provide the class with foundational knowledge of the subject matter, the students are the ones who also have the responsibility to discuss relevant issues and seek understanding for themselves as well as to discover what is most relevant to their own need and applicable to their own situation (1.54 per cent). Such envisaged self-directed judgment and open communication also helps diminish the traditional hierarchy of respect and distance between the teachers and students, a hierarchy which inherently makes conversation difficult in Vietnamese classrooms.

Contrary to the reforming argument above, 33.85 per cent of the participants feel that it is essential to maintain teachers' traditional values, to observe Vietnamese educational traditions and see that learners' contribution must take place in a respectful manner; 10.77 per cent believe that participants in classroom discussion must take their verbal involvement seriously for real learning purposes rather than simply display 'smooth talk' to please the teacher or put on a pre-tense to seek teacher's attention. Besides, contributions must not sound like criticism of the teacher. Two examples of such mindful behaviour, as suggested by 23.08 per cent of the students, are that students should always raise their hands to ask for permission when they wish to speak; and, when permission is granted, their manner of speaking should well tuned so that it stays gentle and humble enough to show respect for the teacher.

The students show sensitivity toward the appropriateness of verbal participation: 6.15 per cent suggest that classroom discipline should take priority over verbal activeness; 41.53 per cent recommend that classroom contributors should be aware of the teacher's presence when they interact with one another and should refrain from disrupting the teacher's lecture. Students should avoid causing disruption by shouting or arguing impatiently; if a large number of students contribute during one session, this may take up excessive class time and interfere with the lesson agenda (6.15 per cent). For this reason, students should be selective in what they ask, putting intelligent or difficult questions to the teacher and saving easy or direct-information questions for friends or for when they consult books; 6.15 per cent feel that unless it is appropriate in time and topic, verbal participation can be pointless, time-wasting and destructive to the whole lesson. Casual and untimely participation may also disrupt teacher inspiration and upset the flow of logic that the teacher hopes to maintain in order to keep the lesson consistent and coherent.

Further ideas relate to the learning environment; these are interesting because they emerge from the student voices in this culture of learning. An often ignored factor among educators in Vietnam is the physical condition of the classroom (3.08 per cent). Many are designed with two doors plus multiple windows and, due to hot weather and a shortage of air conditioning, most teachers tend to keep them wide open for air circulation. This means that teacher talk can easily carry and echo to the next classroom. If many students participate enthusiastically, it is hard to keep the noise level down. Every so often an enthusiastic teacher is faced with angry complaints from the next-door teacher who steps over to demand that the classroom be put under control. This situation partly explains why many teachers remain reluctant to arrange collaborative learning activities in which hearty laughter and debate in the classroom are often frowned upon by their colleagues as a sign of poor discipline.

Some students believe that teachers' traditional values need modification (6.16 per cent); 4.62 per cent believe that progress in education starts through changing classroom practices. As Vietnam is integrating into the global market economy, there is a need for the country's education to be improved, and this can only be done if schools, educators and students are willing to adapt, adjust and transform their way of doing things. Such change should begin in everyday classroom practice where teachers, it is argued, need to consciously question and review their roles to meet learners' varying needs. It was suggested by 1.54 per cent of the students that teachers should be more flexible with the rituals of learner participation and let students know this. For example, students may not need to stand up when they speak. This traditional code of behaviour often makes some students feel too ceremonial in a classroom in which open discussion needs to be spontaneous, improvised and stress-free.

7.5.7 How teachers' traditional role influences participation

The influence of the teacher's traditional role over students' attitudes toward classroom participation is indicated in three tendencies. One view highlights teachers' overused authority as a factor that induces fear and silence among learners. A second view implies that teachers' unchallenged expertise and self-complacency are a cause of poor teaching performance which leads to poor participation. A third view suggests that teachers' positive qualities are a stimulus to active collaboration and enthusiastic participation.

Teachers should not overuse their authority because it can become a main source of inhibiting students' verbal performance (78.46 per cent). Many students are conscious that respect is different from fear, and sometimes they remain more afraid of the teacher than respectful. In particular, teachers need to be more accepting of students' errors (33.96 per cent). Many teachers remain too conservative to accept different ways of viewing the same issue (12.31 per cent); 7.70 per cent of the students comment that many teachers easily lose their tempers and reprimand students by shouting at them when they receive a wrong answer. Such pressure is destructive and psychologically damaging to students' love for learning. It was suggested that teachers should pay more attention to students' emotional needs by being more flexible and by incorporating humor into the lesson wherever possible (13.85 per cent).

Both the flow of teaching content and the consistency of teacher behaviour are of vital importance to students. Disjointed lessons can damage learning in subtle ways (1.54 per cent). The lack of connection between lessons could disrupt learning (1.54 per cent). Before starting a new lesson the teachers might like to give students a chance to reflect on knowledge previously taught, so that students feel motivated to review their knowledge and understanding before the class. Teachers' apparently temperamental behaviour should change (3.08 per cent). Some teachers are said to have a changeable personality, which confuses students and makes the classroom climate feel unsafe. Such teachers allegedly yell at students from time to time without an obvious reason, which makes it hard for the class to enjoy learning. Some teachers are viewed as being unfair when judging, marking or criticizing students' work and even when assessing students' personalities.

Other students say that for teachers' expertise to be improved, it needs to go through some degree of challenge (16.93 per cent). This indicates a direct relationship between teacher performance and the lack of student challenges to it. Historically, it is simply not in the tradition of Vietnamese formal education that students can be critical of issues, disagree with ideas in lectures, suggest changing methods or question the teacher's knowledge. However, without such feedback and the encouragement for teacher performance to be adapted or modified, it is unlikely that instructional quality can improve. In fact, many students are highly critical of their teachers' knowledge, pedagogy and assessment skills; 13.85 per cent of the students comment that some teachers fail to respond to learners' inquiries in well-informed and convincing ways. They also feel that book-oriented pedagogy is fairly common in many classrooms where teaching seems routine and boring. In addition to this, in the views of these students, the way tests are designed and test papers are marked do not reflect fairness and professionalism. It was suggested that teachers need to invite students' opinions and organize more classroom interaction rather than simply transmit factual knowledge from the printed word. From this, it seems essential that teachers become aware of the need to refresh their pedagogical approaches in order to inspire students' learning.

Some students commented on other professional matters. They said teachers' enthusiasm, commitment and morality need to be evident to the learners (16.92 per cent). If teachers demonstrate a high level of dedication and passion in teaching, students are able to pick up these positive signals and respond correspondingly. In fact evidence of teacher commitment can be demonstrated through features such as the tone of speech, well-planned lessons, good classroom management, practical illustrations and anecdotes from life to support knowledge in the lecture. All of these sensitivities are factors that have direct influence over students' motivation to learn, and these students are aware of them.

7.6   Implications and applications

Among the most important results of the study is the fact that the *students differ considerably in their self-perception*. In exploring the students' views of their own classroom behaviour, the majority of students yearn for a more interactive learning mode. Some, however, feel that they are already verbal enough and believe they know how to interact during the lesson if they wish to do so. Individual students differ in their mode of participation, and such diversity requires some flexibility by teachers to accept various styles and set up a classroom environment that supports both silent reflectivity and verbal contribution.

7.6.1   A number of tensions revealed between teachers and learners

These tensions include students' limited ability versus teachers' high demand for perfect performance; students' quiet, somewhat reticent, approach to learning and teachers' lack of motivational strategies; students' communication apprehension and teachers' pressuring behaviour; students' lack of experience in classroom participation and teachers' poor questioning skills; students' expressed need for more verbal interaction and teachers' concern with lectures in order to cover a heavy syllabus; students' desire for the classroom to be enjoyable and teachers' routine teaching methods. Various factors can be considered to boost classroom participation. The conditions that would support an active learning style include more interesting lesson content, greater teacher understanding of individual learning styles, implementing a good rewards system and sustaining a positive classroom atmosphere.

When these students' data were being analysed, it was exciting to see an emerging picture of students voicing how *change should occur in four dimensions: curriculum, management, pedagogy and the need for socialization.* These factors are essential and mutually supportive to the extent that improving only one of them would not be sufficient to bring about change in classroom participation. First, curriculum should be adjusted to leave space for learners to discuss rather than solely for teachers to lecture, and such expectation needs to be spelled out explicitly to students. Second, classroom management should include various methods of inviting learners' participation, depending on the nature and complexity of the issue to be discussed. Third, pedagogy should improve teachers' questioning techniques, ways of supporting students' contributions and of allocating time for students' reflection on issues of their concern. Finally, socialization should be promoted through developing greater approachability for teachers, closer connections between lessons and real-world applicability, syllabus flexibility, having a fresh rather than routine learning environment and sustaining a warmly accepting classroom atmosphere.

7.6.2 Shared responsibilities between teachers and students in modifying their classroom practice

Students should be more aware of how classroom participation constitutes the depth of learning, builds their confidence in self-expression, increases their decision-making skills and attends to their whole-person development. Teachers, meanwhile, should constantly work toward professional development rather than remain complacent with the status quo; they need to develop good judgment and understanding of students' behaviour as well as toleration of students' differing ideas, and to have respect for individual opinions. In short, teachers need to develop explicit awareness of students' cultures of learning and how many (but not all) students want this to develop in the direction of greater classroom participation.

Specific to the Vietnamese educational context is the realization of the need to strike a balance between contemporary and traditional classroom values. Moving away from educational traditions that seem to pose obstacles to an active learning style should be prioritized over preserving the past at any cost. In order to make this possible, teachers need to become more open-minded, retain some degree of authority, tolerate diversity in student viewpoints, develop physical expressions of enthusiasm and friendliness, share explicit rules about participation, renew pedagogy and incorporate more interesting content into the everyday lessons. Students, correspondingly, need to remain respectful while becoming more verbally active, to ask for permission to speak when necessary, to exercise more spontaneity and autonomy, and to prepare well to contribute to every lesson rather than wait for the teacher to take the initiative all the time.

7.6.3   Two recommendations for future research

These recommendations include investigating teachers' views (to complement the voices of the students studied here) and conducting action research studies. Although this project has aimed to provide a scenario of learners' perceptions of the status quo and their aspirations for the future, the picture would be more complete if teachers also have a chance to make their voices heard which, due to the limited time frame, has not been within the scope of this study. In addition, the recommendations presented above would lead to further valuable insights if they were tested through action research projects which investigate classroom cultures over a period of time in school contexts in Vietnam and other Asian settings. Once suggestions similar to those raised by these students are brought into the classroom as methods, strategies and interaction, the teachers and students involved could be invited to reflect on the process. Not only would they have a chance to experience educational attempts to make classroom life more meaningful but, based on what happens, they can also develop a forum to be critical of current practice, exchange viewpoints and propose new ideas that would eventually benefit Vietnamese and other Asian educational systems which share similar contextual features with Vietnam.

References

Bui Ngoc Anh (2004) 'Mot so chien luoc su dung ngon ngu cua giao vien trong viec nang cao tinh tich cuc hoc tap cua hoc sinh' [Strategies in teacher talk to boost learner activeness]. In *Linguistic Issues 2004*. Hanoi: Social Sciences Publisher, pp. 241–51.

Clamb, C. (1996) *The self-directed teachers – managing the learning process*. Cambridge: Cambridge University Press.

Coulthard, M. & Brazil, D. (1981) Exchange structure. In M. Coulthard and M. Montgomery (Eds), *Studies in discourse analysis*. London: Routledge & Kegan Paul, pp. 82–105.

Edwards, A. D. & Furlong, V. J. (1978) *The language of teaching, meaning in classroom interaction*. London: Heinemann.

Hall, J. K. (1998) Differential teacher attention to student utterances: The construction of different opportunities for learning in the IRF. *Linguistics and Education*, 9 (3), 287–311.

Hoang Co Chinh (2000) 'Cai tien quan ly qua trinh day hoc nham thuc hien viec doi moi Phuong phap day hoc' [Improving pedagogy management towards methodological reform]. In *Educational Studies* No 2/2000. Ha Noi: Nguyen Thi Minh Khai Press, pp. 145–72.

Hoang Tue (2002) 'Tim den giai phap cho truong hoc' [Working toward a solution for the educational system]. In H. Tue and L. X. Thai (Eds), *Tieng Viet Trong Truong Hoc [The Vietnamese Language in Today's Schools]*. Hanoi: Social Sciences Press.

Hoey, M. (1993) The case for the exchange complex. In M. Hoey (Ed.), *Data, description, discourse, papers on the English language in honour of John McH Sinclair.* London: Harper Collins, pp. 115–38.

Holliday, A. (1994) *Appropriate methodology and social context.* Cambridge: Cambridge University Press.

Huu Dat (2002) *Phong Cach Hoc Voi Viec Day Van Trong Nha Truong va Ly Luan Phe Binh Van Hoc [Methodology in the Teaching of Vietnamese Literature and Literature Research]*. Hanoi: Hanoi Publisher.

Jin, L. & Cortazzi, M. (1998) Dimensions of dialogue: large classes in China. *International Journal of Educational Research,* 29, 739–61.

Karavas-Doukas, K. (1998) Evaluating the implementation of educational innovations: Lesson from the past. In P. Rea-Dickins and K. P. Germaine (Eds), *Managing evaluation and innovation in language teaching: Building bridges.* London: Longman, pp. 25–50.

Lantolf, J. P. (2000) *Socio-cultural theory and second language teaching.* Oxford: Oxford University Press.

Le Phuong Nga (2002) *Day Hoc Tap Doc o Tieu Hoc [Teaching Reading Skills in Vietnamese Primary Classrooms]*. Hanoi: The Education Publisher.

Le Xuan Thai (1995) *Boi Duong Hung Thu Cua Hoc Sinh Doi Voi Bo Mon Tieng Viet [Increasing Learner Interest in the Vietnamese Language Classroom]*. Hanoi: Social Sciences Press.

Maley, A. (2000) 'One-size theory that does not fit all' in TEFL Supplement in Association with the BBC World Service – *The Guardian Weekly,* September 2000: 01.

Mercer, N. (1995) *The guided construction of knowledge, talk amongst teachers and learners.* Clevedon: Multilingual Matters.

Newman, D., Griffin, P. & Cole, M. (1989) *The construction zone, working for cognitive change in school.* Cambridge: Cambridge University Press.

Sinclair, J. McH. & Coulthard, R. M. (1975) *Towards an analysis of discourse, the English used by teachers and pupils.* Oxford: Oxford University Press.

Sullivan, P. N. (2000) Playfulness as mediation in communicative language teaching in a Vietnamese classroom. In J. P. Lantolf (Ed.), *Socio-cultural theory and second language teaching.* Oxford: Oxford University Press, pp. 115–32.

Tharp, R. & Gallimore, R. (1988) *Teaching, learning, and schooling in social context.* Cambridge: Cambridge University Press.

Tran Vui (2009) Enhancing classroom communication to develop students' mathematical thinking. Hue University, Vietnam. Retrieved Monday 11 May 2009 at http://www.criced.tsukuba.ac.jp/math/apec/apec2008/papers/PDF/21.Tran_Vui_Vietnam.pdf

Wagner, J. (1991) Innovation in foreign language teaching. In R. Phillipson, E. Kellerman, L. Selinker, M. S. Smith and M. Swain (Eds), *Foreign/second language pedagogy research – A commemorative volume for Claus Færch.* Clevedon: Multilingual Matters Ltd., pp. 288–306.

Walsh, S. (2006) *Investigating classroom discourse.* London: Routledge.

Wells, G. (1993) Reevaluating the IRF sequence: A proposal for the articulation of theories of activity and discourse for the analysis of teaching and learning in the classroom. *Linguistics and Education,* 5 (1), 1–37.

Wells, G. (1999) *Dialogic inquiry, towards a socio-cultural practice and theory of education.* Cambridge: Cambridge University Press.

Wertsch, J. V. (1991) *Voices of the mind, a socio-cultural approach to mediated action.* London: Harvester Wheatsheaf.

Willis, J. (1992) Inner and outer: Spoken discourse in the language classroom. In *Advances in Spoken Discourse,* London: Routledge, pp. 162–182.

8

Towards Transformative English Language Education: Evolving Glocalization in Textbooks Used in Malaysia

Hajar Abdul Rahim and Shakila Abdul Manan

This chapter discusses the evolving language and cultural policies in the Malaysian English language teaching (ELT) context. In particular, it analyses the cultural content in English textbooks used in secondary school classrooms in Malaysia to find out the extent to which they are meeting the current outlook on education which researchers believe should be shaped by the main social influence of the twenty-first century, namely, 'glocalization'. The analysis reveals certain realities about the cultural content of the textbooks that have implications for English language teaching materials and methods in the Malaysian context and other similar second language contexts.

8.1 Introduction

The term globalization, whilst considered a fashionable term, is also a much contested one (Block & Cameron, 2002). This arises from the opposing views on globalization: whether it is seen as an overpowering entity from the West that promotes 'an extreme of standardization and uniformity' (Gray, 1998) or as an agent of 'glocalization' (Robertson, 1995) that connects the global and local in a productive and creative manner. Whatever the case may be, globalization is a major social influence of our time that has impacted various dimensions of life and changed human experiences at different levels. The effects of technological developments and the new media, arguably the biggest movers of globalization, are causing change in many important areas of human life, including education. And where language is concerned, as has often been claimed, globalization has spurred on the phenomenal spread of English (Schneider, 2011).

The need to communicate in English for various economic and social purposes has increased the demand for learning it, and has significantly impacted on the teaching and learning of English in second language and foreign language situations (Warschauer & Kern, 2000; Gray, 2002). Some researchers argue that the demands of globalization have raised the bar in terms of the knowledge and skills that learners need to have. Block and Cameron (2002: p. 5), for instance, consider 'the new literacies demanded by new technologies, as well as competence in one or more second/foreign languages, as valuable "linguistic capital" (following Bourdieu, 1991). Others have raised concerns about the ripple effect of globalization in areas of English language teaching: the urgency to learn English has created the high demand for ELT programmes and materials, which has prompted fierce competition in the market to supply ELT materials, such that even countries in Europe and Asia that used to be 'in receipt of British ELT, are now exporting materials or offering their own English language teaching programmes to the rest of the world' (Gray, 2002: p. 156). One of the concerns within this development is the cultural content of ELT textbooks. Past research reveals that the focus on cultural content in ELT textbooks is one of the following three: the learners' culture, the target culture and cultures that are neither the source nor the target culture (Cortazzi & Jin, 1999). Yet the current consensus among academics and educators is for an intercultural approach, one that combines and moves beyond these three foci and helps develop the learner's own identity as well as encourages 'the awareness of others' identities and an element of stabilization in a world of rapid change' (ibid.: p. 219). More recently, researchers have begun to draw a link between the intercultural approach and glocalization. It has been suggested that there is an inherent relationship between the two and that the latter as a social process has implications for language education (East, 2008). Glocalization tends to cause a paradigm shift in education 'from transmissive to the transformative', affecting learning and teaching styles, organizational culture and methodologies (Novak 2005: p. 401). It follows from this that 'glocal' cultural content in ELT textbooks is potentially the medium for transforming English language teaching and learning in native and non-native contexts.

This chapter discusses the issue of glocal cultural content in light of the trends in cultural content in ELT that have evolved over the past three decades with particular reference to intercultural communication. It surveys the global-local-glocal evolution of ELT cultural content, which is claimed to be in tandem with the shift from the native speaker model to intercultural speaker model, and provides an account of the relationship between intercultural communicative competence and glocalization. The argument for a glocal cultural content is based upon the case of an analysis of cultural content in Malaysian English textbooks used in schools. To contextualize the analysis, a brief account of the Malaysian English education system as well as the Malaysian English language syllabus is given. The outcome of the analysis and the implications of this on cultural content in English text-books in Malaysia conclude the chapter.

8.2   Trends in ELT cultural content: From global to glocal

The trend in course book content has also evolved to meet the demand of the English 'global course book'. In his investigation of this brand of ELT books, Gray found that they 'have been subtly deterritorialized' with a shift from native settings, such as Britain, to more international in order to reflect 'a growing sense on the part of the publisher of English as an increasingly global language' (Gray, 2002: p. 157). Ironically, these trends have invariably caused global course books to resemble each other, not just in appearance but also in content. This is the outcome of writers adhering to publishers' guidelines on 'inclusivity' and 'inappropriacy' with regard to content. The former refers to 'the need for a non-sexist approach' in the representation of the different genders in the coursebook, and the latter refers to the avoidance of topics that can 'offend the sensibilities of potential buyers and readers' (ibid.). Whilst these appropriations were generally met with approval by users of the books, Gray also found that a recurring complaint about the 'one size fits all' model of global course books 'is the absence of the *local*' (2002: p. 164). Teachers who use them generally believe that there is a need to bridge 'the world of English with the world of the students[,] ... of the place for the local in the global' (ibid.).

Fortunately, the stifling effects of globalization on ELT course book content are limited to those designed for post secondary learning situations and for English for international purposes (Gray, 2002; Cortazzi & Jin, 1999). In countries where English is a postcolonial variety or used as a foreign language, the materials used in teaching English in schools usually adhere to the national educational aspirations. The 'one size fits all' model of the global course book usually does not apply here because, despite globalization, 'the nation-state as an economic and political entity ... continues to exert significant influence in many areas of its inhabitants' experience, including their experience as users and learners of languages' (Block & Cameron, 2002: p. 6). In these contexts, the agents of the nation state have a hand in language and education planning and policy and 'national differences, the histories they arise from and the conflicts they engender are not rendered insignificant by globalization' (2002: p. 7). The emphasis which national education agendas place on local knowledge and the collective memory of the people suggests that the dominant content of English textbooks in this case is primarily local. Research in this area suggests that in many EFL situations, the focus of textbooks produced at the national level is guided by the stipulations of ministries of education (Gray, 2002). Generally, the predominant culture in these books is the source culture, that is, the learners' culture. Local characters and settings are used chiefly because the aim of teaching English is to help students acquire the skill to communicate with visitors about their own culture. The inclusion of Western cultural content varies in terms of degree and is usually limited to stereotypical roles and function. The emphasis on local culture is mainly 'to help students become aware of their own cultural identity' (Cortazzi & Jin 1999: p. 205). In relation to this view, research in some EFL contexts reveals that educators believe that the motivation to learn English improves if the context is relevant to the students' environment and that the inclusion of Western culture is not necessarily beneficial to students' learning (Adaskou et al., 1990; Suzuki, 1999, cited in McKay, 2004). These findings seem to be supported by recent research in Foreign Language (FL) learning motivation and identity construction. There is evidence to suggest that FL learners are motivated to learn a target language to enact 'possible selves' which are congruent with some social traditions and/or habits in the learners' environment (Dörnyei & Csizér, 2002). In the Malaysian English as a Second Language (ESL) context, research suggests that whilst culturally familiar items facilitate second language learning, teachers must be cognizant of social-cultural issues in textbook materials and select those that are appropriate to their learners' culture. These findings essentially dispute the value of including the target culture in language teaching materials and argue for the benefits of localizing the content.

Whilst there is much support for the localization of ELT content, some researchers have warned of the danger of extreme localization. The focus on local culture and the minimization, if not exclusion, of the target cultures can be disadvantageous to students, particularly if the aim of the curriculum is to develop communicative competence. Cortazzi and Jin (1999) stress this point and argue that the inclusion of the target culture in the textbook is not necessarily harmful. Citing the Lebanese case, they point out that in the 1990s most of the textbooks used there were imported, the cultural content is that of the target culture and many Lebanese are bilingual, yet there is no evidence to suggest that the Lebanese feel that their ethnic identity has been compromised or threatened.

The various studies and findings in the preceding discussion underline the importance that researchers and educators place on culture in language learning. Interestingly, there is also the view that language learning should be completely devoid of cultural content. Prodromou (1992), for instance, concludes this from a study of Greek students' reactions to culture content which found that the inclusion of culture, either the target language or the local culture, does not motivate learning. This is indeed an extreme and contentious claim, given the long-standing view of the inextricable link between culture and language: The two are 'a single universe or domain of experience' (Kramsch, 1991: p. 217), which means that the process of learning a language involves learning the culture of the language, even if not explicitly.

The concerns on localization of cultural content in textbooks seem to be diametrically opposite to issues raised by Gray on the global coursebook.

Localization draws in the learners such that they are quite detached from the target language culture, whilst globalization leaves the learners looking in from the outside and, to some extent, marginalized in the world of English. Either way, it would seem that neither the local nor the global methodology for textbook content is successful in giving students an enriching and effective language learning experience. And if the shortcoming of one is due to the lack of the other, it would seem that the meeting of the two is a feasible alternative. In his final analysis of the global coursebook, Gray states that 'the local is always imbricated in the global' (2002: p. 166). He argues that this process is in fact 'glocalization', the meaningful relationship between global cultures and local cultures (Robertson 1995; Baraldi, 2006). The way forward, therefore, to borrow Gray's term, is to develop a '*glocal* coursebook', one that bridges the world of English with that of the student, allowing 'the possibility of two-way traffic, of cultural exchange, of the place for the local in the global' (2008: p. 164).

8.3   Glocalization and intercultural communication

The literature shows that the concept of glocalization came from Japan (Robertson, 1995). It is derived from the Japanese word *dochakuka*, used in the context of agriculture to refer to adapting a farming technique to suit local needs. The concept of localizing the global underpins the term glocalization, 'a neologism which attempts to capture something of the complexity inherent in globalization by conflating the terms global and local' (2002: p. 166). The word and the idea behind it have become indispensible in discussing the synergistic potential of the global and the local in various areas of knowledge including education. Baraldi, for instance argues that 'glocalization has *intercultural* meaning and is created through *communication*' (2006: p. 54). In fact, glocalization is considered 'a product of *intercultural communication*' (ibid.).

Intercultural communication assumes intercultural knowledge, awareness and competence. Byram's (1977) oft-cited publication, *Teaching and Assessing Intercultural Communicative Competence*, began 'a 'top-down' perspective, to discuss what intercultural communicative competence (ICC) means and then to identify ways in which it could be formulated as teaching and assessment objectives' (Byram et al., 2001: p. 2). Intercultural competence is premised upon crucial factors: attitudes, knowledge, skills and critical cultural awareness (Byram et al., 2001). The first component, attitudes, is the most crucial as it involves 'the attitudes of the intercultural speaker and the mediator' (Byram et al., 2001: p. 5). Someone with intercultural competence 'has an ability to interact with 'others' to accept other perspectives and perceptions of the world, to mediate between different perspectives, to be conscious of their evaluations of difference' (ibid.). In a nutshell, the intercultural speaker has a range of abilities, such as having the skill to close the gap between the local culture with the target culture, being culturally sensitive and having the ability to use a number of strategies in communicative situations with those of other cultures, having the ability to mediate between one's own culture and that of another and having the skill to be understanding of the 'other' and to overcome stereotypes. In language education, the intercultural approach favours a holistic personality development which enriches (and does not threaten) a learner's sense of identity in learning another language. It rejects language learning activities that consider the native speaker as an ideal model that cause 'dis-identificatory moments of non-participation or marginalization' (Murphey et al. 2004, p. 85) and cultivates an 'intercultural' learner 'who is linguistically adept (although not 'native speaker' proficient) who has skills which enable him or her to identify cultural norms and values that are often implicit in the language behaviour of the groups he or she meets' (Corbett, 2007: p. 41).

The reciprocation of us–others which is advocated in the ICC approach is what East argues for in discussing the implications of glocalization in language education. People acquire 'vital skills to build more successful relationships, and understanding the social influences at work' may be the way towards an effective language education (East, 2008: p. 156). In relation to this, East underlines that out of the three main social influences of our time (globalization, localization and glocalization), the impact of glocalization is the reality around which language education should be shaped in this millennium. He argues for glocalization as a construct that has implications for a transformative approach to language education as it reciprocates 'us–others' in learning a new language.

This is the motivation for the present analysis of cultural content in English textbooks used in secondary schools in Malaysia. The content and approach found in the books are guided by the national curriculum and English language syllabus. These, in turn, have been shaped over the years in response to global changes in educational methodologies and various local sociolinguistic, socio-economic and socio-political factors at the domestic level. The following section provides an account of the development of the current English language curriculum for schools in Malaysia.

8.4   English in the Malaysian education system: A brief history

Mufwene theorized that the way English developed in colonized countries depended on the type of colony: 'trade colonies', exploitation colonies' or 'settlement colonies' (2001: pp. 8–9). Where the contact was due to trading between English traders and locals, the variety of English used was not a standard one and would have caused the emergence of pidgins. However, when the nature of the colonizers' presence morphed from trade to exploitation, there was more language contact between the colonial and local languages. Malaysia, a former British 'exploitation' colony, provides an interesting sociological and sociolinguistic setting. This is because it is a multi-ethnic, multilingual, multireligious and multicultural country. The population of 28.7 million in 2011 comprises Malays (50.4 per cent), Chinese (23.7 per cent), the indigenous community (11 per cent), Indians (7.1 per cent) and others (7.8 per cent). The various languages spoken include Malay, English, Chinese (Cantonese, Mandarin, Hokkien, Hakka, Hainan and Foochow), Tamil, Telugu, Malayalam, Gujerati, Punjabi and indigenous languages such as Temiar, Jah Jut, Mah Meri, Iban, Kadazan and so forth (Malaysia Demographics Profile, 2011; Abdullah Hassan, 2004).

In the early nineteenth century the British had recruited the people of Chinese and Indian descent to work as indentured labourers in the mining and plantation industries, respectively. English was brought in by British colonial policies and Christian missionaries. The latter had set up English-medium schools in the thriving urban areas of the then-British Malaya. These schools were multi-ethnic as they were open to children of all ethnic groups in the urban centres. Many of the students were children of rich Chinese and Indian businessmen and Malay royalty. These English-medium schools provided opportunities for the students to obtain prestigious white collar jobs in the various sectors of the economy (Gaudart, 1987). Eventually, the products of these schools became the crème de la crème of Malayan society. The British helped set up Malay-medium schools for ethnic Malays in the rural areas. However, the Chinese-medium schools (for ethnic Chinese) and Tamil-medium schools (for ethnic Indians) were established by the local Chinese and Indian communities, themselves, and not by the British, who did not consider themselves obliged to provide education to an 'alien temporary population' or the 'children of immigrant labourers' (Chang Min Phang, 1973: pp. 17–20).

Unfortunately, this quadrilingual educational system resulted in inter- and intra-ethnic divisions and differences. The vernacular schools helped to reinforce the communal identities of the Malays, Chinese and Indians, whilst the English-medium schools fostered greater cultural integration between the three races (Chai, 1977, in Gaudart, 1987). The common bond for the latter was the English language. However, the English-medium schools weakened the traditional cultural loyalties of each ethnic group, causing social differences to surface between the English-educated and the vernacular-educated, and these social differences had to be gradually removed (Gaudart, 1987).

Long-term language policy planning for national development did not exist then, as the British adopted a 'non-interventionist policy' that allowed the various schools to develop on their own (Kaplan & Baldauf Jr., 1997: p. 197). However, language planning was only formalized in the 1950s with the drawing up of a number of education reports which sanctioned some form of bilingual education, 'English-knowing bilingualism' being favoured until Malayan independence in 1957, and 'Malay-knowing bilingualism' being increasingly promoted after Malay was proclaimed the national language (ibid.). In 1956, the *Razak Report* made an attempt to streamline the education system by proposing the use of a common national curriculum and a common examination system, regardless of the medium of instruction, for all schools. It also made it clear that, although the government intended to introduce Malay as the national language, other local languages will be maintained (Gaudart, 1987). In 1957 these proposals were incorporated in the National Education Policy. This marked the transition 'from a fragmented colonial education system to one which was more integrated along national lines' (Malaysia's MDG 2004: p. 74). Education was seen as an important instrument for integrating the different ethnic groups and for nation building, and huge capital investments supported the development of the educational infrastructure through its successive five year plans (ibid.: p. 75).

Malay was made the national language of the whole country in 1967. English, (the official language till then), was still to be used in parliament and courts of law since the change from English to Malay could not be executed with immediate effect (Asmah, 1987: p. 59). The tragic race riots of 1969 resulted in the swift and strict implementation of the National Language Policy, as it was believed that the political and economic status of the indigenous Malays can only be improved if and when the status of the Malay language is upgraded (Kaplan and Baldauf Jr., 1997: p. 197). A common national language (Malay) was also deemed necessary to forge national unity and cohesion. The process of nationalizing the schools began from 1970 onwards with the gradual phasing out of English-medium schools. In line with this 'nationalistic fervour' (David & Govindasamy, 2003 cited in Tan, 2005: p. 52), these 'national-type schools' would eventually become 'Malay-medium' or 'national' schools by 1985 (Tan, 2005: p. 52). Malay was soon used as the medium of instruction in tertiary institutions and public universities.

After 1970, English was relegated to the status of a second language. However, it was still widely used in the business and banking sectors as well as in public universities, where there was still a heavy reliance on English language reference books and materials. With the switch to Malay-medium national schools, students' competency and fluency in the English language began to decline as English was now taught as 'another school subject', giving these students little opportunity to actually use the language (Nalliah, 1981: p. 16). In the second half of the 1970s, and in keeping with 'worldwide reorientation in language teaching', Malaysian schools began to shift their focus from grammar-based teaching to the teaching of 'communicative skills' in the English language classroom (ibid.). This shift was in line with developments in linguistics that began to focus on the view that language is a communicative tool, and that its rules should be learnt in context by linking them to the various functions of language (David, 1990).

This shift in focus from form to communication was considered too sudden, and it became a bone of contention for several scholars in the field of English language teaching in the 1980s (David, 1990). Without sound knowledge of grammar, students were not able to communicate effectively and efficiently in speech and in writing. As a consequence, students in tertiary institutions in Malaysia, especially the ethnic Malays, were found to be lacking in important skills, and this affected their employability. It has also been argued that the ethnic Malays were 'largely monolingual' and, together with the 'segregation of races' in schools, a shift towards a 'mixed-medium education' in national schools had to be implemented (Tan, 2005: p. 53). In 2003, with the advent of globalization and the steady decline of English in Malaysia, the government implemented a new education policy of teaching mathematics and science in English. The decision to readopt English as a medium of instruction for these two subjects met with much public protest (there were arguments for and against it), but it was implemented. This is an indication that the 'Malaysian education system is a highly centralized and bureaucratic top-down system' (Zuraidah et al., 2011: p. 158). With the passing of the Education Act of 1996, the minister of education had 'greater powers than before in many educational matters' (p. 158).

Interestingly, with regard to this change in medium of instruction for the teaching of science and mathematics, the Education Act of 1996 (amending the Education Act of 1961) signalled a 'shift towards multiculturalism' (See Segawa, 2007), which is very much line with Vision 2020. Implemented in 1991, this is a long-term programme goal of the nation to become a fully developed industrialized country by the year 2020. It also affirmed that all Malaysians are given the freedom to practise their own customs, cultures and religious beliefs and, yet, feel that they are still part of one nation (Segawa, 2007). Importantly, the Education Act of 1996 informs all curriculum policies and matters which must be complied with by all schools. Malaysia's educational goals are enshrined in the Malaysian National Educational Philosophy (1989) which states that 'education in Malaysia is an on-going effort towards further developing the potential of individuals in a holistic and integrated manner so as to produce individuals who are intellectually, spiritually, emotionally and physically balanced and harmonious' (Official portal of the Malaysian Ministry of Education).

8.5   Malaysian English language syllabus and textbooks

The above perspectives and orientations are incorporated in the standardized English language syllabus for all secondary schools in Malaysia. The syllabus provides an overview of the English Language Integrated Curriculum for Secondary Schools (its acronym in Malay is KBSM which stands for *Kurikulum Baru Sekolah Menengah*), which aims to 'extend learners' English language proficiency in order to meet their needs to use English in certain situations in everyday life, for knowledge acquisition and for future workplace needs'. Essentially, the syllabus intends to produce learners who are equipped with the four language skills of speaking, listening, reading and writing as well as 'thinking skills, ICT skills, good values and citizenship education' (KBSM, 2000: p. 1). Since English is a global language, ICT skills are emphasized to enable these learners 'to access knowledge on the [I]nternet and to network with people locally and overseas' (ibid.: p. 3). It is hoped that this will help 'develop their interpersonal skills' in order to prepare them to face the world. Grammar is also given prominence in the syllabus. In the English curriculum, knowledge or the content for learning is obtained from 'subject disciplines such as science and geography' and from 'current issues' as well (ibid.: p. 1).

A small literature component was included in the curriculum in the year 2000, in line with developments in linguistics from the 1980s onwards. Scholars (e.g., Brumfit, 1986) have argued for the inclusion of literature in the ESL/EFL classroom as it is believed that it can help students in terms of their language development (which was considered necessary given the steady decline of English amongst students in schools) and in enabling them to understand 'what we are and what other people are' (Brumfit, 1986: p. 257). The literature component in the Malaysian English language curriculum is meant to encourage students to read 'for enjoyment and for self-development' (KBSM syllabus 2000: p. 1). Importantly, and consonant with Brumfit's view, it is also expected to help develop the students' 'understanding of other societies, cultures, values and traditions that will contribute to their emotional and spiritual growth' (ibid.). However, Zawiah proposes that as a postcolonial nation, it is crucial for this literature to focus on 'both individual growth and national development, something that will produce an individual with a strong sense of national identity, yet still be an enlightened citizen of the world' (1999: p. 10).

Zawiah recommends that texts and methods should be carefully selected so that, at the end of the day, the students will be 'enriched by a knowledge of and love for their own literature, yet able to engage meaningfully with other literatures of the world from their own cultural perspective' (ibid.: p. 10). Hence, she suggests that the core corpus of the literature component should include Malaysian literary texts (English translations of Malay literary texts, literature in English written by Malaysian writers, English translations of the vernacular and contemporary writing by non-Malaysian writers). The regional corpus should include English literary texts, American literature, European literature, Southeast Asian literature in English, new literature and so forth (ibid.: pp. 10–11). Essentially, Zawiah initiated the move to domesticate English studies to serve our 'domestic needs' (ibid.: p. 9). It is important to note that the curriculum emphasizes three main purposes of language use: for interpersonal purposes, for information purposes and for aesthetic purposes. The syllabus designed in this way will help to mould a learner who is self-assured in terms of her/his own cultural identity (considering the literature component) and who is willing to know and learn about other people and other cultures. This is in keeping with current trends in language pedagogy, referred to as 'intercultural language learning': the syllabus makes concerted attempts to fuse 'language, culture and learning into a single educative approach' (Liddicoat et al., 2003: p. 43). This is an approach that will help to develop in learners 'an understanding of their own language(s) and culture(s) in relation to an additional language and culture', and in providing spaces for crucial intercultural dialogue and negotiations (ibid.). In meeting the various global and local requirements, the Malaysian English language curriculum shows features of glocalization.

Importantly, glocalization is, in effect, assured, notionally, in the centralized process of textbook production and use. The ministry lays out strict guidelines and insists that textbooks avoid the use of 'sensitive elements' that would refer to matters that are considered 'discriminatory', 'insulting or offensive as pertaining to race, religion, culture, gender, age or occupation'. They must not include 'negative elements' which would refer to 'matters pertaining to attitudes, thoughts, and behaviour which are contrary to noble values in Malaysian society'. Last, but not least, 'subversive elements' must be avoided. These refer to '(a)ll matters which are contrary to national policies' (Textbook Division, Ministry of Education). Additionally, publishers are expected to adhere to ministry guidelines which are based on the National Philosophy of Education, the Syllabus, and the Curriculum Specifications (Textbook Division, Ministry of Education).

The preceding discussion provides a brief account of the institutionalization process of English in Malaysia as well as of the evolution of English language curriculum in the various historical phases. Table 8.1 provides a summary of the development of Malaysian English language curriculum from pre-independence into the first decade of the twenty-first century.

As illustrated in Table 8.1, there are four distinct phases in terms of the evolution of English language education in Malaysia: before independence (1957), after independence (1970s), the year 2000 and the year 2003. The evolution is observed in terms of the medium of instruction as it was changed from English to Malay and then to a Malay-English mixed medium of instruction, the nationalization of schools and, concomitantly, the relegation of English to the status of a second language as well as a shift from a language-based curriculum to one that is more holistic and transformative. The latter is observed in the emphasis placed by the curriculum on the development of a number of other skills apart from language skills, such as ICT and thinking skills, and the inculcation of good values and citizenship education through the literary component. As a consequence, the

Table 8.1   Evolution of English language curriculum in Malaysia

global → local → glocal curriculum			
monocultural → multicultural & intercultural			
English-medium → Malay-medium → Malay-English mixed medium			
grammar-based teaching → communicative language teaching			
language skills development → holistic & transformative curriculum			

Before Independence (<1957)	After Independence (1970>)	The Year 2000	The Year 2003
English-medium and vernacular schools Fragmented colonial education system	Malay-medium or national schools National Education policy which proposed a common national curriculum English was relegated to the status of a second language	The English language Integrated Curriculum for Secondary Schools (the incorporation of literature in the English language syllabus and the placing of emphasis on language as well as ICT and thinking skills, good values and citizenship education)	Malay-English mixed-medium education (Malay-medium with teaching of mathematics and science in English)

curriculum appears to be much more glocalized and provides opportunities for greater intercultural development.

8.6   Analysing cultural content in ESL textbooks using the ICC framework

Given the earlier discussion of the productive relationship between glocalization and intercultural communication, the potential of the ICC as a framework for measuring intercultural communicative content, and the brief account of English in the Malaysian context, the present discussion turns to its main objective of using the ICC to measure glocal cultural content in English textbooks. The focus of the analysis is on the cultural content in English textbooks used in Malaysian schools. The analysis follows Byram's (1977) model for measuring intercultural competence. The constructs that were measured are summarized here (following Byram et al., 2001: p. 5–7) for ease of reference (see Table 8.2).

To facilitate the analysis of cultural content in Malaysian textbooks, a matrix containing the objectives (based on Byram, 1997) of each component was drawn up. The analysis essentially involved mapping the content of the textbooks against the objectives for each construct. For instance, in analysing the content for intercultural attitudes, the objectives of the component, namely the following: Willingness to engage with otherness, interest in

Table 8.2 The framework of Intercultural Communication Competence (ICC) (after Byram et al., 2001, pp. 4–7)

Intercultural attitudes	Curiosity and openness, readiness to suspend belief about other cultures and belief about one's own. This means a willingness to relativize one's own values, beliefs and behaviours, not to assume that they are the only possible and naturally correct ones, and to be able to see how they might look from the perspective of an outsider who has a different set of values, beliefs and behaviours. This can be called the ability to 'decentre'.
Knowledge	Knowledge of social groups and their products and practices in one's own and in one's interlocutor's country. So knowledge can be defined as having two major components: knowledge of social processes, and knowledge of illustrations of those processes and products; the latter includes knowledge about how other people see oneself as well as some knowledge about other people
Skills	Skills of interpreting and relating: ability to interpret a document or event from another culture, to explain it and relate it to documents or events from one's own. Skills of discovery and interaction: ability to acquire new knowledge of a culture and cultural practices and the ability to operate knowledge, attitudes and skills under the constraints of real-time communication and interaction.
Critical cultural awareness	An ability to evaluate, critically and on the basis of explicit criteria, perspectives, practices and products in one's own and other cultures and countries

discovering other perspectives, willingness to question one's own values and practices and readiness to engage with verbal/non verbal interaction were mapped against the content in the books. Based on the ICC, therefore, the analysis draws instances of culture in the books that match the objectives to measure intercultural communicative competence. In all, five English text-books that are used in secondary 1–5 classrooms in Malaysian schools were analysed: *Kurikulum Bersepadu Sekolah Menengah English Form 1*; *Kurikulum Bersepadu Sekolah Menengah English Form 2*; *Integrated Curriculum For Secondary Schools English Form 3*; *Kurikulum Bersepadu Sekolah Menengah English Form 4*; *Kurikulum Bersepadu Sekolah Menengah English Form 5*. These books are written by Malaysians and based on the Malaysian English Language Integrated Curriculum for Secondary Schools. They are approved for publication and endorsed for use in schools by the Ministry of Education.

8.7   Culture in the English textbooks in Malaysia

The analysis of the textbooks reveals that, of the four components of inter-cultural communicative competence, the knowledge component is given most emphasis. The elements which seem to be given the most attention are: the knowledge of local cultural and religious processes, educational system, geographical space, national identities and institutions and processes of social interactions enacted through discussions of beliefs, local legends, food, and relationship between people and between humans and the environment. There is also emphasis on eminent historical and political figures, cultural icons and well-known humanitarians. These form part of the nation's collective memory – a shared sense of heritage and belonging to be passed on to the following generations.

All five textbooks analysed made reference to these topics, suggesting that the people's collective memory and the social processes in the student's environment in Malaysia are consistently given attention throughout their secondary English language education. Besides this, there is also some emphasis on the knowledge of others, globally. This is mostly in reference to well-known personalities who impacted humanity (e.g., Gandhi, Lincoln, Mother Theresa, Nelson Mandela, Marie Curie) and famous geographies of other nations (e.g., the Amazon forest, national parks in Kenya). Interestingly, the social processes and interactions in other cultures, based on literary works and other documents, also seem to receive some attention in the books (e.g., issues of compassion for others, friendship, viewpoints on ageing, and moral values). There are also some instances involving global issues that affect various localities (e.g., tsunami, storms, landslides) and global forums (e.g., Non-violence for Children of the World) which can be seen as an attempt to bring the global and the local closer. Of the ten objectives in the knowledge component that were analysed, two received the least attention. They are knowledge of dominant social distinctions in one's own and others' cultures as well as conventions of communication. There are two instances of the former (eating habits of different social classes, gendered views) but none at all for the latter, which involves knowledge of types/causes of miscommunication between interlocutors of different cultural backgrounds. Further evolution of glocalization here could, therefore, include explicit features of intercultural communication, both within Malaysia and around the world.

The above essentially confirms past research findings on textbooks that are used in countries with a colonial history. The focus on local culture, social structures, beliefs and understandings is in line with the national education philosophy, which places much importance on national integration. The constant reminder of national identities, various ethnic and religious celebrations, constitutional symbols and popular slogans aims at preserving the nation's collective memory and at perpetuating patriotic feelings, respect for one's country, acknowledgement of other local cultures and love for the country. The emphasis is on multicultural competence within national borders.

Whilst there is much emphasis on local culture, the introduction of the literature component in the syllabus has provided the opportunity for a more global intercultural interaction. As discussed earlier, the Malaysian English language curriculum includes a literature component to encourage students to read to enrich their knowledge of local literature as well as appreciate other literatures. The textbooks include extracts, passages and abridged versions of literary and fictional works in Eastern and Western literary traditions. Among others, the texts include short stories, such as 'The Pencil' by Ali Majod, 'Of Bunga Telur and Bally Shoes' by Che Husna Azhari, 'The Necklace' by Guy de Maupassant, 'The Drover's Wife' by Henry Lawson, the poems, 'Monsoon History' by Shirley Lim and 'School life' by Muhammad Haji Salleh. Novels discussed are *A Jungle of Hope* by Keris Mas, *The Return* by K. S. Maniam and *The Pearl* by John Steinbeck. Together, these texts showcase the importance of universal values, such as love, compassion, loyalty, justice, courage, resilience and resourcefulness that transcend ethnic, religious and national borders. These help to bridge the gap between the 'us' and 'them' as they stress the idea of oneness and sameness. Equally important is the fact that these texts provide an understanding of different societies cultural traditions, customs and beliefs. For instance, *The Jungle of Hope* discusses Malay culture and the Malay community's deep attachment to land and their adherence to religious values. *The Return*, on the other hand, shows how prayers and rituals are observed in the Indian community's daily life and during festivals, and *The Pearl* demonstrates the differences in the lifestyle and values between simple native Indians and cultured European types. Skills to identify, infer and interpret implicit and explicit values in the various cultural practices are being honed through compare-and-contrast strategies, small group discussions and simple dramatizations of certain scenes taken from the literary texts. These skills are in line with those found in the skills component of the ICC. There are two main types: skills of interpreting and relating, and skills of discovery and interaction. The former are skills of identifying ethnocentric perspectives, misunderstanding in an interaction and mediating information, while the latter involves acquiring knowledge and operating in real-time interactions. The analysis of the five textbooks shows that there are instances of the second set of skills. There is also evidence of skills of interpreting and relating at very minimal real-time interactional situations.

The analysis also shows that the components of critical awareness and intercultural attitudes could be made more significant in the Malaysian textbooks. There are three objectives in the critical awareness component: identification and interpretation of values in one's own and others' cultures; evaluation; and interaction and mediation. Instances of critical awareness in the literature component of the textbooks are found in the higher level textbook, that is, the secondary level 5 textbook (e.g., dramatize discussing family love). Cultural interaction that involves intercultural attitudes, as with critical awareness, is concentrated in the literature component of the books. Generally, the approach taken in the textbooks does not fully encourage a critical evaluation of issues, although global knowledge and ideas are introduced at various levels in the textbooks. To develop these features would be a healthy future step in the evolution of glocalization.

8.8   Towards glocal cultural content

The content of the textbooks to some extent helps students view the world, not only from their own cultural perspectives, but through other cultural lenses as well. The literature component, in particular, fulfils the requirement of the current Malaysian English language syllabus to develop intercultural speakers through readings and activities that encourage them to seek opportunities to engage and negotiate with otherness, to cultivate an interest in their own cultural practices as well as other cultural practices. Nevertheless, there is a need to expand the breadth of literary texts by including those that have greater cultural diversity. Postcolonial texts which are rich with linguistic and cultural content are highly suitable as they can help bridge the source and the culture of the other. As these texts use varieties of English, they 'can enrich rather than engulf identity and cultural' (Hung, 2009, cited in Houghton, 2005: p. 91).

Culture that is used in Malaysian English textbooks is fairly diverse in spectrum, comprising the source, target and other cultures. However, it is for the most part presented in a static form, as facts to be transmitted to an interlocutor. What is absent is the dialogue between the text and the learner, and the learner with his/her interlocutor. As regards the latter, the learner compares and contrasts similarities and differences between his/her own culture and the interlocutor's culture in terms of food items, clothes, belief systems, stories and folk tales, geography, history and so forth. These are strategies that can harness critical, evaluative and reflective skills, and these skills can be achieved by exploring cultural diversity in postcolonial texts written in English. Research in this area suggests that 'an interactional view of identity is needed in the classroom as identities start to interact in response to learning activity' (Houghton, 2005: p. 91). This view is consonant with the 'cultural identity approach to intercultural competence' (ibid.).

To achieve the above, attention must also be paid to the 'intercultural learning environment' (Jin & Erben, 2007: p. 295). Since 'total immersion in a foreign cultural environment' is not feasible geographically, the only other alternative is to utilize 'Internet technologies' (ibid.). Studies have shown that an Internet-based intercultural learning through students' 'successful tele-collaborations with native speakers (NSs) of the target culture' can facilitate the development of intercultural communication competence (ibid.: p. 296). This would include the use of emails, discussion forums, IM and other internet-based platforms which are popular with the present tech-savvy generation. Although the use of the Internet as an educational tool can be a contentious issue, the fact remains that young children are already using it as a social networking tool. It can be utilized to hone students' language skills and global intercultural competence as they provide 'an authentic conversational environment' (ibid.: p. 297). It can, to use East's (2008) words, move towards 'us-other'.

Significantly, the Malaysian English language textbooks have included ICT skills as an important skill to be developed. Students are already taught how to use the Internet to look up information and to communicate with their friends through email, but they are only expected to write emails to an 'imaginary' friend. Enabling two-way interaction between students and speakers of English from other cultures and localities can help alleviate their 'sensitivity and openness to cultural differences' (ibid.: p. 297). This point was intimated earlier regarding the dynamism of culture and how culture is created through interaction, and that culture learning essentially involves the ability of a speaker to reflect on herself and her interlocutor and vice versa. The dialogue is important, as it would provide the means to deconstruct one's stereotyped or mythologized view of oneself, as one's culture is now being perceived from an alternative cultural lens.

The above suggests that the move towards glocal cultural content in textbooks essentially requires a redefinition of culture in the context of glocalization, one that includes but goes beyond the use of literary texts and takes into consideration current and important social, political and economic knowledge – both local and global – through conventional non-literary texts and the new media. The engagement with diverse cultural material, that is, glocal cultural content in the textbooks can train learners to be open-minded (Byram et al., 2001), a crucial ability for the global intercultural speaker. It will also help to promote the development of critical reflective skills, of the ability to analyse and assess issues that affect the world, and then to relate them to the learners' own personal experiences. In this regard, such skills are indeed crucial as they have a transformative potential for the learner. Learners would be in a position to articulate how glocal issues and experiences have impacted on them, on their sense of identity and on their perspectives of the world. Personal reflection on issues is important, but it tends to be overlooked in Malaysian textbooks. Priority seems to be given to facts and information that are to be transmitted to, and regurgitated by, the learner when answering reading comprehension exercises. It is through such reflection that one is better able to understand oneself and others, and to accept alternative worldviews or perspectives. Reflection adds an important element of 'criticality' and 'intercultural sensitivity' in learners, and these can and should be further honed in Malaysian textbooks.

Glocalization is, as suggested earlier, the fruit of intercultural competence and awareness. It is a meeting place of 'us-other', cultural exchange and 'two-way traffic' (East, 2008; Gray, 2002). The move toward glocal textbook content, based on the Malaysian experience, is a process that has taken

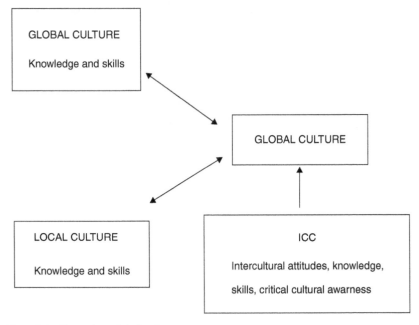

Figure 8.1   Towards a global culture content

various global and local requirements into consideration. Glocal content embraces the global while celebrating and acknowledging the local. As captured in the figure below, glocalization, or glocal culture, is the outcome of intercultural competence and the meeting place of the global and the local. Here, the two forces are non-opposing and in essence are necessary elements that contribute to glocal culture.

8.9   Conclusion

As a social process, glocalization has a tendency to cause a paradigm shift. In ELT, Gray suggests that glocalization which links the global and the local has the potential to bridge 'the world of English with the world of the students' (2002: p. 164). This, as argued earlier, is achievable through the employment of glocal cultural content which includes resources from the students' source culture, the target language culture and others. In relation to textbooks, content from diverse cultures can, besides widening students' cultural windows, transform language learning. Cultural diversity presented in a dynamic manner is an opportunity for exploration and evaluation of social, political and economic understandings, both local and global. It has the potential to harness the critical skills of students in the native and non-native contexts of English language pedagogy and enable them to be citizens of the world.

References

Abdullah, H. (2004) 'One hundred years of language planning in Malaysia: Looking ahead to the future'. *Language-in-India*, 4, 11 November 2004. http://www.languageinindia.com/nov2004/abdulla1.html. Accessed on 30 April 2011.

Adaskou, K., Britten, D. and Fahsi, B. (1990) 'Design decisions on the cultural content of a secondary English course for Morocco'. *ELT Journal*, 44 (1), 3–10.

Asmah H. O. (1987) *Malay in its socio-cultural context*. Kuala Lumpur: Dewan Bahasa dan Pustaka.

Baraldi, C. (2006) 'New forms of intercultural communication in a globalized world'. *International Communication Gazette*, 68 (1), 53–69.

Block, D. & Cameron, D. (Eds) (2002) *Globalization and language teaching*. London and New York: Routledge.

Bourdieu, P. (1991) *Language and symbolic power*, 7th ed. Cambridge (MA): Harvard University Press.

Brumfit, C. J. (1986) Wider reading for better reading: An alternative approach to teaching literature. In C. J. Brumfit and R. Carter (Eds), *Literature and language teaching*. ELBS: Oxford University Press, pp. 256–61.

Byram, M. (1997) *Teaching and assessing intercultural communicative competence*. Clevedon: Multilingual Matters.

Byram, M., Nichols, A. & Steven, D. (2001) *Developing intercultural competence in practice*. Clevedon: Multilingual Matters.

Chai H. C. (1977) *Education and nation-building in plural societies: The West Malaysian experience*. Canberra: The Australian National University.

Chang Min Phang, P. (1973) *Educational development in a plural society: A Malaysian case study*. Kuala Lumpur: Malaya Publishing and Printing Company.

Corbett, J. (2007) *An intercultural approach to English language teaching*. Pasig City, Philippines: Anvil.

Cortazzi, M. & Jin, L. (1999) Cultural mirrors, materials and methods in the EFL classroom. In E. Hinkel (Ed), *Culture in second language teaching and learning*. Cambridge: Cambridge University Press, pp. 196–219.

David, M. K. (1990) 'The bell tolls for communicative language teaching'. *The English Teacher*, 19, MELTA. http://www.melta.org.my/ET/1990/main7.html

David, M. K. & Govindasamy, S (2003) Language education and 'nation building' in multilingual Malaysia. In J. Bourne & E. Reid (Eds), *World yearbook of education 2003: language education*. London: Kogan Page, pp. 215–226.

Dörnyei, Z. & Csizér, K. (2002) Some dynamics of language attitudes and motivation: Results from a longitudinal nationwide study. *Applied Linguistics*, 23 (4), 421–62.

East, M. (2008) Moving towards 'us–others' reciprocity: Implications of glocalisation for language learning and intercultural communication. *Language and Intercultural Communication*, 8 (3), 156–71.

Gaudart, H. (1987) English language teaching in Malaysia: A historical account. *The English Teacher*, 15 (1), MELTA. http://www.melta.org.my/ET/1987/main2.html. Accessed on 1 May 2011.

Gray, J. (1998) *False dawn*. London: Granta Books.

Gray, J. (2002) The global course book in English language teaching. In D. Block and D. Cameron (Eds) *Globalization and language teaching*. London and New York: Routledge, pp. 151–67.

Houghton, S. (2005) The Role of intercultural communicative competence in the development of world Englishes and Lingua Francas. *3L: The Southeast Asian journal of English language studies*, 15, 69–95.

Hung, T. (2009) *How the global spread of English can enrich rather than engulf our national identity and culture. Paper presented at the 15th International Conference of the International Association for World Englishes (IAWE)*. Cebu City: Phillipines.

Integrated Curriculum for Secondary Schools English Form 3; (2004). Choo, W.Y., Low, K. P. & Anthony, S.M. Kuala Lumpur: Elite Teguh Industries Sdn. Bhd.

Jin, L. & Erben, T. (2007) Instant messenger-mediated intercultural learning. *CALICO Journal*, 24 (2), 291–312.

Kaplan, R. B. & Baldauf Jr., R. B. (1997) *Language planning: From practice to theory*. Clevedon: Multilingual Matters.

KBSM (Kurikulum Baru Sekolah Menengah) English Language Syllabus, 2000. http://www.moe.gov.my/bpk/sp_hsp/bi/kbsm/sp_bi_kbsm.pdf. Accessed on 10 June 2011.

Kramsch, C. (1991) Culture in language learning: A view from the states. In K. De Bot, R. B. Ginsberg and C. Kramsch (Eds) *Foreign language research in cross-cultural perspective*. Amsterdam: John Benjamins, pp. 217–40.

Kurikulum Bersepadu Sekolah Menengah English Form 1; (2002). Chitravelu, N., Sitravelu, N. & Hafizah, S.Pahang:PTS Publications.

Kurikulum Bersepadu Sekolah Menengah English Form 2; (2003). Shanta, R, Kurup, U. & Lorenz, S. Petaling Jaya: Setia Emas Publishers.

Kurikulum Bersepadu Sekolah Menengah English Form 4; (2002) Lee, A., Roberts, L. & Chew, M. Johor Bahru: PGI Cipta Sdn. Bhd.

Kurikulum Bersepadu Sekolah Menengah English Form 5; (2003) Lee, A., Roberts, L. & Chew, M. Johor Bahru: PGI Cipta Sdn. Bhd.

Liddicoat, A. J., Scarino, A., Papademetre, L. & Kohler, M. (2003) *Report on intercultural learning*. Canberra: Commonwealth Department of Education, Science and Training.

Malaysian Demographics Profile 2011. http://www.indexmundi.com/malaysia/demographics_profile.html. Accessed on 1 May 2011. Malaysian Ministry of Education. http://www.moe.gov.my/?id=37&lang=en. Accessed on 10 May 2011.

Mufwene, S. (2001) *The ecology of language evolution*. Cambridge: Cambridge University Press.

Murphey, T, Jin, Chen, J, & Chen, L. C (2004) Learners construction of identities and imagined communities. In P. Benson & D. Nunan (Eds), *Learners stories: difference and diversity in language learning*. Cambridge: Cambridge University Press, pp. 83–100.

Nalliah, M. (1981) Communicative approaches to the teaching of English in upper secondary schools in Malaysia. *Southeast Asian Review of English*, 2, 16–25.

Novak, B. (2005) *Transformative school in the glocalisation process. In Managing the Process of Globalisation in New and Upcoming EU Members: Proceedings of the 6th International Conference of the Faculty of Management Koper Congress Centre Bernardin, Slovenia, 24–26 November*, pp. 401–411.

Prodromou, L. 1992. What culture? Which culture? *ELT Journal*, 46 (1), 39–50.

Robertson, R. (1995) Glocalization: Time-space and Homogeneity-heterogenity. In M. Featherstone, S. Lash and R. Robertson (Eds), *Global modernities*. London: Sage Publications, pp. 25–44.

Schneider, E. W. (2011) *English around the World: An introduction*. Cambridge: Cambridge University Press.

Segawa, N. (2007) Malaysia's 1996 education act: The impact of a multiculturalism-type approach on national integration. *Sojourn: Journal of Social Issues in Southeast Asia*, 22 (1), 30–56.

Tan, P. K. W. (2005) The medium-of-instruction debate in Malaysia: English as a Malaysian language? *Language Problems & Language Planning*, 29 (1), 47–66.

Textbook Division, Ministry of Education, Malaysia. http://www.moe.gov.my/bbt/kbsm_proses_en.php#. Accessed on 10 May 2011 United Nations Development Programme Malaysia: Supporting National Development Aspirations.

Malaysia's MDG (Millennium Development Goals) 2. Achieve Universal Primary Education. http://www.undp.org.my/uploads/mdg2.pdf. Accessed on 1 May 2011.

Warschauer, M. & Kern, R. (Eds) (2000) *Network-based language teaching: Concepts and practice*. Cambridge: Cambridge University Press.

Zawiah, Y. (1999) Your language, my culture: Domesticating English literature for the postcolonial classroom in Southeast Asia. In L. J. Mallari-Hall and L. R. Tope (Eds), *Texts and contexts: Interactions between literature and culture in Southeast Asia*. Department of English and Comparative literature. Quezon City: University of the Philippines.

Zaaba, Z. , Ramadan, F. I. M., Aning, I. N. A., Gunggut, H., & Umemoto, K. (2011) Language-in-education policy: A study of policy adjustment strategy in Malaysia. *International Journal of Education and Information Technologies*, 5 (2). http://www.naun.org/journals/educationinformation/19–648.pdf. Accessed on 3 May 2011.

Part III

Learners' Perceptions and Expectations of Teachers

9
Kazakh Students' Perceptions of Good English Teachers: Multiple Heritages in a Culture of Learning

Gulnissa Makhanova and Martin Cortazzi

9.1 Introduction

Every culture of learning is deeply contextualized in local circumstances, traditions and communities and is thus locally constructed and specific; however, the study of particular cultural contexts gives insights into a much wider range of cultures of learning, not least because such research raises our awareness of influential features which may prove to be common elsewhere. The study of a changing situation, like that of language education in Kazakhstan, in which multiple heritages make a complex blend of features helps us to consider other contexts in which complex heritages are becoming normal. Alongside previous internal diversity, many education systems are now increasingly influenced by population movements through which large numbers of incoming learners represent an ever-widening range of cultures.

To know and appreciate students' perceptions of teachers is to understand part of a given culture of learning. The study of learners' perceptions is a key element of current learner-centred approaches, since teachers need to consider students' beliefs and needs in order to facilitate learning activities (Nunan, 1988). Students' expectations can significantly mediate classroom interaction and learning. For instance, they might filter or limit the effect of teaching activities which differ from those expectations (Cortazzi & Jin, 1996, 1999), and they may therefore affect the role of teachers to help perfect students' human and social qualities (Hare, 1993). An examination of Kazakh students' perceptions of good English teachers thus helps us to understand cultures of learning in Kazakhstan, with potential insights for other multiple-heritage contexts.

This chapter first outlines heritages in the educational context in Kazakhstan and approaches to English language teaching and learning (ELT). We then analyse data elicited from Kazakh university students to show how their perceptions of good English teachers have been influenced by changes in the multiple heritages. Here, 'Kazakh' refers to students in Kazakhstan in general; because the Kazakh population is diverse, we will make it clear in the context where 'Kazakh' refers more specifically to the Kazakh language or ethnic group in contrast to other local languages and ethnic groups.

9.2   Education, languages and multiple heritages in Kazakhstan

Kazakhstan, the size of Western Europe in terms of land mass, is a former Soviet country in Central Asia with a multiethnic population of 16 million and two official languages: Kazakh and Russian. Education is compulsory and free for 7- to 17-year-olds. Currently, there is a transition period in higher education: Kazakhstan joined the Bologna Process in 2010 to align its universities with the European degree system of bachelor's, master's and PhD degrees.

With a substantial legacy of being part of a well-educated population, students have high literacy and language skills (OECD, 2007). The UNESCO report, *Education for All*, monitors indicators such as child development, comprehensive primary education, gender equality, literacy development and quality of education, and gives an average sum of such indicators as an Education Development Index: Kazakhstan was ranked in the first position with the highest index among 129 participating countries (UNESCO, 2009).

The complexity of the various cultural heritages that have influenced students in Kazakhstan can be gauged from recent population statistics (The Agency of Statistics, 2010a). Ethnically, 63 per cent of the population is Kazakh, while 24 per cent is Russian (recently the percentage of Kazakhs has risen, while that of Russians has fallen); however, there are still considerable numbers within other smaller groups, notably Uzbeks, Uighurs and Tatars, and virtually all members of all these groups speak the particular language associated with their ethnic group. This contrasts with other ethnic groups of Ukrainians, Germans and Koreans, many members of which do not speak the associated heritage language. In the population as a whole, for the Kazakh language, 70 per cent understand the spoken language (additionally, 13 per cent are learning it), whereas 94 per cent understand Russian. Complexity is recognized in the range of languages used as media of instruction in secondary schools: besides Kazakh and Russian (many schools use both), in areas with significant numbers of speakers of other Turkic mother tongues, media of instruction are also Uighur, Uzbek and Tajik. Changes in the balance within this heritage can be seen in both language and religion. While Russian has long been a lingua franca, the present national policy is to develop Kazakh as a state language so, increasingly, Kazakh is the medium of instruction. While Islam was the major religion until 1730, when Russia annexed the territory, such beliefs were suppressed in Soviet times; they have experienced some revival since the early 1990s. Importantly, however, Islam has been distinctively practiced in Kazakhstan and is less conservative compared to much of the Middle Eastern region: for example, women and men wore traditional Kazakh clothing during the period when Islam was practiced (i.e. until 1730). Within these shifting heritages, English and international influences have assumed increasing roles.

9.3   English language teaching in Kazakhstan

Until the early 1990s, 'English had little significance in North and Central Asia' (McArthur, 2003: p. 20). The situation changed dramatically with the breakup of the Soviet Union (USSR). Since English is, arguably, a global lingua franca (McArthur, ibid.), currently the language has a prestigious status in Kazakh society because knowledge of English enables better career prospects, travel abroad and access to the world. Internationalization of education is officially a national priority as a prerequisite for international competitiveness (OECD, 2007: p. 25). According to the Organisation for Economic Co-operation and Development (OECD) report (ibid.), 'Kazakh students seem keen to study abroad and many clearly have the language competence to do so'. Support for English in its internationalization role is shown in a government scholarship scheme (*Bolashak*) which allows Kazakh students to gain degrees in English-speaking countries, and a 2007 presidential decree says citizens should be able to do business in English and that, consequently, the quality of English language teaching should be improved. Further evidence of the recent growth of English is that 15 per cent of the population 'understand the spoken language' (The Agency of Statistics, 2010a); it is a compulsory subject for university students in their first two years; there is a push for university students to be taught through the medium of English and for staff to publish research in English, rather than in Russian.

With this demand for learning English, the official standards set for the teachers of English are rising: Teachers take regular tests to demonstrate their professional competence and are required to update their skills by attending training workshops. Teachers' professional skills are measured through students' performance, which reflects or confirms a results-oriented assessment of teachers and – as emphasized by William Hare (1993) – the moral and personal qualities of teachers are challenged in the search for efficiency, which dominates in current educational discourses in Kazakhstan, as elsewhere.

Data on the number of English teachers in Kazakhstan are hard to verify. However, the minister of education, interviewed by the newspaper Kazakhstanskaya Pravda (2010), stated that there are 300,000 schoolteachers in Kazakhstan, implying a reasonable estimate of around 30,000 English teachers. As for learners, the number of schoolchildren learning English comprises 95.3 per cent of those studying foreign languages (The Agency of Statistics, 2010b). English is taught in years 5–11 in state schools, but from year one in private schools. There are six English-medium schools (out of 7,702) (ibid., 2010b). Official national statistics do not provide data on the number of students in Kazakh universities, but the OECD report (2007: p. 19) states that in 2004–05 there were 744,200 students in the institutions of higher education. Exemplifying using English for international study, about 4,000 Kazakh students pursue education in the United Kingdom (newspaper, Diaposon, 2010).

9.4   Approaches to English teaching and learning in Kazakhstan

To understand the classroom teaching-learning context in Kazakhstan, we start by describing the Soviet approaches for teaching, which have had a significant impact on the current system of education. The Soviet Union was known for its ideology of collectivism in education; for example, the same course book and methods were used throughout the country (Olcott, 2002; Ter-Minasova, 2005). The educational philosophy was characterized by its 'supervised and rule-ridden' schooling (Smith, 1976: p. 190). Unsurprisingly, this led to the dominance of teacher-centred instruction at all educational levels (Smith, 1976; Ter-Minasova, 2005; McCaughey, 2005). In learning English, the pedagogic emphasis was on drill and 'straight memory work, often unchanged for generations' and special attention was given to 'reading, grammar and penmanship' (Smith, 1976: p. 207). Now outdated, aspects of this teaching tradition are still found in Kazakhstan (Yuzefovich, 2005); significantly, as an outcomes-oriented model of learning is being developed, the outcomes are explicitly defined, *not* as the remembering of facts and performing narrowly defined tasks, but as developing general and specific competencies (World Bank, 2011) – a tacit recognition of the influence of memorization approaches.

However, alongside teacher-centred traditions there was an alternative paradigm stemming from Lev Vygotsky (1896–1934), which shifted the focus to the learner's active role in learning (Smith, 1976; Kerr, 1997). This sociocultural theory of learning had limited dissemination till the 1980s because this Russian scholar's ideas were censored as 'anti-Soviet' (Kerr, 1997). However, when sociocultural theory became available to teachers, it led to wider emphasis on social interaction in language learning; for example, learners engaged in projects working collaboratively in groups independently of teachers (Smith, 1976). Significantly, Vygotsky's colleague, Alexander Luria (1902–1977), had carried out cross-cultural fieldwork around 1930 in Central Asia among people in what is present-day Uzbekistan, who were then undergoing radical social change; this research confirmed their basic sociocultural hypothesis about language's decisive influence to mediate the development of higher cognitive functions (Kozulin, 1996), and sociocultural approaches now form a significant strand in theories about second language learning (Mitchell & Myles, 1998; Lantolf, 2000). Thus, the teacher-centred Soviet legacy had some apparently contradictory interactive practices.

In Kazakhstan, ELT still has features of traditional approaches that do not provide sufficient opportunities for learners to become responsible for their learning – despite the fact that a communicative approach is the officially documented framework of pedagogical instruction (Krasnikova, 2006). Some teachers do adopt a communicative approach; they see themselves as facilitators of the learning process and believe that success depends on the teacher's ability to stimulate interest in English and help learners become autonomous (Krasnikova, ibid.; Mukhamedyarova and Cotter, 2005). These ideas echo Vygotsky's socio-cultural concepts.

This tendency towards more learner-centred approaches in ELT is consonant with the emerging change in educational culture in Kazakhstan from 'transmission-based' toward 'interpretation-based' (Wedell, 2009: p. 33). In the latter, 'knowledge is dynamic and is arrived at through discussion' (ibid.). Rather than a lecture-style transmission of knowledge in which learners are seen as passive recipients, the current objective is to create a collaborative environment for learning English (Mukhamedyarova & Cotter, 2005); this is, inevitably, a challenge for some English teachers. In the experience of this chapter's first author at a teacher training university in Kazakhstan, a communicative approach seems one of the most efficient methods of teaching EFL. However, the relationship of communicative approaches to training in practical pedagogy is not obvious because, reflecting Russian traditions, most teacher training courses emphasize mastering the English language and understanding educational theories. Compared to most European ELT teacher training, methodology courses and teaching practice receive much less attention than theory and are postponed until relatively late in the programme.

Thus, current approaches to ELT in Kazakhstan are shaped under the influence of layers of sociocultural heritages. There are two opposing paradigms of pedagogical foci for language learning. Historically, a structural framework has been more favoured by educators; with the impact of Vygotsky's ideas, however, a sociocultural theory of learning emerged and coexisted alongside structuralism. Kazakh learners' expectations about good teachers are influenced by the current educational practices described above and by other socio-cultural factors to be discussed later. However, given the global status of English and the current ELT associations with active, communicative and learner-centred learning, it may be supposed that English teachers – more than teachers of other subjects, perhaps – are influenced by a third stream of widely accepted practices and ideas from outside Kazakhstan,

184 *Gulnissa Makhanova and Martin Cortazzi*

which should have some influence on their teaching. Indirectly, this third stream should affect students' perceptions of good English teachers.

9.5 The present study

The influences outlined above mean that the present research question of *'What are Kazakh students' perceptions of a good English teacher?'* is worth asking in order to tease out how these multiple heritages have impacted on current students' perceptions, and whether students' perceptions are framed by the more global influence of English and the more learner-centred approaches widely embodied in ELT.

9.5.1 Participants

The participants of the study are 105 undergraduate students of a Kazakh university based in the city of Almaty. They study various social sciences (applied linguistics, business, international relations, etc.) in which English is the language of instruction.

9.5.2 Methodology

There were two data-collection instruments: essays and semi-structured interviews. The students were asked to write one-page essays to answer the following open-ended question: *What do you expect from a good teacher of English?* Open-format items like these essays permit greater freedom of expression and can provide 'richness' of data (Dörnyei, 2003; McDonough & McDonough, 1997). Disappointingly, the students' essays turned out to be relatively short, but follow-up semi-structured interviews explored, in more detail, the students' perceptions and clarified the concepts they were using. Students were asked to give a rank order of the attributes they expected in good teachers.

Because we believe the language of data collection can affect research outcomes (Cortazzi et al., 2011), three languages were used here: English, Russian and Kazakh. Since the students are at an English-medium university, they were initially asked to write essays in English. Those students who found it difficult to express their thoughts in English were given a choice to write in English or in Russian/Kazakh. This approach was applied for interviews, but the students mainly chose to be interviewed in their first languages.

9.5.3 Data analysis

The data were analysed during and after the data collection process (see Kvale, 1996). The analysis during the interview data-collection process involved transcribing each interview as soon as possible after it had been conducted, drawing up an agenda for follow-up interviews and provisionally seeking common patterns in content. After the data collection, for both the essay and interview data analysis, meanings in large blocks of text were sought (see Ryan & Bernard, 2000). Data items were categorized under themes from different perspectives, looking for connections and patterns (Ryan & Bernard, ibid.; Richards, 2003), yielding a frequency order of the attributes of good English teachers mentioned by the Kazakh students.

9.5.3.1 'Good' English teachers

First, we note the central importance of teachers for these students: In our data, 19 students wrote that *learning English depends on good teaching*, while another ten wrote, *Good competent teachers help us to learn English*. A ranked order of characteristics of such 'good' English teachers shown in the students' essays is presented in Table 9.1.

As Table 9.1 suggests, the attributes of a good English teacher as perceived by Kazakh students seem to be in agreement with the list of good language teaching characteristics offered by H.Douglas Brown (1994: p. 430) and can be categorized in terms of technical knowledge, pedagogical skills, interpersonal skills and personal qualities.

9.6   Extended discussion, further results and commentary

It was argued above that multiple heritages in educational practices and Kazakh society may have an impact in shaping the students' expectations of a good English teacher. The ranked attributes in Table 9.1 indicate a relation between the expectations and cultural traditions of the society in which 'a culture of learning' is located (Cortazzi & Jin, 1996: p. 169). In this concept, expectations held by students about good teachers come from the students'

Table 9.1   Kazakh students' characteristics of a good teacher of English (ranked in order of importance) (N = 100)

Characteristics (in order of importance)	Number of students who give significant mentions of these
1. has deep knowledge of English	95
2. has interesting lessons	92
3. is dedicated to their work and is passionate about teaching	86
4. is caring and helpful	90
5. is not too strict but requires students to study	93
6. is fair with giving students marks	94
7. exposes students to cultures of English-speaking countries	84
8. teaches students about life	75
9. is very learned	79

childhood and later experiences of actual teachers in education, but also from general social attitudes and cultural ideas and traditions about education, learning and teaching (Cortazzi & Jin, ibid.). In Kazakhstan, expectations come from socialization in childhood, the students' experience in primary and secondary education regarding teachers in general and English teachers in particular, together with socio-cultural ideas about teachers and language from the web of traditions currently found in Kazakh society. Further ideas are likely to come from the impact on students of actual pedagogic practices of university teachers of English, which in turn may be influenced by international practices and ideas of what constitutes good language teaching.

This correlation between learning and culture as 'frameworks of expectations, attitudes, values and beliefs' (Cortazzi & Jin, 1996) is widely supported in applied linguistics (Harrison, 1990; Byram, 1994; Coleman, 1996; Oxford, 1996; Byram & Fleming, 1998; Hinkel, 1999; Coverdale-Jones & Rastall, 2009). These authors provide evidence that learning cultures are shaped under the influence of socio-cultural phenomena. This study attempts to show that Kazakh students' perceptions of a good English teacher might have been influenced by such broader factors (see Figure 9.1) as:

(1) the Soviet legacy with learner-activity and teacher-centred strands
(2) Islamic conceptions about learning and teaching
(3) a stream of ideas about pedagogy and ELT from outside Kazakhstan

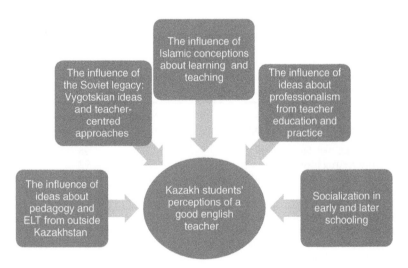

Figure 9.1   Socio-cultural roots of Kazakh students' perceptions of a good teacher of English

(4) teachers' professionalism ideas from teacher training and observed practice
(5) conceptions of teaching and learning imbued through socialization in schooling into local combinations of the above

A sixth area of influence, not explored here, is the possible differences between the various ethnic groups: For this, we would need a much more extensive data set to include reasonable numbers of representatives of each major group. We will examine in detail each of these five strands which emerged as a result of the analysis of students' responses about the attributes of good teachers.

9.6.1 Having deep knowledge

Table 9.1 indicates that 'deep knowledge of English' is the most important attribute which students expect of good English teachers in Kazakhstan. This finding accords with the results of other studies on good teachers in the neighbouring country of China (Cortazzi & Jin, 1996, 2002) and good language teachers in the United States (Brosh, 1996) and Japan (Shimizu, 1995). In their essays, Kazakh students define teachers' deep knowledge of English in the following ways.

A teacher knows vocabulary and can translate words if a student asks; also the teacher should write words on the board without mistakes. The teacher knows rules and exceptions, related to English, and explains them clearly. (KzS 1)
A teacher is able to answer students' questions about the English language without hesitation, for example, new words or grammar. Besides, a teacher should speak English fluently in order to teach it. (KzS 2)
In order to teach us the teacher should know the subject very well, otherwise she won't be able to teach. She should know correct spelling, grammar and should be able to speak English fluently. (KzS 3)
A good English teacher should know his/her subject very well. When a student asks a question about English, a teacher should answer confidently and clearly. (KzS 4)

'Deep knowledge of English' is linked to teachers' ability to answer students' questions about the subject. This is generally expected from a teacher of any subject in Kazakhstan. It is not common for a teacher to say that she or he does not know the answer to a question; typically they will prepare lessons with students' likely questions in mind so that they are in a strong position to answer them. Characteristically, teachers in Kazakhstan are considered to be knowledgeable in their fields.

This perception is similar to that of Chinese students' (Cortazzi & Jin, 1996). In China, students' most common expectation is that teachers should be 'very learned' and 'able to answer all sorts of questions' (Cortazzi & Jin, ibid.: p. 187). This matches with the traditional Chinese notion that 'the central aim of teaching is to provide knowledge for students' (ibid.) and fits practices of training teachers in China, where a significant part of the curriculum is the acquisition of subject knowledge (Gumbert, 1990, cited in Cortazzi & Jin, 1996: p. 188).

Similarly, teacher training programmes for English teachers in Kazakh universities put special emphasis on acquiring the subject knowledge – a legacy of the former Soviet practices. There is a disproportionate time allocation to the linguistic and methodological courses, and deferred practical application, which implicitly declares, as in China (Cortazzi & Jin, 1996), that teachers' primary concern is to provide profound knowledge of the subject.

Although neighbouring Chinese (Cortazzi & Jin, 1996; Cortazzi et al., 2009) and the present Kazakh students expect, above all, that their teacher be knowledgeable, the underlying ground for this perception differs, since there are different sets of beliefs and cultural values. Chinese students' ideas about a good teacher are largely influenced by complex Confucian traditions of learning and teaching (Cortazzi & Jin, ibid.), whereas Kazakh students' expectations might have been framed (in addition to the Soviet tradition) by the impact of Islamic conceptions of learning and teaching. We now explore this possible feature of religious influence.

Islam is the religion of the ethnic majority of Kazakhs and of other Turkic communities in Kazakhstan – 70 per cent of the country's population, compared with 26 per cent Christian, mainly Russian orthodox (The Agency of Statistics, 2010a). However, in common with China, the religious–philosophic influence is tempered by changes in history and secular modernity. Historically, Islam is said to be 'often corrupted by or combined with pre-Islamic practices' (Olcott, 2002: p. 209). While Kazakhstan was first influenced by Islam in the seventh–twelfth centuries, since its annexation to the Russian Empire in the eighteenth century the country has been a secular state, and 'Kazakhstan is the only Central Asian state that can truly call itself secular since it is the only state in the region that has not accorded Islam a special legal role' (Olcott, 2002: p. 209).

Furthermore, Islam in society is not assumed as 'the faith but as traditional Kazakh culture and family practice' (Olcott, ibid.). These practices have kept many pre-Muslim nomadic features, since 'Islam made little impression on Kazakhs until the eighteenth century' (Lapidus, 2002: p. 342). Therefore, Islam in Kazakhstan is different from that of the wider Muslim world (Rumer et al., 2007); it is less obviously a faith practice, and there is an absence of an elaborate system of religious schools (Olcott, 2002). For these reasons, 'Kazakhs have never been *that kind* of Muslim' (Dave, 2007: 12; italics in the original), one who considers Islam as a rigid doctrine to follow, but rather sees the faith as a set of beliefs. Since we focus on perceptions about teachers, we outline Islamic beliefs about knowledge and teachers.

Knowledge has high status in Islam, as illustrated in the following extracts from the *Qur'an*, the most authoritative text and holy scripture for Muslims, and from authoritative *hadith*, or historically transmitted oral traditions (Shakir, 2002):

> Seek knowledge even though it be in China;
> Seek knowledge from the cradle to the grave;
> The acquisition of knowledge is compulsory for every Muslim.

This strong valuation of knowledge in Islam seems to underlie Muslim beliefs about teachers, since teachers are those who help learners 'seek knowledge'. The reason why the students have ranked teachers' deep knowledge of their subject as the most important attribute might also have roots in the following Islamic ideas about teachers (Shakir, ibid.):

> To listen to the words of the learned and to instil unto others the lessons of science is better than religious exercises.
> Scholars should endeavour to spread knowledge and provide education to people who have been deprived of it.

Thus, the ideas about knowledge and teachers could be of Islamic origin, since such verses and sayings are widely known and respected. However, the Soviet ideology also had a notable emphasis on knowledge, and this more recent influence was realized directly through the provision of Soviet education in Kazakhstan, which was free and compulsory. Soviet educational institutions used to highlight Lenin's slogans about the necessity of studying, and the general assumption in society then was that 'Soviet means perfect knowledge of everything' (Ter-Minasova, 2005: p. 447).

Arguably, the Soviet ideology was imposed on Kazakh society from outside, while Islamic conceptions seem indigenous over many centuries but, historically Kazakhs did not generally become Muslims until the eighteenth or even the nineteenth century (Olcott, 2002), whereas Kazakhstan's annexation to the Russian empire had taken place early in the eighteenth century. Therefore, it remains unclear whether the students' expectation of teachers' deep knowledge has Islamic roots or whether the origin of expectations has a blended nature. Still, the likely social balance between these is that the underlying values have more Islamic sources because the ideas of the Soviet educational philosophy circulated in official, more urban circles, whereas those of Islam had apparently more practical influence on ordinary people in daily rural life – even today 46 per cent of the Kazakh population is rural (The Agency of Statistics, 2010).

Further questions remain about why the students have given the highest priority to teachers' knowledge: Have they ranked teachers' deep knowledge as the most important attribute because they had poor examples or, on the contrary, because their good teachers have been visibly knowledgeable? Why do not most research-based studies find this attribute as essential for teaching? Is it because teachers' deep knowledge is taken for granted and, therefore, not reported by the respondents? Such questions could be leading points for further research.

9.6.2   Having interesting lessons

A second most important characteristic of English teachers is that they should have interesting lessons. Other studies on learners' expectations also reported such a finding (Cortazzi & Jin, 1999; Pollard et al., 2000; Oder, 2008). For example, British students ranked teachers' ability to 'arouse students' interest' as the most important (Cortazzi & Jin, ibid.).

For the Kazakh students 'interesting English lessons' mean the following.

Lessons were not just a completion of sentences and similar boring tasks such as copying exercises from the coursebook or replacing one word with another from the given list of vocabulary. I mean that a lesson should have interesting activities which stimulate our thinking, activities which require us to think but not doing the same thing again and again. For example, there was an interesting lesson which I remember. We worked in groups and the task was to decide on a limited number of things we could take to an isolated island where we were going to stay for a long time. We had to justify our decision by strong arguments which created a lot of interesting discussion. (KzS 5)

In my opinion, a variety of things makes lessons interesting. For example, using games in lessons but games should not be just for fun; games should teach us something about English in a way which is not ordinary and that makes a lesson interesting. (KzS 6)

I think an interesting English lesson helps us be more creative and use our imagination. We did a lot of project work on different interesting topics. Once our task was to prepare in groups a presentation on a country where we could spend our holiday and it was interesting. (KzS 7)

To make lessons interesting a good English teacher should use different activities, such as role plays, debates, games and songs which require us to communicate in English and practice it. (KzS 8)

These responses might indicate an application of Vygotskian theory of learning (Vygotsky, 1978): A teacher challenges student's thinking within the 'zone of proximal development' and creates conditions for classroom learning by providing relevant, interesting activities and teaching material relevant to increase motivation (Donato, 1994; Ushioda, 2007). The zone of proximal development is what a learner can do with a teacher's help (or with the help of a more advanced peer) but cannot accomplish alone, and the teacher's aim is that the learner will be independent in this respect later. This zone is thus a social correlate of Stephen Krashen's well-known concept of i + 1 in second language acquisition (Krashen, 1985). It is interesting to note that one of the students' English teachers made Vygotskian ideas on learning explicit to the students.

My teacher would ask us to work in groups and tell each other what we have understood in turns and help each other with things which are not clear. She used to say that when we verbalize what we are thinking, it promotes learning. (Kz S9)

This indicates how a teacher was using Vygotskian concepts on collaborative learning (scaffolding, mediating activities) and made this pedagogical framework explicit to learners. This socio-cultural theory of learning was widely advocated by English teachers in the Soviet Union, and some Kazakh teachers appear to make use of Vygotskian ideas in the teaching and learning processes. The concepts are of Russian origin, although they are now widely elaborated in the West and broadly accepted globally within constructivist practice. Thus, other research accounts of Western students' perceptions (Oder, 2008; Pollard et al., 2000) may indirectly have been influenced by Vygotskian approaches since they have had a deep influence on ideas and practices about language and learning in the West since the 1980s (Lantolf, 1994, 2000). Therefore, this connection may also suggest both a direct Soviet and an indirect Western impact of Vygotskian ideas on students' expectations of good English teachers. Teasing these out within students' expectations could be further research.

9.6.3 Influence of ideas about professionalism

Philosophers of education (Hare, 1993) point out that teaching goes beyond covering the curriculum and meeting the objectives which characterize current results-oriented educational discourses. Hare (ibid.: p. 10) goes on to say that 'education cannot be reduced to a set of "teachable skills"' and teaching should reflect professionalism that is not achievement dominated. It was found in this study that some of these professional attributes, as defined by Hare (ibid.), are expected of teachers by Kazakh students: namely dedication to work and being passionate, caring and helpful.

9.6.4 Dedication to work and being passionate about teaching

This attribute was the third most important as perceived by the students. Below are some students' ideas of how they define being 'dedicated to work' and 'passionate'.

A good teacher should be interested in her/his work. In my opinion, if a person does not truly like his/her work, it is obvious, and this person has an 'I don't care' attitude to others and she/he does not explain properly because it does not interest himself/herself. But if a person is really keen on his/her work and passionate about it, she/he tries to share this passion and enthusiasm. (Kz S10)

On entering the classroom my teacher seems to transform into another person because she gets so enthusiastic and full of energy, she does not simply sit at her desk and give tasks[;] on the contrary, she is very active and is engaged with us, she doesn't frequently check her wristwatch to finish the lesson on time, she does not have that mechanical approach such as entering the classroom, opening the book, doing exercises and that is it – end of the lesson. (Kz S11)

If she is passionate about teaching, in general she has a positive attitude in the classroom and she does not complain about things. She seems happy because she often smiles while teaching. (Kz S12)

The teacher should not just come to the classroom, open the book and approach all the work technically. The teacher should love teaching and be passionate about it. (Kz S 13)

From these students, it is clear that teachers' dedication and enthusiasm are held to be vital for good teaching. Such views – familiar in the literature on good teachers (Hare, 1993; Taylor & Miller, 1996) – are currently threatened by efficiency-oriented educational reforms and special emphasis on teachers' accountability (Hay McBer, 2000). University teachers' workloads are increasing: They are under pressure to implement reforms, meet the standards, produce higher exam results and publish research (Hughes, 1996; Noddings, 2001). While it can be argued that current trends in educational discourses decrease teachers' enjoyment in their work (Hughes, 1996: p. 201), which puts teaching and learning at risk, Kazakh students do expect their teachers to be passionate and dedicated, though Kazakh university teachers are under all these pressures: for example, they are required to have 800–900 hours contact time a year with their students (Matthews, 2012: p. 23).

Teachers' dedication and passion about teaching are followed by the fourth characteristic of being caring and helpful, which also seems to be challenged by the changing ideas about teachers' professionalism.

9.6.5   Being caring and helpful

How Kazakh students' perceive a caring and helpful teacher is shown below.

A good English teacher should be caring and helpful which means that she/he should be attentive to the students' words, behaviour and emotions and react accordingly. For example, if a student approaches a teacher with a learning problem, a teacher should attentively listen to what the student is saying and should try to help by giving more exercises for practice or helping to find another reference/book. (Kz S14)

A teacher should show concern and be considerate to what is happening to a student and if there are problems with the acquisition of the subject, a teacher should not ignore it. For instance, I once had a teacher who was very attentive to students' emotions during the lessons. I remember that whenever I was anxious and struggling to understand a new topic, she would come to my desk and explain a little further or after lessons she would help me by giving more examples/explanations. (Kz S15)

Teachers should consider students' emotions and like a mother should care for their students. For example, if there are learning problems, a good teacher always shows empathy and tries to help. (Kz S16)

If the student has lower level than others, she gives him some extra exercises or some supplementary homework; or she comes to me and explains while others are doing what I didn't understand, she notices if I'm not following the tasks and asks me what I did not get.... (Kz S17)

For these students, attributes like being 'caring and helpful' come together; their view appears to accord well with Hare's (1993: p. 101), that 'a caring person contrasts with one who is indifferent'. Other studies also found this to be a very important characteristic (Hadley, 1996; Oder, 2008; Beishuizen et al., 2001; Nikitina & Furuoka, 2009; Pollard et al., 2000; Morgan & Morris, 1999). However, this virtue of good teachers, is arguably threatened in the present definition of professional teaching 'as teaching that produces specific academic achievements' (Noddings, 2001: p. 102). Under the pressures of results-oriented approaches, teachers may not have time to show a caring attitude toward their students. As Noddings (ibid.) puts it, teachers 'value caring relationships but found themselves unable to establish such relationships'. Similarly, Kazakh teachers face challenges meeting new standards and producing higher test results, which seem to have an impact on learners' expectations of good teachers.

9.6.6   Influences of teacher-centred approaches

Some expectations reported by the students have been apparently influenced by the heritage of teacher-centred approaches. These characteristics are that *a teacher is not too strict, but requires that students should study* (Kz S3); and *a teacher is fair with giving students marks* (Kz S 9).

It is widely accepted in applied linguistics that within teacher-centred approaches learning processes in the classroom are highly directed and structured by the teacher, which results in future conditions for learners' autonomy; however, Kazakh students tend to see themselves as dependent on the teacher.

If the teacher does not push us to study, I find it difficult to force myself. (Kz S12)

A teacher should not be too permissive and too strict but should push us to study. One of my teachers was not too bossy but she always checked if we did our homework and required that we should study. She did not let us do whatever we wanted in the classroom, she always reminded us that our job was to study, otherwise we would not learn anything and as a result would not get good grades. (Kz S18)

Regarding being 'fair' (Table 9.1), it is generally known that teacher-centred approaches tend not to have explicit criteria of assessment and may be subjective, whereas more learner-centred approaches establish clear criteria for learners' assessment (Lantolf and Aljaafreh, 1994), like the widely known example of the Common European Framework of Reference for Languages which explicitly identifies assessment criteria for any European language from beginners to mastery levels.

9.6.7   Influence of ideas about pedagogy and ELT from outside Kazakhstan

English teachers are exposed to a stream of ideas from outside Kazakhstan and widely accepted practices in ELT around the world. Perhaps due to this factor, the students expect their English teacher to *expose students to cultures of English-speaking countries* (Kz S19).

The learners indicate that, besides the English language, they would also expect to learn about cultures of English-speaking countries.

I think a good teacher should teach us about traditions and ways of behaviour in English-speaking countries. Because when we meet a person from an English-speaking country, we should be able to recognize things in conversation which refer to these aspects of culture, so that we know what this person is talking about. (Kz S21)

I like it when a teacher of English covers such topics as holidays in English-speaking countries and how these holidays are celebrated. In that way we learn better about cultures of these countries. In my opinion, it is important to know about such cultural things because we are learning a language of these countries. (Kz S22)

This suggests that the students consider English as a language of English-speaking countries, but not as an international or global language (e.g., see Crystal, 1997), which might imply limited exposure to a wider internationalization through English. Thus, at least some Kazakh students perceive their teacher of English not just as a teacher of language but also as a mediator of English-speaking countries and cultures (though not of cultures globally). Further examples are:

English teachers should be able to show a new world, a new foreign language environment which is full of different peculiarities, something unknown, something that might be completely unusual for you, but which still challenges you to open it and become a part of it. (Kz S23)

A good English teacher should be aware that it is not possible to acquire a foreign language without learning the cultures where this language is native. (Kz S24)

It would be also great if the teacher could teach the peculiarities of different styles of English (British, American, Australian, and so forth.) Of course, knowing the difference involves awareness of the cultural diversity (history, geography, maybe some politics, and so forth.) of the main English-speaking countries. (Kz S25)

In addition, some students reported that they would expect their teacher to obtain a teaching qualification abroad, specifically in English speaking countries, because

a teacher then will be able to show us and share with us cultural experience. In order to master English, knowledge about culture is also important, for example, what to say when a person sneezes and when to say 'How do you do?' and so forth. (Kz S24)

The students' interest to learn about cultures of English-speaking countries can be linked to the teachers' objective to develop a socio-linguistic component of communicative competence which situates the learning of a foreign language in a wider social context where this language is spoken (Savignon, 2007).

9.6.8   Changing images of teachers in Kazakhstan

The results here seem to reflect a changing image of teachers in post-Soviet Kazakh society. Given the long historical involvement with Russian intellectual traditions, it could be argued that teachers in Kazakhstan were respected for their high intellectual abilities. This characteristic is still present in some of the students' conceptualizations of good teachers, but has far less significance than other attributes.

A good teacher of English should not only know the subject very well but also should be erudite which means a teacher should know about the arts, history and literature, know about prominent writers and composers and be aware of their masterpieces; then it means to be aware of various spheres of knowledge: theories in sciences, technologies, and so forth. (Kz S26)

A teacher should know her/his subject very well and be informed of new developments in the world and innovations in technologies. (Kz S27)

Historically, teachers in Kazakhstan were accorded the status of a person of high moral qualities, so they were expected to guide students in life outside the classroom. This is similar to the common Chinese perception of teachers who should 'teach to solve problems in life' and 'help to learn more of the world and about life' (Cortazzi & Jin, 1996: p. 188). Smith illustrates teachers' high status in Soviet society: 'Everyone seemed to accept the idea that school is supposed to know best about bringing up children and that teachers should coach families and set standards for them, not vice versa' (Smith, 1976: p. 190).

However, in contemporary Kazakhstan this idea of respecting teachers as moral examples is not as common as it was previously; this is also clear from Table 9.1. But those who expect a good teacher to teach more than the subject do express deep appreciation for their teachers.

> I suppose that a teacher of foreign language should be more than a teacher, he should be the person who inspires you to do something and to be better; he should advise you about life and therefore I think a teacher should be an example of how to behave in society; we, students, should try to follow a good teacher's example. For instance, one of my favourite school teachers used to quote prominent philosophers' ideas about how to be a good person and that in order to be a good person he or she should have a set of certain qualities. (Kz S28)
>
> A good English teacher like a good teacher of any other subject, first of all, gives his/her students a direction in life, that is, she or he gives valuable pieces of advice how to act in certain situations and which type of conduct to avoid. For example, it is bad to smoke or drink alcohol and use drugs. A teacher should help prevent all those bad things from happening. (Kz S29)

It could be argued that changes in teachers' roles in post-Soviet Kazakhstan were caused by the shifting of ideologies which has led to 'the total collapse of public interest in most forms of higher culture' (Olcott, 1996), and such higher culture includes high moral virtues (ibid.).

Sadly, this situation is not unique to Kazakhstan: Many other societies have experienced changes in the roles of teachers. According to Gordon (2005: p. 459), Japanese teachers are currently facing the decline of their high social status in society due to 'fluctuating economic, political and cultural climate'. Thus, attitudes towards Japanese teachers have been influenced by wider sociocultural factors, as in Kazakhstan.

This precarious position of teachers in society might be due to 'consumer' characteristics of contemporary culture in general (Fairclough, 1995; Bloor and Bloor, 2007; Goatly, 2000), which are now evident in urban Kazakhstan. As the result of a shift within world-leading economies, all the spheres of social life have been reconstructed on a market basis, including education (Goatly, 2000). Some authors even consider teaching as 'essentially a consumer service' (Desai et al., 2001: p. 137). This is heavily reinforced in the United Kingdom by popular use among teachers of such official expressions as 'deliver the curriculum' and to treat schools and universities as agencies of 'service delivery'. Parallel official expressions in Kazakhstan include 'to satisfy demands' and 'to build competitive enterprises' (referring to educational institutions). Does this suggest that, ultimately, a teacher will be yet another person 'delivering' the so-called 'consumer service', profit-oriented like cohorts of sales people? What about the moral significance of teaching? It seems that not without reason such well-known philosophers as Plato, Aristotle and Confucius assert that teaching is a moral activity which is also supported by contemporary teachers (Hughes, 1994; Cortazzi et al., 2009) and researchers (Hansen, 2001). This apparent erosion of students' perceived moral valuation of good teachers warrants further research.

9.7   Applications and implications

The process of exploring beliefs and perceptions with students can raise students' metacognitive awareness and lead to greater self-knowledge which, in turn, accelerates learning (Wenden, 1999; White, 2008). Reflecting on their own perceptions about teachers and discussing peer and teacher perceptions can help students become more successful learners. This point suggests that a productive classroom discussion activity might be to share research results, based on essay writing, to share expectations; this would help students to become better learners – one of the ultimate goals of education and instruction (Wedell, 2009).

The findings have implications for teachers and teacher training. Teachers need to know and understand students' conceptions of teachers, in line with student-centred approaches in which students' ideas are in the centre of teaching instruction (Nunan, 1988). Teacher training programmes in Kazakhstan do not include affective sides of learning, thus knowledge of learners' expectations of good teachers (which include dimensions of care and affect) might be helpful for teachers. However, teachers and teacher trainers should treat such insights with caution because:

What is good teaching in the opinion of a principal may be poor teaching in the view of a pupil or a teacher (Getzels & Jackson, 1963: p. 575) [or vice versa].

Furthermore, learners' beliefs can be limited to idealistic expectations about good teachers, and learners may not be aware of such alternative views as those of the teachers' themselves (Wenden, 1999). Teachers' ideas about good teachers seem to differ from students' inasmuch as teachers' views can be more sophisticated (Morgan & Morris, 1999) and reflect issues of educational reforms (Tang & Choi, 2009; Morgan & Morris, ibid.; Korthagen, 2004). Thus, there is a need for teachers and students to articulate their perceptions of good teachers in collaborative discussions, so that students can adopt a more reflective approach to their own learning (Wenden, 1999; White, 2008) with a view to developing it more autonomously.

Similar insights can be drawn for education administrators. While recognizing the need for systematic assessment of students' beliefs, administrators should be cautious about results of such assessment and balance outcomes with views of teachers and members of the public, including parents.

9.8   Conclusion

Knowledge of learners' perceptions of teachers seems important to develop learner-centred approaches in education and English language teaching. This study has attempted to give voice to learners from Kazakhstan. Insights into what makes a good English teacher in Kazakhstan can help teachers facilitate learning and raise awareness of what is expected from them. It was found that these particular Kazakh students have high expectations of English teachers. Not only should the English teacher know the subject very well and be able to conduct interesting lessons, but they should guide learners to become better human beings, a social role which goes beyond teaching the subject. Such conceptualizations of the teacher seem to have roots in complex and changing cultural traditions about learning and teaching that are present in Kazakh society. These traditions have layers of tensions and apparent contradictions from several sources: the Soviet heritage, Islamic traditions, and modern secular influences, with further tensions from global influences of ELT pedagogies and its associated cultures, which may be modified by other tendencies towards marketization and consumerism in education and an apparent decline of teacher status and threats to the moral valuation of teachers. This is a complex heritage within which learners' perceptions reflect complex layers of cultures of learning: Good teachers, of course, may through their work modify such perceptions and make creative contributions to new cultures of learning.

References

Beishuizen, J. J, Hof, E., van Putten, C. M., Bouwmeester, S. & Asscher, J. J. (2001) Students' and teachers' cognitions about good teachers. *British Journal of Educational Psychology*, 71, 185–201.

Bloor, M. & Bloor, T. (2007) *The practice of critical discourse analysis: an introduction.* London: Hodder Arnold.

Brosh, H. (1996) Perceived characteristics of the effective language teacher. *Foreign Language Annals*, 29 (2), 125–36.

Brown, H. D. (1994) *Teaching by principles: An interactive approach to language pedagogy.* New York: Prentice Hall Regents.

Byram, M. (Ed.) (1994) *Culture and language learning in higher education.* Clevedon: Multilingual Matters.

Byram, M. & Fleming, M. (Eds) (1998) *Language learning in intercultural perspective.* Cambridge: Cambridge University Press.

Coleman, H. (Ed.) (1996) *Society and language classroom.* Cambridge: Cambridge University Press.

Cortazzi, M. & Jin, L. (1996) Cultures of learning: Language classrooms in China. In H. Coleman (Ed.), *Society and the language classroom*. Cambridge: Cambridge University Press, pp. 169–202.

Cortazzi, M. & Jin, L. (1999) Bridges to Learning: metaphors of teaching, learning and language. In L. Cameron and G. Low (Ed.), *Researching and applying metaphor*. Cambridge: Cambridge University Press, pp. 149–76.

Cortazzi, M. & Jin, L. (2002) Cultures of learning: The social construction of educational identities. In D. Li (Ed.), *Discourses in search of members, in honor of Ron Scollon*. New York: University Press of America, pp. 44–77.

Cortazzi, M., Jin, J. & Wang, Z. (2009) Cultivators, cows and computers: Chinese learners' metaphors of teachers. In T. Coverdale-Jones and P. Rastall (Ed.), *Internationalising the University: The Chinese context*. Basingstoke: Palgrave Macmillan, pp. 107–29.

Cortazzi, M., Pilcher, N. & Jin, L. (2011) Language choices and 'blind shadows': Investigating interviews with Chinese participants, *Qualitative Research*, 11 (5), 505–35.

Coverdale, J. & Rastall, P. (Eds) (2009) *Internationalising the University: The Chinese context*. Basingstoke: Palgrave Macmillan.

Crystal, D. (1997) *English as a global language*. Cambridge: Cambridge University Press.

Dave, B. (2007) *Kazakhstan: Ethnicity, language and power*. London: Routledge.

Desai, S., Damewood, E. & Jones, R. (2001) Be a good teacher and be seen as a good teacher. *Journal of Marketing Education*, 23, 136–44.

Decrees of the President of the Republic of Kazakhstan (2007) Retrieved June 3, 2010 from http://akorda.kz/en/speeches/addresses_of_the_president_of_kazakhstan

Diaposon (2010) *Kazakh people abroad*. Retrieved June 5, 2010 from http://www.nomad.su/?a=14–201003240015

Donato, R. (1994) Collective scaffolding in second language learning. In J. Lantolf and G. Appel (Eds.), *Vygotskian approaches to second language research*. Norwood, NJ: Ablex, pp. 33–56.

Dörnyei, Z. (2003) *Questionnaires in second language research: Construction, administration, and processing*. London: Lawrence Erlbaum Associates.

Fairclough, N. (1995) *Critical discourse analysis: The critical study of language*. London: Longman.

Getzels, J. W. & Jackson, P. W. (1963) The teacher's personality and characteristics. In N. Gage, *Handbook of research on teaching*. Chicago: Rand McNally & Company, pp. 506–83.

Goatly, A. (2000) *Critical reading and writing*. London: Routledge.

Gordon, J. (2005) The crumbling pedestal: Changing images of Japanese teachers. *Journal of Teacher Education*, 19 (5), 359–79.

Gumbert, E. B. (1990) *Fit to teach: Teacher Education in International Perspective*. Atlanta, CA: Georgia State University.

Hadley, G. (1996) The culture of learning and the good teacher in Japan: An analysis of student views. *The Language Teacher*, 20 (9), 53–55.

Hansen, D. (2001) Teaching as a moral activity. In V. Richardson (Ed.), *Handbook of research on teaching*. Washington D.C.: American Educational Research Association, pp. 826–57.

Hare, W. (1993) *What makes a good teacher*. London: The Althouse Press.

Harrison, B. (Ed.) (1990) *Culture and the language classroom*. London: Macmillan Modern English.

Hay McBer, H. (2000) *Research into teacher effectiveness: a model of teacher effectiveness*. Report by Hay McBer to the Department of Education and Employment.

Hinkel, E. (Ed.) (1999) *Culture in second language teaching and learning*. Cambridge: Cambridge University Press.

Hughes, M. (1994) Introduction to the edition. In M. Hughes (Ed.), *Perceptions of Teaching and Learning*. Clevedon: Multilingual Matters, pp. 1–5.

Hughes, M. (1996) *Teaching and learning in changing times*. Oxford: Blackwell Publishers.

Kazakhstanskaya Pravda (2010) *Interview with Mr. Tuimebayev*. Retrieved 5 June 2010 from http://thenews.kz/2010/04/24/336882.html

Kerr, S. (1997) *Why Vygotsky? The role of theoretical psychology in Russian education reform*. Annual Meeting of the American Association for the Advancement of Slavic Studies. Seattle: University of Washington. Retrieved 12 June 2010 from http://faculty.washington.edu/stkerr/whylsv.html

Korthagen, F. (2004) In search of the essence of a good teacher: towards a more holistic approach in teacher education. *Teaching and Teacher Education*, 20, 77–97.

Kozulin, A. (1996) The concept of activity in Soviet psychology: Vygotsky, his disciples and critics, In H. Daniels (Ed.), *An introduction to Vygotsky*. London: New York, pp.99–122.

Krashen, S. (1985) *The input hypothesis: issues and implications*. London: Longman.

Krasnikova, L. (2006) *Changing perspectives in teaching and learning languages*. Presented at the conference of National Association of Teachers of English in Kazkhstan. Retrieved 7 June 2010 from http://www.natek.kz.iatp.net/2006/Krasnikova.rtf

Kvale, S. (1996) *Interviews: An introduction to qualitative research*. London: Sage.

Lantolf, J. (1994) Introduction to the special issue. *Modern Language Journal*, 78 (iv), 418–20.

Lantolf, J. (Ed.) (2000) *Socio-cultural theory and second language learning*. Oxford: Oxford University Press.

Lantolf, J. & Aljaafreh, A. (1994) Negative feedback as regulation and second language Learning in the zone of proximal development. *The Modern Language Journal*, 78, 465–83.

Lapidus, I. (2002) *A history of Islamic societies*. Cambridge: Cambridge University Press.

Matthews, D. (2012) The boosters are in place…. *Times Higher Education*, 8 March, 22–23.

McArthur, T. (2003) English as an Asian Language. Some observations on roles and realities in the world's largest continent. *English Today*, 74 (19/2), 19–22.

McCaughey, K. (2005) The kasha syndrome: English language teaching in Russia. *World Englishes*, 24 (4), 455–59.

McDonough, J. & McDonough, S. (1997) *Research methods for language teachers*. London: Arnold.

Mitchell, R. & Myles, F. (Eds.) (1998) *Second language learning theories*. London: Arnold.

Morgan, C. & Morris, G. (1999) *Good teaching and learning: Pupils and teachers speak*. Buckingham: Open University Press.

Mukhamedyarova, Zh. & Cotter, M. (2005) Interactive methods of teaching as a condition for developing students' independent learning skills in Kazakhstan and the U.S. *International Education*, 34 (2), 62–70.

Nikitina, L. & Furuoka, F. (2009) Teacher–Student relationship and the conceptualisation of the 'good language teacher': Does culture matter? *Asian EFL Journal*, 11 (2), 163–87.

Noddings, N. (2001) The caring teacher. In V. Richardson (Ed.), *Handbook of research on teaching*. Washington D.C.: American Educational Research Association, pp. 99–105.

Nunan, D. (1988) *The learner-centred curriculum: a study in second language teaching*. Cambridge: Cambridge University Press.

Oder, T. (2008) The professional foreign language teacher in Estonia: students' and principals' perceptions. *Teacher Development*, 12 (3), 237–46.

Olcott, M. (1996) *Library of congress: Country studies. Kazakhstan*. Retrieved 10 June 2010, from http://lcweb2.loc.gov/cgi-bin/query/r?frd/cstdy:@ field%28DOCID+kz0031%29.

Olcott, M. (2002) *Kazakhstan: Unfulfilled promise*. Washington D.C.: Brookings Institution Press.

Organization of Development and Economic Cooperation (OECD) and World Bank (2007). *Reviews of national policies for education: Higher education in Kazakhstan*. Paris: OECD Publishing.

Oxford, R. (Ed.) (1996) *Language learning strategies around the world: Cross-cultural perspectives*. Honolulu: University of Hawaii.

Pollard, A., Triggs, P., Broadfoot, P., McNess, E. & Osborn, M. (2000) *What pupils say: Changing policy and practice in primary education*. London: Continuum.

Richards, K. (2003) *Qualitative inquiry in TESOL*, Houndmills: Palgrave Macmillan.

Rumer, E., Trenin, D. & Zhao, H. (2007) *Central Asia: views from Washington, Moscow, and Beijing*. London: M. E. Sharpe.

Ryan, G.W. & Bernard, H. R. (2000) Data management and analysis methods. In K. Denzin and Y. S. Lincoln (Ed.), *Handbook of Qualitative Research*. London: Sage, pp. 769–802.

Savignon, S. (2007) Beyond communicative language teaching: What's ahead? *Journal of Pragmatics*, 39, 207–20.

Shakir, M. (translated) (2002) *The Qur'an*. New York: Tahrike Tarsile Qur'an.

Shimizu, K. (1995) Japanese college student attitudes towards English teachers: a survey. *The Language Teacher*, 19 (10). Retrieved 3 May 2010 from electronic version http://www.jalt-publications.org/tlt/files/95/oct/shimizu.html.

Smith, H. (1976) *The Russians*. London: Sphere Books Limited.

Tang, S. & Choi, P. (2009) Teachers' professional lives and continuing professional development in changing times. *Educational Review*, 61 (1), 1–18.

Taylor, P. & Miller, S. (1996) *The primary professional: A study of professionalism in primary education*. Birmingham: Educational Partners.

Ter-Minasova, S. (2005) *Traditions and innovations: English language teaching in Russia*. *World Englishes*, 24 (4), 445–54.

The Agency of Statistics of the Republic of Kazakhstan (2010a) *The results of the national population census in 2009*, Astana: Retrieved 15 March 2012 from http://www.eng.stat.kz/news/Pages/n1_12_11_10.aspx

The Agency of Statistics of the Republic of Kazakhstan (2010b) *Information on pupils learning foreign languages*. Retrieved 2 June 2010 from http://www.stat.gov.kz.

UNESCO (2009) *EFA global monitoring report: Summary*. Paris: UNESCO Publishing.

Ushioda, E. (2007) Motivation, autonomy and sociocultural theory. In P. Benson, *Learner autonomy 3: Teacher and learner perspectives*. Dublin: Authentik, pp. 5–24.

Vygotsky, L. (1978) *Mind in society: The development of higher psychological processes.* Cambridge, MA: Harvard University Press.

Wedell, M. (2009) *Planning for educational change: Putting people and their perspectives first.* London: Continuum.

Wenden, A. (1999) An introduction to metacognitive knowledge and beliefs in language learning: beyond the basics. *System*, 27, 435–41.

White, C. (2008) Beliefs and good language learners. In C. Griffiths, *Lessons from good language learners.* Cambridge: Cambridge University Press, pp. 120–29.

World Bank (2011) Retrieved 15 March 2012: http//go.worldbank.org/VHWF60J860

Yuzefovich, N. (2005) English in Russian cultural contexts. *World Englishes*, 24 (4), 509–16.

10

'He or She?' Examining Cultural Influences on Iranian Language Learners' Perceptions of Teacher Efficacy

Majid Nemati and Shiva Kaivanpanah

10.1 Introduction

This chapter aims to extend our understanding of cultural perspectives on gender in relation to perceptions of effective language teachers by examining how learners view male and female teachers and how these views compare with those of the teachers. Language learners are sometimes asked about *good* teachers, but they are rarely asked about their views of the efficacy of their *male* teachers compared with that of *female* ones – and for a number of reasons. This is an even rarer question, at least in public, when it concerns teachers' evaluation of their colleagues of the opposite sex. Many studies have focused on the concept of teacher efficacy, in general, and some have examined the effect of learners' genders, ages, and language proficiency on their perceptions of teacher efficacy, but few studies have compared teachers' and language learners' perceptions in this regard. An additional complexity is how gender perceptions might be affected by the cultural setting in which teachers work: There is a need to understand how learners' views of effective teachers are influenced by their context of learning, especially when it comes to the gender of the teacher in a gender-sensitive society such as that of Iran. Here, we first provide a brief outline of English language teaching (ELT) and considerations of gender in education in Iran, then focus on gender perceptions of both teachers and learners of English.

In Iran, students begin to learn English as a foreign language (FL) for three years in the 'guidance school' (middle school, from grade 6, at the age of 12); English is compulsory, and this continues in the three years of secondary school and one-year pre-university courses. English is a crucial part of the highly competitive university entrance exams. In schools, there is some emphasis on traditional grammar teaching and on passing exams.

Some students attend language institutes or private schools to enhance their learning of English. Since 2007 a national curriculum has put more emphasis on communicative approaches to learning the language; however, students have little opportunity to practise English outside formal classes, so language input comes predominantly through their teachers. The English teachers are nearly all non-native speakers who have spent four years at university to graduate in English; they teach English to students whose contact with the target language (L2) is limited to the classroom, and whose exposure to authentic language, if any, comes mainly from films or other audio materials: This is also the case for many teachers and is felt to be a constraint. Researchers in ELT and applied linguistics in Iran are, however, generally well-informed and publish their work in local journals as well as international ones. Many have been trained through established local masters and doctoral programmes; some have been trained outside Iran. Nationally, English is considered important for international links and, for many among the Iranian population of over 70 million (two thirds of whom are under the age of 30), English is Iran's primary window on the world.

Outsiders who are unfamiliar with modern Iran may have quite different ideas about the question of gender in Iran (perhaps based on representations in the global media) compared to how the insiders – Iranian students and teachers – perceive gender and good teachers. However, to understand different cultures of learning, it is essential to gain some understanding of the inside views, beliefs and interpretations of experience of the participants in particular cultures. As we gain insights from one cultural context (perhaps one which is less familiar), it should prompt us to reflect on other cultural contexts (those in which we have a primary involvement): We learn about cultures of learning through appreciation of tensions between diversity and universality, between local differences and identities and wider, perhaps global, features.

Regarding female roles in education and society in Iran, there has been some understandable tension between tradition and modernity, between the perceived stability and tranquillity of women's roles in the family and home, and the development of contemporary roles relating to women as citizens who make meaningful socio-economic contributions to society, say through developing advanced knowledge and skills in professional activity. Traditionally in Iran 'typical' characteristics for women are piety, submissiveness, and domesticity, while authority in social behaviour is commonly perceived to be held by men. The images of women in Iran held by outsiders, perhaps disseminated through international media and influenced by external appearances, may reinforce such ideas. However, these social images may be gender stereotypes – conventionally simplified and standardized conceptions or images concerning the typical male and female social roles – both domestically and socially. As the product of social activity, gender stereotypes are neither perpetual nor static. They are influenced by social ideology at certain periods of time; they are changing, even at times reversing, with every significant social transformation. This change and 'crossing' of gender stereotypes will be discussed later.

While female teachers have tended to teach in girls' schools and male teachers in boys' schools, male and female academics in universities teach both male and female students. Statistics may counter some external stereotypes: They show huge advances in gender achievements in education in Iran over recent decades. In schools the gender parity index, based on the male–female ratio, is very high, and female enrolment compares favourably in international contexts (Mehran, 2003). Female teachers comprise around 54 per cent in primary schools and 46 per cent in secondary schools. In secondary schools, there are different gender balances among students in different curricula branches: female students may comprise around 43 per cent in maths and physics but 62 per cent in experimental sciences, 55 per cent in literature but only 30 per cent in technical/vocational branches. At university level, female students have been 50 per cent or more of registered students since 1999; female enrolment can be 70 per cent in some fields, like science and engineering. Clearly, both as learners and teachers, women have significant engagement in education.

This research project investigates participants' perceptions of 'good' teachers and how their gender shapes these perceptions. It was conducted with a sample of university students and English language teachers in Iran. Participants' views concerning teacher efficacy were elicited through a questionnaire, with a particular focus on such components as teacher's knowledge, teaching skills, evaluation, classroom management, behaviour, and appearance among male and female teachers. Students were also interviewed to obtain a more in-depth understanding of what shapes their perception and how these perceptions are rooted in culture.

10.2   Effective teachers

The notion of an effective teacher is a key issue for all participants in education. Teacher *efficacy* relates to teacher effectiveness in producing intended results in student learning, so perceptions of efficacy are a likely influence on how teachers teach and students learn. An understanding of relevant principles should help teachers to be better managers of classroom learning; it should help teacher educators to enable novice teachers to develop sounder pedagogies. So, the present study of teacher efficacy is galvanized by the following assumptions. First, that it is possible to distinguish effective from less effective English language teachers and to glean participants' perceptions relating to the distinction; second, that male and female language learners will have different notions of teacher efficacy, mainly because their socialization in learning contexts might generate differing gender-based expectations; third, non-native speakers language teachers are not as fully proficient in the target language as they would wish to be. This third assumption and related perceptions of teachers are seen by participants as clear constraints on ELT in Iran and are believed to affect how well students are likely to learn the language.

To become a distinctively 'good' language teacher, an understanding of the characteristics that contribute to effective teaching is helpful; this is a key issue for FL teachers because 'language teacher education presupposes an understanding of what specifically it means to be a language teacher and, therefore, insight into the distinctive characteristics of language teachers is central to the work of language teacher educators' (Borg, 2006: pp. 3–4). There is, however, no single, accepted definition for effective FL teaching: Being and becoming such a teacher are different processes compared to teachers of other subjects because, 'In foreign language teaching, the content and the process for learning the content are the same. In other words, in foreign language teaching, the medium is the message' (Hammadou & Bernhardt, 1987: p. 302). Nevertheless, researchers do agree on some dimensions that describe effective teaching, regardless of subject matter (Bell, 2005: p. 259), and many studies have sought to identify these dimensions as perceived by language learners or language teachers. For example, Borsh (1996) includes language teachers' knowledge and command of the L2; their ability to organize, explain and clarify, to arouse and sustain students' interests and motivation; their sense of fairness; and their availability to students.

In the United States, the national association of foreign language teaching supervisors, NADSFL, has set standards relating to communication, connections, comparisons, cultures, and communities (the 5Cs), which include the following characteristics of effective FL teaching (NADSFL, 1999). The teachers should:

- set high expectations; organize learning to engage and motivate all learners in purposeful communication; arrange a predominance of student activity, including individual, pair and group work, and student questioning as well as answering;
- encourage student risk-taking in a supportive environment and handle student errors in appropriate ways that include self-correction and re-teaching;
- develop both formal and informal assessment and hopefully include continuous self-assessment of progress for both students and teachers;
- include cultural components in all activities and develop positive attitudes towards cultural diversity;
- guide students to use all levels of thinking skills to repeat, recognize, and recall, but also to apply, create and predict language, and take account of diverse learning styles;
- use both print (but without being text-bound) and non-print materials, which include authentic target language; use technology appropriately

where it is available; display student work that is instructive, motivational, and informative.

Another organization in the United States which supports new FL teachers, INSTAC (2002), proposes that teachers should

(1) be proficient in the language they teach, understand the language as a system, and the culture(s) of those who use it;
(2) understand how students learn and develop, and be able to relate this to their development of language proficiency and cultural understanding and provide ample learning experiences;
(3) value individual differences and understand that learners differ in their knowledge, experiences, abilities, needs, and approaches to language learning, and create appropriate learning opportunities;
(4) use a variety of strategies to help learners develop language proficiency, build cultural understanding, and develop critical thinking skills;
(5) provide learners with an interactive and supportive learning environment that promotes student self-motivation and, thus, their language learning and cultural understanding;
(6) use effective verbal and non-verbal communication to foster language development and cultural understanding;
(7) plan learning on the basis of teachers' knowledge of the target language and cultures, learners, standards-based curriculum, and the learning context;
(8) use a variety of assessment strategies to monitor student learning, to inform language and culture instruction, and to report student progress;
(9) be reflective individuals who evaluate the effects of their practices on learners and actively look for opportunities to grow professionally;
(10) develop good relationships with their colleagues, learner families, and agencies in the community in order to support students' learning.

Several research studies confirm these characteristics, though in different terms. Borg (2006) studied over 200 FL teachers from different contexts to ascertain any distinctive characteristics of language teachers compared to teachers of other subjects: There were distinctions in terms of the nature of the subject, the content of teaching, the teaching methodology, teacher–learner relationships, and contrasts between native and non-native speakers. Borg raised the need to define FL teachers' distinctive characteristics with reference to specific contexts rather than globally, to compare insider views on such distinctiveness with those of outsiders. Bell (2005), studying teachers of European languages to English speakers, found strong agreement on a number of teacher behaviours and attitudes related to FL teaching and argued that the more we know about teachers' beliefs, the more professionals are able to produce models of teacher preparation and evaluation that better reflect behaviours and attitudes of FL teachers. Reber (2001) examined teacher perceptions of a similar group of teachers and found that there was an emerging professional consensus regarding a number of teacher behaviours and attitudes related to FL teaching. Bauml (2009) analysed the conceptions of pre-service teachers concerning the professional characteristics of effective teachers, their observations of those characteristics in early childhood classrooms, and their personal engagement with those characteristics. Participants identified relational characteristics (such as caring for, respecting, and getting to know students) more frequently than instructional traits (e.g., having high standards; preparing fun lessons) and valued these relational qualities for their impact on student learning and behaviour. This suggests that teachers' relationships with students can foster learning and promote appropriate student behaviour: Professional characteristics of effective teachers can be defined in terms of pedagogical strengths enhanced by interpersonal connections with students.

10.3   Teacher and learner beliefs about effective language teaching

Having realistic and positive beliefs helps teachers to overcome problems and uphold student motivation, while unrealistic or negative beliefs can lead to a decline in student motivation and to frustration and anxiety (Bernat, 2007). Studies examining the relationship of learner beliefs and teacher beliefs have found a considerable amount of mismatch between them. Perhaps this is inevitable; there are potential mismatches between what students see as effective and what is believed professionally to be effective (Brown, 2009), but these beliefs may vary culturally in different contexts and may have different effects, including an effect of classroom tension (Kern,1995). To explore such mismatch areas, Brown (2009) compared teachers' and students' ideals about effective teacher behaviours and found that students seemed to favour a grammar-based approach, whereas their teachers preferred a more communicative classroom. Other mismatches were found regarding target language use, error correction, and group work – implying that teachers should be more willing to know more about their students' belief systems and involve them more in discussions about their own belief systems, an idea elaborated across cultures with reference to reciprocal benefits of articulating cultures of learning (Jin & Cortazzi, 1998; Cortazzi & Jin, 2002).

Some researchers have investigated teacher efficacy through ranking procedures. In Korea, Park and Lee (2006) asked high school teachers and students to rank relevant characteristics according to their importance. Teachers' responses differed from those of students in areas related to English proficiency, pedagogical knowledge, and socio-affective skills. While teachers ranked English proficiency the highest, the students ranked pedagogical knowledge the highest. Male students valued different characteristics from female students concerning socio-affective skills; male students valued teachers' sense of humour more than female students did, whereas females gave higher ranking to pronunciation proficiency, teaching how to learn English, and treating students fairly. The high-achieving students valued teachers' pedagogical knowledge and socio-affective skills significantly more than did low-achieving students. Some teacher characteristics, such as reading and speaking proficiency – arousing students' interest in learning English, and building students' self-confidence and motivation – were considered important by all participants.

Borsh (1996) studied personal, pedagogical, and interactional characteristics of effective teachers among FL teachers and high school students by asking participants to choose three major characteristics from a list and rank them in order of importance. High student–teacher agreement was found regarding teachers' knowledge of the L2 and the ability to transmit this. They also believed that effective FL teachers should have the ability to organize, explain, and clarify, and to arouse and sustain interest and motivation among students; they should be fair to students by showing neither favouritism nor prejudice and be available to students after class. Perhaps, surprisingly, other factors perceived as least important for the effective language teacher included knowledge and positive attitudes toward the L2 culture, conducting the lesson in the L2, having knowledge of the curriculum, a classroom research orientation, readiness for in-service training, a sense of humour – and the teacher's gender and appearance.

In Iran, research on the relationship between learners' and teachers' perceptions of effective FL teachers is largely unexplored. Among the few published studies including gender, Babai Shishavan (2010) asked 59 English language teachers and 215 university or school language learners (in high school or private language institutes) to complete a 46-item questionnaire exploring the characteristics of an effective English language teacher. Significant differences were found between the responses of male and female participants in both the teacher and the learner groups. Female learners focused more than males on teacher characteristics, such as: alleviating students' anxiety and arousing students' motivation. Males agreed more than female teachers that following syllabus tightly, sticking to administrative rules and regulations, and teaching English in students' mother tongues are the qualities of an effective FL teacher. Female teachers, on the other hand, agreed more strongly than did the male teachers that an effective English language teacher should be able to pronounce English well. It was concluded that studying perceptions of male and female teachers and learners is beneficial: It gives insights into whether variables like participants' genders affect their expectations of an effective teacher and how this relates to their status as a teacher or student.

The following questions were addressed in the present study to further investigate the cultural aspects of teacher efficacy:

(1) Is there a significant difference concerning students' views and teachers' views on teaching behaviours and attitudes that contribute to effective teaching?
(2) Does the gender of respondents affect their views on the teaching behaviours and attitudes that contribute to effective teaching?
(3) Do university teachers of the same gender regard themselves as more effective than teachers of the opposite gender?

10.3.1   Participants

The participants in this phase of study (investigating the first and second research questions) were 100 university students majoring in English, French, German, and Japanese as foreign languages in the University of Tehran. All were native speakers of Persian who were learning these languages as part of a BA program. Their ages ranged from 18 to 25. There were also 50 language teachers. For the third research question, 20 university professors, both male and female, were interviewed.

10.3.2   Instruments

The participants received a questionnaire on their perception of effective FL teachers. It was developed by translating Bell's (2005) questionnaire into Persian. Two teachers independently checked the translation, and the questionnaires were piloted with 35 students who were asked to highlight items that were not understandable. The final version comprised 31 items that were grouped into 11 categories. These focused on language form, culture, error correction, practice, the use of L2, grouping, teaching, testing, strategies, the use of L1, and stress management. Participants' responses were recorded on a five-point Likert scale with from 'strongly disagree' to 'strongly agree'.

10.4   Results and discussion

The questionnaire was designed to compare teachers' and learners' perceptions of effective FL teacher practices and to examine the impact of the genders of learners on their perception of effective foreign language teaching and learning.

10.4.1   Students' and teachers' views

We compared the differences between students' and teachers' views on teacher efficacy components and found slight differences between students' and teachers' perspectives. Lack of significant differences shows some congruence between students' and teachers' views about good teachers and about *testing, teaching,* and *the L2 culture.* Significant differences were found between teachers and language learners only regarding *focus on form* (p = 0.04) where students value this focus by teachers more, which indicates learners' expectations about grammar teaching; *the use of L2* (p = 0.05) where, not surprisingly, teachers value the use of the target language significantly more in good teachers; even for students also, high mean scores were observed; and *the use of strategy* (p = 0.000) was valued more by students. An understanding of these differences is important because, as Bernat (2007) notes, mismatches between teachers' and students' beliefs can cause problems such as misunderstanding and miscommunication, students' questioning of their teachers' credibility, learners' engagement in strategies of which the teacher disapproves, and students' withdrawal and feelings of unhappiness. Similarly, it is argued that mismatches between students' and teachers' expectations can negatively affect L2 students' satisfaction with the language class and potentially lead to demotivation and discontinuation of L2 study (Horwitz, 1990; Kern, 1995).

10.4.2 Male and female students' views

The second concern of the study was comparing male and female students' perceptions of their male and female teacher efficacy. The question of how students' gender affects their views of effective teaching has been addressed by many studies. In modern Iran, females have been reported to participate in the national examination for universities and enter universities more than males (Mehr news, 2011; Alef, 2011) and are competing equally, and this recent context in relation to longer-term traditions makes the question of gender particularly relevant.

When the question of gender differences in views of teacher efficacy was of interest, we found *no* significant differences between male and female students on any of the characteristics of effective teachers investigated. The clear implication is that male and female students were not biased to certain features that made their professors more effective; however, the comparison of the means for each category indicates that female teachers are regarded as less effective in all categories except one (teaching). This difference, though it does not reach a significant level, shows that students are somewhat biased toward their female instructors. This finding is consistent with previous studies which show that females are rated lower than the male teachers (Basow & Silberg, 1987; Sandler, 1991).

When examining gender differences of efficacy we thought it might be a good idea to ask students to rate their male and female teachers and to state which of them they regard more successful as language teachers and to state why. Therefore, two intact classes, including 66 students majoring in English language and literature at the University of Tehran, were asked to indicate whether their male teachers are more effective than their female teachers and state why. Although they were supposed to do so anonymously,

11 were reluctant to write on this issue. A summary of the reasons given by the remaining 55 students is presented below.

On the basis of the results, it was found that 17 students regarded female instructors as more effective, 19 regarded male instructors as more successful than female ones. The other 19 argued that teacher efficacy does not depend on gender; rather, characteristics such as knowledge of the subject matter, interaction between the instructor and students, and quality of teaching – among other factors – are of determining importance in deciding teacher efficacy. They argued that most of the time, those of opposite genders are attracted to each other, and it is natural for the students to regard the instructors of the opposite gender as more effective for reasons other than professional practice.

On the whole, it may be concluded that most male and female students preferred male language teachers. The reasons they stated for preferring a male or a female language teacher varied widely from, 'I don't know why', to 'It depends on the level of education. At earlier stages, when language learners are not competent they prefer women, since they are more caring, patient, and attending; at more advanced stages they prefer male language teachers as they are more in control of language class and take their job more seriously'. The reasons cited for the efficiency of male teachers can be summarized as follows:

(1) Male teachers were regarded as more *energetic*; hence, their classes were more fun.
(2) Male teachers were believed to have more *self-esteem, self-control, confidence*; they *behaved respectfully*; they were said to better keep balance between a friendly or strict classroom atmosphere; they had *positive* attitudes.
(3) Male teachers were *not strict* in grading students; they did not have a fixed criterion to evaluate students.
(4) Male teachers had *better teaching skills*: they were more focused and could better convey the subject; they also were said to force students to study.

And the reasons for favouring female teachers were:

(1) the psychological advantages of showing *care* and *interest*, being more *patient and flexible, sympathetic* and *emotional*, more *tolerant* of students' mistakes and misbehaviours;
(2) corresponding gender (females preferred female teachers);
(3) certain perspectives held by females help them teach better; they are *available out of the class* and know what they want to teach; they are *more prepared*;
(4) their *teaching skills* and *being strict*; they are *committed* to their job and can better maintain a friendly and stress-free atmosphere; they are *even-tempered*, they seldom lose control;

(5) married females have *more responsibilities*; some jobs such as teaching or nursing require capacities found in female;
(6) they are more *serious, punctual* and *strict*; discipline is their uppermost concern;
(7) they are *meticulous* in evaluation and scoring; and *analytic*; they have the ability to analyse the class.

Some of the patterns observed here do not conform to the findings of the other researchers. Basow (1994), for instance, notes that:

> Researchers who take into consideration the gender of the rater find a more complex pattern. The ratings of male professors are unaffected by student gender, but female professors frequently receive lower ratings from their male students and higher ratings from their female students. Female professors also appear to be evaluated according to a heavier set of expectations than are male professors, and these expectations affect student ratings. (Para 2)

A large number of students (19 out of 55) stated that the gender of the instructors does *not* make a difference in determining their efficacy; in their opinion, overriding relevant factors are

(1) knowledge, skill, familiarity with technology, experience, and classroom interaction;
(2) similarity in gender of the students;
(3) educational level of learners: at earlier stages women are more successful while at more advanced stages men are;
(4) the ability to establish positive relationships with students;
(5) psychological factors, including patience, devotion, and commitment.

So far we have given a summary of reasons mentioned by the participants. It might be interesting and useful to look into the reasons in the wording of the students themselves. A selection of excerpts is given below, without error correction for the sake of authenticity. While each of the following perspectives has a narrow focus, each has an important bearing on our understanding of how Iranian undergraduate students view gender stereotypes in the Iranian context. These ideas have been shaped during the learning process through several years of education and, like other socialized beliefs, are changeable and not necessarily related to any specific factor. We reiterate that although we asked the students to comment on only language teachers, most of them nevertheless considered teachers in general, irrespective of field of study and discipline. Some excerpts from students' written reflections on gender issues are given below.

A 25-year-old male language learner wrote:

> I found male teachers more confident in their abilities to offer information to their students. They can develop a close rapport with them. The reason may be the fact that women have to meet much more challenges to become a university professor, then they are more likely to adopt a rather dogmatic and tough approach regarding teaching, and although they may be very knowledgeable, they are considered to be less competent, but there are women teachers who have proved the opposite.

Some students seemed to have a realistic perspective, like that of a 22-year-old female language learner:

> Teaching is one of those professions that require some special characteristics. Teachers are expected to face any kind of people in their class. They have to have the ability to get along with all of them. In comparison to women, men are less emotional and sensitive. So they can cope with any situation better. As a result, getting nervous, anxious, or even annoyed would interfere with their job loss. Even if there is a rudest student in their classes, it is no big deal to handle the class. This element is one of the most important requirements that a teacher needs to have and would make men the better teachers.

A 22-year old female student looked at the psychological factors more seriously:

> Female students mostly claim that they prefer male teachers and to support this idea they come up with sentences like, 'Male teachers are far more respectful and tolerant towards girls compared to female teachers'. I myself am a stalwart fan of this belief considering days back at high school that male teachers never wanted to check the homework for they considered it an insult, while female fellows used to ask you to go out if you hadn't done a small part.

Another wrote:

> I think the gender of the teachers can influence the success of teaching and also the success of the students. Some of the students feel more comfortable with the teacher who has the same gender or mostly male students prefer to have a female teacher. For me the gender of the teacher at the university is not important. At the school, maybe the gender of the teacher has some effect but at the university I think knowledge and the degree of connection between teachers and students are important.

Honestly, I should know at the end of the course how much I have learnt and to somehow [what extent] the course was effective for me. At this university we have some knowledgeable professors but they are unable to give the information. Totally, I think the gender at the university is not an important fact and just the relationship between teachers and students to share knowledge and get information is important.

A 22-year old female maintained:

When it comes to talking about good teachers, gender is a feature of paramount concern. Whether a good teacher is male or female is what crosses every person's mind. If you ask me, I'd opt for a male teacher. As for my personal experience, female teachers are much more serious. They go strict on students, are punctual and discipline is their uppermost concern in the classroom. They are also very meticulous in the way they evaluate and grade students. On the other hand, male teachers are much easier and more permissive. They are not as strict and punctual and evaluate students based on their general performance. Educationally speaking, you can learn from a female teacher while getting a good grade from the male teacher. That's why I'd prefer a male teacher at university.

A 21-year old student maintained:

In my opinion men are better teachers than women, indeed. After almost 13 years of education and passing courses with both male and female teachers, I think men can teach better; they can manage a classroom in a better way and the also seem to have better social behaviour [at least in the classrooms]. I think women are more strict in classrooms because it's a situation in which they can experience the power which society has violated them from. Men are free from this thought and they only concentrate on teaching and best trends of it and they don't look at a classroom as a kingdom of theirs [society is their real realm].

Finally, a 22-year old male student wrote:

I believe that male teachers are better than female teachers for three reasons; the first reason is their general attitude; male teachers are generally more tolerant than female teachers and take their job less serious; thus, it is easier to have them as your teacher. Another reason is that male teachers are less limited than female teachers; there are many red lines for female teachers in our society while male teachers do not have many of these restrictions and are able to teach more effectively. And last but not least, is the fact that I'm accustomed to having men as teachers and thus am more comfortable with them teaching me.

An analysis of these excerpts indicates that undergraduate students are biased in evaluating their professors' performance; previous research has shown that females tend to rate their female teachers more favourably than their male teachers (Bachen et al., 1999). Similarly we expected the female students in our study to rate their female professors more favourably. But the results indicated that in an Iranian context, because of the sex role differences, females tend to be biased in favour of their male professors. In this context, because of the dominant role of males, lenience toward the softer sex, and giving high scores to females (these are some of the reasons mentioned by female professors for the popularity of male teachers among female students), they attract the attention of the female students. Female professors, who tend to be stricter, on the other hand, because they adhere to the standards they have set, tend to be less liked by their female students. However, the interesting point is that if we hypothesize that sex plays a role in influencing the evaluation of students, one might expect the male teachers to rate their female professors more favourably. This, however, did not happen. We found that males are more biased in favour of their male professors, the details of which are given next.

10.4.3   In the eyes of colleagues: Male and female teachers' views

At the final stage, the views of teachers with regard to their male and female colleagues were examined. In this regard, 13 male and 7 female university lecturers with varying years of teaching experience were asked about their own evaluation of their colleagues based on their genders. This is a small sample, but it should be recognized that it is not easy to get data on this underresearched topic in Iran. The participants were asked to judge whether their male or their female colleagues were, on the whole, more successful as teachers.

While the beliefs of the language learners may partly result from educational experience and from socialization into social and cultural values, we expected the beliefs of the teachers (although they are also highly proficient learners) to be primarily informed by education and professional training, This, however, did not happen. Analysis of the data showed that 45 per cent of the participants considered men as *more efficient* teachers, whereas 25 per cent found their female colleagues *more successful*, and 30 per cent believed that gender plays no role in the educational environment. Interestingly, at least three men judged their female colleagues as professionally superior. One male teacher said: 'Male teachers I know are mostly a disaster'. However, almost no female lecturers expressed a similar view towards female colleagues: Only one female teacher disfavoured female teachers on grounds other than their professional characteristics; she criticized women teachers' 'crooked behaviour in the work place'. She believed that, at least in Iranian academia, men show a better developed character, but women as university lecturers turn 'somehow snobbish'.

Those who thought men were better teachers mainly included their *personality* and their *social status* and *role* as the primary reasons, rather than their academic capabilities and, of course, these social advantages indirectly boost their professional performance. These reasons can be classified as follows:

- Unlike women, men stick to their teaching and do not get involved in marginal issues.
- Men take risks more often, which make them more creative, 'exploring new horizons'.
- Traditionally, men are not required to help with daily household chores and, therefore, can dedicate more time to their teaching responsibilities. Women need 'more time for family'.
- Men are more humble, level-headed, and principled teachers.
- Men show a stronger sense of leadership and authority so they can control the class better and 'push the students'.

At the other end of the pole, people who considered female teachers more apt for the job focused on certain (perceived) feminine characteristics, like *patience* and *sensitivity*:

- Women teachers can easily establish emotional relations with learners; 'Women can usually connect with the students and touch their feelings more easily'.
- Women are more conscious in keeping learners' attention throughout the class session.
- Female teachers are more obedient to institutional rules and regulations, and that is an advantage since it makes them more 'organized'.
- Teaching is a job which suits ladies more both physically and psychologically, especially in our society and culture.

Besides these two opposing views, there was a third group of professors who did not prefer a certain gender; they instead pointed to advantages and disadvantages for each. They believed that there were many determining factors in teaching which are not related to teachers' genders. However, some believed that gender is quite important in teachers' performance but that there is no advantage for either gender because teachers are usually more efficient when teaching students of the opposite sex. Yet some other were of the opinion that the genders of teachers did play a role in making them more or less suitable for different teaching jobs. In their view, females had better teach young learners and beginners and teach general English courses and literature, whereas men are more successful teaching 'more sophisticated subject matter's, such as mathematics, trigonometry and physics at advanced levels.

10.5   Discussion

Recently there has been a rise in more socially and contextually oriented studies of learners' beliefs in the contexts in which they are shaped. Beliefs are shaped in society and are used for interpreting and acting upon the world. Beliefs are not stable within the individual and are developed in the context that, in turn, influences the way we view the world. Here, learners' beliefs are analysed in relationship to the contexts in which they have been shaped. In this analysis, one of the complicating factors is culture. The culture of a community determines, in part, the way people in that community see the world and interpret it. Unfortunately, in many studies, insiders' views have not been seen as an issue, and complex relationships between different variables have been dismissed as insignificant. We believe that the study of the context of learning, especially the context of language learning, will confirm that context influences the interpretations that we draw, and that context will have consequences for teaching.

As indicated in the responses of university students, the student rating of teacher effectiveness is influenced by factors such as instructor's gender, age, and experience; this endorses previous findings in studies that have mostly been conducted in Western cultures which are regarded as more open to change and criticism. As literature suggests, teacher effectiveness is influenced by factors that include the instructor's gender, age, experience, and academic rank (Young et al., 2009).

Another reason for the lower rating of female instructors by both male and female students might be attributed to expressiveness of female teachers. In the literature, this is called 'the Dr Fox effect', which is defined as 'the overriding influence of instructor expressiveness on students' evaluation of college/university teaching' (Marsh, 1987: p. 331). Female instructors, as observed, were not as expressive as their male colleagues. As Basow and Silberg (1987) note, previous research has found that 'teacher expressiveness strongly influences summary and global student rating, sometimes even more than does lecture content' (313). As Marsh (1987) notes, the results imply that 'an enthusiastic lecturer can entice or seduce favourable evaluations, even though the lecture may be devoid of meaningful content' (331). Hence, in an Iranian context, it might be argued that male teachers are more successful than females because of communicating their enthusiasm.

Comparison of the reasons for efficacy of either male or female teachers at university shows that, in some cases, reasons provided for better teaching by one sex are offered as causes for weaker performance by the other sex. For example, *being strict* is considered by many students a positive attribute of male teachers; however, the same attribute is regarded as a negative characteristic for female instructors. We speculate that this gender bias has been formed over long periods and, like any type of bias, is hidden and unknown even to the possessor. Centra and Gaubats (2000) also refer to this characteristic, arguing that

> [a] second, more general, definition of bias is when a known characteristic of students systematically affects their ratings of teachers. The gender of the student, particularly how it interacts with the gender of the teacher, is an example of this possible bias in student evaluations. Do male students tend to rate women teachers lower than men teachers because of a gender bias, especially in fields that are male dominated, such as the natural sciences? Do female students judge women teachers to be more effective than men because they feel more comfortable with them? These are important questions that directly affect the validity of the evaluations when used for personnel decisions. Ideally student evaluations should be related to what they learn from a teacher and not to gender or to other personal characteristics of the teacher (e.g., age, ethnicity). (17)

Trying to understand the reasons for different ratings of teachers by Iranian university students, one may conclude that students' views and shared beliefs, which are part of their learning culture, may have influenced their perceptions of efficacy. Similarly, one may argue that 'certain personality characteristics influence student evaluations of college professors' (Arbuckle & Willams, 2003: p. 507). In fact, in Iran, more than 60 per cent of those who recently have had the chance to continue their education at university are females (Alef, 2011) who expect to find better job opportunities after they graduate; to achieve this they sometimes tend to work more with those who may help them find a better job. In other words, they regard their male professors as role models for the future. This may partially explain why they tend to regard their male professors as more successful than their female professors and, hence, regard them as more effective teachers. This, in return, might lead them to associate these teachers' characteristics and behaviour with success or as an indication of effectiveness.

10.6 Conclusions

The findings of the present study suggest that students' beliefs were different from those of their teachers; this implies that teachers should not only consider their own views of methodologies and theories in L2 teaching, but also develop an understanding for their students' beliefs and expectations. In order to be aware of their learner's beliefs, teachers should encourage their learners to articulate them explicitly. This can be done by asking them formally (e.g., with interview questions) or informally (e.g., at the end of a class activity). Once they have become aware of their learners' perceptions, teachers can identify mismatches that exist between their beliefs and those of students. An awareness of these mismatches can help teachers to find out their students' expectations, communicate their own ideas to the students, convince them of the usefulness of their teaching techniques, and implement more effective strategies aimed at fostering learners' language development. When teachers explain the reasons for what they do in the classroom, and why, the frustration of students may decrease. Hence, it is crucial to inform students of the rationale behind learning activities so that they fully understand the reasons behind the teacher's actions. This strategy can address the diverse beliefs and expectations students bring to the classroom context about the appropriateness of certain behaviours or teaching materials. However, more research is needed in this area before we can validate the findings and determine the extent to which beliefs are shaped by social factors and change as a result of teacher interventions.

References

Alef (2011) Threats caused by the increasing number of female students entering universities/ A table of experts' views. Retrieved from http://alef.ir/vdcjthevxuqeyiz.fsfu.html?109534

Arbuckle, J. & Willams, B. D. (2003) Students' perceptions of expressiveness: Age and gender effect on teacher evaluations. *Sex Roles: A Journal of Research*, 49 (9–10) 507–516.

Babai Shishavan, H. (2010) The relationship between Iranian English language teachers' and learners' gender and their perceptions of an effective English language teacher. *English Language Teaching*, 3 (3), 3–10.

Bachen, C. M., McLoughlin, M. M. & Garcia, S. (1999) Assessing the role of gender in college students' evaluation of faculty. *Communication Education*, 48, 193–210.

Basow, S. (1994) Student ratings of Professors are not Gender Blind. Reprinted from *AWM Newsletter*, 24(5) September–October 1994.

Basow, S. A. & Silberg, N. T. (1987) Student evaluations of college professors: Are female and male professors rated differently? *Journal of Educational Psychology*, 79 (3), 308–14.

Bauml, M. (2009) Examining the unexpected sophistication of pre-service teachers' beliefs about the relational dimensions of teaching. *Teaching and Teacher Education*, 25 (6), 902–08.

Bell, T. (2005) Behaviours and attitudes of effective foreign language teachers: Results of a questionnaire study. *Foreign Language Annals*, 38 (2), 259–70.

Bernat, E. (2007) *Bridging the gap: Teachers' and Learners' diversity of beliefs in SLA*. Proceedings of the 20th English Australia Education Conference, Sydney, September 14–15.

Borg, S. (2006) The distinctive characteristics of foreign language teachers. *Language Teaching Research*, 10 (1), 3–31.

Borsh, H. (1996) Perceived characteristics of the effective language teacher. *Foreign Language Annals*, 29 (2), 125–36.

Brown, A. (2009) Students' and Teachers' perceptions of effective foreign LANGUAGE teaching: A comparison of ideals. *The Modern Language Journal*, 93 (1), 46–60.

Centra, J. A. & Gaubats, N. B. (2000) Is there gender bias in student evaluations of teaching? *Journal of Higher Education*, 70 (1), 17–30.

Cortazzi, M. & Jin, L. (2002) Cultures of learning: The social construction of educational identities. In D. C. S. Li (Ed.), *Discourses in search of members: In honour of Ron Scollon.* Lanham: University Press of America, pp. 49–77.

Hammadou, J. & Bernhar, E. B. (1987) On being and becoming a foreign language teacher. *Theory into Practice,* 26 (4), 301–06.

Horwitz, E. K. (1990) Attending to the affective domain in the foreign language classroom: Shifting the instructional focus to the learner. S. Magnan (Ed.), *Northeast Conference on the teaching of foreign languages.* Middlebury College: VT, pp. 15–33.

INSTAC (2002) Model Standards for licensing beginning foreign language teachers: a resource for State dialogue. Retrieved from http://www.lhup.edu/evalerio/Web%20 Docs/ForeignLanguageStandards.pdf

Jin, L. & Cortazzi, M. (1998) The culture the learner brings: A bridge or a barrier? In M. Byram & M. Fleming (Eds.), *Language learning in intercultural perspective.* Cambridge: Cambridge University Press, pp. 98–118.

Kern, R. (1995) Students' and teachers' beliefs about language learning. *Foreign Language Annals,* 28 (1), 71–92.

Marsh, H. (1987) Students' evaluation of university teaching: Research findings, methodological issues, and directions for further research. *International Journal of Educational Research,* 11, 253–388.

Mehran, G. (2003) 'Gender and education in Iran', paper commissioned for the EFA Global Monitoring Report 2003–04: 'The Leap to Equality'. Paris: UNESCO.

NADSFL (1999) Characteristics of effective foreign language instruction. Retrieved from 06/2/2007: http://www.nadsfl.org/characteristics.htm

Mehr News (2011) Sex ratio of students entering universities/ provinces with highest number of female students. Retrieved from http://www.mehrnews.com/fa/newsdetail.aspx?NewsID=1337658

Park, G. P. & Lee, H. W. (2006) The characteristics of effective English teachers as perceived by high school teachers and students in Korea. *Asia Pacific Education Review,* 7 (2), 236–48.

Reber, T (2011) 'Effective teaching behaviors and attitudes as perceived by foreign language teachers'. Doctoral dissertation, University of Arizona, Tucson.

Sandler, B. R. (1991) Women faculty at work in the classroom, or, why it still hurts to be a woman in labour. *Communication Education,* 40, 6–15.

Young, S., Rush, L. & Shaw, D. (2009) Evaluating gender bias in rating of university instructors' teaching effectiveness. *International Journal for the Scholarship of Teaching and Learning,* 3 (2), 1–14.

11
Poles Apart: Protocols of Expectations about Finnish and Thai Teachers

Erich Berendt and Maaret Mattsson

11.1 Introduction

No two societies could be so far apart as Finland and Thailand in terms of both physical geography as well as cultural traditions. One is a country in Northern Europe with deep Protestant Christian roots; the other is at the crossroads of Southeast Asia with deep roots in Theravada Buddhism. Each has a strong national language identity, reflecting its historical roots and geographical setting.

In Thai traditional learning culture (Mulder, 1997) the teacher is addressed as *ajarn,* the same as Buddhist monks, but teachers are classified a step just below monks in the social hierarchy. What that means is that the social deference and expectations that are extended to monks are also applied to the teacher to a considerable degree. A teacher/*ajarn* should possess moral goodness *(khun ngaam khanamdee)* and is admired and expected to uphold those moral and social behaviors. The teacher is thus seen as a conduit to give knowledge yet also has obligations regarding the moral life of students. The teacher–student relationship, *ajarn nakrien,* assumes a reverence and respect for the teacher that does not allow the student to question the teacher, who is regarded as the abode of knowledge. This reflects the traditional top-down, monastic valuation in formal learning. The traditional lore of learning which centered in Buddhist Pali texts was to be not only read but memorized, and all knowledge was intended to lead to one's moral realization. The very acts of reading and reciting were grounds for making merit. Formal knowledge, a *saksit,* was learned through ritualistic rote memorization. Even today, when passing a monastic school, you will hear the loud recitative chanting of the lessons, not necessarily in unison; the louder the recitation, the better the student. Thailand today, however, in its trade, tourism and increasing industrialization, is also at crossroads in terms of its pedagogics, where learning needs to be directed to new ends of technology and analytical skills.

Finland shares the European Socratic dialogue mode of critical inquiry as a highly valued learning mode to achieve insight or understanding. A major goal in such education is to acquire analytical skills for creating technical knowledge. Critical thinking in solving problems and discerning hidden patterns, structures and relationships depends upon an interactive process founded upon the give and take of dialogue. While teachers may be mentors, they are also provocateurs who stimulate students' discussion and thinking (Helkamäki & Kyrkkö, 2007).

Erich Berendt (2008b: pp. 73–89) found in his comparative study of the underlying conceptual patterns in Japanese and English discourse on learning that some conceptual metaphoric patterns, such as LEARNING IS A PATH, LEARNING IS AN ENTITY/COMMODITY, are very common in both cultures, but there were other underlying patterns which shaped the discourse of negotiating understanding which suggested strong culturally divergent values about how we learn (the use of capitals here indicates underlying conceptual metaphors rather than simply the surface realization in actual words; the underlying metaphors encompass a variety of surface expressions). The characteristics of LEARNING AS A LIGHT SOURCE/SEEING IS UNDERSTANDING were quite divergent. English focused on discovery, uncovering hidden knowledge, Japanese on illuminating. These poles seemingly reflect the heuristic tradition of the West in contrast to a learning process of seeking an enlightening change in perception. In looking at the conceptual metaphor, LEARNING AS AN ACT OF COMMUNICATING, there were similar divergent patterns in discourse. For example, English often focused on DIALOG and PHYSICAL CONTROL, whereas Japanese focused on passive reception of 'lore', which is valued content learned through the conduit of the teacher. While disciplined training was often valued in each culture, when and how that should take place was construed differently. Such a conceptual metaphoric analysis thus indicated that there might well be distinctive patterns of learning embedded in the respective cultures.

As E. T. Hall (1959, 1976) has observed, all cultures potentially have several modes of learning. He calls these formal, technical and informal: '[P]eople reared in different cultures *learn to learn* differently and go about the process of acquiring culture in their own way. Some do so by memory and rote without reference to 'logic' as we think of it, while some learn by demonstration but without the teacher requiring the student to do anything himself while "learning"'. Hall further argues that it is not just a cross-cultural issue of people who go overseas and try to train locals, but that 'once people have learned to learn in a given way it is extremely hard for them to learn in any other way. This is because, in the process of learning they have *acquired* a long set of tacit conditions and assumptions in which learning is imbedded' (Hall, 1959: p. 47).

Jerome Bruner has also cogently argued for the concept of 'cultures of learning' as being founded in the child's notion of the teacher's mindset.

'Teaching, in a word, is inevitably based on notions about the nature of the learner's mind. Beliefs and assumptions about teaching whether in a school or in any other context, are a direct reflection of the beliefs and assumptions the teachers hold about the learner' (Bruner, 1996: p. 46–47). Learning essentially involves the creation and negotiating of meaning in a society. '(T)he teacher is the vicar of the culture at large. You cannot teacher-proof a curriculum any more than you can parent-proof a family' (Bruner, 1996: p. 84).

11.2 Purpose and method

How modes of learning are manifested in different countries and their cultures can be seen in the concepts of what a GOOD TEACHER's behavior and expectations are. The objective of this study is to examine the respective modern learning cultures in Thailand and Finland in regard to the concept of GOOD TEACHER based on the conceptual metaphoric patterns in Contemporary Metaphoric Theory, following the work of George Lakoff (1987), Lakoff and Mark Johnson (1980) and Raymond Gibbs (1994). This study is particularly informed by the previous study by Lixian Jin & Martin Cortazzi (2008) on the images of the teacher in the Chinese cultures of learning as well as that of Berendt (2008a) Cortazzi and Jin (1999). The focus in this study, however, is only on the conceptual metaphoric patterns in the contemporary discourses on learning in Thai and Finnish (Mattsson, 2010).

To conduct this comparative study of contemporary cognitive metaphors and the expectations which shape the protocols of teacher–student behavior, two sources were initially researched to solicit ideas on GOOD TEACHER which could then be incorporated into a questionnaire. (a) Traditional proverbs on learning from Finnish (Lauhakangas, 2001; Granbom-Herranen, 2008) and Thai societies (Bhamorabutr, 1983; Sorsosodthikul, 1991) were collated, and (b) for contemporary values essays on the theme 'What is a good teacher? What makes a good teacher?' were collected from university students in each country. All essay contributions were from students in faculties of education preparing for the teaching profession both in Thailand and Finland. The essays were written in their respective native languages. Twenty essays were received from the Faculty of Education of Chulalongkorn University, Bangkok, and seven via the Internet service of the Peduca-student organization of the Faculty of Education of the University of Helsinki.

From the data of essays and traditional proverbs a questionnaire of 30 statements on GOOD TEACHER was prepared; this balanced 15 statements of the most salient mentioned items from sources in each country. Statements from each country were alternated in the questionnaire's composition and administered in the respective native languages. Table 11.1 gives the statements used in the questionnaire. The questionnaire was answered by using a five-point Likert scale (1 = strongly agree to 5 = strongly disagree) and the mean scores and F-test for statistical differences were calculated by using Microsoft Excel to determine significant differences.

The questionnaire was administered to students from two universities in each country with different major fields of study to ensure that the results were more balanced and reliable. They were done in classrooms with a researcher present. In both the essays and questionnaires each student's profile for age, gender, nationality, year of university education and major field of study was solicited. Respondents' ages were 18–30 and only ethnic Thais and Finns were included in the data analysis.

In Finland a total of 185 students were from the University of Helsinki and Helsinki University of Technology. In Thailand 187 students responded from Assumption University and Rajamangala Institute of Technology Borpitpimuk Mahamek, both in Bangkok. The universities were chosen for their availability and also because the student bodies were broadly representative of the middle classes in the respective countries and had a broad variety of fields of study, such as business, engineering, law, ICT, humanities and so forth. Some questionnaires had to be eliminated because the respondents did not follow instructions or were out of the age group focused upon. The remainder were 176 from each country. In the Finnish data there were 111 females and 65 males; in the Thai data there were 141 females and 35 males.

11.3 Attitudes toward GOOD TEACHERS

Table 11.1 shows the mean scores for each of the statements in the questionnaire. A comparison of the mean scores shows that the students from Finland and Thailand have a high degree of agreement. Mean scores below 3 imply strong agreement on each statement. Some items, however, show statistically significant differences ($p < 0.05$) and imply that that conceptions about GOOD TEACHER are different in each country. A total of 19 out of the 30 items were significantly different.

There is a noticeable, general pattern in each country in how the respondents answered the questionnaire suggesting a cultural attitude. Among the Thais the responses tended toward the mean about the degree of agreement; whereas among the Finns it broadly ranged over the attitude scale among the items. This is suggestive of a cultural value among Thais to avoid disagreement (a potential loss of face), whereas the individualism of the Finns would encourage a frank, individual expression of their attitudes about their society and way of life. This is reflected in the Finnish data in which respondents often chose a much stronger degree of agreement or disagreement than close to the median, which was most common among the Thais.

In order to discuss the significant patterns found in the data, various statements are now presented in groups by focusing on shared or divergent conceptual patterns. The questionnaire statements, presented in a literal translation in English, are given in bold, conceptual metaphors are given in capital letters, and proverbs in italics.

Table 11.1   The mean scores for rating questionnaire statements about a GOOD TEACHER by students in Finland (N = 176) and Thailand (N = 176)

30 questionnaire arguments	Finns	Thai
A good teacher is a good model for the students	1.883	1.511
A good teacher has an interesting personality	1.993	2.261
A good teacher is patient	1.676	1.563
A good teacher is strict, challenging and demanding	2.476	3.068
A good teacher is a friend	3.264	1.750
A good teacher shows that the teacher is human and compassionate	1.924	1.864
A good teacher is like a parent	4.255	1.994
A good teacher listens to the students and learns from them	1.848	1.574
A good teacher is responsible	1.559	1.290
A good teacher is able to create the joy of learning	1.359	1.449
A good teacher is hard working and dedicated	1.868	2.278
A good teacher demands critical thinking	1.743	1.801
A good teacher sacrifices him/herself	3.228	1.983
A good teacher makes time for learning	1.945	1.795
A good teacher is able to transfer knowledge to the students	1.607	1.250
A good teacher teaches students to be sceptical	2.118	1.909
A good teacher is able to build good character in students	2.597	1.580
A good teacher does not force students to learn	2.387	2.580
A good teacher has the spirit of the teacher	3.021	1.625
A good teacher is logical and consistent	1.618	1.528
A good teacher updates his/her knowledge all the time	1.283	1.784
A good teacher knows that learning never ends	1.528	1.585
A good teacher will receive moral obligation from the students	3.347	1.636
A good teacher lets the students learn individually and not just follow the teacher	1.757	2.034
A good teacher should not hurt the student physically or mentally	1.181	1.483
A good teacher teaches for life, not just for schooling	2.424	1.273
A good teacher loves and cares for every student	3.545	1.449
A good teacher individualizes the teaching	2.369	1.739
A good teacher has the heart of the teacher	2.958	1.494
A good teacher cooperates with other teachers	1.811	1.614

In the Thai essays on GOOD TEACHER, the statement (S-1), **A good teacher is a good model for the student,** was one of the most common items, suggesting an important quality for Thai teachers. The teacher (in Thai *ajarn*) has been seen as an elevated SUPERIOR PERSON, sometimes referred to as a 'GOD SENDER', a conduit for the spiritual goals in life and a person who has therefore greater social responsibilities than ordinary citizens. The teacher is seen as an example in society with consequent higher status as well. The concept of MASTER can be related to this social role and its expectations.

As can be seen from Figure 11.1, not only is there very strong agreement among Thais (more than half) but most of the remainder chose agreement. Finns, too, tend to agree with the statement but at a significantly lesser degree. This is suggestive of how strongly the Thai teacher is seen as a MASTER and that the student is a dependent FOLLOWER, or disciple. In Figure 11.2, **A good teacher is able to build good character in the students** (S-17) shows a slightly greater divergence between the two cultures. But still the results tend to complement those of the previous figure. In Figure 11.2 the Finnish respondents range across the scale, whereas the Thai cluster strongly with agreement. The fact that both cultures tend toward agreement is also probably an indication of the universal expectations about a GOOD TEACHER and molding good character.

A good teacher teaches for life, not just for schooling (S-26) also has a high degree of agreement for Thais (see Figure 11.3). This is a little surprising as this statement was taken from a Finnish proverb which can be translated as: *We do not study for school, we study for life (Emme opiskele koulua varten vaan elänää varten)*. It has been adapted by substituting teaching for studying. It may be surmised that 'teachers' and 'learners' are not necessarily closely related in the Finnish way of thinking. That is, learning is something that is internal, but teaching is something that is external. For Thais, both are derived from the dominant role of the teacher in the relationship.

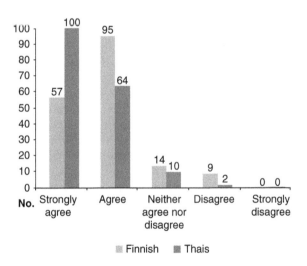

Figure 11.1 A good teacher is a good model for the students (S-1)

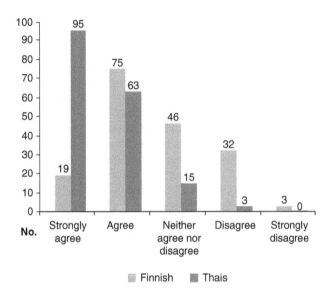

Figure 11.2   A good teacher builds good character in students (S-17)

This also raises the point about the TEACHER AS PARENT, a relationship which is also suggestive of the dominance of MASTER in the learning relationship but with added emotive expectations of dependency. Children, especially younger ones, often see their parents as the source of knowledge; they are dependent on their parents but are expected to treat them with respect.

One the greatest divergences between the Finnish and the Thais can be seen in the Thai-originated statement, **A good teacher is like a parent.** As can be seen in Figure 11.4, the responses are almost poles apart. The metaphors TEACHING AS TAKING CARE OF SOMEONE and TEACHER AS A PARENT occur in other statements as well. Finnish students do not at all identify a teacher with the role of parenthood; rather, teaching is seen as a profession, freely chosen, while parenthood is something obligatory. The Finnish also see the transmission of technical knowledge as the primary purpose of teaching, whereas parents teach 'life'. Thus, a shared conceptual grouping can be seen in the Thai statements: **A good teacher is a good model. A good teacher is able to build the good character of students. A good teacher teaches for life, not just for formal education.**

Another significant Thai statement (S-5) is, **A good teacher is a friend,** which Thais agreed with or strongly agreed with, but the Finns have a neutral or negative attitude regarding this concept. This again can be compared to the Finnish dominant attitude of teaching as a profession. This

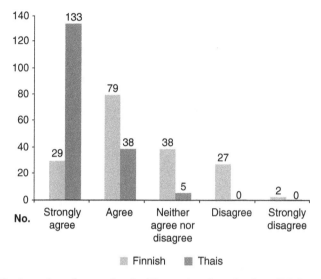

Figure 11.3 A good teacher teaches for life, not just for schooling (S-26)

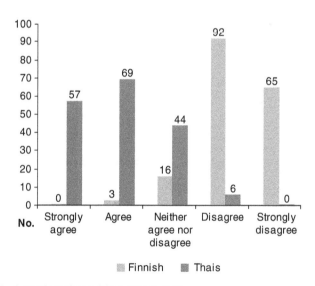

Figure 11.4 A good teacher is like a parent (S-7)

suggests a very different teacher–student relationship in the two cultures. Westerners tend to see the relationship in an emotionally cool or neutral manner. In this regard the TEACHER AS LEADER has probably more emotional impact than TEACHER AS GUIDE. A leader is someone people are likely to have a strong attachment to, as in a religious context or an idealized sense, someone worthy on whom people can be dependent. Associated with the role of TEACHER AS LEADER is a sense of dominating power, whereas the concept of a GUIDE is more likely one of a greater range of impact from the domain of religion (strong) to that of tourism (weak).

The Thai-originated statement, **A good teacher loves and takes good care of every student** (S-5), also shows a similar cultural difference in attitudes (see Figure 11.5). There is a strong difference in expectations between the two cultures: Thais agree with this statement, reflecting the expectation that the teacher will assume a personal interest and concern for the student beyond the domain of academic study, but Finns rather disagree or are neutral about it, although it should be mentioned that some Finnish respondents commented that it depends on the level of schooling under discussion. In a primary school context, teachers are expected to be loving and should take great care of their young charges. Overall the responses in Figure 11.6 (S-27) reflect those noted in the conceptual patterns of TEACHER AS PARENT, TEACHER IS KIND. In contrast, the Finnish respondents do not support these expectations.

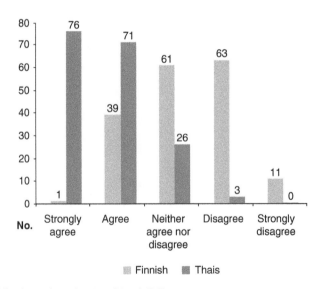

Figure 11.5 A good teacher is a friend (S-5)

On the other hand, the Thai-originated statement, **A good teacher is patient** (S-3), did not show much difference between the Thais and the Finns. Almost all respondents in both cultures agreed or strongly agreed. But it is worth reflecting on what their concept of 'patience' might entail. In the Thai conceptual pattern, TEACHER AS PARENT, it can be said that parenthood implies considerable patience. But Finns may see 'patience' as simply an attribute of a teacher, whereas among the Thais it is more of a total role expectation. Thais have proverbs regarding the importance of 'patience', such as: *Moderation is the way (Tang sai klang pen tang ti se ti sud). Do not catch the fish in both hands (Maw jap plar sawng meu). Rub the stone until it becomes a needle (Fon tang hai pen khem).*

One can raise here the question about the relationship of 'patience' with 'dedication' and 'perseverance'. As the Finnish proverbs suggest, patience in the sense of perseverance or dedication is necessary in learning. For example, *For learning there is no royal shortcut (Oppimiseen ei ole kininkaallista oikotietä). In study time goes (Opissa aika kuluu). There is learning as long as you live (Oppia ikä kaikki).* However, the expected involvement of emotion may be behind the dichotomy found here in the expectations of Finns and Thais. Thais seem to relate patience with kindness or compassion – feelings which are regarded as an essential feature of patience. The Western expectation to separate feelings and rationality would affect these different expectations. This reflects the deeper 'culture of communication' that Berendt and Keiko Tanita (2011) have argued for in their study of English, Japanese and Thai.

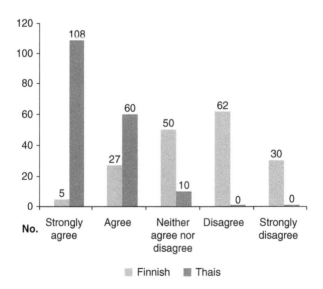

Figure 11.6   A good teacher loves and cares for every student (S-27)

Thais and Japanese, they argue, have an 'interdependent culture of communication' in which attitudes, emotions, relationships, empathy and feelings are integral to each other. The English (Western) is a 'dichotomous culture' in which the 'mind' as the locus of rationality and decision making is separated contrastively with attitudes and feelings with different valuations given to each.

Similarly, **A good teacher is a friend/parent**, is not part of the expectations of a good teacher in the West, as the teacher's position is seen as a profession. Unlike in the West, if there is a relationship in Asian societies, it should involve feelings as well (Triandis, 1989: p. 509). What the rules of behavior are will be dictated by the participants involved, the ideology of the cultures, the degree of formality expected and so on (ibid.; Hofstede, 2009).

The Finnish-originated statement, **A good teacher shows that the teacher is human and compassionate** (S-6), did not reveal much difference in expectations between the Thais and the Finns (see Figure 11.7). Most students agreed to the statement with only a slight variation in degree. The mean score did not indicate any significant difference but the F-test showed a significant difference ($p < 0.001$). While the Thai response can be linked to other conceptual patterns in their expectations, such as TEACHING IS TAKING CARE, TEACHER AS FRIEND, and TEACHING AS PARENT,

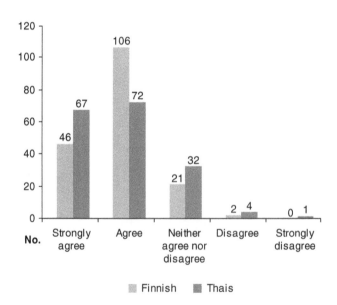

Figure 11.7 A good teacher shows that the teacher is human and compassionate (S-6)

the surprise is in the Finnish responses. Perhaps this Finnish expectation reflects the expected skill of the teachers, a skill of knowing the students' limitations as well as their own, as a sense of limitations is closely associated with the degree of perceived power that the teacher may or may not have. For Finns the teacher's power is viewed as rather limited as an ordinary person in society, rather than reflecting a superior position of the teacher.

The TEACHER AS A SUPERIOR PERSON is a significant conceptual pattern found in the Thai data. 'Superior' reflects not only the idea of a higher position, but also a morally better person. The Thai statement (S-13), **A good teacher sacrifices him/herself**, is an instance of relating the teacher's social and moral superiority to the idea of what is good (even to a perceived perfection). As Figure 11.8 shows, few Finnish students would agree with this, perhaps because in their society such an expectation is considered unrealistic.

The Thai (and perhaps most Asian cultures) have the expectation that one's life is very much bound to work. But Western individualism would downgrade the value of sacrificing oneself for work or the collective good. This sense of sacrificing oneself can be linked to TEACHER AS A SUPERNATURAL FIGURE, a conceptual metaphor noted by Jin and Cortazzi in their study of Chinese cultures of learning (2008: 188). For example, TEACHER IS CONFUCIUS/GOD/THE SAVIOR/SUPERMAN/AND IDOL. Such an adulation of teachers not only places them in a superior position but raises expectations to a level of sacrifice, which is a strong theme in Chinese cultures of learning (Jin & Cortazzi, 2011: p. 85).

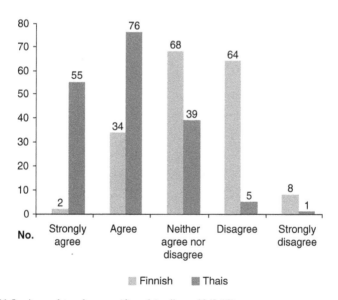

Figure 11.8 A good teacher sacrifices him/herself (S-13)

Another Thai-originated statement has to do with the 'spirit' of the teacher, suggesting a commitment that goes beyond professionalism and approaches a religious vocation. **A good teacher has the spirit of a teacher**, again recalls the conceptual metaphor of THE TEACHER AS SUPERIOR. The concept of 'vocation' (a calling traditionally associated with that of religious belief and religious vocations such as priesthood or entering a convent for religious service), can be related to the deep integration of Buddhism in contemporary Thai culture. The Finnish students mostly chose the middle neutral ground (Figure 11.9), reflecting the relatively low impact of religion in Finnish society today. The professionalism expected of a teacher is seen as institutionally independent of the church. The dichotomy of the rational from the emotive in Western culture would be a complementary attitude to this.

A good teacher will receive moral obligation from students (Figure 11.10, S-23), is a strong tradition in Thai society. This is rather awkward to express in English, as it is related to the Buddhist tradition of expressing one's obeisance, deference and respect in temples, to monks as well as to teachers, since teachers are ranked just below monks in the hierarchy of Thai society. The attitude is visually expressed by the *wai* gesture of respect. There is a special day each year to honor teachers in every school, called *'Wai Khru'* Day. While it is a highly formalized ceremonial occasion, it reflects the expectations of what a GOOD TEACHER is, symbolically. There is even a special traditional song which is sung, called the 'The Third Gratitude'.

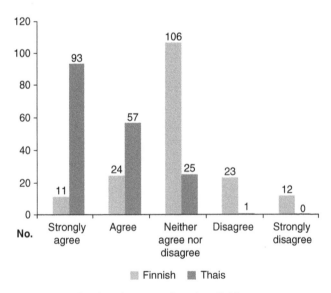

Figure 11.9   A good teacher has the spirit of teacher (S-19)

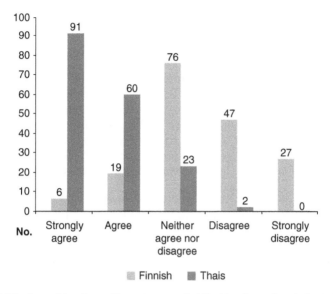

Figure 11.10 A good teacher will receive moral obligation from the students (S-23)

Gifts and flowers are given to teachers on the occasion to express their indebtedness to what the teacher has done for them. In the West, however, rather than gratitude, this might be seen negatively as a bit of payback. For Thais, the whole affair is cloaked in the aura of the Buddhist religion, a vital part of one's daily activities, but for Lutheran (Protestant Christian) Finland religion does not play a major role in the daily life rituals of most people.

The Third Gratitude
(trans. by Chatree Changthongsirir)
The respectable master who gives us knowledge
Trains our mind to know right from wrong
Before we sleep, we chant and pray each time
May virtues and merits bring happiness to him
The master is owed debts of gratitude, we pay him high respect
He teaches us and trains us without rest
He is devoted and does not think of hardship
Teaches us until we know, always guides and hides nothing
The third gratitude, magnificent and bright
But who, oh who, compared the master to a ferry
If we were to think, the more we think, we see it is wrong
Is there anyone who can show us this part like the master?

The merits made in our past lives, we give to him
May virtues and merits bring him happiness forever
Bring him happiness forever.

Not surprisingly, the results in Figure 11.10 show that Thais strongly agree with this expectation of the GOOD TEACHER, and Finns are neutral or disagree reflecting the fact that there are no cultural traditions or symbolic ceremonies which represent such an attitude. Finnish students feel little moral obligation to their teachers, partly because the learning is probably seen as their own achievement not that of the teacher. But, still, there were 25 out of 176 Finns who did agree, reflecting a degree of gratitude to their teachers.

The Thai statement, **A good teacher is hard working and dedicated** (S-11), shows a significant difference in the F-test ($p < 0.01$), although the mean score shows a minimal difference (see Figure 11.11). Even though this statement was derived from the Thai sources, there is a stronger agreement among the Finnish. There is a greater degree of skepticism among the Thais with 62 who either disagree or do so strongly compared to only 25 among the Finns. Underlying these figures, undoubtedly, is the general cultural attitude about hard work.

Responsibility is a universal social value, but how it is perceived in specific cultures may be significantly different. The conditions, relationships, the degree or limitations of obligations to carry out responsibilities will vary

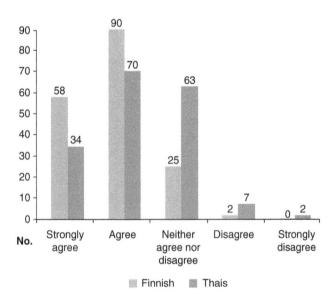

Figure 11.11   A good teacher is hard working and dedicated (S-11)

from society to society. There is also the question of fate as a condition of not being obligated, an escape from the burdens of responsibility. The statement, **A good teacher is responsible**, may seem facile but the F-test of the responses suggest that Thais and Finns have significantly different expectations ($p < 0.05$). It can only be suggested that the difference may lie in the role of fate in judging the degree of responsibility. Westerners tend to assume individual responsibility with recognition of circumstantial conditions which allow for obligations to be changed according to changing situations. In contrast, Thais tend to avoid taking responsibilities, as they are seen in a more absolute, non-conditional obligation. But there are also varying degrees of obligation, depending on the relationships involved (family, friends, colleagues, leader, boss, etc.). In Japanese culture, the negotiations regarding who takes what responsibility are elaborate and tend toward finding conditions for not having to take responsibility, as there are few conditions to ameliorate the obligations of responsibility once it is taken.

Enjoyment as a social value, known as *sanook*, is very important in Thai culture. But students in both countries responded positively to: **A good teacher is able to create the joy of learning**. In this, there are no statistical significant differences between Finns and Thais (see Figure 11.12). They share the conceptual pattern, GOOD LEARNING SHOULD BE A JOY/PLEASURE.

The Finnish-originated statement, **A good teacher has an interesting personality** (S-2), did not show any significant difference. Generally, the role of personality was seen as a good thing, although Thais tended toward a more neutral median expectation.

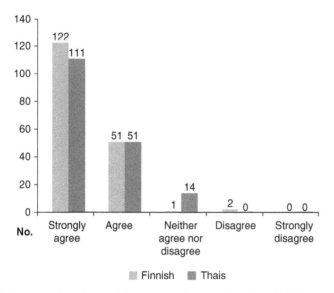

Figure 11.12 A good teacher is able to create the joy of learning (S-10)

The statement, **A good teacher is strict, challenging and demanding** (S-4), is a kind of continuum with what has been observed about the teacher's characteristics and skills. In Figure 11.13, half of the Finnish students agree with the statement, unlike Thais who seem rather scattered in their opinion, although half of the Thais chose the median, neither agreeing nor agreeing.

There are many Finnish proverbs focusing on discipline and learning through practice. *The harder the master of the school, the clearer is the learning (Jota koulumestari kovempi, sitä oppi selkeämpi). No one is a blacksmith when they are born (Ei kukaan seppä syntyessään). For learning there is no royal shortcut (Oppimiseen ei ole kininkaallista oikotietä), and so forth.* These also relate to the conceptual metaphor, TEACHER AS GUIDE. The teacher shows the way, but students need to go and do it themselves. The comparable Thai metaphor would be TEACHER AS LEADER, as has been discussed above. Thais do have a proverb reflecting that LEARNING IS HARD WORK/DIFFICULT. For example, *Rolling a great cannon up a hill (Khen krok keu phu kaw)*. But Thais sense that life should be *sanook* (enjoyable/fun) and *sabai sabai* (comfortable/relaxed) which is a counter value on the degree of how much is expected.

The statement from Finnish, **A good teacher demands critical thinking** (S-12), is equally agreed upon by Finns and Thais. There is no divergence in the mean score nor any significant difference. Nonetheless, there are some potential contradictions in what actually is meant by 'critical thinking',

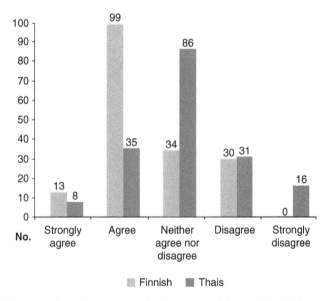

Figure 11.13 A good teacher is strict, challenging and demanding (S-4)

which is currently highly valued as an educational tool. For Finnish students, the TEACHER AS GUIDE, is seen as being demanding and challenging, concepts which the Thai students disagree with. For critical thinking to be achieved, an agonistic relationship is necessary to some degree. But, for Thai students, the predominant expectation is one of comfort, the role of TEACHER AS PARENT, the TEACHER AS CARING.

Related to the above, are other statements, such as, **A good teacher teaches students to be skeptical** (S-16); and, **A good teacher lets students learn and not just follow the teacher** (S-24). In both statements there was a similarity in the respondents' expectations. Proverbs reflecting such values can be found in both languages. Finnish proverbs reflecting S-16 are: *Do not believe before you see (Älä usko ennen kuin nä). Do not think bone is meat or buck's head is roast (Älä luule luuta lihaksi, pässin päätä paistikkaaksi). Learning is better than supposition (Oppi parempi kuin luulo). Supposition is a hole of falsehood (luulo on valheen kranni).* Thai proverbs for taking a skeptical attitude are: *Four legs may slip, a sage may be mistaken (se tin yang ru plad nak prad yang ru plang). A thousand friends will eat with you but hardly one will die with you (Phang gin ha ngai hua dai ha yak). A student betrays the teacher (Sui sit kid lang kru).* Nonetheless, the Thai proverbs which revealing the student's dependency on the teacher in the student's thinking (cited previously) demonstrate a countervailing cultural value. But Thai society and educational culture is undoubtedly changing with the major changes in the past 20 years.

A good teacher is logical and consistent (S-20), comes from Finnish sources, but there is only a negligible difference with the Thais. Almost all students agree with the statement. The underlying conceptual pattern of LEARNING IS A PATH, in which learning is viewed as a step-by-step process, would help to frame this conceptualization of expecting logical and consistent teaching. The statement, **A good teacher knows that learning never ends** (S-22), is also related to LEARNING IS AN ENDLESS JOURNEY. There was again close agreement on this between Thais and Finns, supporting the increasingly common expectation that learning is a lifelong endeavor.

LEARNING IS TIME-CONSUMING is also shared by the Thai and Finnish respondents in the Finnish-originated statement, **A good teacher makes time for learning** (S-14). These are reflected in proverbs: the Finnish, *Throughout life we learn and unfinished we die*; the Thai, *Slow work produces a fine knife (Cha cha dai phra leun ngai).* Although both groups share in their expectations, the F-test ($p = 0.005$) suggests there is a significant difference, perhaps related to underlying concepts about time.

The Thai statement, **A good teacher updates his/her knowledge continuously** (S-21), is largely shared between the two groups (Figure 11.14), although the Finnish students very strongly value this much more than do the Thais. The statement reflects the conceptual metaphors of TEACHER AS A SOURCE OF KNOWLEDGE and A GOOD TEACHER HAS DEEP KNOWLEDGE.

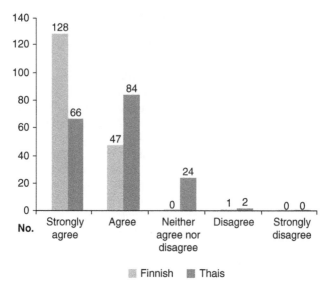

Figure 11.14   A good teacher updates his/her knowledge continuously (S-21)

In the area of the teacher's responsiveness to the student's needs, there are the Finnish statements: **A good teacher listens to the students and learns from them** (S-8), and **A good teacher individualizes the teaching** (S-28). In both of these Finnish-originated statements the Thai and Finnish attitudes are close. Figure 11.15 shows even greater (stronger) agreement of expectation in the latter statement. This suggests the conceptual pattern of GOOD TEACHING IS LEARNING.

Cooperation is something that is usually highly valued in collectivist societies, a characteristic often associated with Asian cultures, such as Thai and Japanese. But the statement, **A good teacher cooperates with other teachers** (S-30), was derived from the Finnish essays. However, little difference is shown between the Finnish and Thai groups. This commonality of expectations could imply the conceptual metaphor of TEACHING IS SHARING, or THE TEACHER'S TASK IS TO SHARE KNOWLEDGE. These also reflect the conduit conceptual metaphor, as in the statement, **A good teacher is able to transfer knowledge to students** (S-15). This reflects the expectation of getting KNOWLEDGE AS AN ENTITY, in which quantification of what is being learned can be transmitted down the line, top to bottom. Another related image is the big pitcher filling the little one. While statement S-15 originally was from Thai sources, Finnish students had a high degree of agreement, only 14 not concurring (see Figure 11.16). This may reflect the modern tendency to see learning as a commodity, a valued entity rather than as other underlying concept in learning, such as journey or dialog.

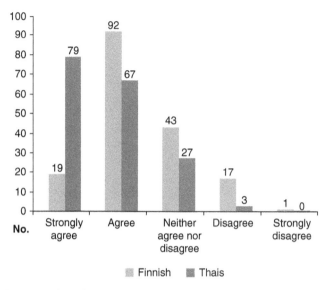

Figure 11.15 A good teacher individualizes the teaching (S-28)

A good teacher does not force students to learn (S-18), comes from Finnish proverbs, one of which states that the keys of learning are in the learner's hand, not the teacher's. Other related Finnish proverbs are: *No one is deafer than those who do not want to listen (Ei kukaan ole kuurompi kuin se, joka ei tahdo kuula). Antlers do not stick to the head (Sarvet eivät tartu päähä).* In Thai, too, there is the proverb, *Hard work he denies, light work he rejects (Ngan nak mai au ngan bau mai su).* Surprisingly, many students (53 Finnish and 67 Thai), chose neither to agree nor disagree. These uncommitted responses may reflect the fact that the statement was worded in the negative. But, in contrast, **A good teacher should not hurt the student physically or mentally** (S-25), received very strong agreement from both groups. For the Finnish, it was almost the entire group (see Figure 11.17).

A number of proverbs, however, reflect traditional values in which violence is condoned in teaching. For Thais, there is, *To love the cow, you must tie it. To love the child you must beat it.* In Finnish culture, proverbs which imply some violence or threatening include: *The good child will bring its own switch, the bad will not get better even by being hit (Hyvä lapsi tuo itse vitsansa, paha ei lyödenkään parane).* These may reflect past, not present, attitudes.

At the heart of the Thai learning discourse is a style of communication which links their relationships, feelings, attitudes and decision making. It is frequently expressed through a wealth of metaphors centering on the HEART, or *JAI* (Moore, 2010). This has been discussed above in conjunction with THE GOOD TEACHER AS PARENT and the research of Berendt and

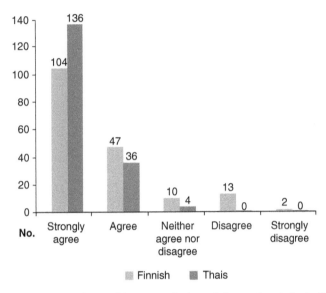

Figure 11.16   A good teacher is able to transfer knowledge to the students (S-15)

Tanita. Christopher Moore (1992) has collated over 700 heart/*jai* metaphoric expressions in the Thai language. The very Thai statement, **A good teacher has the heart of the teacher** (S-29), reflects thus the Thai language and culture in this regard. The Thai culture of communication sees human relations, feelings, and decision making all being interdependent, so a teacher possessing such 'heart' is seen as having PARENTAL CARING, KINDNESS and COMPASSION, supportive rather than agonistic in teaching. A GOOD TEACHER IS A MASTER, very knowledgeable and willing to share.

Figure 11.18 shows that none of the Thai students disagree with this statement and two-thirds strongly agree. While few Finnish agree, the range of their responses undoubtedly reflects the lack of a coherent cultural concept in using heart metaphors in Finnish learning discourse. In the Finnish language, the heart-related metaphoric expressions tend to be restricted to feelings, such as liking something or someone. Some Finnish students did think that GOOD TEACHING should be something 'from the heart', or something which we like.

11.4   Protocols of Caps expectations

From the data discussed above, the concepts of what constitutes a GOOD TEACHER in Thai and Finnish cultures both share some expectations but also reveal a number of significant differences. Since we are dealing here with the underlying attitudes about teachers, the impact upon classroom

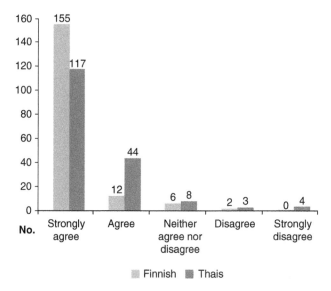

Figure 11.17 A good teacher should not hurt the student physically or mentally (S-25)

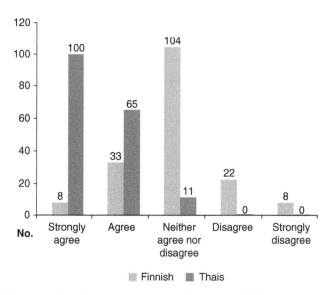

Figure 11.18 A good teacher has the heart of the teacher (S-29)

behavior needs to be considered. The discourse of the classroom will be affected (Berendt, 2009), and one can assume it will be facilitated or hindered to various degrees, by the different perception of the underlying cognitive patterns, shown conventionally here in capitals (caps), both from the students' perspective as well as the behavior of the teacher. From the data, we can say that the Finnish students strongly assume the teacher's role to reflect TEACHING AS A PROFESSION, THE TEACHER AS GUIDE, TEACHING AS DEMANDING, but the teacher is seen as AN ORDINARY PERSON. For the Thai, the TEACHER AS MASTER/SUPERIOR, someone who expects to be followed, reflecting a strong power relationship, is complemented with TEACHER AS PARENT/FRIEND, and being COMPASSIONATE and CARING. How teachers relate to their students will affect their style of teaching: for example, interactive versus lecture; Socratic, critical dialog versus proclamation of facts and obligations; questioning versus passive listening, and so forth. The atmosphere in the classroom as a social microcosm will also be significantly different; if fun (*sanook*) and parental care are expected, this allows considerable leeway from a restricted and disciplined style of classroom management. Expectations of the teacher to provide a kind of parental care would allow the student considerable leeway in a psychological attitude of dependence. What constitutes being 'demanding', or the degree of allowing individual expression as opposed to deferential behavior, are things which need to be negotiated when there are no norms(or only weak norms) of expectation. In today's multicultural environment, both in Europe and Southeast Asia, the assumed norms and possible conflict of expectations need to be understood. The following tables (Tables 11.2–11.6) (20–24) are a summary of potential protocols in

Table 11.2 Significant statements showing areas of cultural differences. (F-test $p < 0.05$)

A good teacher is a good model for students (S-1)
A good teacher has an interesting personality (S-2)
A good teacher is a friend (S-5)
A good teacher is a kind and compassionate person (S-6)
A good teacher is like a parent (S-7)
A good teacher is hard working and dedicated (S-11)
A good teacher makes time for learning (S-14)
A good teacher is able to transmit knowledge to students (S-15)
A good teacher is able to build good character in students (S17)
A good teacher updates his/her knowledge all the time (S-21)
A good teacher will receive moral obligation from students (S-23)
A good teacher lets students learn, not just follow the teacher (S-24)
A good teacher should not hurt students physically or mentally (S-25)
A good teacher teaches for life, not just for schooling (S-26)
A good teacher loves and cares for every student (S-27)
A good teacher has the heart of the teacher (S-29)

our expectations regarding a GOOD TEACHER, as they contain culturally divergent expectations.

Each of these underlying conceptual patterns provides a basis for protocols of teaching, reflecting the priorities of what is valued in each culture as well as what is more generally shared. The protocols need to focus on (a) what is expected in the teacher–student relationship, (b) classroom management, (c) the social role identity of the teacher and his/her character, (d) the nature of how knowledge is created, transmitted and achieved from the previous two and (e) the emotive qualities which are valued and should be part of the learning process and teacher–student relationship. Where there are clear cultural differences (as in international educational institutions and within classrooms where there may be a dichotomy in expectations between the local student body and the outside teacher), an awareness of culturally dependent expectations and behaviors which are influenced from them becomes an important tool to facilitate cross-cultural learning.

Table 11.3 Finnish conceptual patterns

TEACHING IS A PROFESSION
THE TEACHER AS GUIDE
THE TEACHER AS AN ORDINARY PERSON
THE TEACHER AS STRICT/DEMANDING
LEARNING REQUIRES PATIENCE

Table 11.4 Thai conceptual patterns

THE TEACHER AS SUPERIOR/'GOD SENDER'
THE TEACHER AS MASTER
THE TEACHER AS LEADER (TO BE FOLLOWED)
THE TEACHER AS FRIEND
THE TEACHER AS PARENT
THE TEACHER HAS HEART
THE TEACHER IS COMPASSIONATE/KIND
TEACHING IS CARING FOR STUDENTS

Table 11.5 Shared conceptual patterns

THE TEACHER HAS THE KEY TO KNOWLEDGE
THE TEACHER IS A CONDUIT OF KNOWLEDGE
TEACHING IS SHARING
TEACHING IS LEARNING
LEARNING IS A PATH/AN ENDLESS JOURNEY
LEARNING IS HARD WORK/DIFFICULT
LEARNING SHOULD BE A JOY

Table 11.6   Conceptual focus areas for protocols on GOOD TEACHER

The teacher's social role (relating to power and social obligations)
Teacher's personal qualities (affective, attitudinal, behavioral)
Concept of the teacher's role in having and transmitting knowledge
The conceptual basis for the learning processes
The teacher's awareness of student needs and cultural/social background

An example could be made of how questions are used in the classroom (see Jin & Cortazzi, 2008). Not only can questions be power tools, managing classroom learning and roles in the teacher's discourse, but they may have different impacts on students' willingness to cooperate. Open-ended questions that allow individual students to display their knowledge may be desirable in developing critical thinking and encourage a competitive environment in the classroom (e.g., in Finland), but they may have a negative effect on student face requirements, or be perceived as a threat to the teacher's face/position (e.g., in Thailand), such as questioning the teacher's superior knowledge which violates the student's sense of obligation to always honor the master teacher.

References

Berendt, E. A. (2008a) Cultures of learning. *JATLAC Journal*, (2), 37–42, Tokyo: Waseda University.

Berendt, E. A. (Ed.) (2008b) *Metaphors for learning: Cross-cultural perspectives*. Amsterdam: J. Benjamins.

Berendt, E. A. (2009) The discourse and epistemology of ideas: The role of metaphors. *Asian journal of literature, culture and society*. Bangkok: Assumption University Press.

Berendt, E. A. & K. Tanita (2011) The 'Heart' of things: A conceptual metaphoric analysis of *Heart* and related body parts in Thai, Japanese and English. *Intercultural Communication Studies*, 20 (1), International Association for Intercultural Communication.

Bhamorabutr, A. (1983) *Thai proverbs*. Bangkok: Assumption University Press.

Bruner, J. (1996) *The culture of education*. Cambridge, MA: Harvard University Press.

Cortazzi, M. & L. Jin (1999) Bridges to learning: Metaphors of teaching, learning and language. In L. Cameron & G. Low (Eds), *Researching and applying metaphor*. Cambridge: Cambridge University Press, pp. 149–76.

Gibbs, R.W. Jr. (1994) *The poetics of the mind: Figurative thought, language and understanding*. Cambridge: Cambridge University Press.

Granbom-Herranen, L. (2008) *Proverbs in pedagogical discourse: Tradition, upbringing, indoctrination?* Jyväskylä: University of Jyväskylä Press.

Hall, E. T. (1959) *The silent language*. New York: Anchor Books.

Hall, E. T. (1976) *Beyond culture*. New York: Anchor Books.

Helkamäki, T. & J. Kyrkkö (2007) *On the way to become a good teacher: Me, a good teacher?* Last accessed 9 March 2009. http://oa.doria.fi/bitstream/handle/10024/7192/jamk_1183543704_3.pdf?sequence=1

Hofstede, G. (2009) *Cultural dimensions* . Last accessed 2 March 2010 http://geert-hofstede.com/hofstede_finland.shtml and http://geert-hofstede.com/hofstede_thailand.shtml

Jin, L. & Cortazzi, M. (2008) Images of teachers, learning and questioning in Chinese cultures of learning. In E. Berendt (Ed.), *Metaphors for learning: Cross-cultural perspectives.* Amsterdam: J. Benjamins, pp. 177–204.

Jin, L. & Cortazzi, M. (2011) More than a journey: 'learning' in the metaphors of Chinese students and teachers. In L. Jin and M. Cortazzi (Eds), *Researching Chinese learners: skills, perceptions and intercultural adaptations.* Houndmills: Palgrave Macmillan, pp. 67–92.

Lakoff, G. (1987) *Women, fire and dangerous things.* Chicago: University of Chicago Press.

Lakoff, G. & M. Johnson (1980) *Metaphors we live by.* Chicago: University of Chicago Press.

Lauhakangas, O. (2001) The Matti Kuusi International Type System of Proverbs. http://lauhakan.home.cern.ch/lauhakan/cerp.html. Last accessed 12 November 2009.

Mattsson, Maaret (2010) *A Study of the Concept of a GOOD TEACHER in the Learning Cultures of Finland and Thailand.* Unpublished masters thesis, Graduate School of English, Assumption University, Bangkok, Thailand.

Moore, C. G. (2006) *Heart talk: Say What you feel in Thai.* Bangkok: Heaven Lake Press.

Mulder, N. (1997) *Thai images: The culture of the Public World.* Chiang Mai: Silkworm Books.

Sorsosodthikul, R. (1991) *Supasitang kridkam sonkhon thai timekwam hmay klyklungkan (The Similarities of English and Thai Proverbs)* (8th edn). Bangkok: Chulalongkorn University Press.

Triandis, H. C. (1989) The self and social behaviour in differing cultural contexts. *Psychological Review,* 96, 506–20.

12
Problematizing the Culture of Learning English in Vietnam: Revisiting Teacher Identity

Le Thi Thu Huyen and Phan Le Ha

English language learning in Vietnam has often been criticized for its 'not yet satisfactory' quality, which is ascribed to a range of 'traditional' factors, such as large class size and inefficient and inadequate teacher training. Especially, the 'problematic' learner tends to be the main target of blame: In the literature, prevailing epithets for learners are 'passive', 'traditional', 'mechanical', 'reactive', 'dependent', 'reticent', 'reluctant'. These learners are said to lack confidence, to be dependent upon memorization and prone to errors, to lack communicative skills and critical thinking. This alleged 'culture of learning' is viewed as being 'difficult to change', as it has, supposedly, deep roots among Vietnamese learners and in the culture. This conceptualization seems problematic, not least because it seems to portray the learner as having a fixed unitary identity. This chapter takes this as an issue for investigation, and it draws on a qualitative case study with Australian-trained, ethnic Vietnamese teachers of English to ascertain whether and how the stereotyped culture of learning ascribed to Vietnamese learners persists for these teachers; the teachers have been exposed to English as an international language (EIL), which should offer space for alternative frameworks within which learners and teachers could view each other differently.

12.1 Overview of English language teaching and learning in Vietnam

Recently, much literature about English Language Teaching (ELT) in Vietnam has pinpointed how it is 'problematic' to enhance the quality of learning and teaching English. One of the perceived causes may be ascribed to inadequate teaching methodology or 'faults' of teaching methodology which is grammar-based, textbook-focused, and examination-centred (Hoang, 2008; Le, 2004). Other suggested causes are, for example, the shortage of well-trained teachers (Bui, 2006; Dang, 2006), the inadequacy of teaching facilities and resources, and the lack of English speaking environment. As Nguyen Xuan Vang (2004) points out, while the textbooks in use have attempted to incorporate communicative language teaching (CLT), in Vietnam English is rarely used in speaking or writing outside the classroom, so there is no local English-speaking environment in which students might practise and reinforce classroom teaching. This is one of the perceived obstacles faced by teachers in ELT in Vietnam and in many other countries which has courses of English as a foreign language (EFL). It means, for example, that in terms of developing communicative skills there is a large gap between the rhetoric and the reality (Nunan, 2003). The slogan 'communicative', with an integrated four-skill focus, is the prevailing rhetoric in Vietnam; however, the real focus is exclusively on reading (Nunan, 2003). ELT in classrooms is best described as mostly 'traditional', with more focus on accuracy, form and reading skills than on fluency, meaning and integrative skills (Bui, 2006; Le, 2001; X.V. Nguyen, 2004). More problematically, language learners in Vietnam are often portrayed as 'passive learners' whose roles are 'to attend class, listen to the teacher's explanation, finish the assignment and pass the final examinations' (Pham, 2000). As is evident in Dang Van Hung research (2006: p. 162), such words and phrases as 'passive', 'traditional', 'mechanical', 'reactive', 'reticent', 'reluctant' and 'lack of confidence' frequently emerge in the data as descriptors of students' ways of learning. Moreover, the rhetoric of the 'deteriorated' quality of English teaching in Vietnam has been compounded by the traditional perception that there is a monolithic English language methodology with the usual parameters of fluency and accuracy. Deborah Cameron (2000) emphasizes a threat to the dominant discourse in language teaching: the communicative model. She argues that this model bears a simplistic and impoverished view of language learning: the problems confronted by the learner are not just technical or mechanical ('How do I say X in this language?'), but involve complex issues of identity ('Who am I when I speak this language?') – a non-linguistic aspect (ibid.: p. 91). The communicative approach, with its parameters that measure values of foreign language proficiency, seems to govern local values in teaching methodology. This fails to encourage the particularities of local situations, problems and issues which are what critical pedagogies aim to develop.

In this chapter, we will focus on English language teacher identity, which is deemed a crucial role to foster the learners' identity. If a student fails to thrive, the teacher the engagement with students rather than powerlessness (Norton & Toohey, 2004). The concepts of teacher and learner identity should be discussed in tandem with English as an international language (EIL): this shift in terminology from EFL to EIL reflects a tendency which offers a platform for teachers and learners to understand themselves (and their own identities) and the process of learning and teaching English in an age of globalization. The Vietnamese participants in this study who received training overseas and then returned to Vietnam to teach English are considered 'multipliers' in ELT in Vietnam: their role is extremely critical, as they have been facing the dilemma between 'local' and 'global' standards to foster an appropriate culture of learning in Vietnam.

12.2   Professional identity of English language teachers

Identity has been approached by many scholars from different angles, depending on the goals of their research. Identity has been viewed as multiple, shifting and in conflict – a site of struggle, and subject to change (Duff & Uchida, 1997; Norton-Peirce, 1995). Furthermore, teacher identity is not context-free, yet it is socially constructed (Duff & Uchida, 1997) as 'the formation, negotiation and growth of teacher identity is fundamentally a social process taking place in institutional settings such as teacher education programs and schools' (Varghese et al., 2005: p. 39). Teachers' professional identity is developed and accentuated by being compared with others (Tang, 1997). From a different perspective, teacher identities may be well constructed alongside core identities which are necessarily culture-driven or locality-driven (Phan Le Ha, 2008) or integral to cultural identity (H. T. Nguyen, 2008).

12.2.1   Professional identity formation: factors influencing non-native speaker teachers' professional identity

In the field of ELT, studies on teacher cognition, teacher knowledge, teacher learning and teacher development have been extensive over the past few decades (Calderhead, 1996; Woods, 1996). However, only recently have studies focusing on teacher identities and their professional identities begun to appear. These studies explore, in particular, the identity formation of non-native speakers (NNS) who are teachers of English (Duff and Uchida, 1997; Norton, 2000; Pavlenko, 2003; Phan, 2008; Sharifian, 2009; Varghese, 2005; Zacharias, 2010). These studies provide thorough insights into teacher identities and see identity as a critical component in the sociocultural and sociopolitical contexts of the classroom and as a professional development tool. The present study focuses the discussion on teacher identities as it creates grounds for the notion of critical pedagogies (Canagarajah, 2005; Norton & Toohey, 2004) which posit that the 'good' pedagogy and 'effective' methods of learning cannot be found without taking a socioculturally situated perspective into consideration. Likewise, there would not be 'good' pedagogy and 'effective' methods without teachers addressing issues of agency, identity, creative appropriation and resistance of local social actors when they are confronted with the task of teaching English in their specific local contexts (Lin et al., 2005: p. 217). The concept of 'applying' the 'right' methodology in order for the students to acquire the language was merely something as 'technical', surfacing through the process of teaching. What is salient is the need to understand teachers. As Manka Varghese et al. argue, 'in order to understand language teaching and learning we need to understand teachers: the professional, cultural, political and individual identities which they claim or which are assigned to them' (2005: p. 22).

In line with Varghese, Phan Le Ha (2008) posits that understanding what teachers want, how they perceive themselves and how they are often represented is crucial to the success of ELT teacher training courses and to an EIL pedagogy in global and local contexts.

Prevalent in the literature on NNS teachers, factors influencing their professional identity revolve around their self-positioning in their professional community, teachers' sense of competence, language proficiency and pedagogical competence. These factors have been identified as influential to teachers' professional identity. Regarding self-positioning in a professional community, Yasuko Kano and Bonny Norton (2003) argue that it is the teachers' self-positioning that may impact on their actions and self-evaluation. For NNS educators of the English language, if they perceive themselves in terms of having a self-imposed 'peripheral' role in the profession, this can limit their future development. On the other hand, if they perceive themselves as legitimate or multi-competent teachers, this may open up more opportunities for their professional development. Phan's study (2008) aims to understand teacher identity formation with English language teachers studying for master's and doctoral degrees in programs overseas. She argues that their identities were reshaped and negotiated with their awareness of differences, showing a degree of mixing and adjusting. Also, her participants' identities were subject to reconstruction but along the lines of existing values embedded in them, showing a sense of connectedness and fluidity in the negotiation of values.

Regarding language and pedagogical competence, many, perhaps most, non-native speakers (NNS) English teachers have experienced a lower self-image and something of an inferiority complex due to their self-perception that they lack language proficiency in the language they teach compared with their native-speaking (NS) counterparts (Jenkins, 2005; Llurda & Huguet, 2003; Péter Medgyes, 1999; Tang, 1997; Tsui & Bunton, 2000). However, their pedagogical skills as professionals in the ELT community have enabled NNS English teachers to gain confidence, hence enhancing their professional identity (Liu, 1999; Llurda, 2004; Peter Medgyes & Reves, 1994; Sifakis & Sougari, 2005).

12.3   From teaching English as a foreign language (EFL) to teaching English as an international language (EIL)

EFL is strongly criticized for its orientation towards native speaker norms, given the fact that globally learners of the language outnumber its native speakers. When EFL is measured against the standard of a NNS, few EFL learners will ever be perfect. Within the traditional EFL methodology there is an inherent ideological positioning of the learner as an outsider, and as a failure in a process that David Graddol (2006) criticizes as the ideology 'designed to produce failure'. Such an ideology and positioning within EFL frameworks would entail some consequences in the teaching of EFL. Learner identity tends to be largely ignored in traditional EFL methodology. EFL learners are more likely to be assigned as having 'deficit' skills in their language ability.

12.3.1   English as an international language and teacher professional identity

Some applied linguists have suggested that the development of English as an international language (EIL) has the potential to redefine the professional competence of all English teachers (Jenkins, 2005, 2007; McKay, 2003; McKay et al., 2008), which may impact on English teachers' self-image, inform their professionalism, and change their beliefs about teaching pedagogies. Many researchers (Alptekin, 2002; Hempel, 2009; Jenkins, 2007; McKay, 2003; Seidlhofer, 2004) have proposed a new pedagogic model which deviates from a monolithic perception of English language and culture. Given the fallacy of the EFL model informed by standardized native speaker norms (McKay, 2003) or constraining views of communicative competence (Alptekin, 2002), salient features of the EIL model take into account a theory of language learning and teaching that caters to divergent demands of English users with reference to lingua franca status of English, that re-conceptualizes the stable norms and goals entrenched in a traditional foreign language teaching framework, and seeks to develop appropriate pedagogies, instructional materials and the ownership of English. Pedagogic models in EIL thus open up avenues for both learners and teachers of English to perceive and define themselves differently.

12.4   The study

Inspired by critical pedagogy which fosters local issues and particularities in relation to English language teaching, this chapter examines how Vietnamese teachers of English who were trained in Australia through master's courses and returned to Vietnam to practise their profession, have conceptually changed themselves in terms of their teaching profession and their perception of their own learner identity, and how such conceptual changes contribute to nurturing a culture of learning appropriate for the teaching context in Vietnam.

The chapter addresses two issues:

- How does the advanced professional training in Australia contribute to the re-conceptualization of teacher identity?
- How is the learner perceived by these Australian-trained ethnic Vietnamese teachers of English?

The study draws on case studies with ethnically Vietnamese Australian-trained teachers of English to explore how they negotiate between 'local' (Vietnamese, EFL) and 'global' (EIL) to appropriate their teaching methodology when they returned to Vietnam to teach English. Case study data rely on extensive, multiple sources of information in data collection derived from in-depth interviews, classroom observation, reflective writing, document reviews and email communication.

12.4.1 The data

The data obtained through the interviews, reflective guided journal and classroom observations, reflected that the participants' transnational training experiences in Australia helped them boost their professional identity in terms of their professional status as non-native speaker teachers, and attitudes towards language proficiency and pedagogical competence. We use pseudonyms to refer to the participants in this study. Most of the data were given in English – significantly, the participants chose to express themselves in English throughout the data collection process – and so we leave the data as it is to respect the voices of the participants.

12.4.2 How does the training in Australia contribute to the reconceptualization of teacher identity?

Most of the participants underwent change in their overall philosophy and approaches to English language teaching. The following excerpts shed light on how the teachers in the study negotiated and appropriated their practice of teaching English, since their completion of the master's course in Australia. Their perceptions of their teacher's identity are communicated through such negotiation and appropriation, accordingly.

Most of the participants did not indicate any worries or tensions in being an EFL teacher, or conducting a 'traditional' role. As they reported, they were able to accommodate confidently different roles in their context without experiencing the pressure to adopt Western-based theory and teaching philosophy. The boundary between English as a foreign language (EFL) and English as an international language (EIL) is not a clear-cut distinction, but it becomes mingled, which required a sensitive negotiation of practices and assumptions of teaching English in a culturally specific context (Matsuda, 2009). Seeing herself as a proactive teacher with nearly ten years' working experience at tertiary level, Khanh highly valued her opportunity to be trained in Australia, revealing that the master's course in Australia has bought her to a bigger horizon. She is proud of being a Vietnamese teacher who, she confirmed, has been formed from her Vietnamese culture, in which she had been acculturated from primary school to high school and later when she became a teacher. She has brought all that culture to her teaching style, and it has established her role in the classroom. This teacher shared her conceptual change in thinking toward the concept of teaching English:

> Before I went to Australia, I thought teaching English was a career very simple like teaching maths or physics or any subjects, but when I came back to my home country in Vietnam, it changed. I think teaching English is teaching a language, a culture and it is not a subject but it is a way to communicate. It links people to people, culture to culture. Language is the way to communicate to people so we teach someone to know how to communicate and we teach them how to communicate appropriately not rightly or not wrongly.

She viewed her teaching of English as moving away from the standard norms with linguistic parameters, such as grammatical correctness, but more about a way for empowering learners through language:

> We should not talk to them, we should not lecture to them, but we should create real situations for them and by group work, and we should give chances or opportunities to them to explore themselves in the language.

What was obtained during the classroom observations of her classes confirmed what she had revealed in the interviews: she did not talk and lecture much to her students who were encouraged to take control of the class atmosphere.

Ho is another participant who developed his teaching methodology in the same way. He proactively applied what he obtained in his training course overseas to make changes in his teaching, such as integrating technology into language teaching and learning. He shared in the interview his stance that communicative language teaching is not always good because this approach is rather old; he viewed his teaching not as mainly a technical act, based on the traditional discourse of linguistic competence:

> Previously, I thought teaching English was just to teach syntax, grammar and we focus on linguistic aspects, now I should look more at socio aspects such as how students learn from the other, learn by working in pairs, in groups to exchange ideas. And by doing that they can improve their communication in their language they are learning. So it is very interesting, but I have to make so-called local adaptation. For example, I also supply my students with some grammar points when I teach them. If I just focus too much on communication without linguistic input, then my students may feel unconfident.

Lan commented on her experience of being exposed to a new learning context in Australia. Such exposure did not affect the way this participant perceived herself as an English teacher with an inferiority complex; instead, this led to her revised identity as a non-native speaker teacher, reframing her prior non-native identities in a new and positive light:

> I always think I tried to imitate, tried to have the voice of the native speaker because I think that only by that way you can be a good teacher also needs to speak like a native speaker, your sound, your pronunciation everything should be American standard or British standard, but when I went there, I witnessed that all of the senior lecturers and professors, they come from everywhere in the world; they can be a senior lecturer in an internationally recognized university and they speak with their accents, but the point is everyone, every student can understand them so I think, okay, this relieved my burden.

As such, her previous burden of the EFL teacher identity was relieved of the laborious process of acquiring native-like English pronunciation; this induced her to change the preconceived beliefs of English teaching to her students. Acquiring native-speaker English was no longer an attempt to negotiate her competence and identities:

> [W]hen I returned home, I also told my students that we don't try to speak like a native speaker; it is good to do that but it doesn't need that, The point is that I just want to make people understand, make myself understandable. That is the point that will help me a lot, and I feel more confident; I don't care about my accent because everyone has their own accent. We try to pronounce correctly and make people understand you well, so that helps me a lot, makes me confident.

Most of the participants, when asked about the effect the training course had on their professional development, tended to view the course process positively in terms of their new appreciation towards an exposure to a new culture of learning and teaching. Some teacher participants admitted that such exposure was really necessary for an EFL teacher, as this enabled them to immerse themselves deeply into cultural features related to language use; however, this did not mean that all the knowledge or theory acquired was of great help in their context. As in the case of Ngoc, who admitted in her interview:

> I tried to read a lot of theory during the course which I think I was going to apply, but I think there was something wrong somewhere. In my opinion, theories are not magic tricks that could help the teacher perform in classroom. They cannot help teachers to control the real situation when they come into their real class. I just ignore theory and do something instinctively from the experience of the teacher and the learner.

Ho also reflected in a guided journal, in which he wrote about his exposure to different ideologies and teaching and learning approaches.

> During my Master course in Australia, I was exposed to some other modern approaches, especially CLT. However, I don't think that such exposure has affected my teaching a lot.... I am quite conscious of my teaching context in which my students, at different levels of English, have to study English together in a non-language environment.

It is seen from the data above that these Australian-trained EFL teachers experienced growth in their professional identity. Such a revised professional identity developed, but not necessarily because the training in Australia had enlightened them in terms of pedagogical competence. To put it differently, although they admitted that they had been exposed to different ideas and ideologies in teaching, such 'new' ways of teaching or exposure to Western scholarship also enabled them to be critical of their 'newly acquired' pedagogical skills. They did not adore Western theory, but they used it as a basis to look more deeply at their professional selves. This provides some evidence to confirm the argument that teachers' professional identities are socially constructed (Duff & Uchida, 1997) and their formation, negotiation and growth are a matter of social practice which takes place in teacher education programs (Varghese, 2005), as in the cases mentioned. In fact, these teacher participants challenged the dominant theories and assumptions in the prevailing language teaching frameworks. Ho challenged the 'merits' of communicative language teaching (CLT), which are frequently documented in the literature, and he acknowledged that a local adaptation was more desirable in his teaching. Also, language proficiency did not appear to hamper a process of teacher professional identity being reified as one of the important factors influencing professional identity (Liou, 2008). Intelligibility, rather than 'standard' pronunciation acting as professional indicator in the teaching context, was revealed in Lan's case.

It is noted that the 'being' and 'becoming' (Phan, 2008) in the teacher professional identity clearly demonstrated that teacher identity may be well-constructed alongside core identities which are culture-driven or locality-driven. See, for example, in Khanh's case. Teacher identity is not one stable identity and not just about changing and fragmentation, but it incorporates continuity, fluidity and connectedness, creating dynamic change within the wholeness (Phan, 2008). Khanh valued her identity as a Vietnamese teacher, an identity constituted from her primary to tertiary education. Her experience, condensed from experience as a learner which coalesced with that of a teacher in the Vietnamese education system, formed her professional identity. To her, local values forming teacher professional identity might enable her to enact a more effective role as a teacher, which reflects *continuity and fluidity* in teacher professional identity (Phan, 2008).

The EFL teachers' self-positioning in Australia as learners and as English teachers in their teaching context contributed to their reconceptualization of professional identity. They became more critical of their prior teaching experience, thus boosting their self-image of being Vietnamese educators. It can be seen that they did not consider their professional role 'peripheral' (Kano & Norton, 2003), but confirmed their confidence as a result of exposure to Western ideology and scholarship. The teachers' professional growth was not totally formed from the assimilation of Western ideology and theory in teaching and learning, but from their critical construction of knowledge which is culture-driven or locality-driven (Phan, 2008).

12.4.3 ELT professionals and their professional roles in local teaching contexts

Although there has been some conceptual change among these teachers of English away from a monolithic perception of English language and culture of learning, and toward positive attitudes regarding their professional identity, there are still some inconsistencies in their beliefs regarding their professional role. Dominant Western-based discourses in language teaching and learning seem to govern and orientate their perceptions in their local teaching context.

Minh is among the few participants here who challenged, with power, his status as a teacher. He is a university professor who had the longest teaching experience, and he had held managerial positions at tertiary level. He was awarded master's in education and a PhD in TESOL (Teaching English as an International Language) in Australia, where he believed his exposure to English not only benefited him but also empowered him, both in learning and practising the teaching of English. 'Learning English in a democratic country like Australia, with liberal-minded people here certainly greatly influenced my thinking and practising teaching as a career', he revealed. He admitted that the change in his power and status as a teacher really made a difference in the local context in Vietnam. He expressed his awareness of building up his own learner identity as a result of his training in Australia. He gave one example that illustrated how he had boosted his student identity to empower his students so that they would have opportunities to think about themselves and feel worthy in themselves.

What was obtained from the classroom observations at Minh's classes confirmed his effort to empower his students and give them a greater feeling of self-worth.

It is common in a Vietnamese classroom that students give their answers to such types of questions in a cliché way, such as gaining knowledge, being knowledgeable. However, I shared my thoughts with the students about their learning. I thanked my students for their presence in class so that I got paid to support my family. In this way, I think, I tried to empower my students in a sense that they feel a worth of their learning and feel responsible for their ownership of learning.

Also, in his reflective journal he revealed there was a tension somewhere in applying ELT theory in a language class in Vietnam and, in order to remove such tension, ELT practitioners needed to think about modifying the roles that both teachers and learners may take. This view was reflected in his journal:

> Teachers in Vietnam used to and are thought to take the model role in classroom where there is a gap between teacher and learners. A change in thinking will help to remove such a barrier. A change will take place in many aspects: teacher and learner role, teaching methodology, learning styles and a respectful challenge to the teacher's questions and ideas. Teachers have to accommodate themselves with these changes about their status and power in class.

His experience and effort of trying to surrender the self of 'status' and 'power' of a Vietnamese teacher reflected the desire to change the identity of a 'teacher-controlling' and 'directing' self commonly associated with the characteristics of Vietnamese teachers, and such a status in his perception was something *problematic* in a Vietnamese classroom. He mentioned, in his reflective journal, the potential effect of changing this 'problematic' identity: 'Teachers seem to be more vulnerable because their role, respect might be challenged'.

Coming into contact with different ways of learning and teaching approaches in Australia, Lan felt excited about such *new* and *empowering* methodology to develop the learners' autonomy, which seems to be a value that needs to be fostered in her teaching. The so-called *domination* in her teaching profession should be replaced by a *managerial* role.

> Considering the student as the center of the learning and teaching process, at the beginning of every course, I often make an interview or deliver questionnaires to find out what the students expect and how they are motivated when attending the course. From these initial understandings, I can add/remove some sections from the materials so as to meet their expectations. In the classroom, I have created favorable conditions for the student to get actively involved in class participation, encourage them to ask questions and challenge their ideas. I base part of the student's grade on oral participation; courses are often organized around classroom discussions, student questions, and informal lectures. In some courses (for example, Cross-Cultural Communication), I have only a 'managerial role' and the students do the actual teaching through discussion and presentations. And to encourage the learner autonomy in language learning, a variety of tasks are often given to my students; for instance: group project, group presentation, reading assignment, peer counseling, etc.

12.4.4 How is the learner perceived by these Australian-trained Vietnamese teachers of English?

To the majority of the participants, in their perceptions a stereotypical culture of learning ascribed to both learners and teachers still persists. Learners of English in Vietnam are still viewed as deficient, passive, error-prone and preconceived with stable norms and ideology in language learning. When asked about their students, most of these teachers admitted that, although their students worked hard and were willing to participate in learning and teaching activities, they were quite shy in class discussions and this was, as they believed, a common characteristic of Vietnamese students. Such a preconception is inherently embedded in the teacher participants' minds as one strand of a local culture of learning. Khanh still believed that the kind of interaction/communication she experienced in her class in Australia was more 'prestigious' than the classroom atmosphere in Vietnamese classrooms, which presented a big obstacle in her teaching.

> My students are second year ones and I am teaching American culture; in some ways, they are senior, so they are quite confident in class. However, we are Asian people, so my students have something unlike Western students. That is one of the problems that will affect communication in class, different from communication in class in some other countries like Australia or US.

Such an entrenched belief is also found in Linh's response:

> My students are interesting; they are intelligent, but somehow because of the culture of Vietnam, when they participate in English classroom, they are a little bit shy. This is one of the disadvantages of my teaching. The culture roots in themselves. So it is very difficult to change their point of view or their style in learning. This is one of the obstacles that most of the Vietnamese teachers meet when they teach English in Vietnam.

The excerpts above clearly showed the participants' deeply entrenched beliefs about the learner in Vietnam in particular and Asian students in general. Linh and Khanh gave more weight to the Western style of teaching and tended to view traditional teaching in Vietnam as something problematic affecting communication negatively.

Another participant, Ha, described her students as follows:

> I must say their English level is not very good. The second thing, their motivation is not very high. Sometimes you feel frustrated because it seems that they don't want to learn even though you try your best to find good learning materials. You think that they will be interesting enough,

but in fact, students may not be interested so sometimes I really feel frustrated about their learning habits, their motivation and their English level. I must say their English level is not very good.

Ha felt frustrated because her students were not highly motivated. When asked about the reasons why the participant's students lacked motivation in class, Ha mentioned that wrong placement through university entrance exams were to blame for demotivation among her students.

Different reasons why. We have selected these students, I don't think in an appropriate way. Again, it relates to the way how university entrance exams are conducted because we test them based on grammar and reading skill and their speaking skill and listening skills are not good enough. So when they go to listening and speaking classes, maybe their level is not good enough. They don't understand. I have some students who told me that they didn't understand a thing in my class although the listening activities are not difficult at all because they never learn listening before. I think the first reason is their proficiency, their English level is not good enough in class, so they don't feel highly motivated to do thing.

Unfortunately, it was such inappropriate placements that directed the teacher's frustration toward to the learner themselves. Students were to blame for having a *'problematic'* learner identity which was considered a big obstacle to teaching and learning a foreign language.

The data above suggest that the participant's professional identity is constructed by comparing it with that of others (Tang, 1997). The example given in Lan's and Minh's cases demonstrate this argument. They may think the *status, domination, teacher-controlled* and *power* associated with a Vietnamese teacher are something they need to change when compared with a democratic learning environment like Australia or other English-speaking countries where students feel free to address teachers by their first names and ask questions, and they assume that such factors affect the quality of teaching and learning in the Vietnamese context. However, as Vietnamese teachers, their status and power are values that come from the social tradition in which teachers are highly respected and are important values in the culture of learning in Vietnamese education. If these values are considered problematic and are held to affect the quality of teaching, this may go against Suresh Canagarajah's (2005) argument that 'local is a relational and fluid construct[;] ... paralleling the appropriation of the global by the local, the global has absorbed local knowledge and resources for its own purpose' (p. 10). Canagarajah also warns of the risk of giving a low estimation of local knowledge, causing impediments to alternative development. Also evident in Lan's interview is the conceptualization of the dominant discourse's *managerial role*. It can be seen from the data that local knowledge of competence, expertise and professionalism in language teaching seems to be viewed as one-sided from the perspective of a 'Western' ELT orientation and understanding of teaching. As Jack Richards (2010) argues, teaching is sometimes said to be 'situated' and can only be understood within a particular context and, hence, the nature of effectiveness in teaching is not always easy to define, as conceptions of good teaching differ from culture to culture.

With the current spread of English, EFL learners should not be viewed as deficient or error-prone non-native learners (McKay, 2003). Also, given the local and international contexts as settings of language use, English learners who have inclined to be ascribed to fixed identity have been repositioned (Alptekin, 2002). In theory, EIL really opens up avenues for both learners and teachers of English in the more peripheral contexts of global English to perceive and define themselves differently; however, in practice, stable norms and goals are still entrenched in teaching and learning discourses in such contexts (see Figure 12.1).

While the training courses in Australia helped these ELT professionals to enhance their professional identity in terms of pedagogical competence, they appeared to hold certain assumptions about their role as ELT professionals in their own teaching context and stereotypes about their learners. Why did they still hold such conceptions in mind? One reason might be because dominant discourses in language teaching and learning theories are so powerful and well-established that they take longer to be erased than we anticipate; or this may seem to be the case because we as teachers – and as researchers – are interpreting the local through global lenses and not vice versa. The global values are considered the point of reference in Western theories or standards against which local values are weighed up (Canagarajah, 2005). However, the formulation of 'cultures of learning' as reciprocal learning about the cultural ways of learning by participants in intercultural contexts can potentially resolve this problematic when the discourses are seen as part of a two-way process of both mediating learning and locating educational identities (Cortazzi & Jin, 2002). This formulation can apply to these teachers and their students in Vietnam – and to the researchers – to mediate for a synergy within the tensions between the local and global while giving respect to and understanding of the need for the values of both.

12.5   Implications for TESOL professionals

Based on the findings and discussion, some suggestions can be made for the ELT field. EFL teachers in their teaching context should be made aware of their professional selves in continuity and fluidity from their prior learning and teaching experience. In this way, their professionalism can be more legitimate and richer as the norms, values of practice and language ideology shift away from the monolithic view in language teaching and learning.

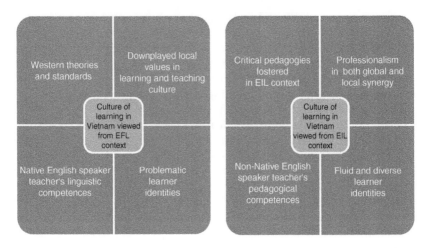

Figure 12.1   The matrix shows the contrastive perspectives regarding the formulation of 'culture of learning' as reciprocal learning in intercultural contexts

This would benefit their teaching philosophy in a more informed manner which dynamically combines the local and global.

The data also help ELT courses to respond better to local contexts of non-native speaker ELT professionals. Such courses should be an arena for ELT professionals to raise their voices regarding local constructions of knowledge in language teaching and learning, which needs to be redefined and respected in a synergy with global practices (Cortazzi & Jin, 2002). Furthermore, this study opens up space for both Western and Eastern scholars to work more on the validity of EIL approaches and their application in EFL contexts (see Figure 12.1).

Another important implication of our study is that English language teachers need to view the learner through a different lens with institutionalized standards so that both the learners and teachers become empowered in their learning and teaching contexts. Furthermore, this research helps to raise awareness among teachers who are desperate for change in their teaching practices for the sake of the future of their students, and it suggests more insights into the complex, non-linear nature of teachers' conceptual change regarding their resistance, struggle and adaptation to accommodate change in teaching approaches.

References

Alptekin, C. (2002) Towards intercultural communicative competence in ELT. *ELT Journal,* 56 (1), 57–64.

Bui, T. M. H. (2006) Teaching speaking skills at a Vietnamese University and Recommendations for Using CMC. *Asian-EFL Journal,* 14.

Calderhead, J. (1996) Teachers: Beliefs and knowledge. In D. C. Berliner and R. C. Calfee (Eds), *Handbook of educational psychology.* London: Macmillan Publishers, pp. 709–25.

Cameron, D. (2000) Difficult subjects. *Critical Quarterly,* 42 (4), 89–94.

Canagarajah, A. S. (2005) *Reclaiming the local in language policy and practice.* Mahwah, NJ: Lawrence Erlbaum Associates.

Cortazzi, M. & Jin, L. (2002). Cultures of learning: The social construction of educational identities. In D. C. S. Li (Ed.), *Discourses in search of members in Honor of Ron Scollon.* Lanham: University Press of America, pp. 49–77.

Dang, H. V. (2006) *Constructions of active language learners in English as a Foreign Language (EFL) teacher education in Vietnam.* Unpublished Doctoral Thesis, University of South Australia, Adelaide.

Duff, P. A. & Uchida, Y. (1997) The negotiation of teachers' socio-cultural identities and practices in postsecondary EFL classrooms. *TESOL Quarterly,* 31 (3), 451–85.

Graddol, D. & British Council (2006) English next. Why global English may mean the end of English as a foreign language, p. 132. Available from http://www.british-council.org/learning-research-englishnext.htmz

Hempel, M. (2009) *Global English: English is changing the world: In what way is the world changing the English language and the way it will be taught?* Munich: GRIN Verlag.

Hoang, V. V. (2008) The current situation and issues of the teaching of English in Vietnam. Retrieved from http://www.ritsumei.ac.jp/acd/re/k-rsc/lcs/kiyou/pdf_22–1/RitsIILCS_22.1pp.7–18_HOANG.pdf

Jenkins, J. (2005) Implementing an international approach to English pronunciation: The role of teacher attitudes and identity. *TESOL Quarterly,* 39 (3), 535–43.

Jenkins, J. (2007) *English as a lingua Franca: Attitude and identity.* Oxford: Oxford University Press.

Kano, Y. & Norton, B. (2003) Imagined communities and educational possibilities: Introduction. *Journal of Language, Identity and Education,* 2 (4), 241–49

Le, C. V. (2001) Language and Vietnamese pedagogical contexts. *Teacher's Edition,* 2001 (7), 34–39.

Le, C. V. (2004) From ideology to inquiry: Mediating Asian and Western Values in ELT. *Teacher's Edition,* 15, 28–34.

Lin, A., Wang, W., Akamatsu, N. & Riazi, M. (2005) International TESOL professionals and teaching English for glocalized communication (TEGCOM). In A. S. Canagarajah (Ed.), *Reclaiming the local in language policy and practice.* Mahwah, NJ: L. Erlbaum Associates, pp. 197–224

Liou, I. Y.-S. (2008) 'English as an international language and teachers' professional identity'. Unpublished Doctoral Thesis, Deakin University, Melbourne.

Liu, J. (1999) Non-native English-speaking professionals in TESOL. *TESOL Quarterly,* 33 (1), 85–102.

Llurda, E. (2004) Non-native-speaker Teachers and English as an international language. *International Journal of Applied Lingustics,* 14 (3), 314–23.

Llurda, E. & Huguet, A. (2003) Self-awareness in NNS EFL primary and secondary school teachers. *Language Awareness,* 12 (3–4), 220–33.

Matsuda, A. (2009) Negotiating ELT assumptions in EIL classrooms. In J. Edge (Ed.), *(Re-) locating TESOL in an age of empire.* Basingstoke: Palgrave Macmillan, pp. 158–70.

McKay, S. (2003) Toward an appropriate EIL pedagogy: Re-examining common ELT assumptions. *International Journal of Applied Lingustics,* 31 (1), 1–22.

McKay, S. & Bokhorst-Heng, W. (2008) International English in its sociolinguistic contexts: Towards a socially sensitive EIL pedagogy. New York: Routledge.

Medgyes, P. (1999) *The non-native teacher* (2nd edn). Ismaning: Hueber.

Medgyes, P. & Reves, T. (1994) The Non-native English speaking EFL/ESL teacher's self-image: An international survey. *System,* 22 (2), 353–67.

Nguyen, H. T. (2008) Conception of teaching by five Vietnamese American preservice teachers. *Journal of Language, Identity & Education,* 7 (2), 113–36.

Nguyen, X. V. (2004) English teaching in Vietnam today. In W. K. Ho and R. Wong (Eds.), *English language teaching in East Asia today: Changing policies and practices* (2nd edn). Singapore: Eastern Universities Press, pp. 447–54.

Norton-Peirce, B. (1995) Social identity, investment, and language learning. *TESOL Quarterly,* 29 (1), 9–31.

Norton, B. (2000) *Identity and language learning: gender, ethnicity and educational change.* Harlow: Longman.

Norton, B. & Toohey, K. (2004) *Critical pedagogies and language learning.* New York: Cambridge University Press.

Nunan, D. (2003) The impact of English as a global language on educational policies and practices in the Asia-Pacific region. *TESOL Quarterly,* 37 (4), 589–613.

Pavlenko, A. (2003) 'I Never Knew I Was a Bilingual': Reimagining teacher identities in TESOL. *Journal of Language, Identity & Education,* 2 (4), 251–68.

Pham, H. H. (2000) *The key socio-cultural factors that work against success in tertiary English language training programs in Vietnam.* Paper presented at the the Fourth International Conference on Language and Development, Hanoi.

Phan, H. L. (2008) *Teaching English as an international language: Identity, resistance and negotiation.* Clevedon: Multilingual Matters.

Richards, J. C. (2010) Competence and performance in language teaching. *RELC Journal,* 41 (2), 101–22.

Seidlhofer, B. (2004) Research perspectives on teaching English As a lingua franca. *Annual Review of Applied Linguistics,* 24, 209–39.

Sharifian, F. (2009) *English as an international language: Perspectives and pedagogical issues.* Bristol: Multilingual Matters.

Sifakis, N. C. & Sougari, A.-M. (2005). Pronunciation issues and EIL pedagogy in the periphery: A survey of Greek state school teachers' beliefs. *TESOL Quarterly,* 39 (3), 467–88.

Tang, C. (1997) The identity of the Non-native ESL teacher on the power and status of non-native ESL teachers. *TESOL Quarterly,* 31 (3), 577–80.

Tsui, A. B. M. & Bunton, D. (2000) The discourse and attitudes of English language Teachers in Hong Kong. *World Englishes,* 19 (3), 287–303.

Varghese, M. M., B.; Johnston, B. and Johnson, K. A (2005). Theorizing language teacher identity: Three perspectives and beyond. *Journal of Language, Identity & Education,* 4 (1), 21–41.

Woods, D. (1996) *Teacher cognition in language teaching: Beliefs, decision-making, and classroom practice.* Cambridge: Cambridge University Press.

Zacharias, N. (2010) *Stories of multilingual English teachers: Negotiating teacher identities in the land of the 'natives'.* Saarbrücken: VDM Verlag Dr. Müller Aktiengesellschaft.

Part IV

The Dynamics of Socialization and Motivation in Cultures of Learning

13

Cultural Models, Children's Beliefs and Parental Socialization: European American and Chinese Learning

Jin Li

No doubt the world is changing, and changing fast. As globalization broadens and deepens, it is only understandable that we feel the world is shrinking into an ever more-downsized village. Such sweeping change may render any attempt to distinguish cultural variations in human lives as futile and superfluous. There is little wonder that some would like to collapse all accumulated human knowledge and wisdom into a grand consilience (Wilson, 1998). However grand that ambition that may be, research on human psychology indicates quite the contrary (Henrich et al., 2010; Phinney & Baldelomar, 2011). It appears that the more the world is globalized, the more people strive to maintain, protect, and sanctify their cultural and ethnic distinction, as the case of the diversity-saturated America demonstrates. Clues from other increasingly diverse cultures indicate a similar pattern (Grigorenko & Takanishi, 2009).

There are many reasons why this seemingly strange counterforce against change exists. However, it is not the goal of this chapter to enumerate all the reasons. Relevant to this chapter's central theme is one main reason: the need for distinction as an indispensable part of human identity that is inherently coalesced with cultural values. Every person develops an identity. In the core of our identity is the notion of distinction and uniqueness (Damon & Hart, 1988). It is erroneous to assume that just because many cultures endorse the interdependent self (Markus & Kitayama, 1991), their people have no need for distinction and uniqueness. Of course, the specific configurations of distinction and uniqueness may differ across cultures. Furthermore, the notions of distinction and uniqueness do not merely apply to individuals but also to groups to which individuals belong. A significant outcome of successful identity development is cultural/ethnic pride, self-respect, and dignity that further nurture and sustain people's lives. This basic human need is likely the reason why cultures continue to endure and adapt rather than diminish and voluntarily destroy themselves.

In this chapter, I focus on one essential part of cultural maintenance, transmission, and continuity: cultural learning models. Research in recent decades has provided clear evidence that cultural learning models exist (Chan & Rao, 2009; Li, 2003; Watkins & Biggs, 1996, 2001). They can be traced back to the long-standing intellectual traditions that were formed in the process of development of individual cultures throughout history. As part of a particular culture's core values, these learning models shape children's learning beliefs and learning outcomes. When children become adults and parents, they use their culturally based learning beliefs to socialize the next generation. The importance of cultural learning models is apparent in education and childrearing across time and world regions. Although cultural learning models may change in response to external forces, their core values tend to endure. In order to show the existence and functions of cultural learning models, children's learning beliefs, and parental socialization, I review relevant research and the empirical methods used to conduct such research. I conclude the chapter by discussing future research directions.

13.1   Cultural learning models as a repertoire of cultural meaning system

The idea of cultural models was introduced and studied by anthropologists (D'Andrade, 1995; Harkness & Super, 1996; Shweder, 1991). They examined components of a given culture that serve to structure people's lives with regularity. Such structured components are called cultural models because they provide relatively stable contexts, scripts, and patterns for people to lead their lives. As such, cultural models enable people to anticipate, participate in, explain, predict, and interpret their activities and interactions (D'Andrade, 1992; Quinn & Holland, 1987). For example, the notion of family is a cultural model containing set meanings that people formulate within a given culture. Since learning is a universal human activity but takes place within specific cultures, learning is also thought of as contextualized, scripted, and patterned according to cultural values and processes (Li, 2003, 2012), thus the term *cultural learning models* (CLMs).

How do we know that different CLMs exist? There are many ways to ascertain this knowledge. We could, for example, search the database for published articles on the topic, review the research, and construct a composite picture of learning models across cultures. We could also conduct in-depth interviews and observations of learning and derive learning models thereof. Despite the high validity of these research efforts, they are costly and time-consuming. One way to achieve the goal of understanding CLMs is to use the so-called *prototype method* commonly employed in cognitive science. This particular empirical approach examines the living language of a cultural group. Through accessing the lexicon that refers to learning, we can obtain concepts and meanings contained in such a lexicon. The ways in which these meanings are organized allow us a glimpse into CLMs.

Although previous research documented cultural variations of learning, little research existed on CLMs. My own research has tried to fill this research gap (Li, 2003). My particular focus was on similarities shared, and differences between, Chinese and European American (EA) learning models. These cultures were chosen because they both have comparably long intellectual histories, both emphasize learning, and both invest heavily in their children's education. Yet, despite these similarities, these two cultures differ markedly in their intellectual outlooks and values attached to learning and education. Taken together, they offer an excellent empirical basis for understanding the role of culture in shaping learning models.

To document Chinese and EA CLMs, I asked EA and Chinese college students to list terms in their respective languages they freely associated with the English term *learn/learning* and its Chinese equivalent *xuexi* (学习) (this age group was preferred because of the high demand in this task on their ability to differentiate fine meanings of words) (see Li, 2003, for details). This procedure produced nearly 500 terms from each culture, which total was further reduced to 205 English and 225 Chinese terms by using a rating procedure to ascertain the degree of each term's relevance to learning. The consensus for each culture's list was regarded as representing core cultural terms. These core terms were sorted further by a different group of college students from each culture, who arranged the terms according to similarity in meaning. With the statistical procedure of cluster analysis, the sorted groupings resulted in a conceptual map of learning in each culture.

Next, I asked EA and Chinese students to describe their ideal learners in order to obtain accounts of learning images as embodied in real people beyond the learning terms in my lexicon study (Li, 2002). Ideal learner images are assumed to exist in people's minds through the process of their upbringing. As such, members of the culture use these images consciously or unconsciously to guide their own learning and to socialize their own children (Bruner, 1986). Participants wrote about four dimensions: (a) ideal learners' thinking on their purposes and processes of learning, (b) their views of the relationship between learning and one's moral development, (c) their learning behaviors in routine situations, such as facing high achievement, failure, and boredom, and (d) their emotional patterns associated with good or poor learning. Cluster analyses of these written descriptions yielded four profiles corresponding to the four sets of probes for each culture (see Li, 2002, for more details).

The basic findings from the two studies reveal comprehensive pictures of the two cultures' learning models. Each culture's model contains four dimensions of learning: purpose, agentic process, achievement, and affect. With regard to purpose, the EA model centers around the finely differentiated functions of the mind in order to understand the world, develop personal skills, and realize personal goals. To pursue these purposes, one engages in the learning process that is characteristically active, such as reading, hands-on construction of scientific models, and participation in volunteer work. Thinking in all forms (deductive and inductive logic), levels (brainstorming and analysing), and dimensions (comparing and contrasting) assumes key importance. A pivotal step is inquiry that guides one to examine and question the known and to explore and discover the new. In these processes, one also needs to communicate in order to understand as well as to make others understand one's own learning results. A high premium is placed on the act of self-expression, such as arguing, debating, and presenting one's thoughts and feelings. Such learning is powered by personal curiosity, interest, and intrinsic enjoyment throughout the learning process. Among the learning affects, a challenging attitude on the part of the learner is highly prized. Those who challenge authority and the existing canons of knowledge are often regarded as the best learners. EA learning aims at understanding the essentials of a given topic and/or developing expertise in a field, personal insights and creative problem solving in real life, and being the best one can be. When these goals are realized, one feels, not merely happy, but proud of oneself. However, when experiencing failure, one feels disappointment, indifference, and low self-esteem.

In contrast, the Chinese model elaborates on perfecting oneself morally and socially as a main purpose of learning, followed by acquiring knowledge and skill for oneself, and contributing to society. Embedded in these purposes are commitment, love, passion, and thirst for knowledge which may or may not be intrinsic in origin as understood in the West. To pursue those purposes of learning, one needs to develop the so-called learning virtues of diligence, self-exertion, endurance of hardship, perseverance, and concentration. These virtues are seen as more essential than actual learning activities, such as thinking, asking questions, practicing, or doing research. Chinese learners believe that once the learning virtues are there, one can apply them to all learning activities and processes. Since these virtues are by their nature volitional attitudes, affect is implicit in each virtue. An additional affect in the learning processes is respect for knowledge and teaching authority, which does not mean obedience and blind acceptance of what is taught. Respect for teaching authority is receptivity to learning and willingness to put one's ego to the side in order to improve oneself continuously. Such learning aims at breadth and depth or mastery of knowledge, application of knowledge to real life situations and problems, and unity of one's knowledge and moral character. When learners achieve learning, they remain calm and humble; they also watch out for signs of complacency and arrogance in order to continue self-perfecting. When encountering failure, they feel shame and guilt, not only themselves but also in reference to those who nurtured them. However, given that the ultimate purpose of learning is a lifelong process, failure does not lead to prolonged disappointment, indifference, learned helplessness, or low self-esteem. Instead, mistakes and failures may motivate learners to work harder to self-improve.

Based on the above studies, CLMs define what learning is, what purposes it serves, what people think it takes to learn something, what achievement standards people ought to pursue, how people feel about learning and achievement, what rewards people receive for good learning and what consequences people anticipate for poor learning, how people feel about high achievers versus low achievers and, finally, who supports their learning.

Because the learning lexicon leans heavily toward the mind and its functions, the EA learning model has been referred to as a mind-oriented model. Owing to the common intellectual origin and historical development, this learning model is also understood as the general Western learning model (Li, 2005), with the caution that the 'West' clearly includes much diversity in approaches to learning. This initial claim has been confirmed by recent extended research involving Europeans (Kühnen et al., 2009). Likewise, because the Chinese model emphasizes learning virtues, this model has been referred to as a virtual-oriented learning model. Although there may be subtle differences among East Asian learning orientations, research in general indicates that the so-called Chinese model may be more accurately called 'Confucian-heritage' model which applies also to other East Asian cultures such as Korea, Japan, and Vietnam beyond the culturally Chinese societies of Taiwan, Hong Kong, and Singapore (Watkins & Biggs, 1996).

13.2 Children's learning beliefs as reflection of their cultural models

How do cultural learning models influence children's learning beliefs? Here I use the term *children's learning beliefs* (CLBs) instead of cultural learning models, to differentiate the fact that individual children do not internalize the entire learning model of their culture. Cultural learning models exist at the cultural, that is, collective, level. Compared to cultural learning models, CLBs are fewer in quantity and less comprehensive and complex. CLMs are cultural resources for individuals to appropriate according to their development and needs, and they serve as guides for child development and learning. Thus, CLBs should reflect their CLMs.

In order to trace developmental origins of CLBs, I conducted a number of studies with 93 Chinese and 93 EA preschool children (with a total of 188 children 4–6 years of age, balanced for each age and gender) (Li, 2004a, 2004b; Li & Wang, 2004, for more technical details). Children were told story beginnings and asked to complete the stories. One set of stories depicted a protagonist child who liked to go to school and another child who did not. Another set showed a child who achieved best in his or her class. A third set presented a hardworking bird who tried hard to learn how to fly and succeeded, as well as a bear who tried to learn how to catch fish but gave up in the end. The final set presented a child who is doing homework at home but is distracted by children playing outside. The first set of stories elicited children's perceptions of the purposes of school learning; the second set tapped children's perceptions of their achieving peers; the third set focused on their construals of what the learning process involves; and the fourth set probed children's views of the conflict between the need to learn and the desire to play (Li, 2012).

Based on the CLMs summarized in the previous section, we hypothesized that for learning purposes, EA children would focus on mind, mental functions (e.g., 'learning makes you smart'), and fun, whereas Chinese children would elaborate on self-growth (e.g., 'learning makes me grow'), social purposes (e.g., 'you learn and you can tell others why they should not fight'), and seriousness (e.g., 'you can't just play in school; you have to learn'). For children's perceptions of achievement, we anticipated that both groups of children would know that achieving well is positive for the protagonist, parents, and teachers. However, EA children would be more sensitive to the social cost of high achieving in that low achieving peers would express negativity toward high achieving peers. By contrast, Chinese children would not express such negativity but, instead, admiration and the desire to emulate high achievers. Chinese children would also be concerned about high achievers as being more vulnerable to arrogance, whereas EA children would not have such a concern. For the learning process, we expected that EA children would be oriented toward mind and its functions, such as 'smart' and 'ability', open exploration, and creative strategy use. Chinese children would be oriented toward learning virtues such as diligence (i.e., frequent practice), persistence (i.e., carry out an activity from the beginning to the very end without stopping), and concentration. Finally, for response to the conflict between homework and play, we predicted that EA children would see effortful learning and play as having equal weight for them, but Chinese children would regard effortful learning as a non-negotiable commitment (Li, 2012).

Data analysis proceeded in a laborious, multilayered, and multicycled process for deriving codes – a branch of content analysis. Established codes were used to code the data into frequencies of thoughts and feelings by native speakers. These coders were unaware of the above hypotheses.

Results showed that, consistent with our hypotheses and their associated CLMs, EA children talked more about smartness (i.e., emphasizing the mental), literacy, friendship, and play as their purposes for going to school. Chinese children mentioned more the need to self-improve morally, mastery of knowledge (defined with a moral component), social contribution, and social respect/economic reward as their purposes. Regarding their perceptions of the achieving peers, EA children mentioned the achiever's intellectual development and positive affects (e.g., happiness, pride) felt by the achiever and his or her parents and teachers. But they expressed significantly more concerns about negative consequences of achieving well in school (e.g., rejection and social isolation from peers) than did Chinese children. Chinese children talked more about the social respect the high achievers received and their ability to help others with their knowledge. Although Chinese students voiced more negative parental concerns about lack of achievement among other students in the class than did EA students, they often expressed respect for their high-achieving peers and a desire to emulate them. The high achievers were also perceived as having a need to be humble in order to improve themselves further.

In their construals of the learning process, EA children referred more to ability and related mental processes, to exploration in order to increase of the chance of success, and to creative strategies. Chinese children mentioned more the virtues of diligence, persistence, and concentration. In response to the conflict between homework and play, EA children expressed the belief that work and play are equally important, and that it is up to them to negotiate with their parents to determine which of these to prioritize. Chinese children expressed more the notion that homework must be completed before they should play.

These trends became more consistent in each higher age group. These developmental data suggest that the respective CLMs are likely to shape the beliefs and learning orientations of children. Such an influence can be observed in children as young as four years of age. These age-related findings have important educational implications for early childhood education.

13.3   Parental socialization and their shaping power

It is clear that children develop learning beliefs that resemble their cultures' learning models. However, the missing link for our understanding is how, specifically, CLMs enter children's minds and become their own beliefs. Children are not born with set beliefs, but they acquire them as they grow older. How does this process unfold? Research on socialization in general points to what parents do at home as a main source of child development (Bornstein, 1995; Harkness & Super, 1996). Although children are exposed to outside influences, parental socialization is undeniably most crucial. The simple reason for this is that young children spend much more time with their caregivers than with other people or in virtual places such as the Internet. The younger the child is, the stronger is the influence of parents. As noted previously, parents were once upon a time children themselves. While they were brought up by their caregivers, they internalized their culture's learning models. When children become adults and assume the parental role, they naturally use their knowledge and beliefs, or 'ethnotheories', as conceptualized and researched by Sara Harkness and Charles Super (1992), to socialize their children. Moreover, the way parents socialize their children is mostly implicit, as a matter of daily routine. Anthropologists refer to this very powerful process as *enculturation* (LeVine, 1990). Socialization is essentially the same process except that it emphasizes structured, explicit, and deliberate guiding and teaching. Formal schooling is an example of socialization rather than enculturation. In today's education-heavy world, enculturation and socialization join forces in childrearing. Parents both enculturate and socialize; for this reason they are the most committed, effective, and successful transmitters of cultural values. To paraphrase Richard Shweder's (2011) metaphor, if cultural values are prescriptions for people to follow, caregivers and parents are the prime executors of such prescriptions for children.

To study what A or B is or is not is much easier than studying how A *becomes* B, especially when the becoming is a gradual process. The paradox is that we can hardly see the change in a given moment or on a given day, but we can see the change over time. Furthermore, to attempt to capture the flow of parental socialization is to ladle the rolling water in a river. No sooner has one taken a specimen, than the water is no longer the same, it has flowed forward. This is the phenomenon famously noted long ago by the Greek philosopher Heraclitus: 'You could not step twice into the same river'. This enigmatic nature of parental socialization poses serious challenges to empirical research on this essential process.

However, thanks to advancement in developmental science, we now have some effective research methods that enable researchers to peek into this process. Researchers on children's memory development as a function of parent-child co-construction of recalled experiences use the method of parent–child conversations (Fivush & Nelson, 2006; Van Abbema & Bauer, 2008). Either naturally occurring or simulated daily conversations are recorded. These conversations take place in real time on actual, lived experiences, thereby providing a good window for understanding socialization process. When parents and children talk with each other, culturally encoded concept, ideas, and affects are expressed (Wang, 2001, 2004). Moreover, what is valued and not valued as well as parental attempts to instruct, encourage, model, correct, and discipline – as well as children's responses – are revealed. Finally, disagreements, negotiations, harmony, or disharmony between parents and children are fully displayed (Miller et al., 2001).

Research on parental socialization of CLBs is scarce because research on CLMs and CLBs is a relatively new line of inquiry. To my knowledge, no one has studied this topic. In order to address this research limitation, my collaborator Heidi Fung and I (Li et al., 2008) used mother–child conversations about learning (MCCs) to explore cultural differences in parental socialization of CLBs. Since this research is more recent, I take more space to describe it and report our findings.

We recorded the MCCs between EA and Taiwanese (TW) mothers and their children aged 6–10. The sample consisted of 218 mother–child pairs (102 EA and 116 Taiwanese) all of whom were from middle-class backgrounds. There were 100 boys (43 EA and 57 TW) and 118 girls (59 EA and 59 TW) and 53 6- or 7-year olds, 74 8-year olds, 62 9-year olds, and 29 10-year olds. We targeted this age range of children because they were early elementary school students who had some education experience that was needed for recording MCCs.

We hypothesized that each culture's mothers would use their culturally based learning beliefs (as found in our previous studies) to socialize their children. Accordingly, EA mothers would emphasize the mind and mental functions and learning strategies, positive affect, but talk less about learning virtues as well as downplay negative affect (Ng et al., 2007). By contrast, TW mothers, being members of a Confucian-heritage culture, would elaborate on learning virtues more than mental functions and learning strategies. They would also be more open to addressing negative affect in learning.

We asked each mother to identity a positive and a negative learning attitude or behavior that she knew her child showed and then to talk to her child about each. The order of the positive and negative attitudes/behaviors was randomly determined by having the mother choose a topic from the two. For convenience, we refer to the positive topic as 'good learning' and the negative topic as 'poor learning'. The topic prompt for good learning is as follows:

> Recall an actual incident where your child showed, in your judgment, good attitudes/behavior in learning. It could be in school or outside school. The incident does not need to be something that you personally witnessed. But you should know about it in some detail to talk about it with your child. You have unlimited time to talk about this incident, and the conversation can go in any direction.

The topic prompt for poor learning is identical to that for good learning except the word 'good' was replaced with 'not perfect'

EA pairs were interviewed by native English speakers from the United States and TW pairs by native Mandarin speakers in Taiwan. The English and Chinese versions of the prompts were developed simultaneously by a team of fully bilingual and bicultural researchers. The prompts were piloted and revised to ensure comprehension and compatibility before data collection began. These MCCs lasted anywhere from a few minutes to more than 30 minutes. They were transcribed verbatim for analysis.

We conducted two sets of analyses: structural and sequential. For structural analysis, we tallied the number of turns that the mother and the child took, the length of each MCC, and volume (subject–verb output in a given MCC in order to establish the linguistic equivalence of English and Chinese; see Fivush et al., 2000, for this technical detail). We found no differences in these structural elements by culture, gender, or age. Thus, any differences we found were not because of these elements, but something else.

Sequential analysis is used to track the likelihood of a given topic by a conversation starter, referred to as a 'given' that is followed by the partner, referred to as a 'lag' (Bakeman & Gottman, 1997). In order to conduct such analysis, the data needed to be coded into 'events'. An event is a topic; for example, a mother starting to talk about how the child liked reading. Based on previous research on these cultures' learning models and individuals' learning beliefs, we generated an initial list of topics. Then, two coding teams, each comprising two coders for each culture, read 20 per cent of a randomly selected sample of the data to trial the coding according the initial list of topics. Within each culture, the two coders read the identical set of data, but each coder's reading of the data was independent of that of the other coder. When the coders encountered new topics from each culture that could not be accommodated by the initial list of topics, they met and, through discussion, reached consensus whether to add new topics to the list. Through this laborious process, we generated a final list of 30 topics that accommodated all of this 20 per cent of the data.

Because sequential analysis constrains how many events and turns can be used for a given set of data, we needed to group the 59 topics into four sets of topics: (a) when the mother or the child mentioned the mind and its functions and learning activities (e.g., reading, homework, thinking, and ability), abbreviated as *mental*, (b) when both partners talked about positive affect (e.g., happiness, liking, pride, and interest), abbreviated as *positive*, (c) when both discussed negative affect (e.g., frustration, dislike, anger, and boredom), abbreviated as *negative*, and (d) when both referred to learning virtues (e.g., diligence, earnestness, persistence, and concentration), abbreviated as *virtue*. Our data allowed us to compute four turns.

In order to compute the cultural differences (Bakeman & Quera, 1995) in how a given topic from a starter is followed by the partner, we set each of the four topics by mother first and then by child again. This means that we examined how a topic initiated by the mother was followed for three steps (starting plus three turns following) and, likewise, setting a topic mentioned by the child first, and tracked how that topic was followed by the mother. Since each topic could have been followed by the partner with any of the four topics, we examined all possible sequences. Thus, we have a sequence of the mother as the starter→child→mother→child for each topic with a total of four sequences for good learning and a second sequence of the same mother–child chain for poor learning, resulting in eight sequences. Then we repeated the analysis for the sequence of the child as the starter→mother→child→mother for both good and poor learning, resulting in another eight sequences. Therefore, there were 16 sequences, half for good and half for poor learning.

The specific statistics we used were odds of each given versus each lag by constructing two X 2 tables, and then odds ratios between EA and TW for each topic. In order to calculate statistical significance level, we set the odds ratios at 95 per cent confidence interval and $p < 0.05$. Any odds ratio that was smaller or greater than 1 and any confidence interval that did not include 1 was significant.

To provide the overall picture of the distribution of EA versus TW MCCs, I present Figure 13.1 for good learning and Figure 13.2 for poor learning by culture. As can be seen in Figure 13.1, the two cultures' MCCs for good learning did not differ much. In general, mothers (m) talked most about mental (M), followed by positive (P), virtue (V), and negative (N) last. It makes sense that mothers would focus on positive rather than negative affect since they recalled with their children a *good* learning attitude/behavior. Still, it is noticeable that TW MCCs talked more about virtue than did their EA counterparts. Tests for odds ratio further confirmed no statistically significant differences in the four pairs of codes between the two cultures' children. However, there were two significant differences between the two groups of mothers. EA mothers talked more about positive affect and TW mothers more about virtue.

For poor learning, the distribution in Figure 13.2 is quite different. There were significant cultural differences for every set of topics. First, EA mothers (m) and children (c) still talked most about mental (M) followed by positive (P), then virtue (V), and negative (N) last. TW mothers talked most about virtue, and next about mental, negative, and positive last. It seems that EA mothers stressed mental and positive affects over learning virtue. Negative affect was to be avoided. By contrast, Taiwanese mothers focused on virtue and then on mental. Unlike their EA peers, TW mothers elaborated more on

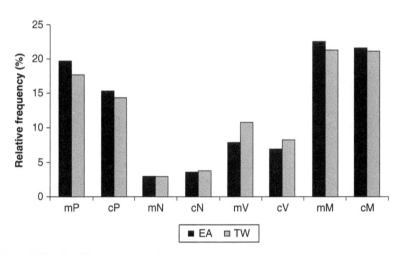

Figure 13.1 Good learning by culture

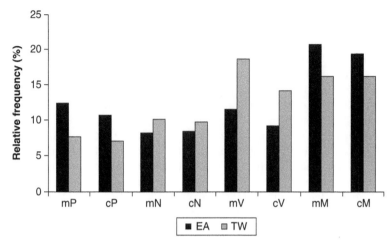

Figure 13.2   Poor learning by culture

Table 13.1   Sequences of EA and TW mothers starting to talk about their children's poor learning for four turns

	EA				TW		
Turn 1: Mother	**Turn 2: Child**	**Turn 3: Mother**	**Turn 4: Child**	**Turn 1: Mother**	**Turn 2: Child**	**Turn 3: Mother**	**Turn 4: Child**
Mental →	Positive →	Positive →	Both positive/ mental	Mental →	Mental →	X	Virtue
Positive →	Mental →	Both positive/ mental	Mental	Positive →	X	Virtue→	Virtue
Negative →	Positive →	Positive →	Positive →	Negative →	X	Virtue→	Virtue
Virtue →	Positive →	Positive →	Positive	Virtue →	X	X	X

Note: Mental = mental functions and learning activities, positive = positive affect, negative = negative affect, and virtue = learning virtue. Arows indicate significant turns for the cultural groups all based on odds ratio at 95% confidence interval, $p < .05$.

negative affect with their children. Positive affect, in comparison, was least emphasized. Tests for odds ratio further confirmed these findings.

Owing to space limitations, I present a table (Table 13.1) based on significant *sequences* (not overall distribution of MCCs), showing EA and TW mothers as starters for poor learning. The remaining statistics for the other sequences show the same cultural patterns.

Table 13.2 EA and TW examples of mother–child conversations for good learning

EA	TW
M: You were learning things but it was <u>fun</u>, wasn't it?	M: ..., why did you <u>feel it hard</u> to spell words, but now you feel easy? Before <u>you were afraid</u> of Chinese, and you didn't like it, but why did you change to liking it now?
C: Yeah.	C: ..., because I did well on my tests,and understand the teacher in class so I like it now.
M: ... do you think it's better when you're doing things ... that like having a play or something, do you think that's better to learn than sitting there and reading a book? <u>Do you think its more fun, or do you can learn more, you just think it's just more fun?</u>	M: That'swhy <u>mom urges you to hold on to persistence toward things, ... the attitude, you need to have seriousness toward learning anything, not afraid of difficulties,</u> don't I?
C: <u>I think</u> it's better to learn....	C: Yes.
M: You think it was easier to learn, when you're ... speaking your lines, going over the lines every day.	M: Like <u>you were afraid</u> of the? standard sound of Chinese..., right
C: Yeah.	C: Mm-hmm.
M: Cause I'm sure, you going over those lines every day, doing the play, I betcha you would <u>remember more</u> than just reading it in the book once or doing a little eassy about it. ... <u>Don't you think?</u>	M:
C: Yeah.	C:

Note: Underline show emphasis on EA mental activities and positive affects vs. TW learning virtues of persistance, seiousness, and courage in learning and negative affect. M = mother and C = child.

In the EA part of Table 13.1, when mothers began talking about mental, children followed up with positive but not mental, but their mothers continued to talk more about positive in the third turn, which was followed by children also talking more about both positive and mental. A similar pattern also emerged for maternal talk of positive first. The turns alternated between positive and mental by the two conversational partners. More striking is the fact that when mothers began with virtue and negative affect, their children still steered the conversation more into positive affect, all the way to the fourth turn.

By contrast, when TW mothers started to talk about mental, their children followed up more with mental. But mothers switched to talk about virtue that continued to be followed up by children with virtue. Similarly, when mothers began to talk about positive or negative, the remaining sequences were likely to move to virtue talk again. However, when both EA and TW mothers started with virtue talk, there were no differences in the follow-ups on virtue (but EA sequences went to more positive instead, as noted before).

In order to give some concrete sense of what these MCCs were like, I present two segments of two MCCs, one EA and one TW on their children's good learning (see Table 13.2). The underlined parts of each segment show the parental socialization focus characteristic in each culture.

Taken together, the sequential analyses compel us to conclude that both groups' mothers and children talk about all four topics. While the follow-ups on the topic of learning virtues do not differ that much between the two cultural groups, the follow-ups on the other three topics are quite revealing. EA mother–child conversations about learning center around positive affect and learning activities/mental functions, regardless of what topic the mother or the child brings up first. In contrast, TW conversations are mostly followed up with learning virtues, also irrespective of what topics the conversation partners begin with.

13.4　Conclusion

The forgoing research on cultural learning models, children's learning beliefs, and parental socialization provides evidence that not only do these models and beliefs exist, but they also exert powerful influences on children. These models and beliefs are likely to persist despite sweeping, dramatic changing currents in the world that are impinging upon long-held cultural values. To the extent that they are tenacious forces at home and school, it is important that we understand what they are and how they operate. This understanding is necessary for early childhood educators before we contemplate changes, their desirability, and implementation.

The research that has been conducted covers only a small fraction of the vast area that awaits further illumination. To continue research in this area, one general direction is suggested as the most pressing issue in today's fast changing world. Within the Confucian-heritage cultures, the force of 'modernization' is deepening: China is the most dramatic example. The term 'modernization' can basically refer to the Western model of organizing life, ranging from political systems to industry, commerce and finance, urbanization, and education. Every cultural community that desires modernization faces the challenge of how to retain its own cultural traditions while simultaneously adapting successfully to changes. This challenge, introduced earlier, threatens the maintenance of cultural tradition that has everything to do with the identity of its people and the culture itself, seen holistically.

To put this question succinctly: Should the Chinese abandon their way of learning and socializing (laying aside the question of whether this is possible)? If so, to what end? What would be the costs if such a massive undertaking were to take place? Is there a clear gain after all? We may recall the effects of an existing cultural experiment in the not too distant past: the Chinese Cultural Revolution (1966–76). There is broad agreement within and outside China, official or otherwise, that this experiment, in which the Confucian learning model was fiercely attacked and abandoned, left generations of students deprived of formal education and other developmental opportunities. The consequence was disastrous (see Li, 2012, for further discussion).

Thus, researchers and practitioners are urged to contemplate this problem carefully. A constructive way to do so is to engage in research. First and foremost, we need to delve into the nature of these basic cultural patterns of child development, learning, teaching, and education. These essential questions have long been neglected, yet large-scale cultural and social experiments have been launched, regardless. In my opinion, only after we have a good grasp of the first question are we in a position to evaluate cultures of learning regarding what to retain, what to jettison, what to borrow, what a 'successful' mixture looks like, how to achieve such a mixture, and how to scale it up across the population. Without this foundational knowledge, we are likely to remain blind, repeating the vicious cycle of plunging into acts that come back to haunt us and later generations.

The seriousness of this challenge pertains not only to people within East Asian societies, but also to children and families who migrate to the West. In most people's minds, immigration from a less well developed country to an advanced one ought to make people's lives better because the destination seems affluent, democratic, scientific and technologically oriented, and efficiently run with a fair judicial system, protected personal rights, free education, and mostly free (except in America) healthcare. But much research shows quite the opposite: the newcomers, the first-generation immigrants, who were born and grew up outside the host country but landed in the West against all odds, surprisingly fare better all round (although not better than non-immigrants in the host country). However, their children, the second-generation, who speak fluent English and enjoy all the benefits from the host country, do worse in health, education, career, and so forth. Sadly, their children, now the third-generation, do even worse. This puzzling phenomenon is aptly dubbed as the 'immigration paradox' (Garcia Coll & Marks, 2009; Portes & Rumbaut, 2001; Suárez-Orozco et al., 2008).

This pattern also applies to Chinese immigrant children and families despite the fact that many attend renowned universities. For example, research shows that children and parents grow apart, witnessing deepening conflict, emotional distancing, and breakdowns in communication, which leaves both children and parents in a state of loss, confusion and, frequently, desperation (Qin, 2006, 2008). Our own recent research on Chinese immigrant preschoolers also indicates that when they attend EA schools, their quietness is associated with lack of learning engagement and dislike by EA peers, as rated by teachers. However, not only do quiet Chinese children attending schools with a preponderance of Asian students not experience negativity, but they also learn and adjust better to school while not being affected differently by peers. Still, the difficult reality is that most Chinese children are seen as more quiet due to culturally based childrearing practices. As a result, they live under undue negativity in EA schools. Yet, most parents, schools, and Chinese communities are unaware of these hidden costs of immigration. This knowledge has become available only recently. Asian immigrants have been settling in the United States for over a century, yet, until recent documentation by this research, we did not know how their children fared in school and how early negativity associated with quietness befell them.

It is thus my hope that more research can be conducted on cultural learning models, children's learning beliefs, and socialization both inside and outside home and, further, to study children's schooling process in conjunction with continued research on home socialization. Such research will undoubtedly help parents and educators to guide children, families, schools, and cultural communities through our testing times.

References

Bakeman, R. & Gottman, J. M. (1997) *Observing interaction: An introduction to sequential analysis* (2nd edn) Cambridge: Cambridge University Press.

Bakeman, R. & Quera, V. (1995) *Analyzing interaction: Sequential analysis with SDIS and GSEQ.* New York: Cambridge University Press.

Bornstein M. H. (Ed.) (1995) *Handbook of parenting, applied and practical parenting,* vol. 4. Hillsdale, NJ: Lawrence Erlbaum.

Bruner, J. (1986) *Actual minds, possible worlds.* Cambridge, MA: Harvard University Press.

Chan, C. & Rao, N. (Eds) (2009) *Revisiting the Chinese learner: Psychological and pedagogical perspectives.* Comparative Education Research Centre (CERC), University of Hong Kong and Springer Press.

Damon, W. & Hart, D. (1988) *Self-understanding in childhood and adolescence.* New York: Cambridge University Press.

D'Andrade, R. G. (1992) Schemas and motivation. In R. G. D'Andrade and C. Strauss (Eds), *Human motives and cultural models.* New York: Cambridge University Press, pp. 23–44.

D'Andrade, R. G. (1995) *The development of cognitive anthropology.* New York: Cambridge University Press.

Fivush, R. & Nelson, K. (2006) Parent–child reminiscing locates the self in the past. *British Journal of Developmental Psychology,* 24 (1), 235–51.

Fivush, R., Brotman, M., Buckner, J. & Goodman, S. (2000) Gender differences in parent-child emotion narratives. *Sex Roles, 42,* 233–53.

Garcia Coll, C. T. & Marks, A. (2009) *Immigrant stories: Ethnicity and academics in middle childhood.* New York: Oxford University Press.

Grigorenko, E. L. & Takanishi, R. (Eds) (2009). *Immigration, diversity, and education.* New York: Routledge.

Harkness, S. & Super, C. (1992) Parental ethnotheories in action. In I. Sigel, A. McGilliguddy-Delisi and J. J. Goodnow (Eds), *Parental belief system: The psychological consequences for children.* Hillsdale, NJ: Erlbaum, pp. 373–91.

Harkness, S. & Super, C. M. (Eds) (1996) *Parents' cultural belief systems: Their origins, expressions and consequences.* New York: Guilford.

Henrich, J., Heine, S. J. & Norenzayan, A. (2010) The weirdest people in the world? *Behavioral and Brain Sciences, 33,* 61–83.

Kühnen, U., van Egmond, M., Haber, F., Kuschel, S., Özelsel, A. & Rossi, A. (2009) Mind and virtue: The meaning of learning across cultures. In G. Gunderson and J. Berninghausen (Eds), *Lost in TransNation: Towards an intercultural dimension on campus.* Bremen, Germany, Kellner.

LeVine, R. A. (1990) Enculturation: A biosocial perspective on the development of self. In D. Cicchetti and M. Beeghly (Eds) *The self in transition: Infancy to childhood.* Chicago: University of Chicago Press, pp. 99–117.

Li, J. (2002) A cultural model of learning: Chinese 'heart and mind for wanting to learn'. *Journal of Cross-Cultural Psychology, 33* (3), 248–69.

Li, J. (2003) U.S. and Chinese cultural beliefs about learning. *Journal of Educational Psychology, 95* (2), 258–67.

Li, J. (2004a) 'I learn and I grow big:' Chinese preschoolers' purposes for learning. *International Journal of Behavioral Development, 28* (2), 116–28.

Li, J. (2004b) Learning as a task and a virtue: U.S. and Chinese preschoolers explain learning. *Developmental Psychology, 40* (4), 595–605.

Li, J. (2005) Mind or virtue: Western and Chinese beliefs about learning. *Current Directions in Psychological Science, 14* (4), 190–94.

Li, J. (2012) *Cultural foundations of learning: East and West.* Cambridge: Cambridge University Press.

Li, J. & Wang, Q. (2004) Perceptions of achievement and achieving peers in U.S. and Chinese kindergartners. *Social Development, 13* (3), 413–36.

Li, J., Fung, H., Liang, C.-H., Resch, J., Luo, L. & Lou, L. (2008) When my child doesn't learn well: European American and Taiwanese mothers talking to their children about their children's learning weaknesses. In J. Li & H. Fung (chairs), *Diverse paths and forms of family socialization: Cultural and ethnic influences.* Symposium paper presented by biannual conference of the International Society for the Study of Behavioral Development, Würzburg, Germany.

Markus, H. R. & Kitayama, S. (1991) Culture and the Self: implications for cognition, emotion, and motivation. *Psychological Review, 98,* 224–53.

Miller, P.J., Sandel, T. L., Liang, C-H. & Fung, H. (2001) Narrating transgressions in Longwood: The discourses, meanings and paradoxes of an American socializing practice. *Ethos, 29* (2), 159–86.

Ng, F. F.-Y., Pomerantz, E. & Lam, S.-F. (2007) European American and Chinese parents' responses to children's success and failure: Implications for children's responses. *Developmental Psychology, 43* (5), 1239–55.

Phinney, J. S. & Baldelomar, O. A. (2011) Identity development in multiple cultural contexts. In L. Arnett Jensen (Ed.), *Bridging cultural and developmental psychology:*

New syntheses in theory, research and policy. New York: Oxford University Press, pp. 161–86.

Portes, A. & Rumbaut, R. G. (2001) *Legacies: The story of the immigrant second generation*. Berkeley: University of California Press.

Qin, D. B.-L. (2006) 'Our child doesn't talk to us anymore': Alienation in immigrant Chinese families. *Anthropology and Education Quarterly*, 37 (2), 162–79.

Qin, D. B.-L. (2008) Doing well v. feeling well: Understanding family dynamics and the psychological adjustment of Chinese immigrant adolescent. *Journal of Youth and Adolescence*, 37 (1), 22–35.

Quinn, N. & Holland, D. (1987) Introduction. In D. Holland and N. Quinn (Eds), *Cultural models in language and thought*. New York: Cambridge University Press, pp. 3–40.

Shweder, R. A. (1991) *Thinking through cultures*. Cambridge, MA: Harvard University Press.

Shweder, R. A. (2011) Commentary: Ontogenetic cultural psychology. In L. A. Jensen (Ed.), *Bridging cultural and developmental psychology: New syntheses in theory, research and policy*. New York: Oxford University Press, pp.303–10.

Suárez-Orozco, C., Suárez-Orozco, M. & Todorova, I. (2008) *Learning a new land: Immigrant students in American society*. New York: Belknap.

Van Abbema, D. L. & Bauer, P. J. (2008). Autobiographical memory in middle childhood: Recollections of the recent and distant past. *Memory*, 13 (8), 829–45.

Wang, Q. (2001) 'Did you have fun?' American and Chinese mother-child conversations about shared emotional experiences. *Cognitive Development*, 16, 693–715.

Wang, Q. (2004) The emergence of cultural self-constructs: Autobiographical memory and self-description in European American and Chinese children. *Developmental Psychology*, 40 (1), 3–15.

Watkins, D. A. & Biggs, J. B. (Eds) (1996) *The Chinese learner: Cultural, psychological, and contextual influences*. Hong Kong: Comparative Education Research Centre.

Watkins, D. A. & Biggs, J. B. (Eds) (2001) *Teaching the Chinese learner: Psychological and pedagogical perspectives*. Hong Kong: Comparative Education Research Centre.

Wilson, E. O. (1998) *Consilience: The unity of knowledge*. New York: Knopf.

14
Social Network Relations in Omani Students' Motivation to Learn English

Sami Dadi and Lixian Jin

Social network relations are important in a culture of learning because within them significant others are likely to have an influence on learners' personal choices and engagement in interaction for learning, which will in turn be factors affecting students' motivation. This can be seen not only in teacher–student relations but also in student–student relations and in the out-of-class informal interactions in which learners engage. Such social networks are likely to be particularly significant in a traditional collective society, such as that of Oman, where – despite modernization in many spheres – family relations and friendships are generally held to be of great importance within the local culture and are likely to influence learning directly or indirectly.

This chapter describes the English Language Teaching (ELT) context in Oman and relates this context to social network relations as a feature of motivation within a culture of learning. The chapter employs questionnaire and interview data to analyse the effects of social network relations on students' motivation to learn English. The attitudes expressed by parents, brothers/ sisters, other relatives, friends, and teachers are shown to have an effect on the students' learning of English as a second language (L2). Significantly, the analysis of the expressions employed by participants reveals some local features of the linguistic mechanisms used to produce change in other people's motivation to learn English. In turn, this suggests ways in which teachers or family members may draw on these mechanisms to catalyse change in motivation and, perhaps, in local cultures of learning.

14.1 Introduction

In a particular socio-cultural context, the motivation to learn English as an L2 is an aspect of the local culture of learning. Social relations exert their influence on the culture of learning by influencing the dynamics of motivation. These dynamics are, in fact, embodied in the locally defined most significant constructs and factors of L2 learning motivation. Hence, cultures of learning determine, in part, these constructs and their type of influence on students' motivation to learn English as L2. The Omani socio-cultural settings reveal an important role for social influence on individuals' choices and interests. These influences are enacted through social network relations within occasions of social interaction. The present study shows the extent of influence of social networks on Omani L2 learners' motivation. It investigates how the cultures of learning formulate the motivational factors among secondary school students. It also identifies a number of mechanisms of effective influence employed for this purpose.

14.2   L2 motivation research

Motivation research was for a long time almost entirely assigned to the domain of psychology. This apparent monopoly resulted in a large number of theories and paradigms that were of little real practical value to L2 learning motivation. Even with the emergence of education-specific models and theories (e.g., Gardner & Lambert, 1959), the socio-cultural parameter was rarely given its due weight. This was mainly owing to the lack of contextualization and (at the time) to ignoring the specificity of each socio-cultural setting. However, there is a relatively recent shift to the socio-cultural dimension (Dornyei, 2001). This has not, however, fully incorporated psychological elements into the specificities of the socio-cultural context of L2 learning motivation. Motivation remains an inclination that needs context-specific elements of cultures of learning.

Among the features of this dimension was the recent concept of L2 Self. Ema Ushioda and Zoltan Dornyei (2009) have attempted to eradicate the claims of integrative motivation by introducing the concept of L2 Self. This is, essentially, the self-concept of the L2 learner, which seeks to transcend cultural affiliations. English is the language of a globalized world; it does not necessarily represent Western civilization, and any people who use it regularly may align themselves with it. However, we cannot prevent learners from associating a target language with its original socio-cultural context. It is difficult to teach a language without cultural references. Many word meanings, for example, reveal aspects of cultural definitions. Being 'honest' refers to specific concepts of favourable evaluation which are culturally bound. What makes a person honest in one specific cultural context can evoke the opposite behaviour in another. So, cultural affiliation is deeply embedded in the mind of the learner, even with English having the status of the language of globalization. Therefore, instead of attempting to transcend the socio-cultural context, it is wiser to attend to it and examine its influence on the students' motivation. In practice, the effects of this socio-cultural context on learning are generally produced and maintained through social network relations.

14.3   Social network influence

Socio-cultural communities share a number of social norms. The diffusion of these norms is assured through social network relations. The social network context is the venue in which a socio-cultural influence is enacted. Values, on the other hand, determine the acceptability of certain behaviour or thought (Lapinski & Rimal, 2005: 129). Whereas the network relations are realized in codes of conduct, values determine acceptability. These two areas seem to be in interaction with interest and efficacy beliefs. In fact, motivation to learn English is an aspect of the norms and values of a social group. Social networks affect these norms and values essentially through efficacy and interest beliefs. The decision to perform certain activities, such as language learning, is based on the judgment of capability: Expectations of capability to achieve, in fact constitute a source of *Self-efficacy* (Bandura, 1986, 1997). Practically, the environment in which individuals live determines their judgments of capabilities (Cottrell, 1996). Also, the acceptability of the outcome of learning determines the interest in pursuing a task. *Interest*, as a complementary factor, is also influenced by social network relations: Interpersonal relations are sources of influence on *Interest* (Kandel, 1978). Since social groups share common interests, it is not strange to find communities with similar choices and attitudes to learning. This is due to the effects of social networks on the creation of common interests and attitudes, which are realized through different mechanisms.

Cotterell (1996) mentioned urging and teasing as two devices that peers use to influence each other. The peer encouragement to pursue some specific activities is another way to reinforce interest (Deci, 1992). From another perspective, the influence on *Interest* is an aspect of social adjustment (Wentzel et al., 2004). Young people need to integrate within their social groups, even if this means adjusting their choices and interests. Academic interest is thus influenced by the company students keep.

Therefore, *Interest* and *Self-efficacy*, as two significant components of motivation, are influenced by the system of social beliefs. These beliefs are diffused by social network relations. Unlike the general concept of social relations, social networks refer to the systematic study of the structure of these relations (Seed, 1990).

The social network is a metaphor which describes the system of relations within a social group. This concept facilitates the description of these social relations. One major aspect of this mapping is that it is necessary to analyse the system of social relations within patterns (Cotterell, 1996). This perspective employs concepts of *closeness* to determine the degree of influence among network members. While frequency can be quantified, the strength of contact remains a quality with a normative value (Seed, 1990). The closer within a network actors are, the more influence they are expected to receive or exert.

Closeness is a general aspect of social networks, an aspect which is more likely to be determined by the qualities of networks. Seed (ibid.) presents a list of relationship qualities – namely esteem, sentiment, and influence – which are mainly affective in nature. They determine the level of closeness and the influence on other social network relations. Sentiments among network agents influence their choices and interests. If a person who is respected has a favourable attitude towards English, others are likely to exhibit a similarly favourable attitude to it. Like sentiments, esteem also gives a highly respected person a special influential position within the community: hence, his/her attitudes influence the choices and interests of others. From these two qualities, we understand the likelihood of influence of network relations. However, the quality of influence attributed to social network relations is best explained through the mechanisms that induce this change in interests and attitudes. In our case, the effects of social network relations on students' motivation to learn English need to be elucidated through the mechanisms of influence. These mechanisms are within the environment, and the system, of social network relations. This influence emerges through the main manifestation of social networks, namely social interaction.

14.4   Social interaction

Social interaction is the manifestation of the relations within social networks. Along with its communicative role, social interaction has a mental function which represents the choices, interests, and attitudes of the individuals (Watson-Gegeo, 2004). Hence, social interaction evokes learners' motivation to learn English by influencing their *Interest* and *Self-efficacy* levels.

Social interaction refers to any form of interpersonal communication between members of a social community. This communication is either non-verbal or verbal which, in terms of education is essentially a source of influence that initiates changes (Kindermann, 2007). In fact, the influence derives from the fact that verbal interaction mediates the construction of the identity of the social group/community (Bucholtz & Hall, 2005). Social realities are defined through linguistic constructions, which are collectively designed and negotiated. Hence, verbal interaction is more likely to be at the origin of the set of interest and attitudes we share with our social community. This is not only an aspect of how the cultures of learning are formed and maintained, but also a source of mechanisms of influence on our motivational forces.

Since social interaction, in general – and linguistic interaction, in particular – largely determines our interest and attitudes, its effects on motivation to learn English as an L2 are reasonably high. Within our social group, we share aspects of interest in particular tasks and the pursuit of certain general goals. Thus, our interest in learning English is partly formulated by the general interests of the community in education, foreign languages, job seeking, and so forth. This is part of the social culture of learning, which determines to some extent what we are interested in learning and the efforts we are likely to exhibit to learn these things. The way these interests are openly expressed in instances of linguistic interaction reveals not only the content but also the devices employed to ensure conformity and maintain group homogeneity.

Linguistic interaction plays an important role in influencing our motivation for particular tasks. Engagement in L2 learning is consequently largely influenced by linguistic interaction. The effectiveness of these desired influences depends on the effectiveness of the mechanisms employed. Generally, normal interaction can aim at producing an effect that transcends the surface level semantics of the discourse. Polite messages, for example, are not always employed to give the same effect. Diamond (1996: 49) gives the examples of the types of mechanisms used to express 'solidarity politeness', revealing attachment to a social group, and 'deference politeness', expressing a difference in status. Apart from the discourse aspect, linguistic interaction reveals the effects which interlocutors aim at producing through language. However, interactive effects on the addressee are not limited to expression of status and affiliation: they may extend over aspects of interest in particular tasks and the efficacy beliefs about the capability to perform them. In order to perform this, interaction employs a number of linguistic devices. Cotterell (1996) gives the example of how some children use urging to raise other peers' feeling of confidence in their capacities. They also use teasing to lower their interest in school subjects.

Linguistic interaction becomes more effective when the degree of closeness between network members is high. Conversely, a linguistic interaction also reveals the nature of the social network and the social status of participants (Diamond, 1996). These aspects are essential to determine the strength and directionality of the effects within a level of network ties. Closeness was used in social network research to designate the kinship and geographical as well as the high frequency kinds of ties. Here, closeness is viewed as a high level of trust that does not necessarily require a kinship relation. This closeness is also likely to reflect a high frequency of meetings and can entail emotional proximity between the network members. McPherson et al., (2001) reviewed a number of studies which found strong links between homogeneity, including religious similarity, and closeness. Nonetheless, this was discussed within the concept of 'homophily', which is believed to have a strong influence on attitudes (ibid.). However, in a society where local people share nearly everything – religion included – closeness is more of an affective feeling than an aspect of homogeneity. Hence, closeness, as a determiner of influence on motivation, is likely to make the influence of verbal interaction not only possible but also strong. However, verbal interaction, specifically, and social influence in general, is not confined to closeness alone: Distant network members may possibly cause influence on motivation to learn English as L2. Within this new socio-cultural component of the L2 motivation concept, a new conceptualization of motivation is required.

14.5   A contextualized view of L2 learning motivation

In an attempt to study the effects of the cultures of learning, a more accurate conceptualization of motivation requires the inclusion of the socio-cultural context. Models and paradigms directly derived from concepts of mainstream psychology have usually resulted in generalizations. For example, applying the general concepts of the Expectancy–Value Theory (Wigfield, 1994) has not added any real value or practical implications to the study of L2 motivation in the Omani context. The principles of this theory tend to be applicable in many contexts; however, no practical guidelines or recommendations have been made to serve the field of researching L2 motivation in this socio-cultural context.

The attempts made by Gardner and Lambert (1959) to include the social context by adopting a socio-educational perspective also were not of much relevance for the teaching practitioners. This socio-psychological model acknowledged the importance of motivation, yet the idea of integrative motivation was generalized to apply to all learners of L2, which led to an oversimplified relevance of the integrative motive. The original Canadian context was generalized: As a result, Gardner and Lambert's work lacked contextualization because the integrative motive construct applies to a socio-cultural context in which integration in the target language community represents a positive attitude. However, this is not necessarily the case: Not every language learner will find this attitude favourable, and an integrative motive may not affect willingness to learn in some contexts. Therefore, a reconceptualization of L2 motivation seems essential.

This reconceptualization should include an emphasis on the socio-cultural dimension and its integration with the psychological element. It needs to adopt a local depiction of the relevance of the motivational constructs. It starts from the assumption that some psychological factors are more effective than others, in particular socio-cultural contexts. The conceptualization of goals is in constant interaction with social structures. Personal goals are, in fact, manifestations of socio-cultural conceptual structures (D'Andrade, 1992). Hence, the importance of psychological factors is related to each social and cultural context.

In the Omani context, the two most relevant constructs are *Interest* and *Self-efficacy.* The latter refers to the person's evaluation of his/her capabilities to perform a task (Bandura, 1977). This evaluation largely depends on the social influences and collective conceptualizations: In order to know how well individuals can do in a particular task, they consciously or unconsciously refer to others' evaluations of their capabilities. This is even more significant in a collective society, like that of Oman, which values social relations and social integrity. Individuals pay special care to what others say about them, which makes judgments important in determining efficacy–self evaluations. Thus, *Self-efficacy* is a much more significant determiner of Omani students' motivation to learn English as an L2, and it is related to the society's values. On the other hand, developing *Self-efficacy* leads to a high *Interest* level (Bandura, 1977). *Interest* is the other most important factor of motivation to learn English, at least in the Omani socio-cultural context. What makes this construct vastly different from the other motivational factors is that it represents the relationship between the person (the learner) and the object of interest (English). The latter is an aspect of general social conceptualizations (Valsiner, 1992). Objects of interest are negotiated at the societal level. In highly collective groups, the conformity of individuals tends to be more significant, which leads to the development of common interests achieved through social interaction (Krapp, 2002). Therefore, *Interest* and *Self-efficacy* are two constructs deeply rooted in the social component of motivation: This is in harmony with the pillars of the local socio-cultural fabric. Their contextual relevance is also related to social interaction. Part of this conceptualization was Brophy's definition of motivation as a competence acquired through experience and influenced by significant others (Brophy, 1987).

This new conceptualization of L2 learning motivation leads to the acknowledgement of the role of social network relations in learning English. These relations not only determine the significance of *Interest* and *Self-efficacy*, but also gauge their levels of influence on L2 learners' motivation. Social network relations were recognized as having a real effect on motivation within L2 motivation research figures, including William and Burden (1997), who maintain that social interaction influences motivation (ibid.: 121). The way this influence is enacted can be explained by the mechanisms of influence exerted by social – albeit linguistic – interactions. Seed (1990) suggested some qualities of social networks (like sentiment, esteem, and influence) enable social network relations to spread influence. They are also the means through which the spread of ideas and beliefs is achieved. Further, they reveal the affective dimensions responsible for the mechanisms of influence. Therefore, the new reconceptualization of motivation has to take into consideration not only the socio-cultural context, but also the influence of the social network relations, which employ psychological factors. The socio-cultural context determines the constructs whose influence is particularly significant and also the forces and mechanisms of influence. Ultimately, the study of these mechanisms reveals a pattern of influence on students' motivation. In order to understand the effects of the cultures of learning and monitor their effects, as part of a local educational plan, these operating forces should be clearly exposed.

Meanwhile, cultures of learning – as part of the larger social conceptualizations – are spread through social interaction. This interaction is a product of the structure of network relations and also a channel through which attitudes and engagements are conceptualized at the social level. The motivation to learn English as L2 is one aspect of these attitudes and engagements. The way this social system of motivational concepts is negotiated is through social network relations and social interaction. Hence, motivation represents two sides of the coin: one psychological and the other socio-cultural. These are inseparable, as one depends on the other, and un-generalizable, since the context usually determines the quality and the magnitude of the interplay between these factors. This contextualized view of motivation to learn English as L2 addresses the following research questions:

(1) Are *Interest* and *Self-efficacy* the main motivational orientations for Omani students learning English?
(2) How do the cultures of learning influence the motivation for learning English as L2?

14.6   Method of the study

14.6.1   Subjects

The subjects who participated in this study were Omani public school students from grades 9 to 11 (aged 15–19). The country initiated an educational reform in the early 2000s by introducing a basic education program: Starting English in first grade was one of its major features. Previously, students started learning English as an L2 in fourth grade. Their English proficiency level was estimated to be around low-intermediate, or intermediate in some cases, to be more optimistic. Socially speaking, these students are from Arab–Muslim backgrounds. Social relations are generally conservative and mainly determined by kinship or geographical neighbourhoods. Social network ties are still strong. This is manifested by social gatherings for frequent casual meetings, during which rituals showing respect and traditional values are enacted. Social support and solidarity are also revealed in social occasions in both good and bad times. Given these features, Omani society can be portrayed as a traditional one. Although social change and modernization have weakened old extended family structures, features of individualism are not prominent in Omani society, as a whole.

14.6.2   Data collection instruments

This study opted for a mixed methodology. First, consistent with the theoretical background presented above, this study views motivation as an aspect of social processes for which traditional self-reports are not adequate as the sole measurement tools. Hence, the use of the motivation questionnaire is limited to the verification of some basic hypotheses. Second, the aim of the study partly requires a deep investigation of the linguistic and non-linguistic mechanisms of influence. This necessitates a follow up procedure that self-report questionnaires alone are not able to realise. In order to investigate the real mechanisms, interviews were employed.

The principle behind the alternation of research instruments is that each one informs the next for the sake of consistency. First, a semi-structured interview was conducted in order to verify the structure and importance of social relations in general terms. Some situations were included to determine the nature and effects of social contacts as well as the structure and the content of the questionnaire. Ten students were randomly selected for these interviews. Second, a questionnaire was administered to 450 students from different social and geographical categories and belonging to male and female schools (there are separate institutions for male and female learners). The questionnaire's role was essentially to verify the first hypothesis of the study. Third, another round of interviews was conducted with 29 students (15 males and 14 females).

14.7   Analysis and discussion

The questionnaire data were analysed using correlation and linear regression. The correlations shown in Table 14.1 indicate the relationship between the variables of the study, making the totality of motivational factors under study here. The general motivation indicator factor gauges the extent to which individual students believe they are motivated. Hence, the higher the correlation between this general indicator and another factor, the more this second factor is likely to represent the student's type of motivation. Several such factors can represent main aspects of these students' motivation. As Table 14.1 shows, *Interest* (column two: 0.685) and *Self-efficacy* (column three: 0.542) correlate highly with the general motivation indicator (row three; $p < 0.000$). These high correlations show the extent to which these two motivation constructs reveal the motivational dimension of Omani students.

Further, the next highly significant correlation between *Interest* and *Self-efficacy* (0.496; $p < 0.000$) shows a clear interrelatedness between them. The level of one factor depends on the other: The rationale behind this interaction will be discussed later. General motivation also correlates highly with the Intrinsic/Extrinsic factor (column seven: 0.349, p, 0.000). Also significant is the correlation between the general motivation indicator and the Social Relations factor (column four: 0.191; $p < 0.000$). The latter (row four) seems to maintain a quite constant level of correlation with the rest of all variables, indicating a high and generalizable association with all the components of motivation. There are also less important, but still high, correlations among all the other variables. *Interest* highly correlates with the Intrinsic/Extrinsic factor (0.414; $p < 0.000$). The correlation of the Intrinsic/Extrinsic factor with *Self-efficacy* is also important (0.349; $p < 0.000$). The scatter plot figures (Figures 14.1 and 14.2) show the relationship between *Interest*, *Self-efficacy*, and the general motivational factor.

In order to understand the nature of the relationship between the variables discussed above, a linear regression test is made between the general motivational factor, from the one side, and these factors, from the other. The linear regression test ($R = 0.398$) indicates a weak positive correlation between these two aspects.

Table 14.1   Correlations between the motivation factors and components

		Correlations							
INTEREST	Pearson Correlation	1	.496**	.685**	.251**	.174**	.414**	.281**	.127**
	Sig. (2-tailed)	.	.000	.000	.000	.000	.000	.000	.000
	N	5381	5381	5381	5381	5381	5381	5381	5381
SLFEFFCY	Pearson Correlation	.496**	1	.542**	.245**	.200**	.349**	.230**	.108**
	Sig. (2-tailed)	.000	.	.000	.000	.000	.000	.000	.000
	N	5381	5381	5381	5381	5381	5381	5381	5381
GENMOT	Pearson Correlation	.685**	.542**	1	.191**	.207**	.349**	.286**	.102**
	Sig. (2-tailed)	.000	.000	.	.000	.000	.000	.000	.000
	N	5381	5381	5381	5381	5381	5381	5381	5381
SCLRLTNS	Pearson Correlation	.251**	.245**	.191**	1	.229**	.257**	.257**	.224**
	Sig. (2-tailed)	.000	.000	.000	.	.000	.000	.000	.000
	N	5381	5381	5381	5381	5381	5381	5381	5381
GOALS	Pearson Correlation	.174**	.200**	.207**	.229**	1	.323**	.317**	.173**
	Sig. (2-tailed)	.000	.000	.000	.000	.	.000	.000	.000
	N	5381	5381	5381	5381	5381	5381	5381	5381
INTEXTRN	Pearson Correlation	.414**	.349**	.349**	.257**	.323**	1	.323**	.156**
	Sig. (2-tailed)	.000	.000	.000	.000	.000	.	.000	.000
	N	5381	5381	5381	5381	5381	5381	5381	5381
INTGINST	Pearson Correlation	.281**	.230**	.286**	.257**	.317**	.332**	1	.244**
	Sig. (2-tailed)	.000	.000	.000	.000	.000	.000	.	.000
	N	5381	5381	5381	5381	5381	5381	5381	5381
EXPCTVAL	Pearson Correlation	.127**	.108**	.102**	.224**	.173**	.156**	.244**	1
	Sig. (2-tailed)	.000	.000	.000	.000	.000	.000	.000	.
	N	5381	5381	5381	5381	5381	5381	5381	5381

Now, if the regression test is applied to the relationship between *Interest* and the general motivation and between this one and *Self-efficacy*, the strength of these two factors can be determined. The regression coefficient between *Interest* and general motivation is positive (R = 0.685). The one

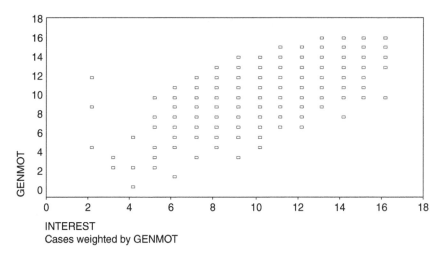

Figure 14.1 Interest and the general motivation indicator

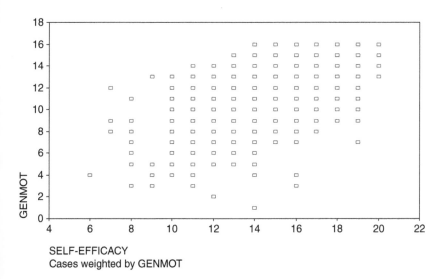

Figure 14.2 Self-efficacy and the general motivation indicator

between *Self-efficacy* and general motivation is also positive (R = 0.542). The charts (Figures 14.3 and 14.4) show the positive relationship.

The intercept level, at around 3.00, and the mean at 16.00 reveal that the initiation of motivation requires the least level of *Interest*.

If we compare the intercept level for *Self-efficacy*, which is just below 8.00, with that of *Interest*, around 3.00, motivation seems to depend more on *Interest*. In fact, this looks logical since the interest in the activity is likely to precede the level of efficacy, which would normally be known after engaging in a given task. Meanwhile, the influence of social relations on the general motivation indicator was not significantly important (R = 0.191). Due to the inherent limitations in self-report questionnaires, the type of direct questions, designed to ascertain the effects of others on the respondent, cannot always capture the real effects. Admitting that others influence the respondent may imply a negative judgment of self-confidence. As a whole, the statistical analyses performed so far indicate the significance of *Interest* and *Self-efficacy* and their role in determining the level of general motivation to learn English as L2. The other motivational factors discussed in the literature review section were, statistically, not able to capture the main motivational orientations of these Omani students. This seems to confirm

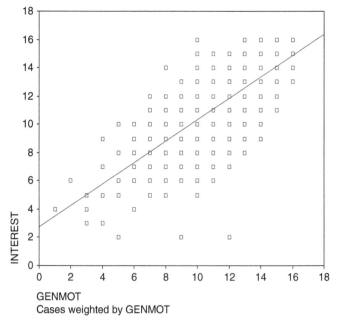

Figure 14.3   Interest and general motivation regression line

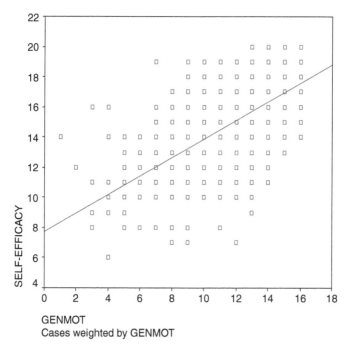

Figure 14.4 Self-efficacy and general motivation regression line

that *Interest* and *Self-efficacy* represent the main motivational orientations for Omani L2 learners. However, the way the local cultures of learning influence these two dimensions of motivation remains to be addressed through the qualitative data.

For the sake of reliability, the interviews conducted employed the same interview questions. These questions aimed at investigating the effect of the cultures of learning, through social network relations, on Omani students' motivation to learn English. Starting from the assumption discussed in the literature review, attitudes towards particular actions as well as the engagements in them, including learning an L2, are largely conceptualized at the societal level. This broad context determines the cultures of learning and influences the main orientations of individuals. What these cultures of learning generally represent includes the main motivational concepts, which are liable to interpersonal mechanisms of influence. Hence, using the qualities of social relations (Seed, 1990), the sources of this influence can be traced. In order to analyse these effects, students' answers to the following interview questions were mainly analysed:

(1) Who is likely to influence you more in learning English, a parent, a distant or a close friend, a teacher, or anybody else?
(2) How do people influence your interest and confidence to learn English?
(3) Tell me in what ways people who can influence you help you to be interested in English and feel confident in it?
(4) Tell me how your interaction with others influences your interest and confidence to learn English?
(5) What do people actually say to influence your English learning?
(6) How do these expressions influence your interest and self-confidence?

Generally speaking, there was broad consensus that parents, family, relatives, friends, teachers, and other people were the main sources of influence on the students' motivation to learn English. The main aspect of the influence of social network relations derives from the affective dimensions. The model of discourse analysis developed by Martin and Rose (2003) will be used to analyse the effects of social network relations. The extent of influence largely depends on the degree of closeness with the network members. The following chart shows the sources of influence and their levels of importance:

Teachers constitute the main source of influence on students' motivation. A number of expressions were used to explain the influence of teachers on students' motivation. Teachers' influence is said to be: 'the most influential' (F11–1, M11–2), 'the most important and basic one' (M10–4), having 'a big role' (M9–1), or even playing 'an essential role' (F9–2). Parents are the second most important source of influence. Their effect was described as being: 'great' (M11–1), 'more' [influential] (M9–4), 'positive' (M10–1, M9–2), but sometimes 'negative' (M9–2, F11–1). However, their type of influence often depended on the provision of necessities, learning materials, and private tuition (M10–1, M10–3, M11–1, M9–4). In fact, in some cases parents were explicitly considered 'less influential than teachers' (F9–2). That parents are more influential than friends is not strange, but it does not support that influence is mainly a matter of kinship proximity, given the relatively higher importance allocated to friends compared to family members other than parents. The importance of friends lies in the closeness effect, which reflects intimacy and familiarity. Hence, there was a general agreement that distant friends are less influential than close ones. In fact, the respondents defined a 'close friend' by using frequency of meetings (F11–2, M9–2), attitude towards learning (F11–3), the degree of trust (F11–3) and the level of intimacy (M10–6). Lastly, the general category of relatives was the last but one in order of importance. This indicates that influence does not essentially depend on family relations or kinship closeness alone.

Sources of Influence

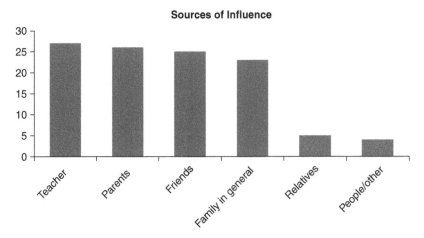

Figure 14.5   Number of cases supporting the different sources of influence on motivation

The main aspect of the influence of social network relations derives from the affective dimensions, particularly through different sources of advice and encouragement.

14.7.1   Encouragement

The term 'encouragement' constantly arose in the data. Parents and teachers were the main sources of expected, or provided, encouragement. The main thing that brothers and sisters can do is to provide encouragement. Friends' encouragement was more emphasized through the frequency of 'encourage' and the use of related terms: the verbs 'urge' and 'reassure'. Friends were sources of urging and reassurance (F10–1, F10–2, F11–1, F11–2, F11–5, among others). While 'urge' has a stronger meaning than simply 'encourage', 'reassure' has a psychological association, denoting more support. Good teachers were expected to encourage students in order to make them motivated to learn English. The manifestations of the teacher's encouragement were directly related to *Interest* and *Self-efficacy*. When the teacher provides encouragement to students, this improves 'self confidence' (F10–2). This also reveals to students that 'English is important' (F11–6) and increases their interest in it. Encouragement shows that English as L2 is important, worthy of interest, and that the student is expected to be able to learn it. It also exhibits a positive evaluation of the respondents' capability to acquire it. However, any lack of encouragement correspondingly results in a lack of motivation.

14.7.2   Help, support and advice

Among the qualities of good teachers, the provision of help, support, and advice are the most important qualities. Their effects on students directly apply to their main motivational constructs, which affects what they feel about the importance of English. More importantly, their need for affective support maintains their *Self-efficacy* at a significant level. Apart from acting as models of success, brothers and sisters provide help, especially when they have some knowledge about English. A number of respondents confirmed the improving effect of the help they provide (F11–4, F11–5, F9–2, M11–2, M9–50). This help either initiates *Interest* or makes students feel that their levels in English can improve. Other aspects of help include working as a team (F11–3) and exchanging ideas and help (F11–1).

14.7.3   Negative effects

The failure to meet students' expectations from their social network relations results in negative effects which can be seen in relation to teachers and parents. The negative profile of a teacher is perceived to have aspects that include being 'nervous', providing 'no encouragement', or not having 'a good relationship' with students. Such a teacher also 'neglects' his students. These descriptors indicate an unsupportive teacher who has a less affective relationship with students, but the affective weight which underlies the supportive expectations teachers in this socio-cultural context are expected to provide. In addition, kinship relations can be very disappointing as well. Relatives can use teasing language which implies strong accusations against the integrity of those interested in learning English: Such students are seen as imitating Westerners, converting to a new religion or adopting a new way of life, which strongly questions the identity of the students. This not only creates a negative affective situation, but also directly affects *Interest* in English and the efficacy beliefs. In both cases the affective dimension is a negative mediator between the received messages and the motivation outcome. Based on the above classification of the aspects of influence, there is a new definition of the concept of closeness of network members.

14.8   The concept of closeness

Closeness is in fact the basis for the sources of influence to produce their effects on the students' motivation. These effects are through the trust the learners have awarded to actors in the network relations. Unlike previous work which defined closeness based on kinship or neighbourhood (e.g., Granovetter, 1973), this study finds closeness strongly related to the concept of trust. Other factors like intimacy, the frequency of meetings and the attitude towards the subject matter are also aspects of this closeness. However, the concept of trust was widely used by participants as a reason for accepting others' influence, especially when it is felt to be positive. If we take advice as a potential port of influence, the ideas expressed by social network agents are accepted only when they have good intentions. The fear that any piece of advice can be misleading always mediates its acceptability. Hence, only messages originating from trustworthy parties are valued. This is what makes certain network relations more influential than others (e.g., parents, teachers). Although teachers do not seem to have much direct informal rapport with students, they enjoy a special influence through the trust many students have in them. Teachers are depicted by using verbal intensifiers that show valued generalized judgments: 'the most influential' (F11–1, M11–2), 'the most important' (M10–4), and playing 'an essential role' (F9–2).

In fact when this trust fades, a list of complaints is raised against teachers. Friends and brothers/sisters could be closer than teachers, for instance, but parents and teachers are objects of trust. In fact what differentiates a close from a distant friend or makes the latter sometimes more influential is the degree of trust allocated to them. More significantly, negative and undesired influences are often attributed to distant friends, to 'others', 'people',

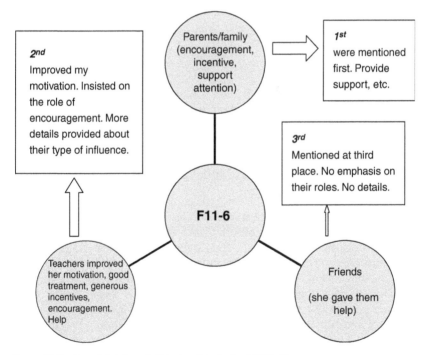

Figure 14.6   A social network diagram for student (F11–6)

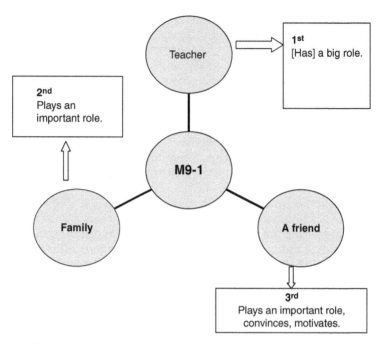

Figure 14.7   A social network diagram for student (M9–1)

or 'other people'. Figures 14.6 and 14.7 are examples of the role of closeness in influencing particular individual students' motivation. Respondents show that closeness depends on the concept of trust rather than on kinship, likeness (friends), or geographical proximity (neighbours) alone.

14.9   L2 Motivation Osmosis Model and the cultures of learning

Cultures of learning influence students' motivation to learn English as L2. This influence is assured not only by the enforcement of norms, but also through social network relations. Chang (2010: 130) discussed the role of the group norms in providing a learning environment that influences L2 learners' motivation. While 'good groups' were proven to have a positive effect on students' motivation, 'bad groups' provide less enthusiasm for learning (ibid.: 149). Although this study used *Self-efficacy* as a motivation construct and supported the argument that the surrounding social milieu influences L2 learners' motivation, this influence is limited to group norms. However, the real effect is larger than social norms: It extends to the whole socio-cultural background manifested in the cultures of learning. Also, there was no attempt to reveal the agents and mechanisms of influence, for a better understanding of the L2 motivation phenomenon. Thus, it is more important to look at how the societal, the social, and the cultural are integrated in L2 learning research.

Cultures of learning are in constant interaction with the motivation to learn English as L2. The cultural facet refers to the acquired knowledge, behaviours, and shared beliefs about norms of conduct and appropriateness. *Cultures of learning* refers to this aggregate of information, beliefs, values, and habits. Vryonides (2007) reviewed Bourdieu's work on the concept of social products (Bourdieu, 1986, 1990). These products, which constitute the main capitals of the society, are social, cultural, and economic. The latter corresponds to the material property available. Whereas the social capital is exhibited by the totality of social network relations in a society, the cultural capital is generally conceived as the internalized knowledge and habits and behaviours in operation within a social setting (ibid.). In order to examine the role of social and cultural capital, Vryonides (2003, 2007) acknowledges the role of the study of social networks. The relationship between social and cultural capital is directly related to social network relations. These relations represent how the social capital interacts with the cultural capital to influence the concepts internalized from the socialization process. Meanwhile, the cultural capital is an aspect of the cultures of learning operationalized at the group level. Hence, social networks, as an apparatus of interaction, operate the manner in which the cultural capital influences cultures of learning. Within this framework, the latter are, then, conceived as the outcome of the effects of social interaction – within social networks – and the totality of the social capital.

The L2 Osmosis Model (Figure 14.8) visualizes the effects of social network relations on students' motivation to learn English as an L2. Motivation is represented by the two most influential factors, namely *Interest* and *Self-efficacy*. The influence of social networks on these two factors determines the learners' motivation for the L2 learning task. However, this influence can go in both directions: The individual can be both a receiver and an agent of influence. In fact, the level of influence depends on the ability and possibility of infiltrating the other person's motivational system. Hence, the efficiency of the linguistic mechanisms partly determines the directionality of the effects. Closeness and the mechanisms employed play important roles in influencing students' motivational orientations. Meanwhile, these effects largely depend on certain internal mental and affective processes, which moderate the dimension of the influences.

This description not only likens the motivation processes to the osmosis mechanisms in the body cell, but also faithfully demonstrates how the most effective mechanisms interact in order to determine the learner's

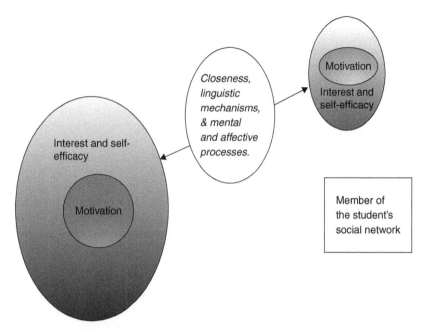

Figure 14.8   Motivation osmosis model of social network influence

motivational determinations. The cell membrane in the biological mechanism is represented by *Interest* and *self-efficacy* SE components in the L2 Motivation Osmosis Model. The interaction between social networks and motivation is mediated by two main categories of factors: the linguistic interaction mechanisms and the mental and affective dimensions. The closer the person is the more likely that their influence becomes more effective. Therefore, the influence capacity depends on how effective the mechanisms can trigger the mental and affective factors responsible for establishing the levels of interest and SE within a certain level of closeness.

The conceptual framework in Figure 14.8 places more significance on the role of social network relations in realizing the prevailing cultures of learning within a society. Hence, the cultures of learning represent the resulting conceptualizations of significant aspects of L2 learning in Omani society, including the conceptualization of the motivation to learn English and its effective factors. The results of the present study show the role of social networks in influencing students' motivation.

Both the sources and aspects of this influence are manifestations of the learning cultures. The sources of this influence – family, teachers, parents, friends, and so forth – represent different voices of the local cultures of learning. Motivation, as an aspect of the cultures of learning, is often influenced by what teachers do. This explains why students have different images of teachers, depending on social backgrounds (Jin & Cortazzi, 2008). The roles of other social agents – including families, parents, friends, and other people – are also manifestations of the different voices within society. Another aspect of these cultures of learning is the broad socio-cultural factor reflected in the effects and mechanisms of influence. The mechanisms, as explained above, are usually linguistic. Social network actors produce influence by using some linguistic devices to produce the desired effect of persuasion. The aspects of this influence are also related to the cultures of learning. That these aspects have an affective dimension shows the extent to which the need for help, support, and encouragement are deeply embedded in the social capital.

14.10   Conclusion

The motivation to learn English as L2 is constantly related to the cultures of learning of almost any society. These cultures of learning are part of the socio-cultural background which determines the most influential motivational factors and the extent to which the societal as well as the socio-cultural interact with the psychological to produce the level of motivation of an individual learner. The concept of closeness is influenced by the degree of trust that allows influence to operate. However, the sources and aspects of this influence are related to the deep need for help, support, and encouragement felt on the students' side. Hence, students' affective needs determine the extent of the need for trust, which in turn defines closeness and the magnitude of influence of social network members, which in turn influences motivation. The L2 Motivation Osmosis Model demonstrates the relationship between these aspects and shows how personal (psychological) and interpersonal (social network, social psychological) factors interact to determine the level of L2 learning motivation the student exhibits. All these interrelated factors are aspects of the cultures of learning and part of the socio-cultural background of the learners of English as L2.

References

Bandura, A. (1977) *Social Learning Theory*. New York: General Learning Press.
Bandura, A. (1986) *Social functions of thought and action: A social cognitive theory*. NJ: Prentice-Hall.
Bandura, A. (1997) *Self-efficacy: The exercise of control*. New York: W. H. Freeman and Company.
Bourdieu, P. (1986) The form of capital. In J. G. Richardson (Ed.), *Handbook of theory and research for the sociology of education*. New York: Greenwood Press, pp. 241–60.
Bourdieu, P. (1990) *The logic of practice*. Cambridge: Polity Press.
Brophy, J. (1987) Synthesis of research on strategies for motivating students to learn. *Educational Leadership*, October 1987, 40–48.

306   *Sami Dadi and Lixian Jin*

Bucholtz, M. & Hall, K. (2005) Identity and interaction: A socio-cultural linguistic approach. *Discourse Studies*, 7 (4–5), 585–614.

Chang, L. Y. (2010) Group processes and EFL learners' motivation: A study of group dynamics in EFL classrooms. *TESOL Quarterly*, 44 (1), 129–54.

Cotterell, J. (1996) *Social networks and social influences in adolescence*. London: Routledge.

D'Andrade, R. G. (1992) Schemas and Motivation. In R. G. D'Andrade and Strauss (Eds), *Human motives and cultural models*. Cambridge: Cambridge University Press, pp. 23–44.

Deci, E. (1992) On the nature and functions of motivation theories. *Psychological Sciences*, 3 (3), 167–71.

Diamond, J. (1996) *Status and power in verbal interaction*. Amsterdam and Philadelphia: John Benjamin's Publishing Company.

Dornyei, Z. (2001) *Teaching and researching motivation*. Essex and London: Longman.

Gardner, R. C. & Lambert, W. E. (1959) Motivational variables in second language acquisition. *Canadian Journal of Psychology*, 13, 266–72.

Granovetter, M. S. (1973) The strength of weak ties. *American Journal of Sociology*, 78, 1360–80.

Jin, L. & Cortazzi, M. (2008) Images of teachers, learning and questioning in Chinese cultures of learning. In Erich A. Berendt (Ed.), *Metaphors for learning*, London: Continuum, pp.177–202.

Kandel, D. (1978) Homophily, selection and socialization in adolescent friendships. *American Journal of Sociology*, 84, 427–36.

Kindermann, T. A. (2007) Effects of naturally existing peer groups on changes in academic engagement in a cohort of sixth graders. *Child Development*, 78 (4), 1186–1203.

Krapp, A. (2002) An educational-psychological theory of interest and its relation to self-determination theory. In E. L. Deci and R. M. Ryan (Eds), *The handbook of self-determination research*. Rochester: University of Rochester Press, pp. 405–27.

Lapinski, M. Kn. & Rimal, R. N. (2005) An explication of social norms. *Communication Theory*, 15 (2), 127–47.

Martin, J. R. & Rose, D. (2003) *Working with discourse: Meaning beyond the clause*. London: Continuum.

McPherson, M., Lynn, S. & James, M. (2001) Birds of a feather: Homophily in social networks. *Annual Review of Sociology*, 27, 415–44.

Seed, P. (1990) *Introducing network analysis in social work*. London: Jessica Kingsley.

Ushioda, E. & Dornyei, Z. (2009) Motivation, language identities and the Le self: A theoretical overview. In Zoltan Dornyei and Ema Ushioda (Eds), *Motivation, language identity and the L2 Self*. Bristol, Buffalo and Toronto: Bilingual Matters, pp. 1–8.

Valsiner, J. (1992) Interest: A metatheoretical perspective. In K. A. Renninger, S. Hidi & A. Krapp (Eds.), *The Role of Interest in Learning and Development*. Hillsdale, NJ: Erlbaum, pp. 27–41.

Vryonides, M. (2003) *The role of social and cultural capital in choice making for post-secondary destinations: The case of contemporary Cyprus*. Unpublished PhD thesis, University of London.

Vryonides, M. (2007) Social and cultural capital in educational research: Issues of operationalization and measurement. *British Educational Research Journal*, 33 (6), 867–85.

Wentzel, K. R., Barry, C. M. & Caldwell, K. A. (2004) Friendships in middle school: Influences on motivation and school adjustment. *Journal of Educational Psychology*, 96, 195–203.

Watson-Gegeo, K. A. (2004) Mind, language and epistemology: toward a language socialization paradigm of SLA. *The Modern Language Journal*, 88, 331–50.

Wigfield, A. (1994) Expectancy-value theory of achievement motivation: A developmental perspective. *Educational Psychology Review*, 6, 49–78.

Williams, M. & Burden, R. L. (1997) *Psychology for language teachers.* Cambridge: Cambridge University Press.

15
Demotivating Factors Affecting Iranian High School Students' English Learning

Rahman Sahragard and Zahra Alimorad

15.1 Introduction

A multitude of positive and negative factors affect the learning behaviours and learning outcomes of English language learners. The available literature, however, reveals that, in the context of Iran, researchers and practitioners have been more interested in investigating the effects of positive factors (e.g., Alavi, 2004; Asghari, 1998; Fazel, 2003; Hasani, 2005; Neisi, 2007; Ramazanian, 1998; Roohani, 2001; Samaie, 2006; Sedaghat, 2001), and little or no attempt has been made to examine complementary negative factors. Those who are interested in investigating English as a foreign language (EFL) students' motivational behaviours might pose questions such as these: Why do some foreign language learners lose their motivation to continue studying the target language with the passage of time? What are some of the causes which lead to students' reduction of motivation? Such questions point to the negative or demotivating factors which affect students' learning behaviour. Examining the causes of demotivation may be intriguing, not only for researchers, but also for many practitioners who see some learners becoming demotivated in their classrooms. For researchers, investigating demotivation sheds light on and leads to a better understanding of theories on motivation; teachers may want to understand the possible causes of their students' demotivation in order to try to mitigate these demotivating factors in their classroom practices (Sakai & Kikuchi, 2009).

Dörnyei (2001) defined *demotivation* as 'various negative influences that cancel out existing motivation' (p. 142) or 'specific external forces that reduce or diminish the motivational basis of a behavioural intention or an ongoing action' (p. 143). However, demotivation is not solely external, and many researchers (e.g., Arai, 2004; Falout & Maruyama, 2004) included internal factors such as lack of self-confidence and negative attitude within learners themselves to complement external sources. Despite his definition of demotivation, even Dörnyei himself listed reduced self-confidence and a negative attitude toward the foreign language as sources of demotivation (Dörnyei, 2001). Therefore, that original definition may need to be expanded to cover both internal and external demotivating factors which reduce or diminish the motivation to study English (Sakai & Kikuchi, 2009).

Demotivation, however, is different from *amotivation*: Demotivation refers to a situation in which motivation must exist before there can be a subsequent decrease, while amotivation is the absence of any motivation and is marked by passivity. Amotivated people feel a lack of competence or control over their external environments, a feeling of helplessness caused by lack of contingency between behaviours and outcomes (Vallerand & Ratelle, 2002). Recently, a further concept has been introduced by researchers in the field of L2 motivation, namely, *remotivation* (see Chapter 17, Falout et al., 2009), which refers to taking steps to bring back L2 learners' lost or reduced motivation.

Over the past decade, demotivating factors have been examined mostly in the area of instructional communication; for instance, demotivators in lectures on communication at North American universities (Christophel & Gorham, 1995; Gorham & Christophel, 1992; Gorham & Millette, 1997) and in university lectures in China, Germany, Japan and the United States (Zhang, 2007). In the field of language teaching, Chambers, Rudnai, Ushioda and Dörnyei (all cited in Dörnyei, 2001) were among the early attempts to investigate demotivation. Recently, however, many researchers have attempted to investigate demotivation of learners of English, especially in the context of Japan (Arai, 2004; Falout & Maruyama, 2004; Hasegawa, 2004; Ikeno, 2002) and more recently Sakai and Kikuchi (2009) and Falout et al. (2009).

In the first of the latter studies, Sakai and Kikuchi (2009) reported a survey which explored demotivating factors for Japanese high school students. A 35-item questionnaire was completed by 656 Japanese high school students. Through a principal axis factor analysis, five demotivation factors were extracted: (a) *Learning Contents and Materials*, (b) *Teachers' Competence and Teaching Styles*, (c) *Inadequate School Facilities*, (d) *Lack of Intrinsic Motivation* and (e) *Test Scores*. The results showed that the *Learning Contents and Materials* and *Test Scores* factors were demotivating factors for many Japanese high school students, especially for less motivated learners. Contrary to what previous research suggested, *Teachers' Competence and Teaching Styles* was not a very strong cause of demotivation compared to *Learning Contents and Materials* or *Test Scores* for both more and less motivated groups. The study also showed that both more and less motivated learners did not perceive *Inadequate School Facilities* as demotivating.

In the second study, Falout et al. (2009) surveyed 900 university learners of English to investigate the demotivating factors in learning EFL in Japan, and the relationship between past demotivating experiences and present proficiencies. Affective states and capacity to self-regulate learning were compared among learners with varying academic interests, experiences, and proficiencies. Demotivating factors were grouped into three categories: external conditions of the learning environment, internal conditions of the learner, and reactive behaviours to demotivating experiences. Internal and reactive factors were shown to correlate with long-term EFL learning outcomes. Findings indicated that beginning, less-proficient learners among non-English majors were least likely to control their affective states to cope with demotivating experiences.

Reviewing the literature on demotivation, we felt a strong need to examine demotivating factors in the context of Iran, where there is a lack of such research. To fill this lacuna, this study examines the common negative factors affecting Iranian EFL high school students' motivational behaviours which lead to the reduction or a complete loss of their motivation to study English.

15.2   The Iranian learning culture

Nowadays, English constitutes an undeniable aspect of many people's lives worldwide because of its status as a global lingua franca and its widespread use in international conferences, scholarly periodicals, foreign trade and business, the Internet, and many other domains. This can be observed in Iran where 'despite the ideological stance of the state's policy towards English culture and language, which intends to keep it at a minimum level, there is nevertheless a strong need for the use of English language' (Riazi, 2005: p. 113). In such a context, English constitutes an obligatory subject to be studied in schools utilizing the books produced by the Ministry of Education. Public school teachers are deemed responsible for teaching those textbooks which are introduced and prepared by ministry authorities; they have no voice in choosing the teaching materials. Students are required to study English from the first year of guidance school (a three-year period between elementary school and high school in the Iranian educational system) to the last year of high school on the basis of centrally determined language policies and planning.

Despite such strict attention to English, it is still largely taught on the basis of traditional approaches, emphasizing 'usage' at the expense of 'use', especially in the public schools. The dominant method of English teaching is a form of grammar–translation. Classes are mostly teacher-centered with little or no verbal participation by learners (Moradi, 1996; Rahimi, 1996; Razmjoo & Riazi, 2006; Yarmohammadi, 2000). The use of such technology as the Internet, language laboratories, videos, CDs, computers, and so forth is nonexistent in public schools, and students have to memorize extensive decontextualized, inauthentic, and isolated vocabulary items and grammatical rules. As Riazi (2005: p. 110) rightly puts it:

> We might describe the present approach towards teaching and learning in Iranian schools as fulfilling the features of a more quantitative approach rather than a qualitative one in which learners might come up with new visions and insights. The difference between learners and teachers is that of quantity rather than quality. Teachers are supposed to know more rules and a greater number of words than students, and students in their learning process should do their best to reduce this gap. Thus, the more rules and words they learn the closer they get to the experts.

Never are students allowed to convey their own ideas or be involved in making decisions regarding what and how to study. Students are required to memorize the content of books taught to them, and most of the tests they take are, in fact, tests of memorization rather than understanding. Student achievements are evaluated based on their test scores; their learning achievements are seen in a product- rather than a process-oriented view. This trend especially prevails in the public schools where the number of students in classes is too large and teachers have neither sufficient time nor the necessary resources to evaluate all of the students' achievements in a gradual, step-by-step manner during the whole semester. As a result, summative rather than formative evaluation is highly dominant (Riazi, 2005). Rarely or never are new teaching techniques employed in public schools, where the main aim is to cover the textbook content in the limited amount of time allotted. 'The centralized system of education assigns the same textbooks, the same teaching methods, and the same testing procedures to all parts of the country regardless of their geographical, social and cultural differences' (Riazi, 2005: p. 111). That is, a 'one size fits all' method in ELT is still accepted and adopted in the context of Iran, especially in the public schools. The outcomes of such instructional procedures are that students are generally not able to use the target language productively and communicatively; rather, they have a superficial knowledge of grammatical structures and vocabulary.

15.3 The significance and objectives of the study

The issue of demotivation and the factors which contribute to students' demotivating behaviours have been largely ignored in the context of Iran. To the best of our knowledge, no study has investigated demotivation and its effects on students' learning behaviour in Iran. Previous studies have focused on motivation and the way it influences learning or its relationship with other factors (e.g., Alavi, 2004; Asghari, 1998; Fazel, 2003; Hasani, 2005; Neisi, 2007; Ramazanian, 1998; Roohani, 2001; Samaie, 2006; Sedaghat,

2001). So, it seemed imperative to study demotivation to fill this gap and thus to further our knowledge of motivation.

In addition, most researchers in Iran have focused on university students and elicited learners' reports about their motivation in their past English learning experiences. In order to further explore internal and external factors contributing to student demotivation, it is important to elicit data from a range of different learners of English. Thus, it is necessary to examine, not only university students, but also high school students learning English. Therefore, this study focused on high school students in their last four years at school and attempted to investigate their possible causes of demotivation in learning English as a foreign language. To this end, this study seeks to answer the following research questions:

(1) What are the demotivating factors in English classes for Iranian senior, junior, sophomore, and freshmen high school students?
(2) To what degree do less motivated and more motivated learners differ in terms of factors they find demotivating?

15.4   Method: participants

A convenient sample of 194 high school students (male = 80, female = 114) from two schools in Shiraz, Iran, participated in the study. They were selected from public schools rather than private institutes because it was envisaged that those who attend private institutes may be more internally motivated to learn English (since they register voluntarily in the institutes) while public school students might be more demotivated because they *have to* learn English as a compulsory subject as part of their education. All of these participants were native speakers of Persian in different instructional levels: Their ages ranged from 15 to 18. They agreed to participate because they were convinced that the results of this study will help improve the learning conditions and reduce the demotivating factors as far as possible, or at least will be informative to those who are responsible for decision making regarding English teaching practices.

15.4.1   The research instrument

The EFL Demotivation Questionnaire used in this study (Appendix A) comprised two sections. The first was a demographic section that recorded name, gender, instructional level, and age. The second section comprised 48 questions about demotivation, formatted with a five-point Likert scale. It was prepared in the students' mother tongue (Persian) to ensure that they understood the items perfectly, since less proficient learners might not be able to understand items in English, which might jeopardize the findings. The Persian version was back-translated into English by two translation experts for validity purposes. The original and the back-translated versions were then compared to ensure a high degree of overlap in terms of concepts and functions of the questions. The questionnaire items were designed to measure six constructs which were derived from previous studies: about teachers, characteristics of classes, experiences of failure, class environment, class materials, and lack of interest. The instructions for this part were: 'How much are the following statements true for you as demotivating factors?' The participants were required to choose one of the alternatives:

(1) Absolutely wrong;
(2) Mostly not true;
(3) Neither true nor wrong;
(4) To some extent true; and
(5) Completely true.

The questionnaire also included one question about motivation to learn English: 'How do you rate your own motivation to learn English?' The participants were required to choose one of the alternatives:

(1) I have almost no motivation;
(2) I have a little motivation;
(3) I have moderate motivation; and
(4) I have high motivation.

Based on the responses to this question, the participants were divided into less motivated and more motivated learners. Finally, the participants were asked to note any ideas or suggestions they might have regarding English and how it is taught in public schools. Using Cronbach's alpha formula, the researchers obtained a relatively high reliability index of 0.81 for this questionnaire.

15.5   Data collection and analysis procedures

The questionnaire (Appendix 15.1) was administered to 194 high school students aged 15–18. They were asked to be honest in responding to the items and were given assurance that their answers to the questions would be kept confidential and would not have any negative consequences for them or any impact on their English exam scores.

To explore the underlying constructs of the questionnaire, an exploratory factor analysis was performed. Following this, the mean scores of items loading on each factor were calculated and seven independent t-tests were run to find out whether less motivated and more motivated learners showed any statistically significant differences in terms of factors they found demotivating. To correct for multiple comparisons, with a Bonferroni adjustment, the alpha level was set at .007 for each test.

15.6 Results

Figure 15.1 shows mean distribution for each item of the questionnaire.

A total of 32 items had means below average (suggesting that students were comparatively more motivated regarding these items), but the following items had higher means: *I seldom have chances to speak English*; Mean = 3.02, item 1; *Most of the lessons focus on translation*, Mean = 4.06, item 4; *Most of the lessons focus on grammar*, Mean = 3.25, item 5; *Most of the lessons are university entrance examination oriented*, Mean = 3.23, item 6; *I am expected to use grammatically correct English in speaking or writing*; Mean = 3.49, item 7; *English passages in the textbooks are too long*, Mean = 3.21, item 21; *Computer equipment is not used*, Mean = 4.42, item 25; *Visual materials such as videos and DVDs are not used*, Mean = 4.47, item 26; *The Internet is not used*, Mean = 4.48, item 27; *Language laboratory equipment is not used*, Mean = 4.30, item 28; *Audio materials such as CDs and tapes are not used*; Mean = 4.2, item 29; *Teachers don't have enough time for expressing all of the materials and practicing them*, Mean = 3.23, item 31; *English is easily forgotten*, Mean = 3.03, item 44; *Summer vacations contribute to forgetting everything that I have learned*, Mean = 3.01, item 45; *English spelling is difficult to learn*, Mean = 3.00, item 47. In other words, the participants considered these items as relatively more demotivating than the rest.

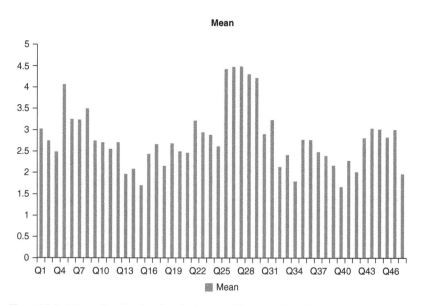

Figure 15.1   Mean distribution for the items of the questionnaire

In order to further investigate the underlying factors, a principal axis factor analysis using a varimax rotation procedure was performed on the 48 questionnaire items. Based on the screen plot and the interpretability of the factor solution, a seven-factor solution was selected. Seven factors were rotated. Appendix 15.2 indicates the pattern structure of the factor analysis and items loading on each factor.

The first factor contains eight items with factor loadings above 0.39 (items 9, 10, 11, 33, 41, 44, 45 and 46). The items concern lack of self-confidence (9, 10, 11, 33 and 41) and difficulties of learning English (44, 45 and 46). This factor was labeled *Lack of Self-confidence*. The second factor was named *Teachers' Competence and Teaching Styles* because the items concerning the teachers' ability (12), way of teaching (13), and the way they behave in the classroom (14, 15, 17, 18, 19, 32 and 34) loaded on this factor. The third factor was defined by eight items (16, 22, 36, 37, 38, 39, 42 and 43) related to the students' lack of interest in English language and English societies, whose factor loadings were above 0.42. Thus, this factor was labeled *Lack of Interest in English*. The other factor, the fourth, was defined by five items (25, 26, 27, 28 and 29) whose factor loadings were above 0.59 and were concerned with lack of supplementary equipment and facilities at schools. Therefore, this factor was called *Lack of School Facilities*. The fifth factor consisted of 7 items with factor loadings above 0.36 (1, 6, 8, 21, 23, 30 and 48) of which items number 6, 21, 23 and 48 related to course books which Dörnyei (2001) and Sakai and Kikuchi (2009) also identified as a demotivating factor. The remaining items were related to the uncomfortable classroom environment, so this factor was named *Learning Contents and Context*. Five items defined the sixth factor: 2, 3, 7, 24 and 35. Their factor loadings were above 0.36, and they were concerned with the use of English in students' lives; thus, this factor was labeled *Focus on English Usage*. The seventh and last factor contained 6 items (4, 5, 20, 31, 40 and 47) and concerns teaching methodologies used in the classrooms; therefore, it was named *The Focus of Teaching*.

The participants were divided into two groups based on the responses to the question about motivation to study English: less motivated learners (N = 27) who answered *I have almost no motivation* or *I have a little motivation* and more motivated learners (N = 167) who answered *I have moderate motivation* or *I have high motivation*. Based on the result of the factor loadings and the answers to the final questionnaire item, the mean distribution of factor loadings for 'less motivated' and 'more motivated' learners were calculated, which appear in Figure 15.2:

Overall, and according to Figure 15.2, the mean score of factor 4 (the fourth pair of bars) is relatively high (4.42 and 4.37 for less and more motivated learners respectively), followed by factor 1 (the first pair of bars), 3 (the third pair of bars) and factor 7 (the seventh pair of bars) (3.56, 3.26 and 3.01 respectively) for less motivated learners; and factor 7 (the seventh pair of bars), factor 5 (the fifth pair of bars), and factor 6 (the sixth pair of bars)

(2.93, 2.84 and 2.83 respectively) for more motivated learners. The mean score of factor 2 (the second pair of bars) (2.25), *Teachers' Competence and Teaching Styles,* was the lowest for less motivated learners, while the mean scores of factors 2 and 3 (both 2.41) were the lowest for more motivated learners.

In order to examine the statistical difference between less motivated and more motivated learners, seven independent samples t-tests were performed. With a Bonferroni adjustment, the alpha level was set at .007 for each test. Results of these t-tests are presented in Appendix 15.3).

As is evident from Appendix 15.3, statistically significant differences were found between the two groups of less motivated and more motivated learners only for the first factor (*Lack of Self-confidence,* M = 7.83, t = 6.53, p =0.000), whereas there were no statistically significant differences between the two groups for factor 2 (*Teachers' Competence and Teaching Styles,* M = 0.94, t = 0.64, p = 0.522), factor 3 (*Lack of Interest in English,* M = 13.68, t = 1.96, p = 0.061), factor 4 (*Lack of School Facilities,* M = 4, t = 1.12, p = 0.271), factor 5 (*Learning Contents and Context,* M = 5.77, t = 0.79, p =0.432), factor 6 (*Focus on English Usage,* M = −0.41, t = −0.67, p = 0.503) and factor 7 (*The Focus of*

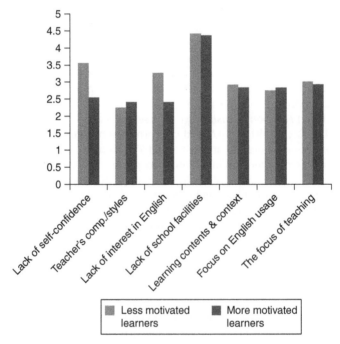

Figure 15.2 Distribution of means of factor loadings for less motivated and more motivated learners

Teaching, M = 0.45, t = 0.77, p = 0.439). To sum up, no group differences were found for *Teachers' Competence and Teaching Styles*, *Lack of Interest in English*, *Lack of School Facilities*, *Learning Contents and Context*, *Focus on English Usage* and *The Focus of Teaching*. Less motivated learners considered only the first factor to be more demotivating. That is, lack of self-confidence can be more demotivating for less motivated learners than for more motivated ones.

15.7 Discussion

The present study intended to identify common demotivating factors affecting Iranian EFL high school students who attend public schools in Iran. To this end, it sought to answer two research questions. The first question was concerned with the salient demotivating factors for Iranian high school students. The extracted factors were as follows: (a) *Lack of Self-confidence*, (b) *Teachers' Competence and Teaching Styles*, (c) *Lack of Interest in English*, (d) *Lack of School Facilities*, (e) *Learning Contents and Context*, (f) *Focus on English Usage* and (g) *The Focus of Teaching*.

Among these seven factors extracted, factor 4, namely, *Lack of School Facilities*, has the greatest mean for both less motivated and more motivated learners. In Iran, public schools do not provide their students with instructional equipment necessary for students' learning improvement. Hence, most of the participants perceived the shortage of school facilities as a cause of their demotivation to study English. Following this factor, less motivated learners perceived factors 1, 3 and 7 (*Lack of Self-confidence*, *Lack of Interest in English*, and *The Focus of Teaching*) as demotivating. Taking these factors into account, one can suggest that the absence of instructional devices and equipment along with an emphasis on English 'usage' at the expense of 'use' has made these students uninterested in learning English and this, in turn, has led to their lack of self-confidence. Although more motivated learners are more self-confident than less motivated ones, they, too, pointed to similar problems related to teaching conditions in Iran. For them, factors 7, 5 and 6 (*The Focus of Teaching*, *Learning Contents and Context*, *Focus on English Usage*) are demotivating, respectively, after the fourth factor. That is, the more motivated students, too, perceived the focus on 'usage' rather than 'use', the kinds of materials taught, and the way they are taught as the causes of their reduced motivation.

Although the questionnaire was constructed on the basis of a six-factor model, seven factors were extracted with the factor analysis. While it was assumed that characteristics of lessons and class environment constitute two factors, both loaded as one factor; that is, *Learning Contents and Context*. Other factors were similar to what they were initially assumed to be.

The second research question asked whether there were differences in demotivating factors between less motivated and more motivated learners. Only for factor 1 (*Lack of Self-confidence*), were there statistically significant differences between the two groups, while there were no statistically significant differences for the other six demotivating factors (2, 3, 4, 5, 6 and 7). In other words, participants with almost no motivation and with a little motivation found the first factor to be more demotivating than did participants with moderate motivation and those with high motivation. This means that *Lack of Self-confidence* was more demotivating for less motivated learners than for more motivated ones. This finding is in contrast to the findings of Hasegawa (2004), who concluded that the experiences related to teachers were the most frequently cited as a source of demotivation for both junior and senior high school students. She maintained that inappropriate teacher behaviours may exert a 'strong impact' on student demotivation (p. 135). This study concludes that this factor is not all that much demotivating in the context of Iran.

The finding that low motivated learners projected the responsibility for their loss of motivation onto internal rather than external causes is in contrast to the findings of Ushioda (1998 cited in Dörnyei, 2001), who came to the conclusion that:

> [b]y projecting the responsibility of their loss of motivation onto external causes in this way, learners may be better able to limit the motivational damage and dissociate the negative affect they are currently experiencing from their own enduring motivation for wanting to learn the language. The process of affirming this sense of motivational autonomy becomes the process of self-motivation, or as one subject puts it, the process of *getting your motivation on line again*. (p. 86)

In contrast to the results of previous research, *Teachers' Competence and Teaching Styles* was not a very strong cause of demotivation compared to *Lack of Interest in English, Learning Contents and Context, Focus on English Usage,* and *The Focus of Teaching* for both more and less motivated groups. Contrary to the findings of Sakai and Kikuchi (2009), the present study also revealed that both more and less motivated learners did perceive *Lack of School Facilities* as highly demotivating.

15.8   Conclusion

This study showed that *Lack of Self-confidence* was a demotivating factor for many Iranian high school students, especially for less motivated learners. In other words, less motivated learners perceived internal factors as more demotivating than external ones. For example, they indicated that their lack of self-confidence is a stronger cause of demotivation than teachers' knowledge or the way teachers teach, students' disinterest in English language or English-speaking communities, inadequate school facilities, problems related to textbooks or class environment, and problems related to teaching methods. With respect to these external forces, there were no statistically significant differences between less motivated and more motivated learners: They are equally demotivating for all students.

Considering the English learning culture of Iran, one can conclude that most of these demotivating factors are rooted in the way English teaching is viewed and practised in Iranian public schools. Although researchers all over the world have examined different teaching methods and have propagated many new ideas and theories about how to teach foreign languages communicatively, the Iranian public school teachers of English are still following the traditional teaching methods of the pre-1970s, especially the grammar–translation method. Teachers' pedagogic knowledge base is in fact out-of-date, leading to their reluctance to try new, up-to-date, and (to them) innovative teaching techniques which are prevalent all over the world. To the extent that these problems persist, there is no way of eliminating the implicated demotivating factors. Consequently, steps need to be taken by responsible authorities to bring about a huge change in English teaching pedagogies and practices currently dominant in public schools of Iran.

On the basis of the findings of this study, the following suggestions can be adopted to mitigate students' demotivation, especially in EFL contexts similar to Iran:

(1) Teachers need to be careful about their behaviour in the classroom environment; that is, they must behave in such a way as to encourage all students to enhance their self-confidence and not lose their motivation.

(2) Responsible authorities need to consider a fair and dignified picture of the English-speaking communities and reflect this in policies and pedagogic materials accordingly so that students' interest and motivation to learn English can be enhanced.

(3) Lack of self-confidence was found to be more demotivating for less motivated learners. Taking this factor into account, teachers can help these students strengthen their self-confidence by evaluating their performance based on their class activities in addition to their test scores, that is, teachers can utilize a formative rather than a summative evaluation, especially in the case of less motivated learners. In this way, with enhanced self-confidence, they might become more motivated and strive to learn English more successfully.

(4) Teachers are not the only individuals who are responsible for their students' demotivation. Low motivated learners themselves are also responsible to search for the causes of their demotivation and let their teachers be aware of them in order for the teachers to help them find suitable solutions for their problems, if possible.

(5) Parents can also be of great help in this process. Their attitude toward the English language and English-speaking people might affect their children's attitude; logically, if parents regard English as an important subject to be studied, they can help their children become more interested and motivated to study it.

(6) Public school teachers need to acquire new, up-to-date, and innovative teaching techniques in their pre- and in-service teacher education programs. Additionally, in order to be able to motivate their students, first of all, they themselves must be well motivated. Therefore, their problems must be taken into consideration and solved if this is feasible; if teachers themselves are demotivated, they cannot help increase their students' motivation.

(7) Finally, although the above points might be helpful and necessary, they are not sufficient. The most important contribution in eliminating demotivating factors in public schools can be made by responsible people who have the necessary decision-making power.

15.9   Limitations and suggestions for further research

Like most empirical research, the present study is not definitive, but is based on a certain sample of learners in a particular context in a particular language program learning a specific language. Clearly, further research is needed in which all of these factors are more systematically explored for definitive answers on the factors affecting second language learning motivation. The data presented here do suggest, however, certain directions that research can take in examining the nature of demotivating factors.

The following can be considered the limitations of the present study which limit the generalizability of the results to other contexts and other populations. First, the number of participants was relatively small (N = 194). Second, this sample was a convenient sample. Third, the instrument used in this study included only 48 items resulting in the exclusion of other demotivating factors. For instance, items might be added to find out if there is any relationship between participants' motivation and their perception of what demotivated them. Further research is needed in which all of these limitations would be taken into account.

Despite these limitations, we hope that the findings here will illustrate the complexity of factors that demotivate English learners elsewhere in the world. However, more research in this area is needed in order for us to deepen our knowledge of L2 learners' demotivation. These studies can have theoretical implications for researchers who are investigating cultures of learning, and there are practical implications for the teachers who see many students becoming demotivated in their classrooms.

Appendix 15.1 Demotivation questionnaire in English

	Absolutely wrong	Mostly not true	Neither true nor wrong	To some extent true	Completely true
1. I seldom have chances to communicate in English.					
2. English language has no use in my daily life.					
3. English language has no use in my future job.					
4. Most of the lessons focus on translation.					
5. Most of the lessons focus on grammar.					
6. Most of the lessons are entrance examination oriented.					
7. I am expected to use (or speak and write) grammatically correct English.					
8. I was forced to memorize the sentences in the textbooks too often.					
9. I have difficulty memorizing words and phrases.					
10. I get low scores on tests (such as midterm and final examinations).					
11. I get confused when I want to self-study English.					
12. Teachers' pronunciation of English is poor.					
13. Teachers' method of teaching is not good.					
14. Teachers ridicule students' mistakes.					
15. English classes are callous and not interesting.					
16. Teachers' explanations are not easy to understand.					
17. Teachers shouted or got angry.					
18. Teachers discriminated among strong and weak students.					
19. Teachers do not encourage us for learning English.					
20. Topics of the passages used in lessons are not interesting.					

Appendix 15.1   (Continued)

	Absolutely wrong	Mostly not true	Neither true nor wrong	To some extent true	Completely true
21. English passages in the textbooks are too long.					
22. English sentences dealt with in the lessons are difficult to interpret.					
23. A great number of textbooks and supplementary readers are assigned.					
24. Topics of the English passages used in lessons are old.					
25. Computer equipment is not used.					
26. Visual materials (such as videos and DVDs) are not used.					
27. The Internet is not used.					
28. Language lab equipment is not used.					
29. Audio materials (such as CDs and tapes) are not used.					
30. The number of students in classes is large.					
31. Teachers don't have enough time to express all of the materials and practice them more.					
32. Teachers are not motivated enough to work harder with us (e.g., because their salaries are low).					
33. I cannot do as well as my friends on tests.					
34. I don't like my classmates.					
35. My friends don't like English.					
36. English is a compulsory subject.					
37. I've lost my understanding of the purpose of studying English.					
38. I've lost my interest in English.					
39. I no longer like to be like an English native speaker.					

continued

Appendix 15.1   (Continued)

	Absolutely wrong	Mostly not true	Neither true nor wrong	To some extent true	Completely true
40. My classmates will make fun of me if I answer well in the class.					
41. I am weak in English and cannot learn it.					
42. I am not talented enough to learn English.					
43. I don't like countries in which English is spoken and their people (e.g., because they have put political and economic pressures on us).					
44. English is easily forgotten.					
45. Summer vacations contribute to forgetting everything I have learnt.					
46. English questions don't have clear answers.					
47. Learning the spellings of the English words is difficult.					
48. I don't like the books that are taught.					

How motivated are you to learn English?
1: I have almost no motivation.
2: I have a little motivation.
3: I have moderate motivation. 4: I have high motivation
If you have any other ideas or suggestions regarding English, its method of teaching or the problems of learning it, please mention them.

Appendix 15.2 Factor analysis of demotivation (48-Items)

No. of Item	F1	F2	F3	F4	F5	F6	F7
Factor 1: Lack of self-confidence							
10. I get low scores on tests (such as midterm and final examinations).	.721						
41. I am weak in English and cannot learn it.	.702						
33. I cannot do as well as my friends on tests.	.638						
45. Summer vacations contribute to forgetting everything I have learnt.	.635						
11. I get confused when I want to self-study English.	.594						
9. I have difficulty memorizing words and phrases.	.522						
44. English is easily forgotten.	.463						
46. English questions don't have clear answers.	.390						
Factor 2: Teachers' competence and teaching styles							
12. Teachers' pronunciation of English is poor.		.701					
18. Teachers discriminated among strong and weak students.		.667					
17. Teachers shouted or got angry.		.650					
14. Teachers ridicule students' mistakes.		.638					
13. Teachers' method of teaching is not good.		.606					
15. English classes are callous and not interesting.		.577					
19. Teachers do not encourage us for learning English.		.547					
32. Teachers are not motivated enough to work harder with us (e.g., because their salaries are low).		.531					
34. I don't like my classmates.		.300					
Factor 3: Lack of interest in English							
36. English is a compulsory subject.			.594				
43. I don't like countries in which English is spoken and their people (e.g., because they have put political and economic pressures on us).			.577				
37. I've lost my understanding of the purpose of studying English.			.576				
39. I no longer like to be like an English native speaker.			.556				
42. I am not talented enough to learn English.			.539				
38. I've lost my interest in English.			.521				
22. English sentences dealt with in the lessons are difficult to interpret.			.452				
16. Teachers' explanations are not easy to understand.			.426				

Factor 4: Lack of school facilities

Item	Loading
27. The Internet is not used.	.888
26. Visual materials (such as videos and DVDs) are not used.	.853
25. Computer equipment is not used.	.791
28. Language lab equipment is not used.	.719
29. Audio materials (such as CDs and tapes) are not used.	.590

Factor 5: Learning contents and context

Item	Loading
21. English passages in the textbooks are too long.	.604
30. The number of students in classes is large.	.589
48. I don't like the books that are taught.	.494
23. A great number of textbooks and supplementary readers are assigned.	.450
1. I seldom have chances to communicate in English.	−.390
6. Most of the lessons are entrance examination oriented.	−.361
8. I was forced to memorize the sentences in the textbooks too often.	.361

Factor 6: Uselessness of English in EFL context

Item	Loading
35. My friends don't like English.	.619
3. English language has no use in my future job.	−.417
2. English language has no use in my daily life.	.400
24. Topics of the English passages used in lessons are old.	.395
7. I am expected to use (or speak and write) grammatically correct English.	.361

Factor 7: The focus of teaching

Item	Loading
5. Most of the lessons focus on grammar.	.696
31. Teachers don't have enough time to express all of the materials and practice them more.	.538
47. Learning of the spellings of the English words is difficult.	−.354
4. Most of the lessons focus on translation.	.342
40. My classmates will make fun of me if I answer well in the class.	−.330
20. Topics of the passages used in lessons are not interesting.	.313

Appendix 15.3   Independent samples t-tests for less motivated and more motivated learners

	Levene's test for equality of variances						
	F	Sig.	T	df	Sig. (two-tailed)	Mean Difference	Std. Error Difference
F1 Equal variances assumed	2.81	0.095	6.53	192	.000	7.83	1.19
F2 Equal variances assumed	1.00	0.318	0.64	192	0.522	0.94	1.47
F3 Equal variances not assumed	14.25	0.000	1.96	26.206	0.061	13.68	6.97
F4 Equal variances not assumed	5.20	0.024	1.12	26.493	0.271	4.00	3.56
F5 Equal variances not assumed	4.60	0.033	0.79	27.930	0.432	5.77	7.23
F6 Equal variances assumed	0.95	0.329	−0.67	192	0.503	−0.41	0.62
F7 Equal variances assumed	0.17	0.679	0.77	192	0.439	0.45	0.58

References

Alavi, S. (2004) 'A multi-variate causal model of motivation in second/foreign language learning'. Unpublished doctoral dissertation, Shiraz University, Iran.

Arai, K. (2004) What 'demotivates' language learners? Qualitative study on demotivational factors and learners' reactions. *Bulletin of Toyo Gakuen University*, 12, 39–47.

Asghari, N. (1998) *The role of intrinsic, extrinsic motivation and amotivation in Iranian students of English language.* Unpublished master's thesis, Shiraz University, Iran.

Christophel, D. & Gorham, J. (1995) A test-retest analysis of student motivation, teacher immediacy and perceived sources of motivation and demotivation in college classes. *Communication Education*, 44, 292–306.

Dörnyei, Z. (2001) *Teaching and researching motivation.* Harlow: Longman.

Falout, J. & Maruyama, M. (2004) A comparative study of proficiency and learner demotivation. *The Language Teacher*, 28, 3–9.

Falout, J., Elwood, J. & Hood, M. (2009) Demotivation: Affective states and learning outcomes. *System*, 37, 403–17.

Fazel, E. (2003) *Effects of instrumental/integrative motivation on oral proficiency among Iranian female students of English at Shiraz University language center.* Unpublished master's thesis, Shiraz University, Iran.

Gorham, J. & Christophel, D. (1992) Students' perception of teacher behaviors as motivating and demotivating factors in college classes. *Communication Quarterly*, 40, 239–52.

Gorham, J., & Millette, D. (1997) A comparative analysis of teacher and student perceptions of sources of motivation and demotivation in college classes. *Communication Education*, 46, 245–61.

Hasani, H. (2005) *The relationship between intrinsic, extrinsic motivation and Iranian EFL students' gender, level of university instruction and EFL proficiency.* Unpublished master's thesis, Shiraz University, Iran.

Hasegawa, A. (2004) Student demotivation in the foreign language classroom. *Takushoku Language Studies,* 107, 119–36.

Ikeno, O. (2002) Motivating and demotivating factors in foreign language learning: A preliminary investigation. *Ehime University Journal of English Education Research,* 2, 1–19.

Moradi, F. (1996) *An investigation into the problems of teaching and learning English in Tehran province.* Unpublished master's thesis, Shiraz University, Shiraz, Iran.

Neisi, S. (2007) *Relationship between self-esteem, achievement motivation, FLCA and EFL learners' academic performance.* Unpublished master's thesis, Shiraz University, Iran.

Rahimi, M. (1996) *The study of English language instruction at the secondary schools of the Isfahan province.* Unpublished master's thesis, Shiraz University, Shiraz, Iran.

Ramazanian, M. (1998) *The motivation for language learning among Shiraz University undergraduate students of English as a foreign language.* Unpublished master's thesis, Shiraz University, Iran.

Razmjoo, A. & Riazi, A. (2006) Is communicative language teaching practical in the expanding circle?: A case study of teachers of Shiraz high schools and institutes. *Journal of Language and Learning,* 4, 144–71.

Riazi, A. M. (2005) The four language stages in the history of Iran. In A. M. Y. Lin and P. W. Martin (Eds), *Decolonization, globalization: Language in education policy and practice.* Clevedon, U.K.: Multilingual Matters Ltd., pp. 100–16.

Roohani, A. (2001) *An investigation into EFL students' motivation in Shiraz state and Islamic Azad University.* Unpublished master's thesis, Shiraz University, Iran.

Sakai, S. & Kikuchi, K. (2009) An analysis of demotivators in the EFL classroom. *System,* 37, 57–69.

Samaie, M. (2006) *A critical discourse analysis of Gardner's theory of attitudes and motivation.* Unpublished doctoral dissertation, Shiraz University, Iran.

Sedaghat, M. (2001) *The effects of attitude, motivation (instrumental and integrative) and proficiency level on the use of listening comprehension strategies by Iranian female EFL students.* Unpublished master's thesis, Shiraz University, Iran.

Vallerand, R. J. & Ratelle, C. F. (2002) Intrinsic and extrinsic motivation: A hierarchical model. In E. L. Deci, E. L. and R. M. Ryan (Eds), *Handbook of self-determination research.* Rochester, NY: University of Rochester Press, pp. 37–63.

Yarmohammadi, L. (2000) Reflection on the treatment and contextualization of pronunciation practices and language functions in the pre-university textbooks in Iran. *Journal of Teaching Languages,* 1, 1–21.

Zhang, Q. (2007) Teacher misbehaviors as learning demotivators in college classrooms: A cross-cultural investigation in China, Germany, Japan, and the United States. *Communication Education,* 56, 209–27.

16
Japanese EFL Learners' Remotivation Strategies

Joseph Falout, Tim Murphey, Tetsuya Fukuda and Maria Trovela

16.1 Introduction

In *Teaching and Researching Motivation*, Zoltán Dörnyei and Ema Ushioda (2011) marvel at the 'wave of research in Japan where demotivation among learners of English seems to be a major educational concern' (p. 150). Japanese learners of English as a foreign language (EFL) start off with healthy motivations in primary school, with curiosity and intrinsic motivation moving statistically hand-in-hand, but no longer by junior high school, as curiosity, enjoyment, mastery-orientation, and both intrinsic and extrinsic motivations decline as learners progress across the school years (Carreira, 2011). Even teacher *demotivation* is becoming a concern in Japan, as Toshiko Sugino (2010) reports that five of the top seven *de-motives* of university English teachers in Japan relate to student attitudes. Stephen Ryan (2009) sums up the stressful dynamics learners face as they progress through the hoops in the educational system:

The reality of the English-learning experience for most Japanese people is that a great deal of time and effort is devoted to the study of a form of English based on the subject's central role in the examination system, but much of the discourse surrounding the provision of English education focuses in the failing nature of this system and the primacy of English as a language of international communication. This leaves the learner with the challenge of somehow bestowing meaning on their efforts and reconciling the two versions of English education (p. 410).

The present study will investigate how learners are able to reverse this trend of increasing cognitive dissonance (feeling uncomfortable tensions caused by conflicting beliefs) and decreasing motivation by looking at the strategies they use to cope with the pressures, to make meaning of their situations and actions, and to revive their motivation to learn EFL – the processes of their *remotivation*. By analysing these strategies within the context of their learning, we hope to impart some reasoned suggestions for teachers and policymakers, as they conscientiously perform their many roles and functions each busy day, to make meaning for themselves and act cooperatively as agents whose common aims are in optimizing environmental conditions within the educational system that promote the psychological vitality of its learners. For, '[t]he essence of language teaching is providing conditions for language learning...'. (Rivers, 1976: p. 96).

16.2   EFL Education – action and inaction

EFL learners in Japan are caught between two contrasting aspects of language learning culture. On the one hand, they study English for an extended period without even the brief inclusion of studying another foreign language. The Ministry of Education, Culture, Sports, Science and Technology (MEXT) has been increasingly promoting an EFL education that focuses on developing communicative abilities by issuing successive guidelines, starting with the Course of Study in 1994, the New Course of Study in 1997, and in 2003 an action plan 'to cultivate Japanese [people] with English abilities' (MEXT, 2003). Almost all students in Japan compulsorily study English for at least six years, from the seventh to twelfth grades (MEXT, 2011a). MEXT introduced a new education system in 2011, in which the compulsory age to start learning English was lowered to fifth grade (MEXT, 2011b). This means students will learn English for at least eight years, predominantly using only textbooks that MEXT certifies.

While the number of schools that have classes for foreign languages other than English (LOTE) has been increasing in recent years (MEXT, 2010), they remain only minor subjects. Every year more than half a million students take a standardized examination called the Center Test, a Japanese version of the well-known American Scholastic Assessment Test (SAT). In it, almost every student takes a foreign language, and 99.8 per cent of them choose English. Increasingly, learners are choosing LOTE, notably Chinese, but only at a current rate of 0.2 per cent (NCUEE, 2011). For most Japanese people, studying a foreign language means studying English.

On the other hand, Japanese society tends to be indifferent to learning English, in spite of the general feeling among Japanese people themselves that they are studying English very hard. Japanese mothers of young children are a lot less willing to teach their children English than are their counterparts in other East Asian countries. According to one study (Benesse, 2010), the rate of mothers sending their preschool children to English classes was 11.5 per cent in Tokyo, while it was 33.6 per cent in Seoul, 31.6 per cent in Beijing, and 33.9 per cent in Shanghai. Another study (Benesse, 2007) indicated that in Japan the more rural the area, the more parents think that English education offered at their children's regular schools is enough. Japanese adults seem to show little interest in learning English themselves. Another study (IIBC, 2007) shows that even though most Japanese businesspeople say that it is most important to become able to express yourself when you learn English, 76 per cent of them said they were doing nothing to improve their English.

One of the reasons that Japanese people lack interest in learning English, even though they study it for a long time, is that they often get demotivated. There are many factors behind this tendency, such as the prevailing grammar–translation method (Fushino, 2004; Hino, 1988; Torikai, 2011) and big class sizes (Otani et al., 2004; Yoneyama & Murphey, 2007) from primary through tertiary education. Perhaps the most fundamentally detrimental factor is the pressure students feel when they prepare for examinations, especially for university entrance (Hirano, 1989). Students who want to get into a prestigious university have to prepare for a long time to pass the entrance examination. To be accepted by the University of Tokyo, for example, they have to take two different exams, the Center Test and the Tokyo University exam. In both tests, English is regarded as an important subject. Every applicant – apart from a few per cent coming from abroad as foreign exchange students or returnees – has to take these exams, and no other considerations, such as academic records from high school, volunteer experiences, or recommendation letters are accepted. These exams do not include essays or interviews, either. Thus, to most Japanese learners, studying English does not so much mean the joy of acquiring a new skill or preparation for their future career, but only as a subject to study for the entrance exam.

Learners remain ambivalent toward English, and formulating whether or not they like English becomes complex. In his data, Ryan (2009) often found learners in secondary and tertiary education who said they liked English, but their reasons fell short as simply culturally implanted platitudes, without further elaboration. For the few who could offer an explanation, they felt English was charming in a superficial way; liberating from the restricted modes within Japanese communication; fulfilling as a means to self-develop and extend oneself toward the world community; and enabling admiration from others and higher social status. However, Ryan (2009) concluded,

> the value of English as social capital is uncertain[;] ... some individuals experience conflicting reactions towards the social value of English, at times regarding it as being prestigious or cool but at others viewing it as a marginalizing force, alienating them from the main social body. (p. 417)

16.3   Demotivation

Emerging models of motivation share *socio-dynamic perspectives* (Dörnyei & Ushioda, 2011) that conceptualize motivation as a flexible state, rather than a stable trait: Motivation grows and subsides – adapts – within its situated contexts and across various phases of experience through non-linear and multiple co-constructive contingencies. Motivation can be particularly sensitive to social interactions and milieu – those who learners are learning from, with, and for – notably (and not necessarily in this order) teachers, peers, and L2-speaking communities – as well as attitudes about L2 learning within the L1-speaking community. Motivation also shifts across temporal phases, including both short periods – that is, pre- through post-learning tasks – and long periods – that is, from first encounter in formal education through to use in professional venues. In sum, motivation to learn is involved in mutually influencing, complex interrelationships of aspects such as people, time, place, activities, experiences, and aspirations (Dörnyei & Ushioda, 2011). Some of the complexities about motivation can be seen in studies on learner demotivation – when motivation decreases. Currently much of this research focuses on EFL learning in Japan (Dörnyei & Ushioda, 2011). In this context, the predominant demotivator – something that causes demotivation – appears to be the overuse of the grammar-translation method (Falout et al., 2009; Kikuchi, 2009; Murphey et al., 2009). This learning centers on teachers lecturing about grammar rules, as applied through sentence diagramming, which learners are expected to memorize and replicate in tests (Gorsuch, 2000). While this may seem to be one common factor of demotivation, there are different ways learners might interpret how it lowers their motivation. For example, some learners may find this way of learning inherently difficult, and thus blame the subject of study, thinking along the lines of 'grammar is boring stuff' or 'learning English requires too many words to memorize'. This is an example of external attribution. Others may instead make internal attributions, meaning they blame themselves, with ideas like: 'I'm just not good at memorization', or 'foreign languages are not my forte'. Still others may focus their attributions elsewhere, such as on the teacher: 'This guy is boring' and 'he can't teach', or on something more abstract, as in 'what's the purpose to all this?' and 'how can anyone call this language learning?' The demotivation which learners feel might stem from a similar source, but their different interpretations bring attendant differences of influences on their motivations.

Bernard Weiner's (1979, 2000) attribution theory offers insights into learner psychology relating to demotivation. Attributions are causal inferences that learners make of their experiences with success or failure – the reasons that they assign or associate with their learning outcomes. Attributions occur in three dimensions: locus, stability, controllability. Locus refers to the attributed source, whether it is *internal* or *external*, something inside or outside of one's self – that is, whether demotivation is believed to be one's fault or not, which can influence emotions such as pride, self-esteem, and guilt. These emotions, in turn, influence learning behaviors positively or negatively. Stability refers to whether the cause of demotivation is perceived as lasting or not, *stable* or *unstable*. Believing how long demotivating conditions can last will affect one's expectations of the future. Past research links negative expectations of the future with anxiety and depression. Positive expectations are linked to trying and persisting to improve undesirable situations – that is, altering the causes or state of one's own demotivation.

Controllability distinguishes whether wilful intervention is thought to be possible, whether the undesirable situation could be changeable through intention or luck, *controllable* or *uncontrollable*. A sense of controllability leads to proactive behaviors (Weiner, 1979, 1990) which, for demotivated learners, could help them to remotivate.

Joseph Falout and Mika Maruyama (2004) asked 164 Japanese learners, majoring in science and just entering college, about what had demotivated them in learning EFL prior to college. Based on their scores from the college's proficiency test, 86 were placed in the lower third of their respective academic departments, while 78 were placed in the upper third, dividing the participants into lower proficiency (LP) and higher proficiency (HP) groups. In responding to the open-ended question, 'Were there any specific experiences or incidents which demotivated you?' the LP group more often attributed internal causes, compared with the HP group. Most of these attributions centered on disappointment in performance, most notably for inability to memorize vocabulary by rote. LP learners appeared more likely to indicate stable attributions; they believed their innate abilities prevented them from doing better. In contrast, HP learners appeared to display more control over their demotivation, with greater use of specific descriptions within their attributions of demotivation, alongside greater likeliness to include positive aspects of their capabilities to learn. Therefore, LP learners were more likely to attribute their loss of motivation to internal, stable, uncontrollable causes – a pattern that is consistent with learned helplessness (Seligman, 1975). 'They delved no further into the problem, seeming to throw their hands up at it all' (Falout and Maruyama, 2004: p. 6), stated the researchers, who also noted that the HP group appeared more likely to be in control of their affective states for dealing with motivational struggles (Falout & Falout, 2005).

This speculation led to a confirmation study of 900 college learners from widely different academic disciplines and English proficiencies (Falout et al., 2009). The study accounted for various sources and frequency of past demotivation, related affective states, self-regulating behaviors as reactions to demotivating experiences, and the learner's year in school. When other variables were controlled, the best predictor of proficiency was the likeliness for seeking enjoyment that in some way relates to English (such as listening to music or watching movies) when facing demotivation. The second best predictor was whether learners did not blame themselves for their demotivation. These findings add evidence that HP learners are not only more able to control their affective states when experiencing demotivation but also their self-regulating behaviors.

Other demotivational factors are related to long-term learning outcomes. Studies in Japan link incidence of demotivation early in formal education, predominantly in the second year in junior high school (Falout & Maruyama, 2004; Carpenter et al., 2009), with long-term negative affect toward learning EFL, which can last into university study (Carpenter et al.,

2009; Falout & Maruyama, 2004; Falout et al., 2009). This degree of affect correlates with level of proficiency: The more positive the affect, the more proficient the learner (Falout et al., 2009). Also correlating with proficiency are the *antecedent conditions of the learner* (ACL); these are a core set of self-beliefs in relation to one's past experiences with a specific school subject (Carpenter et al., 2009).

This concept derives from Joan Gorham and Mika Christophel (1992), who found that learners in the United States without negative ACLs at the beginning of the semester, across various disciplines, were more likely to have experienced an increase in motivation by the end of the semester through self-motivation. Moreover, the ACL levels of the learners could become more positive after one semester if the course structure, teacher behaviors, and classroom environment held motivating elements, particularly the chance to participate actively in class and to receive teacher feedback (Christophel & Gorham, 1995). In Japan ACLs were also shown to increase over one semester in university EFL classrooms though positive group dynamics, and to correlate with present investment in learning (both inside and outside of class) and visions of themselves in the future using English (Murphey et al., 2012). In other words, this internal factor, ACL, is a strong predictor of how experiences within the external environment can influence motivation. ACLs in this sense function as emotional baggage that learners carry with them into every potential learning situation (Carpenter et al., 2009).

16.4 Remotivation

Christopher Carpenter et al. (2009) investigated how 285 university learners in Japan had remotivated after demotivation. The learners reflected back to their English classroom experiences in junior high and high school and marked levels of their motivation on a grid for each year in the past. Three groups were made for comparison: learners with high positive, low positive, and negative ACLs. These motivation timelines were then averaged by group. Learners with negative ACLs by university actually started off with about the same motivation as the other groups in junior high school, but their motivation soon dropped across junior high and into high school, and only slightly recovered upon entering university. Low positive ACLs showed a similar drop, but to a much lesser degree, which rose during high school, resulting in higher motivation by university than in junior high. High positive ACLs started at about the same motivational point in junior high school as the other ACL groups, but their motivation rose upward all the way into university. From their progressively upward motivation timeline it seems that high ACLs had never experienced demotivation, unlike negative ACLs. However, these timelines depicted averages from each group. Individually and on a day-to-day basis, both positive and negative ACLs had faced ups and downs, challenges to their motivation. But positive ACLs had dealt with them more adaptively than negative ACLs.

Those with different ACLs had become demotivated and remotivated differently. Negative ACLs were more likely demotivated by the difficulty of their courses (Carpenter et al., 2009) and loss of self-confidence (Falout, in progress), whereas positive ACLs were more likely demotivated by overuse of the grammar–translation method (Carpenter et al., 2009; Falout, in progress) and poor teaching (Carpenter et al., 2009). As ACL and proficiency levels are highly correlated, these results corroborate earlier findings that HP learners more often think critically of their teacher's teaching abilities and methods, while LP learners struggle emotionally with learning hurdles and related negative self-beliefs (Falout & Maruyama, 2004; Falout & Falout, 2005).

To remotivate, positive ACLs are more likely to involve cognitive-affective and out-of-class self-regulation, while negative ACLs feel helpless to do so. Use of strategies for remotivation is developmental: Positive ACLs react adaptively to demotivation quicker and with more fluid application and volitional use of strategies. Positive ACLs also tend to benefit from direct assistance and unintentional positive influences of teachers, peers, and family members, whereas negative ACLs usually do not (Carpenter et al., 2009; Falout, in progress). What could have helped negative ACLs with their demotivation, they most often report, was support from their social environment – the very thing they lacked most, compared with positive ACLs (Falout, in progress). Positive ACLs may be learning adaptive strategies from their social networks (*social capital*), while the largest portion of their top remotivators – out-of-class self-regulation – included the use of music and movies, made by native-speakers of English, as mood-boosters and sources of self-identification (Carpenter et al., 2009), their *imagined social capital* (Quinn, 2010).

Pierre Bourdieu (1985) identified the value of connections within social networks as social capital. Imagined social capital (ISC) is defined as 'the benefit that is created by participating in imagined or symbolic networks' (Quinn, 2010: p. 68). ISC can stir a desire to belong to a network of professionals or peers to which one does not yet belong but is motivated toward belonging. Similarly, learners aspiring to move from the margins toward the center of an L2 speaking community strive harder to reach this goal, motivated through their *imagined communities* (Norton, 2001). ISC can also bring a sense of belonging *now*; joining with others, although they might not be there (such as making deep-felt connections with authors by reading their work) and even animals, objects, and the natural or surrounding environment (i.e., landscape or cityscape) can be felt as accessed through imagined networks, imparting powerful transformations of self, as 'the imagined and the material co-produce each other' (Quinn, 2010: p. 142). How learners use their social capital and ISC within EFL contexts to remotivate themselves will be investigated here.

16.5   Methods: research questions

Research is starting to show the complexities of EFL learner motivation in Japan. But so far it brings only rudimentary understandings of the relationships between motivational processes, self-concept, and the social environment. The present study will attempt to build upon the direction taken from past studies to confirm and expand upon this knowledge by asking the following research questions (RQ):

(1) What are the relationships between self-concept and processes of demotivation?
(2) What are the relationships between self-concept and developmental processes of remotivation?
(3) What are the effects of social influences on the developmental processes of remotivation?

16.5.1   Instrument and participants

First, 285 university EFL learners wrote their English language learning histories. Then they filled in motivation timeline grids and questionnaires during class time or at home (see Carpenter et al., 2009). The questionnaire contained a mixture of question types, including a six-point Likert scale, circle-if-it-applies, and open-ended items. Apart from calculating ACL levels, the Likert- and circle-type questions were intended to seed participants' thinking about their past motivational struggles, while the open-ended questions were primarily for attaining learner descriptions of their motivational fluxes for analysis; One was specifically for demotivation and seven for remotivation. The purpose of the seven questions about remotivation was to allow for time and different angles for learners to reflect on how they had remotivated, particularly for those who don't readily recognize or understand their remotivational processes.

Questionnaires with missing data for ACL levels, and those with the same number checked across Likert items (indicating lack of sincere thought or effort to complete the survey meaningfully), were culled, as were cases when respondents claimed to have never been demotivated (a prerequisite of remotivation), resulting in 265 participants for the present study. Their majors ranged across language arts, business management, law, and physical sciences, with a total of 173 males and 92 females (Tables 16.1 and 16.2). Marks made on the motivation timeline grids were converted onto a six-point scale for even-interval data ($-3 = 1$, $-2 = 2$, $-1 = 3$, $1 = 4$, $2 = 5$, $3 = 6$), then averaged.

16.6   Analysis

Although the original data came from our earlier study (Carpenter et al., 2009), in which we only coded answers to four open-ended questions, for the present study we analysed answers to all of the ten open-ended questions and developed a new analytical approach based on the following principles and methods.

All descriptions from the open-ended questions were read with the understanding of motivation and its fluctuations as a holistic, ongoing story, still emerging. Answers were kept in context within the frame of the open-ended questions, but sometimes the stories and descriptions were not contained within a one-question, one-answer format, and therefore were answered across questions, and shifting back and forth in time. The analysis allowed for coding as many adaptive and maladaptive processes as were indicated in the responses. These coping processes were further coded for development over time. If it looked like the students were coping near the early period of demotivation (i.e., during high school, for many), then this was for the short term. Coding for long-term coping processes was for when students were using these processes for years after (even into university), as a way to remotivate and maintain their motivation. This holistic interpretation of answers from numerous open-ended questions brought rich descriptions of motivational processes available for coding.

For coding demotivation, multiple coding was allowed by collapsing the codes from Carpenter et al. (2009): *Difficulty of learning* included grades, scores, personal performance, lack of understanding, course pace and speed (usually reported as too difficult; in a few cases too easy), bored with the lecture method, course structure, and so forth. *Grammar-translation* included boredom with lessons, focus on the entrance exam, and too much lecturing, grammar, and vocabulary. Sometimes the teacher is blamed for the pedagogy, but this is not necessarily the same as the teacher's personality. *Teacher personality*: referred not to teaching method but to teachers who nag, blame, or otherwise behave poorly toward students. *Lost personal relevance*: when learners no longer thought English was important, meaningful, or related to them in a way that shapes their identity. A split could be determined between internal and external for the primary or initial cause of demotivation, so an additional coding was performed for attributional locus.

For coding remotivation, a framework of higher-order families of coping and adaptive processes from Ellen A. Skinner and Melanie J. Zimmer-Gembeck (2007) was adopted (Figure 16.1). A corresponding table (Figure 16.2) was made, offering specific descriptions of coping with EFL demotivation from this data set within the Skinner and Zimmer-Gembeck (2007) coping framework.

The following four categories were created for further, multiple coding to expand and offer interpretable data analysis for the ways learners used their social networks: *Lived social capital (LSC)* referred to social networks with actual people, such as teachers, friends, parents; *imagined social capital (ISC)*

	Problem-solving	Information-seeking	Self-reliance	Support-seeking	Accommodation	Negotiation
Family of coping	strategizing Instrumental action Planning	Reading Observation Asking others	Emotion regulation Behavior regulation Emotional expression Emotion approach	Contact-seeking Comfort-seeking Instrumental aid Social referencing	Distraction Cognitive restructuring Minimization Acceptance	Bargaining Presuassion Priority-settimg
Family function in adaptive process	Adjust actions to be effective	Find additional contigencies	Protect available social resources	Use available social resources	Flexibly adjust Preferences to options	Find new options
Also implied	Watch and learn Mastery Efficacy	Curiosity Interest	Tend and befriend Pride	Procimity-seeing Yearning Other alliance	Pick and choose Secondary control	Compromise

(Adaptive processes)

	Helplessness	Escape	Delegation	Social isolation	Submission	Opposition
Family of coping	Confusion Cognitive interference Cognitive exhaustion	Behavioral avoidance Mental withdrawal Denial Wishful thinking	Matadaptive help-seeking Complaining Whining Self-pity	Social withdrawal Concealment Avoiding others	Rumination Rigid preservation Intrusive thoughts	Other-blame Projection Aggression
Family function in adaptive process	Finf limits of actions	Escape noncontingent environment	Find limits of resources	Withdraw from unsupportive contact	Give up preferences	Remove constraints
Also implied	Guilt Helplessness	Drop and roll Flight Fear	Self-pity Shame	Duck and cover Freeze Sadness	Disgust Rigid perseverance	Stand and fight Anger Deerence

(Maladaptive processes)

Figure 16.1 Links between higher-order families of coping and adaptive processes (adapted from Skinner and Zimmer-Gembeck, 2007: p. 126)

included TV and movie stars, the voice in the music – the lyrics, the singers. This is also the future self in context, working or somehow interacting with people in the future (relates to future, possible self); *intentional* referred to when students initiated or relied on this primarily for their remotivation, and *unintentional* when students accepted help initiated by others, or relied on this secondarily for their remotivation.

The final step in the analysis was to calculate and separate ACL levels, which until this point had been the only data that were kept blind during the coding, done explicitly to prevent the influence of research bias during coding. The five Likert-scale items comprising the ACL factor were averaged: 75 participants had values below 3.50, representing an average negative ACL. There were more than twice as many positive ACLs, so this group was further divided into 92 participants in the low positive group, and 98 participants in the high positive group, with the cutoff points from 3.60 to 4.40, and 4.60 to 6.00, respectively.

16.7 Results

Results show that the more positive their ACLs, the more likely the learners are to be language arts majors (Appendix 16.1) and also likely to be slightly

Adaptive processes

Family of coping	Problem-solving	Information-seeking	Self-reliance	Support-seeking	Accommodation	Negotiation
Process of coping with EFL demotivation	Prepare and review lessons Learning strategies Experience success Specific plans for learning	Asking advice from others Self-reflection Other-modeling Take extra calsses (i.e. oram school)	Routines, habits, lifestyles Boosting emotions (i.e. music)	Empathy and encouragement from significant others Interactions about or with L2 Emotional contagion Positive competition Imagined social capital	To think positively, enjoy, change thinking Following joys (i.e. movies) Resting Self-scaffolding confidence	Goal-setting (i.e. tests) Imagining possible self

Maladaptive processes

Family of coping	Helplessness	Escape	Delegation	Social isolation	Submission	Opposition
Process of coping with EFL demotivation	Think it's impossible Efforts are wasted or useless	Sleeping in class Give up studying	Self-blame, whining complaining	Dislike others, input	Study just becuase it's a must Wishing things had been different Should've wanted, wished I'd...	Fighting with teacher Rejecting the L2

Figure 16.2   Descriptions of coping with EFL demotivation, from this data set, within the coping framework

older (Appendix 16.2). The ACL factor was reliable at $\alpha = 0.85$, with significant differences between ACL levels at $p < 0.0001$ for each item (Appendixes 16.3 and 16.4).

The motivation grid (Figure 16.3) shows the tendency of learners with high-positive ACLs to maintain and increase their motivation over the years in school, whereas low-positive and negative ACLs struggle more with their motivation, showing demotivation trends across junior high (roughly ages 13–15) and high school (roughly ages 16–18), with the tendency to remotivate thereafter as they prepare for and enter university. They became demotivated differently: the more positive the ACL, the more likely they externalized their attributions (Figure 16.4). Much of the short-term remotivation processes appeared similar (Figure 16.5), whereas in the long term it was negative ACLs who more often reported coping using remotivation processes (Figure 16.6). The most salient difference across all the codings came from a more careful look at the social processes in remotivation, in which positive ACLs were twice as likely as negative ACLs to report benefiting from the unintentional use of social support for remotivation (Figure 16.7).

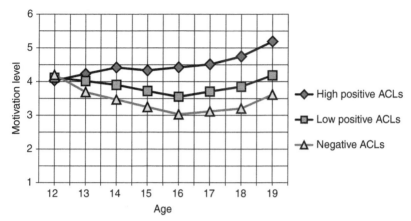

Figure 16.3 In-class motivation timeline by ACL group

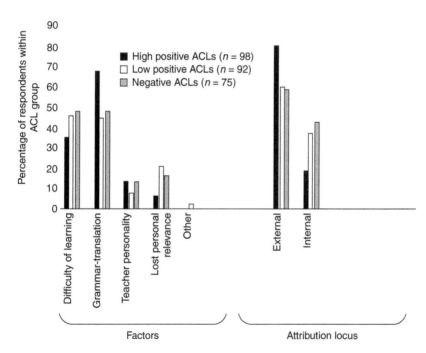

Figure 16.4 Demotivation processes

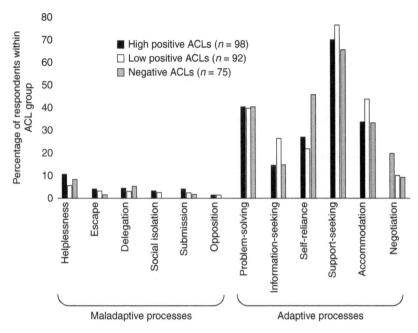

Figure 16.5 Short-term coping processes for remotivation

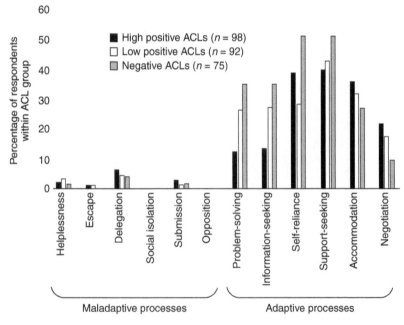

Figure 16.6 Long-term coping processes for remotivation

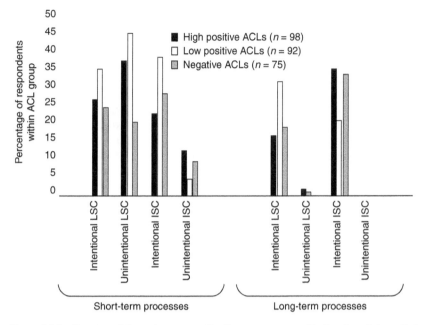

Figure 16.7 Short- and long-term remotivation processes with lived social capital (LSC) and imagined social capital (ISC)

16.8 Discussion of research questions

RQ 1. What are the relationships between self-concept and processes of demotivation?

There are small differences between the ACLs about *what* demotivated them, but bigger differences in the *ways* it happened (Figure 16.4). High-positive ACLs seem more likely than their counterparts to have been demotivated by boredom with repetitive classroom lectures (the grammar-translation method). They are also less likely to report being demotivated from difficulty with learning or from loss of personal relevance. Even larger differences appear in their attributions. The more positive their ACL, the more likely learners are to attribute their demotivation to external sources; conversely, the more negative their ACL, the more likely learners attribute their demotivation to internal sources.

This kind of attribution can explain the connection between low proficiency and loss of self-confidence as contributors to demotivation (Falout et al., 2009). When students become lost in their comprehension of English, itself, in the ways to learn it and use it successfully within their given situations, if they start blaming themselves they become further at risk of staying lost in their studies.

RQ 2.   What are the relationships between self-concept and developmental processes of remotivation?

Across the various coping processes used for short-term remotivation, there are few noticeable differences between ACL levels (Figure 16.5). Perhaps this shows that what has more lasting effect is the way that learners are demotivated. Those who attribute demotivation to external sources tend to end up with positive ACLs, meaning positive self-concepts that relate to learning English, and higher levels of motivation. If the processes of remotivation are similar, then the differences in resulting motivation may be accounted for by how much is needed to remotivate to get to the same levels (i.e., how much they had been previously demotivated) or by how effective these processes are in relation to the nature of the problem (i.e., whether the types of remotivation strategies will work or not, depending on the types of motivational problems).

It is helpful to remember that these codings for remotivation do not necessarily represent the frequency of attempts to remotivate; rather, these data show the likeliness of whether or not learners have tried out the strategies. Therefore, the results need to be interpreted cautiously. One possible interpretation is that positive ACLs are not just throwing a barrage of strategies haphazardly into use, but apply the necessary strategies for their desired effects: They are metacognitively more proficient in using motivational strategies, perhaps even in subtle but powerfully effective ways. This leads to the next interpretation, that while negative ACLs are attempting to remotivate similarly, their motivational struggles may be less effective. Perhaps an additional influence is their lack of beliefs in the strategies, situations, or themselves, so their doubts become self-fulfilling prophecies.

Over the long term, positive ACLs seemingly require, or apply, remotivation strategies less than negative ACLs; maybe, with their lower motivations, negative ACLs need them more, struggling harder to remotivate in the long term (Figure 16.6). If so, this provides evidence that once one's motivation has been substantially lowered, it becomes more difficult to increase it again. Meanwhile, the positive ACLs may have a motivational momentum that requires less maintenance. These results seem to contradict findings from Carpenter et al. (2009) and Falout (in progress), in which positive ACLs are more likely to use remotivation strategies, and in a wide variety, over the long term. The differences in these findings might be accounted for by the different research methods in the present study, which uses numerous open-ended questions about remotivation and holistic interpretation of the participants' responses. Moreover, variety of specific strategy use is not shown in the present study, as the analysis tended to flatten out variety through a more generalized categorization in the coding framework than in Carpenter et al. (2009). Falout (in progress) proposes that it is not their use of a wide variety of strategies that works for positive ACLs, but their adeptness to match, with fluidity and flexibility, the right motivational strategy for the problem.

The present study does indicate a difference in the type of long-term remotivation strategies needed (Figure 16.6). Negative ACLs are, in a practical way, solving their lower proficiency and other learning problems by seeking out help from peers and teachers, by learning how to keep a regimen of study, and by picking up and using learning strategies. Positive ACLs may already have those things down, and to keep their motivation going they are more reliant on focusing on their goals (negotiation) and taking breaks (accommodation) when needed in order to recharge their batteries; they take a rest from learning so they can come back to it with fresh perspective and ample effort to keep learning.

RQ 3. What are the effects of social influences on the developmental processes of remotivation?

As suggested in Carpenter et al. (2009), a salient factor for remotivation appears to be one which is unintentional: Learners receive help from those in the social environment, particularly during the early stages following demotivation (Figure 16.7). Both low- and high-positive ACLs were twice as likely to report becoming remotivated unintentionally through the care of teachers, friends, and families. It is not clear whether positive ACLs had been more motivationally receptive to it or had been more circumstantially lucky, but either way the help they received early on seems to have made the biggest difference for their self-concept, motivation, and proficiency outcomes.

16.9 Implications

In general, it would appear that learners, teachers, and administrators often treat the English performances of learners in essentialising or entifying ways (Dweck, 2000) by judging and labeling students as "good" or 'bad'; that is, you *are* what you have done. As Weiner (2000) has shown, self-attributions can be determining; so too can the attributions that others place on learners, as these can become internalized beliefs. If learners are not good on a test, then they are pronounced bad at English and begin their lifelong demotivation in a negative affective cycle of internal attributions and poor learning outcomes.

The main implication is that somehow we need to help learners understand that nobody is really good at something before they have tried it for a while, and that not knowing and making mistakes are normal processes in learning. As we help learners understand this, we need to convince teachers to promote more incremental ways of teaching and understanding language learning progress. While many Japanese people do report how they liked their first few classes of English, which are often playful with songs and bolstered with scaffolded interactive activities, teachers soon turn to their major methods of grammar and vocabulary teaching and testing, especially in junior and senior high school. It seems that when English becomes a subject of exams that students apparently become 'good' or 'bad', accepting that a test score really shows their value.

Second, letting learners know that their journey of learning will certainly have ups and downs, and that this is part of the road, allows them to anticipate some bad times and still work for the good times. An interesting contrast is that this understanding is central to how many Chinese learners understand their own journeys of learning English (Jin & Cortazzi, 2011). Teachers in Japan need to let learners know that challenges can make us stronger, and nobody knows it all at first. Additionally, learners might share their own journeys together for creating collaborative agency and acting as social models to help get over learning hurdles (Murphey & Carpenter, 2008).

Third, we need to offer learners metacognitive strategies for recognizing demotivation and doing something about it. With our own students, simply looping the list of student remotivation strategies (made by the learners) back to them to read (Murphey & Falout, 2010) allowed some of them to regain motivation and see lights in what they had thought was just a long, dark, hopeless tunnel.

Fourth, students are telling us repeatedly that when they have friends, remotivation is much more effective. Teachers need to attend more to the good group dynamics of classes (Murphey, 1998; Dörnyei and Murphey, 2003) and allow friendly socialization in the EFL classroom so that learners become resources for each other. To promote more in and out of class cooperation, teachers can structure homework that requires collaboration, and provide the scaffolding and assistance (including metacognitive strategies for good group dynamics) that learners will need to satisfactorily make the switchover from doing homework alone to completing some of it in groups (Falout, 2010).

Fifth, teachers themselves need to look seriously at ways to form better relationships with their students and create environments that are more conducive to interaction in and out of the classroom (Lee et al., 2009; Murphey, 2011), and employ materials that are at their level. To do this teachers need to be able to exercise their own judgments about the appropriate materials and goals for their classes that will engage the learners. Especially in Japan, newly employed teachers just exiting from universities are usually the most capable in applying fresh methodologies, and yet they seem to be mostly tied to strict guidelines and materials rather than being allowed to adapt to their students. Thus, our final implication:

Sixth, we think MEXT should loosen their controls on schools and curriculum, allowing teachers to be more flexible in their approaches to teaching and learning, and build meaningful relationship-based teaching.

16.10 Conclusion

The results of the present study imply that demotivation in EFL learning in Japan could be reduced if learners were prevented from becoming lost in their learning due to difficult courses and the overuse of the grammar-translation teaching methodology. For healthier motivation, learners need to be challenged in learning without becoming overwhelmed; to experience variety in learning, if not to alleviate boredom, then to stimulate interest; and to understand the relevance of learning English. The most salient element appears to be whether learners attribute early demotivating experiences to internal or external causes; internal attributions more often lead toward long-term, low-level motivation.

Contrary to past research findings, the present study indicates that positive ACLs (those who have been less demotivated) appear to be spending less effort at remotivation in the long term. Perhaps this is due to their existing high motivation levels or perhaps they are more effective at applying motivational strategies that suit their situations. Learners with positive ACLs are more likely than negative ACLs to remotivate in the long term through positive thinking, taking breaks, and focusing on goals. However, the salient element appears to be the help and care of others, such as family, teachers, and peers, who unintentionally remotivated learners during early demotivating experiences.

These results emphasize the importance of a socially supportive environment from early learning experiences onward. Implications include having smaller class sizes and developing decentralized educational policies. Such changes may not ensure uniform EFL curricula but they would certainly promote better conditions for motivation to flourish.

Appendix 16.1 Participants' subject majors by ACL level

ACL level	Male	Female	Language Arts	Business/Law	Sciences
High positive	55.10 (54)	44.90 (44)	55.10 (54)	30.61 (30)	14.29 (14)
Low positive	65.22 (60)	34.78 (32)	23.91 (22)	39.13 (36)	36.96 (34)
Negative	78.67 (59)	21.33 (16)	6.67 (5)	52.00 (39)	41.33 (31)

Appendix 16.2 Participants' year in school by ACL level

ACL level	Freshmen	Sophomores	Juniors	Seniors	Masters	Mean age
High positive	37.76 (37)	46.94 (46)	11.22 (11)	3.06 (3)	1.02 (1)	19.28
Low positive	38.04 (35)	40.22 (37)	15.22 (14)	6.52 (6)	–	19.41
Negative	52.00 (39)	34.67 (26)	9.33 (7)	4.00 (3)	–	19.11

Appendix 16.3 Descriptive statistics for the ACL items

ACL level		(a) Generally, I think that I enjoy learning English in class.	(b) Generally, I think that I enjoy learning English out of class.	(c) I like studying English now.	(d) Even if English was not a compulsory subject, I would choose to study it.	(e) I am confident in learning English now.
High positive	Mean	5.39	4.92	5.43	5.59	4.20
n = 98	SD	0.69	0.93	0.61	0.68	1.00
	Skewness	−1.07	−0.91	−0.56	−1.80	−0.05
	Kurtosis	1.29	1.83	−0.58	3.20	−0.41
Low positive	Mean	4.66	3.78	4.12	4.63	2.90
n = 92	SD	0.74	1.01	0.61	0.96	0.86
	Skewness	−0.17	−0.06	−0.06	−0.38	−0.12
	Kurtosis	−0.18	0.29	−0.30	−0.16	−0.04
Negative n = 75	Mean	3.45	2.55	2.89	2.73	1.88
	SD	1.06	1.00	0.96	1.26	0.80
	Skewness	−0.80	0.53	−0.52	0.32	0.38
	Kurtosis	0.23	0.92	−0.26	−0.58	−0.90

Appendix 16.4 ANOVA for ACL groups

Item		Sum of Squares	df	Mean Square	F	Sig.
(a)	Between Groups	239.67	2	119.84	123.81	0.000*
	Within Groups	253.59	262	0.97		
	Total	493.26	264			
(b)	Between Groups	275.72	2	137.86	260.17	0.000*
	Within Groups	138.83	262	0.53		
	Total	414.55	264			
(c)	Between Groups	351.79	2	175.89	184.50	0.000*
	Within Groups	249.77	262	0.95		
	Total	601.56	264			
(d)	Between Groups	234.68	2	117.34	143.69	0.000*
	Within Groups	213.96	262	0.82		
	Total	448.64	264			
(e)	Between Groups	239.67	2	119.84	123.81	0.000*
	Within Groups	253.59	262	0.97		
	Total	493.26	264			

*Significant at $p < 0.0001$

References

Benesse (2007) Dai-ikkai shogakkou eigo ni kansuru kihon chosa hogosha chosa houkokusho [The first basic survey on parents about English education at primary school]. *Kenkyu Shoho*, 42, 23.

Benesse (2010) Youji no seikatsu anketo higashi ajia go toshi chousa 2010 [Survey on lifestyles of infants conducted in 5 East Asian cities 2010]. Benesse jisedai ikusei kenkyuujo [Benesse Next Generation Nurture Research Institute]: Tokyo.

Bourdieu, P. (1985) The forms of social capital. In J. G. Richardson (Ed.), *Handbook of theory and research for the sociology of education*. New York: Greenwood, pp. 241–58.

Carpenter, C., Falout, J., Fukuda, T., Trovela, M. & Murphey, T. (2009) Helping students repack for remotivation and agency. In A. M. Stoke (Ed.), *JALT2008 conference proceedings*, Tokyo: JALT, pp. 259–74.

Carreira, J. M. (2011) Relationship between motivation for learning EFL and intrinsic motivation for learning in general among Japanese elementary school students. *System*, 39 (1), 90–102.

Christophel, D. M. & Gorham, J. (1992) A test-retest analysis of student motivation, teacher immediacy and perceived sources of motivation and demotivation in college classes. *Communication Education*, 44, 292–306.

Dörnyei, Z. & Murphey, T. (2003) *Group dynamics in the language classroom*. Cambridge: Cambridge University Press.

Dörnyei, Z. & Ushioda, E. (2011) *Teaching and researching motivation* (2nd edn). Harlow: Pearson Education.

Dweck, C. S. (2000) *Self theories: Their role in motivation, personality and development*. Philadelphia: Psychology Press.

Falout, J. (2010) Purojekuto gata kagaku gijitsu eigo kyoiku: Kyoin to gakushuusha kan no sougo gakushuu kouka [Project-based science English education: Reciprocal learning among teachers and students]. *Learning Learning*, 17 (1), 22–29.

Falout, J. (in progress) Coping with demotivation: EFL learners' remotivation processes.

Falout, J., Elwood, J. & Hood, M. (2009) Demotivation: Affective states and learning outcomes. *System*, 37 (3), 403–17.

Falout, J. & Falout, M. (2005) The other side of motivation: Learner demotivation. In K. Bradford-Watts, C. Ikeguchi, and M. Swanson (Eds), *JALT2004 conference proceedings* Tokyo: JALT, pp. 280–89.

Falout, J. & Maruyama, M. (2004) A comparative study of proficiency and learner demotivation. *The Language Teacher*, 28 (8), 3–9.

Fushino, K. (2004) Students in college English reading classes: A survey. In M. Swanson and K. Hill (Eds), *JALT2003 conference proceedings*. Tokyo: JALT. pp. 119–34.

Gorham, J. & Christophel, D. M. (1992) Learners' perceptions of teacher behaviors as motivating and demotivating factors in college classes. *Communication Quarterly*, 40 (3), 239–52.

Gorsuch, G. (2000) EFL educational policies and educational cultures: Influences on teachers' approval of communicative activities. *TESOL Quarterly*, 34 (4), 675–710.

Hino, N. (1988) Yakudoku: Japan's dominant tradition in foreign language learning. *JALT Journal*, 10, (1 & 2), 45–55.

Hirano, M. (1989) Nyushi ni taisuru – Sugakuteki kousatsu [Mathematical evaluation on entrance examinations]. *Yamanashi Medical University Kiyo*, 8, 34–43.

IIBC (2007) Kokusai bijinesu nioite motomerareru eigoryoku ni kannsuru anketo [Survey on English abilities required in international business]. Kokusai bijinesu komyunike-shon kyoukai [The Institute for International Business Communication]: Tokyo.

Jin, L. & Cortazzi, M. (2011) More than a Journey: 'Learning' in the metaphors of Chinese students and teachers. In L. Jin and M. Cortazzi (Eds), *Researching Chinese Learners; skills, perceptions and intercultural adaptations.* Houndmills: Palgrave Macmillan, pp. 67–92.

Kikuchi, K. (2009) Listening to our learners' voices: What demotivates Japanese high school students? *Language Teaching Research*, 13 (4), 453–71.

Lee, N., Mikesell, L., Joaquin, A. D. L., Mates, A. W. & Schumann, J. H. (2009) *The interactional instinct: The evolution and acquisition of language.* New York: Oxford University Press.

MEXT (2003) *Action plan to cultivate 'Japanese with English abilities'.* 31 March 2003. Monbu kagaku sho [Ministry of Education, Culture, Sports, Science and Technology]: Tokyo.

MEXT (2010) Koutougakkou tou ni okeru kokusaikouryuu tou no jyoukyou nit suite [About International Exchange at High School]. Monbu kagaku sho [Ministry of Education, Culture, Sports, Science and Technology]: Tokyo.

MEXT (2011a) Gimu kyoiku no mokuhyo no meikaku [Clarification of the purpose of compulsory education]. Retrieved 30 June 2011, from http://www.mext.go.jp/b_menu/shingi/chukyo/chukyo0/gijiroku/05052801/002/003.htm

MEXT (2011b) Shin gakushu shidou youkou—Ikiru chikara [New course of study: The power to live]. Retrieved 30 June 2011, from http://www.mext.go.jp/a_menu/shotou/new-cs/index.htm

Murphey, T. (1998) Friends and classroom identity formation. *IATEFL Issues*, 145, 16–17.

Murphey, T. (2011) The L2 passionate interactional imperative (for short 'The L2 pie'): It's hot or it's not! *Studies in Self-Access Learning Journal*, 2 (2), 87–90.

Murphey, T. & Carpenter, C. (2008) The seeds of collaborative agency in language learning histories. In P. Kalaja, V. Menezes, and A. M. F. Barcelos (Eds), *Narratives of learning and teaching EFL.* New York: Palgrave Macmillan, pp. 17–34.

Murphey, T., Falout, J., Elwood, J. & Hood, M. (2009) Inviting student voice. In R. Nunn and J. Adamson (Eds), *Accepting alternative voices in EFL journal articles.* Busan, Korea: Asian EFL Journal Press, pp. 211–35.

Murphey, T., & Falout, J. (2010) Critical participatory looping: Dialogic member checking with whole classes. *TESOL Quarterly*, 44 (4), 811–821.

Murphey, T., Falout, J., Fukada, Y. & Fukuda, T. (2012) Group dynamics: Collaborative agency in present communities of imagination. In S. Mercer, S. Ryan and M. Williams (Eds), *Psychology for language learning: Insights from research, theory and practice.* Basingstoke: Palgrave Macmillan, pp. 220–238.

NCUEE (2011) Daigaku nyuushi senta shaken jisshi kekka no gaiyou [Overview of the results of national university entrance examination]. Daigaku nyushi senta [National Center for University Entrance Examinations]: Tokyo

Norton, B. (2001) Non-participation, imagined communities and the language classroom. In M. P. Breen (Ed.), *Learner contributions to language learning.* Harlow: Longman.

Otani, Y., Hayashi, K., Aikawa, M., Azuma, M., Okihara, K., Kawai, T., et al. (2004) *Sekai no gaikokugo kyouiku seisaku [Language teaching policy in the 21st century].* Tokyo: Toshindo.

Quinn, J. (2010) *Learning communities and imagined social capital: Learning to belong.* New York: Continuum.

Rivers, W. (1976) *Speaking in many tongues: Essays in foreign language teaching.* Rowley, MA: Newbury House.

Ryan, S. (2009) Ambivalence and commitment, liberation and challenge: Investigating the attitudes of young Japanese people towards the learning of English. *Journal of Multilingual and Multicultural Development*, 30 (5), 405–20.

Seligman, M. E. P. (1975) *Learned helplessness.* San Francisco: W.H. Freeman.

Skinner, E. A. & Zimmer-Gembeck, M. J. (2007) The development of coping. *The Annual Review of Psychology*, 58, 119–44.

Sugino, T. (2010) Teacher demotivational factors in the Japanese language teaching context. *Procedia Social and Behavioral Sciences*, 3, 216–26.

Torikai, K. (2011) *Kokusai kyotsuugo toshiteno eigo* [*English as the lingua franca*]. Tokyo: Kodansha.

Weiner, B. (1979) A theory of motivation for some classroom experiences. *Journal of Educational Psychology*, 71 (1), 3–25.

Weiner, B. (1990) History of motivational research in education. *Journal of Educational Psychology*, 82 (4), 616–622.

Weiner, B. (2000) Intrapersonal and interpersonal theories of motivation from an attributional perspective. *Educational Psychology Review*, 12 (1), 1–14.

Yoneyama, S. & Murphey, T. (2007) The tipping point of class size: When caring communications and relationships become possible. *JALT Hokkaido Journal*, 11, 1–28.

Index